Fun with the Family™ Connecticut

Praise for the *Fun with the Family*™ series

"Enables parents to turn family travel into an exploration."

—Alexandra Kennedy, Editor, *Family Fun*

"Bound to lead you and your kids to fun-filled days,
those times that help compose the
memories of childhood."

—Dorothy Jordon, *Family Travel Times*

Help Us Keep This Guide Up to Date

Every effort has been made by the author and editors to make this guide as accurate and useful as possible. However, many changes can occur after a guide is published—establishments close, phone numbers change, hiking trails are rerouted, facilities come under new management, etc.

We would love to hear from you concerning your experiences with this guide and how you feel it could be improved and be kept up to date. While we may not be able to respond to all comments and suggestions, we'll take them to heart and we'll make certain to share them with the author. Please send your comments and suggestions to the following address:

The Globe Pequot Press
Reader Response/Editorial Department
P.O. Box 480
Guilford, CT 06437

Or you may e-mail us at: editorial@GlobePequot.com

Thanks for your input, and happy travels!

INSIDERS'GUIDE®

FUN WITH THE FAMILY™ SERIES

fun WITH the Family™

CONNECTICUT

HUNDREDS OF IDEAS FOR DAY TRIPS WITH THE KIDS

DOE BOYLE

FIFTH EDITION

INSIDERS'GUIDE®

GUILFORD, CONNECTICUT
AN IMPRINT OF THE GLOBE PEQUOT PRESS

INSIDERS'GUIDE®

Copyright © 1995, 1998, 2000, 2002, 2004 by Doe Boyle

Insiders' Guide is a registered trademark of The Globe Pequot Press.
Fun with the Family is a trademark of The Globe Pequot Press.

Text design by Nancy Freeborn and Linda Loiewski
Maps by Rusty Nelson © The Globe Pequot Press
Spot photography throughout © Photodisc

ISSN 1540-2169
ISBN 0-7627-2977-5

Manufactured in the United States of America
Fifth Edition/First Printing

For Tee, who still believes it can be done.

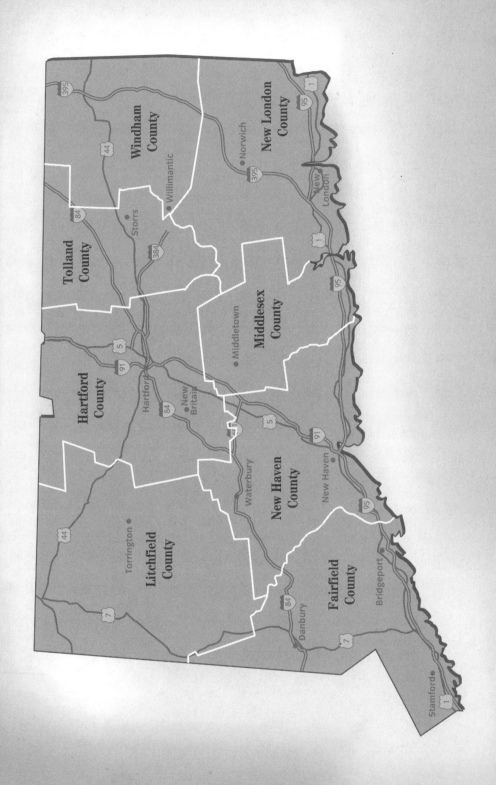

Contents

Preface

In Noah Webster's 1828 *American Dictionary of the English Language,* the word *adventure* is defined, in part, as follows: "an enterprise of hazard; a bold undertaking in which hazards are to be encountered and the issue is staked upon unforeseen events." What better description exists of the social phenomenon known as the family day trip, where two or fewer adults headily depart for an outing with an assemblage of one or more children, a map, a travel guide, maybe a camera, a jugful of lemonade, a six-pack of sandwiches, and an abundance of high expectations for fun?

In most families, a variety of ages, interests, and tastes need to be considered at the outset, or the family day trip will threaten to collapse under the weight of varying expectations even before the family car has left the driveway. On some days, simple variables like weather and traffic conspire against the best-laid plans for an enjoyable day.

Perhaps no certain way exists to predict the hazards that may beset your family adventures, but *Fun with the Family Connecticut* will at least reduce them. Basically, it is a presifted collection of destinations selected by a team of family-fun experts. All the treasures of Connecticut are, in fact, too numerous to be covered in a book this size—even in this thoroughly updated fifth edition. Some categories—annual fairs and festivals, for instance—could fill a book of their own. The selection process, therefore, was both objective and subjective. In some cases, inclusion represents a unique or outstanding attraction, superior facilities, or a broad range of appeal. Exclusion usually represents a decision to limit similar attractions within a certain radius or to reduce what might otherwise result in an overemphasis on one category in the book as a whole. Nearly every town in Connecticut, for example, has a wonderful historical society or historic home. Nearly every county has more than one nature center, bird sanctuary, or wildlife preserve. Christmas tree farms and pick-your-own farms are everywhere as are toy shops, so-called amusement arcades, and family-friendly eateries. The selection process has resulted in a final list of more than 400 attractions and events, nearly all of which were recently visited by the author and her team of experts. In addition to these are more than 300 suggestions for lodgings and restaurants. Your team of experts should peruse the options and pick those that suit you and your family best.

Even a cursory look through the pages of this book will reveal an obvious emphasis on the state of Connecticut itself and on its varied attractions. Don't be deceived, however. Less obviously, the spirit of the book resides in the heart of its title—it is a celebration of family and a celebration of fun within the context of that unit. How lucky you are that Connecticut is the tool you will use for insight into yourselves as a family. Not only will you learn much about science, nature, and history as you travel the picturesque byways of this pretty New England state, but you will also learn much about each other.

Since the first edition of this book, written in the summer of 1994, my family has changed rapidly. Most of the differences are in the evolving interests of my children as they mature, and over the years we've sampled a wide range of activities to accommodate their varied tastes for adventure. I figure as long as we're on the planet together, we're not lost, and by venturing outward as a pack, so to speak, we may discover what we need to know to understand one another before life's divided highways separate us.

As you read this guide, be assured that I have made every effort to be clear in my descriptions and evaluations of the attractions, restaurants, and accommodations selected for inclusion in these pages. I have been a Connecticut resident for forty years of my life and a mother for twenty. I've made it my business to explore this state thoroughly and thoughtfully with the interests of my children and yours in mind. The task of writing this guide has been approached with both enthusiasm and integrity, and I've written the reviews of each entry as positively and fairly as I am able. No matter how appealing or interesting the reviews may seem, you alone as the user of this guide are best equipped to consider the ages, interests, dispositions, and physical and intellectual development of your children. You alone can decide whether a certain attraction may enchant and delight your children or frustrate and disappoint them. *Fun with the Family Connecticut* will, I hope, help you make happy choices, but be sure to trust your own instincts and knowledge of your family.

Scientist and naturalist Rachel Carson wrote, "If a child is to keep alive his inborn sense of wonder, he needs the companionship of at least one adult who can share it, rediscovering with him the joy, the excitement, and the mystery of the world we live in." In that vein, I invite you to use this travel guide to your own advantage. Urge each other toward new experiences. Challenge yourselves to explore what you have not yet discovered. Learn more about a topic you have never been taught. Open your eyes to sights you have never before paused to consider. Most important, use this guide to nurture the curiosity, the playfulness, and the imagination of every member of your family. These are the gifts that will sustain you.

Enjoy the journey.

Doe Boyle
2004

Acknowledgments

Many thanks are owed to the scores of people associated with the attractions listed in these pages. Space restraints prevent a listing of their names, but all—from executive director to publicity manager to docent—provided to us a gracious welcome, much information, and the opportunity to enjoy their facilities as "ordinary" families would.

Thanks are also due the folks at the tourism districts throughout the state, who keep me on their mailing lists and Web updates. All of them are prompt, encouraging, and professional in providing cheerful and generous assistance.

Credit must be given to the dedicated rangers of the Connecticut State Park and Forest System, who renewed my faith in the possibility that we can preserve and protect our land and educate and entertain our citizens at the same time. Each one of these knowledgeable individuals was friendly, enthusiastic, and committed to maintaining the parks for family use.

The folks at The Globe Pequot Press are owed thanks as well. The work of project editor Jennifer Quint and copy editor Jane Merryman is in truth as important as my own. I am grateful for their attention to both the bones and the spirit of this work.

For their great leads, advice, and opinions, I thank the legions of friends and other folks who tell us their adventures, clip articles and reviews, and send us scurrying to see what they had seen. For his unflagging optimism and affection, I thank my husband. His loving support is essential to the happy completion of my work.

Most especially, I thank my daughters. Every day I cherish their company and revel in their astonishing development into young women. As I have written before, I cannot think of finer traveling companions through this book, this world, this life. I love you all, my daughters, most deeply.

Introduction

Connecticut's Bounty

You're already a step ahead of many travelers if you've chosen to tour Connecticut. The rich history of the region has woven a tapestry of attractions that range from typically Yankee to uniquely sophisticated. Among these are boat, train, and trolley rides; science centers and planetariums; canoe trips and river raft races; amusement parks and carousels; art museums; zoos; beaches; skiing and skating centers; and performing arts.

Many attractions reflect Connecticut's remarkable multicultural populations and their histories. Once home to dinosaurs and mastodons, the prehistoric fertile valleys were later roamed by the nomadic ancestors of the Algonkian people. The Mohegan tribe of the Algonkian nation called the region *Quinnehtukqut,* meaning "along the long tidal estuary." The area's indigenous population is represented in many exhibits and festivals throughout the state.

The arrival of the Dutch in 1614 and the establishment of the Hartford Colony by Thomas Hooker in 1636 led to the founding of the Connecticut Colony in 1639 and the subsequent decimation of the native population. Despite the shameful nature of that transition, much of value about the European influence can be learned today. Wave after wave of immigrants enriched the development of the state. Scholars, inventors, artists, industrialists, and others whose deeds made American history have left their mark. So, along with go-kart tracks, miniature golf courses, and water slides, museums and historic sites appear with regularity on the list of attractions families will enjoy. In fact, you may have trouble deciding where to visit first.

Using this Book

Arranged by county in a roughly west-to-east progression and then by geographic proximity of towns within each of the eight county chapters, each entry includes basic information such as addresses, telephone numbers, Web sites, hours, and admission rates. Then there is a brief but detailed review of what families can expect to see (or learn or explore). Bear in mind that the age recommendations are somewhat subjective based on the author's experience or suggested guidelines.

The maps at the beginning of each chapter are a quick reference to the towns covered in each county. Not intended to replace a good highway map or to provide routes for driving tours, the maps should help you gain a general sense of the area.

At the end of each chapter are listings of additional sources of information.

Rates

In the sections listing "Where to Eat" and "Where to Stay," dollar signs provide a sense of the price range at those establishments. For meals, the prices are per individual dinner entrees; for lodging, the rates are for a double room, European Plan (no meals), unless otherwise noted. In addition, guests are charged state sales tax, not included in the room rate. Keep in mind that meal prices generally do not change seasonally, but that lunch

Connecticut's State Parks
and Historic Sites

Although the rangers at Connecticut's state parks are some of the most dedicated professionals employed by the State of Connecticut and although they are committed to preserving safe public access to state-owned lands, they are at the mercy of recent state budget cuts that have compromised their ability to keep our parks open and accessible to visitors. The same is true for state employees of four of the historic sites owned by the state and operated under the agency of the former Connecticut Historical Commission, now folded into the new Connecticut Commission on the Arts, Tourism, Culture, History, and Film. While some state parks and museums listed in this book are fully operational and well staffed, others are closed to visitors or have had their services or hours of operation limited. Some state parks have had their services reduced: trash collection, lifeguards, trail maintenance, picnic tables, drinking water, and toilet facilities may be limited in some parks; some have closed or limited the hours of nature centers or historic museums. Before you set out on a trip to any of Connecticut's state parks or historic sites, be sure to call and ask about current hours and services. Always carry a heavy-duty plastic bag to pack out trash; bring along drinking water and toilet tissue. Do not allow children to swim when no lifeguards are present. Obey signs that indicate closed trails and rest rooms. Look for news about closings or delayed openings in spring 2004 and beyond. You can check the CT State Parks Web site (dep.state.ct.us/stateparks) or call the Parks Hotline (866–CT–PARKS).

may be less expensive than dinner. Lodging rates usually *are* seasonal, with higher rates prevailing during the warm months, at holiday and school vacation times, or in winter near ski centers. Be sure to inquire about special rates.

Rates for Lodging		Rates for Restaurants	
$	up to $50	$	most entrees over $10
$$	from $51 to $75	$$	most $11 to $15
$$$	from $76 to $99	$$$	most $16 to $20
$$$$	$100 and up	$$$$	most over $20

If you are planning to stay at an inn or a bed-and-breakfast, call in advance of your visit and be honest about the number and ages of the children in your family. In hotel rooms with two double beds and perhaps a couch and plenty of floor space, families may be able to sleep three to four small children, for whom there may be no extra charge. In the smaller hostelries, however, space in guest rooms is often more modest; many rooms contain only one double or queen-sized bed. Cribs and rollaway cots are available at all of the listings in this book, and a charge of $15 is usually added for each.

Please note that as of April 2004, all restaurants in Connecticut are smoke-free.

Special Needs and Equipment

If your family has special needs, call before you depart. Families with infants and toddlers may also benefit from an inquiry about the use of strollers, knapsacks, child carriers, and so on. Inquiries about the use of cameras and audio and video equipment may also spare you any disappointment.

A Word to the Wise

While the hours and prices listed in this guidebook were confirmed at press time, we strongly recommend that you call ahead to obtain current information before traveling. Exhibits and facilities change—even locations shift and, unfortunately, some places close down altogether. Restaurants and lodgings are especially changeable. Don't hesitate to let us know if you discover changes you'd like to pass along for future editions.

Attractions Key

The following is a key to the icons found throughout the text.

SWIMMING		**FOOD**	
BOATING / BOAT TOUR		**LODGING**	
HISTORIC SITE		**CAMPING**	
HIKING / WALKING		**MUSEUMS**	
FISHING		**PERFORMING ARTS**	
BIKING		**SPORTS/ATHLETICS**	
AMUSEMENT PARK		**PICNICKING**	
HORSEBACK RIDING		**PLAYGROUND**	
SKIING / WINTER SPORTS		**SHOPPING**	
PARK		**PLANTS / GARDENS / NATURE TRAILS**	
ANIMAL VIEWING		**FARMS**	

Fairfield County

Gold Coast and Green Woods

W idely known as Connecticut's wealthiest, busiest, and most densely populated area, Fairfield County offers a distinctive mix of attractions that belies the stereotyped reputation that gave parts of it the nickname the Gold Coast. True, vast estates fight for space alongside sleek corporate headquarters and manicured suburban enclaves, but much more is also here along this coastal plain, the gateway to New England.

Out-of-state visitors looking for a taste of New England within 60 miles of Manhattan can stop here to sample the Yankee charms of industry, prosperity, and abundance so evident in Fairfield County. This part of the state has long been popular as a playground for those seeking the forest, fields, and flowers in spring; the sea and sun in summer; the glorious foliage and bounties of the harvest in autumn; and the snowy serenity of the lanes

TopPicks for fun in Fairfield County

1. The Bruce Museum

2. Audubon Center at Greenwich

3. Stamford Museum and Nature Center

4. The Maritime Aquarium at Norwalk

5. Westport Country Playhouse children's series

6. *Seaport Islander* Cruise to Sheffield Island Lighthouse

7. The Beardsley Zoological Gardens and Carousel

8. The Barnum Museum

9. Devil's Den Nature Preserve

10. Squantz Pond State Park

FAIRFIELD COUNTY

and pastures in winter. Throughout the seasons, the famed Gold Coast offers a multifaceted gestalt of glitz and glade to suit all tastes and ages.

Some families may wish to search for fun in the county's "metropolitan" areas. The urban movers and shakers of Stamford, Norwalk, and Bridgeport woo travelers wary of the city by providing state-of-the-art museums, aquariums, playgrounds, and performing-arts stages equal to those in Boston and New York. Families adventuring among the city-based destinations will find well-marked streets, good lighting, safe parking, and top-notch facilities to ensure worry-free enjoyment of the city.

Families on the lookout for activities centered on the aquatic and nautical delights of Long Island Sound will find myriad opportunities for fun on and in the waters off the Gold Coast. First-time visitors may want to get their feet wet, so to speak, aboard tour boats that range from an ecological research vessel to a steam-powered cross-Sound ferry or a replica three-masted schooner. Families with their own boats can enter the Sound at a score of docks, marinas, and public launching sites. Fishing charters, daylong and overnight cruises, and sailboat and kayak rentals can be arranged through many operators. Families content with simpler pleasures can take beach gear to any of several public areas for castle-building and beachcombing in the sand.

When the charms of life on the water no longer float your boat, trade your sea legs for a landlubber-ly stroll through attractions wholly or partly dedicated to the marine and tidal ecosystem. You'll gain Sound-related education at Greenwich's Bruce Museum and at Norwalk's Maritime Aquarium and the Stepping Stones Museum.

Care to leave behind the bustle of both city and seaside? Fairfield County has hidden pleasures north of the I–95/Route 1 highways. Nature centers, wildlife refuges, and bird sanctuaries also provide shelter for world-worn seekers of solitude.

If you can't go far, at least take the slow lane to the back roads of Greenwich, New Canaan, Stamford, Westport, and Fairfield. If you can, go farther—to Easton, Redding, Ridgefield, Bethel, Brookfield, and the roads that lace around Candlewood Lake in New Fairfield. A yearlong tribute to Mother Nature lies around each bend of these pretty-as-a-picture roadways. Perfect for hiking, bicycling, and cross-country skiing, these trails, paths, and byways meander through maple and conifer forests, farmlands and orchards, and alongside rivers, streams, and waterfalls. Far from the clamor to the south, families who take these roads less traveled can savor the joys of outdoor recreation in the Eastern Woodlands.

A Heart-to-Heart Chat about Arteries

Lower Fairfield County has some interesting road signage on its main arteries, signage that may prove confusing to newcomers. The three main routes that run the length of the county from its New York border on the west throughout the remainder of the county as it extends east are U.S. Interstate 95 (also called the New England Thruway and the Connecticut Turnpike), the Merritt Parkway (State Route 15), and U.S. Route 1 (also known as the Boston Post Road, the Post Road, King's Highway, or as East or West Main Street or Avenue, *or* as some other name altogether). All these roads run east–west, but they have signs that say they go north–south. This smacks of some twisted Yankee humor along the lines of "You can't get there from here," but it's not. The roads are labeled that way because in general they lead north from New York and south from Boston. To confuse matters further, in Fairfield County the entrance signs to both the Merritt Parkway and I–95 usually read "North—New Haven" and "South—New York." Pull out a map and look at the names of the towns and cities along both routes. Be sure that you know whether you intend to travel east or west to or through these towns. Then, when you hop up on the highway or parkway, go north if you mean to go east and go south if you wish to go west. It's a perverse little system, ain't it?

A Word to the Driver

The main arteries for visitors traveling through Fairfield County are also the main arteries for commuters traveling from their jobs in New York and New Haven to their bedrooms in suburbia. Traffic, especially northbound, on I–95 and the Merritt Parkway (Route 15) is nearly always heavy from 4:00 to 7:00 P.M. on weekdays year-round. Heavy-but-steady becomes stop-and-go or even bumper-to-bumper on Fridays and before holidays from Memorial Day through Columbus Day as city dwellers hit the road in search of sun and fun in New England.

Whenever possible, avoid I–95 and the Merritt during these hours. Instead, stay busy in one place—dinnertime is a convenient excuse for staying put—or take Route 1 if you *must* head out at this time.

Should you become enmeshed in wall-to-wall machinery at some point, it is often best to stay on the road you have chosen—just rock steady with good tunes to pass the time. The other road is as likely to be crammed as the one you exit, although switching *can* be effective if an accident has caused the delay. Tune the radio to a station with a traffic report and get the scoop. If you are near Stamford, Route 137 (Washington Boulevard to High Ridge Road) will take you between I–95 and the Parkway. In Norwalk, Route 7 or Route 53 will get you on a true north–south track between the two highways. In Fairfield, Route 58 (Black Rock Turnpike) connects the two roads, and in Bridgeport the so-called Route 25 Connector is the route to take.

Greenwich

Visitors approaching Fairfield County from the New York border won't have far to drive for a full day of family-perfect activities. Home to corporate executives, artists, writers, athletes, and actors, the prestigious town of Greenwich is enriched by the varied interests and talents of its wealthy inhabitants.

Adding to Greenwich's riches are its most beautiful assets: rolling hills, verdant woodlands, and 32 miles of shoreline along Long Island Sound and its estuaries. Although much of the coast and woods is privately owned, there is plenty that visitors can share in this top-drawer community, especially now that Greenwich beaches have been legally opened to out-of-town visitors.

The Beaches **of Greenwich**

Greenwich's former policy of restricting public access to its beautiful beaches to residents of the town has been overturned by the courts—good news for non-resident visitors, if not for the beaches themselves. Now responsible use and limited parking space will prove the best tools for protecting this valuable environment. Nonresidents willing to pay the day-use fees, charged only in-season from April 14 through November 15, can enter the town beaches as long as parking spaces on any given day are available. Nonresidents pay $20 per car, plus $10 per person over the age of 4 in that vehicle. Beach passes must be purchased at the town hall or the civic center; they are not available at the beaches.

The 147-acre park at **Greenwich Point** is a good bet for families. Excellent for fishing and birdwatching, it also features a large swimming beach with concessions, rest rooms, and play areas; the **Seaside Center** (see page 6), run by naturalists working for the Bruce Museum; ponds; a seaside garden; an arboretum; and biking paths. Open from dawn to sunset, the park is connected to the mainland by a strip of land known as Tod's Driftway. Take Sound Beach Avenue south 1.8 miles from Route 1 to a right turn on Shore Road, then onward to the park entrance. You can also go to Byram Beach (Byram Shore Road) for the same fees. It has a freshwater pool and tennis.

Great fun, too, are the beaches at **Great Captain's Island** and **Little Captain's Island.** The ferry service (mid-June to September; $2.00 per person) at the **Arch Street Dock** takes visitors to **Island Beach** on the three-acre island or to the more primitive seventeen-acre island, where families may enjoy swimming, picnicking, and walking the trail to the nineteenth-century lighthouse. One caveat: to board the ferry, you need to be the guest of a Greenwich resident who can show a beach card and you pay $6.00 per person plus the $2.00 ferry fare. A concession operates on Little Captain's Island, but pack a picnic and beverages for a day on Great Captain's Island. For information on beach passes, call the Beach Card Office at (203) 622–7817. For Ferry Service information, call (203) 661–5957. To sort through the details at your leisure, check www.greenwichct. org/ParksandRec.

Bruce Museum of Arts and Science (ages 5 to 12)

1 Museum Drive; take I–95 exit 3 or Merritt exit 31; (203) 869–0376; www.brucemuseum. org. Open year-round, Tuesday to Saturday 10:00 A.M. to 5:00 P.M. and Sunday 1:00 to 5:00 P.M. Closed Monday and major holidays. $5.00 adults; $4.00 children 5 through 12; children under 5 free. Free to all on Tuesday.

One of the most sophisticated, state-of-the-art museums in the region, the Bruce houses approximately 15,000 objects in three categories: fine and decorative arts, cultural history, and environmental sciences. Pre-Columbian and Native American artifacts, American paintings, including CosCob Impressionist works, prints, and sculpture, French and American costumes, pottery, Tiffany glass, and more are in the art galleries. Changing exhibitions feature such diverse collections as textiles, dollhouses, photography, and mechanical banks.

The science galleries focus on the past 500 years of local history and ecology, taking visitors from ancient to modern times. Within this wing, the cavelike minerals gallery preserves a collection of ores, crystals, precious stones, and fluorescent minerals. An archaeological dig tucked into the coastal exhibit depicts the discovery of the Manakaway site on Greenwich Point and includes artifacts unearthed during the excavation. Interactive exhibits allow visitors to experience the evolution and ecology of Long Island Sound. These galleries also include a simulated wigwam of the Eastern Woodland Indians, a cross-section of a tidal marsh ecosystem, a marine touch tank, a diorama that takes audiences from dawn to dusk in a coastal woodland ecosystem, and an Ecological Awareness gallery focusing on tree and water communities.

The Bruce also offers a museum store and a continuous schedule of festivals, workshops, concerts, and children's programs. The Bruce also runs a small nature center at the beach at Greenwich Point. Perfect for families with young children, the **Seaside Center** offers **free** educational activities about the environment for all ages of visitors. A touch tank is maintained at the site along with other modest displays on marine life, but the best parts of a visit here are the guided beach and marsh walks, sensory hikes, nature crafts, beach-seining activities, and environmental games. Seaside Center is open July 1 to September 5 on Wednesday through Sunday from 10:00 A.M. to 4:00 P.M. Nonresidents should contact Anne Burns at (203) 869–6786, extension 338, for information on access to Greenwich Point and the schedule of programs.

Connecticut Impressionist **Art Trail**

The Connecticut Tourism Council has developed a guide to Connecticut museums with American Impressionism artworks. Three sites are in Fairfield County, where some say the movement was born. All of the sites are covered in this book. They are the Bruce Museum (Greenwich), Bush-Holley House (Greenwich), Weir Farm National Historic Site (Wilton), Yale University Art Gallery (New Haven), Florence Griswold Museum (Old Lyme), Lyman Allyn Art Museum (New London), William Benton Museum of Art (Storrs), Wadsworth Atheneum (Hartford), Hill-Stead Museum (Farmington), New Britain Museum of American Art (New Britain), and the Mattatuck Museum (Waterbury). A series of outdoor exhibits called *Viewpoints* features reproductions of American Impressionist paintings on large display panels at or near the sites where the artists actually worked. Look for these at Sherwood Island State Park in Westport, the Hadlyme Ferry Landing, Kent Falls State Park in Kent, and Windham Mills Heritage Park in Willimantic. For a free brochure on the trail, call the Convention and Visitor Bureau at (800) 866–7925 or send a business-size SASE to CIAT, P.O. Box 793, Old Lyme, CT 06371.

The Bruce Memorial Park and Playground (all ages)

Immediately adjacent to the Bruce is a great place to rest, run, or picnic. Views of a tidal marsh and Long Island Sound provide the backdrop. Leave your car at the museum or park on the street.

Audubon Center in Greenwich (all ages)

613 Riversville Road at John Street, Merritt exit 28; (203) 869–5272; www.audubon.org/ local/sanctuary/greenwich. Open year-round daily 9:00 A.M. to 5:00 P.M. Interpretive Building closed Easter, Thanksgiving, Christmas, and January 1. $3.00 adults, $1.50 children and seniors; free to National Audubon Society members.

In Greenwich's northern reaches, 15 miles of trails lead through 686 acres of woodlands, meadows, ponds, and streams. The Interpretive Building houses an exhibit gallery, a demonstration beehive, a bird observation window, a model backyard wildlife habitat, and the excellent Environmental Book and Gift Shop.

Several loop trails provide options for varying schedules and hiking abilities. None of the trails are strenuous, but some are moderately difficult. The Discovery Trail leads past a pond replete in summer with bullfrogs, duckweed, and dragonflies. Stay on the trail long enough and you'll walk right across the top of a pretty waterfall at the edge of Mead Lake. The landscape here is extraordinarily pretty and restful, and the trees are among the most awesome specimens in Connecticut. Return in autumn for the spectacular foliage and for the annual hawk migration that can be observed from the Quaker Ridge Hawk Watch Site.

Audubon Center offers hikes, bird-watching activities, butterfly programs, aquatic studies, day camps, and workshops for children and adults. Call for a calendar of these events. The center asks that you leave pets at home, that you leave flora and fauna undisturbed, and that you do not picnic on the grounds.

Fairchild Connecticut Wildflower Garden (all ages)

North Porchuck Road. Open daily, dawn to dusk. Free.

Audubon Center visitors are welcome to walk the trails of a second parcel just a mile away on North Porchuck Road. This 127-acre tract offers 8 miles of trails through native flowering plants and ferns. Established by Benjamin Fairchild in the early 1900s as an example of naturalistic landscaping, Fairchild Garden is especially lovely in the spring. On the two properties, more than 900 species of plants, 35 species of mammals, and 160 species of birds have been recorded.

Bush-Holley Historic Site and Visitor Center (ages 7 to 12)

39 Strickland Road in Cos Cob; (203) 869–6899; www.hstg.org. Visitor center and museum shop open year-round Tuesday through Sunday, noon to 4:00 P.M. Bush-Holley House open

year-round by tour only at 12:15, 1:15, 2:15, and 3:15 P.M. Tuesday through Sunday from March through December and on weekends only in January and February. Closed Easter, July 4, Thanksgiving, Christmas, and January 1. Tours of the house, $6.00 adults; $4.00 students 12 and over; children under 12 free. Visitor center and shop, free to all.

If pre-Revolutionary history or colonial lifestyles interest you, visit here. A National Historic Landmark run by the Greenwich Historical Society, the 1732 structure is a classic central-chimney saltbox. Once home to farmer and mill owner David Bush and later a boarding-house operated by the Holley family, the house is the site of one of the first American Impressionist art colonies. Childe Hassam and J. Alden Weir, among others, painted here from 1890 to 1925. Examples of their works are displayed, along with an authentic re-creation of Elmer MacRae's studio and a fine collection of household implements, tools, furniture, and textiles. A charming Visitor Center orients families to the house as well as to the art colony and local history. Three tableaus feature life-sized figures in light and sound presentations describing the history of the site, and five interactive stations offer hands-on displays about local history and arts. Changing and permanent exhibitions such as 2003's *Voices from the Civil War* are also launched annually. Check the Web site to see what is up currently. If you tour the house, be sure to ask for the Colonial Fun Pack cards that help youngsters get the most out of a visit here. The Vanderbilt Education Center is a new facility for lectures, educational workshops, and other special programs for children. There, on the last Saturday of every month from noon to 3:00 P.M., is a free program called Historic Fun for Families, in which you and the children may try fishing pole crafting, papermaking, wool spinning, cooking, or other such history-oriented activities. Reservations are highly recommended.

Children may also attend a two-week history camp annually during the month of July to learn about eighteenth-century colonial life, history, and art. Hearth cooking, needle-work, sheep shearing, painting, drawing, and other art may be among the activities. At Christmastime, the house is decorated in a Victorian theme for candlelight tours.

Putnam Cottage (ages 7 to 12)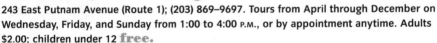

243 East Putnam Avenue (Route 1); (203) 869–9697. Tours from April through December on Wednesday, Friday, and Sunday from 1:00 to 4:00 P.M., or by appointment anytime. Adults $2.00; children under 12 free.

Built circa 1692, Putnam Cottage was used during the Revolution as a meeting place of military leaders, including former resident General Israel Putnam, second in command to George Washington. Restored to appear as it might have in 1700, its unusual fish-scale shingles, its fieldstone fireplaces, and an eighteenth-century herb garden are among its special features. The cottage's collection includes Putnam's desk, Bible, glasses, the mirror through which he supposedly saw the British coming, and his military uniform.

Children may enjoy visiting on the last Sunday in February for the reenactment of Putnam's famous ride down the steep stone cliff east of the cottage; they will be delighted to see Redcoats and rebels—in full regalia—skirmish on the grounds.

Where to Eat

Penang Grill. 35 Lewis Street; (203) 861–1988. Judged "very good" by the *New York Times* in 2001, this popular and inexpensive Malaysian restaurant will suit any food explorers with a taste for spicy Thai/Indonesian/Chinese favorites. Lunch and dinner daily. $–$$

Pasta Vera. 48 Greenwich Avenue; (203) 661–9705. Open daily for lunch and dinner, this is the best place for pasta and pizza. Adults will enjoy favorites with excellent sauces. Salads, housemade desserts. $–$$

Sundown Saloon. 403 Greenwich Avenue; (203) 629–8212. Homemade lemonade and root beer floats. Butcher paper on the tables and plenty of crayons. Sheriff's badges for the kids. Little Dudes' menu with favorites like Sheriff's grilled cheese, Little Joe's pasta, and quesadillas. Plenty of choices for adults, too. Open daily, lunch and dinner; Sunday brunch. $–$$

Meli Melo. 362 Greenwich Avenue (203) 629–6153. This very French, very friendly creperie is great fun for kids and incredibly delicious. Try the ham and swiss cheese crepe or the fabulous banana and Nutella wheat crepe. Magnifique. Fresh-made soups, salads, sorbets. Open daily from 10:00 A.M. to 10:00 P.M. $

Where to Stay

Howard Johnson Greenwich Hotel. 1114 Boston Post Road, in the Riverside section; (203) 637–3691 or (800) 654–2000. Standard best bet for families. 104 units, restaurant, outdoor swimming pool. Kids stay **free.** Complimentary continental breakfast. $$$

Hyatt Regency Greenwich. 1800 East Putnam Avenue, Old Greenwich; (203) 637–1234 or (800) 233–1234. Luxurious, tasteful, convenient to everything. 373 rooms (13 suites), restaurants, health club, indoor pool, day spa. Complimentary continental breakfast. $$$$

Harbor House Inn. 165 Shore Road, Old Greenwich; (203) 637–0145; www.hhinn.com. 22 rooms, including 3 suites in Victorian mansion near the beach. Private baths, some with whirlpool, complimentary breakfast. Nonsmoking; no pets. Bicycles available. $$$$

Stanton House Inn. 76 Maple Avenue; (203) 869–2110. 22 rooms, with 2 suites, in vintage mansion close to town. Breakfast included. Private baths, outdoor pool, beach passes. No smoking. $$$$

Stamford

The glitziest city in Fairfield County, Stamford offers excellent opportunities for family fun in both its southern and northern extremes, along with a handful of lesser-known choices in between. The museums, galleries, performing arts centers, shops, and restaurants sprinkled among the downtown office towers that rise just 5 miles east of Greenwich make the city's center sparkle with a sophisticated vitality. Its shoreline urges visitors to tarry awhile near the marinas and beaches and on the waves of the Sound. Lastly, its northern hills lure families to the hidden pleasures of Stamford's surprising woodlands. In every season, there's a reason to visit Stamford.

Stamford Center for the Arts (all ages) ♫

The Rich Forum, 307 Atlantic Street; The Palace Theatre, 61 Atlantic Street; (203) 325–4466 or (203) 358–2305; www.onlyatsca.com.

The Rich Forum and the Palace Theatre add a dash of panache to Stamford's cultural attractions. From September through June, the Rich Forum's lush performing arts complex hosts highly acclaimed theater productions featuring top performers from around the world. Many of these full-stage performances from Broadway and London are suitable for the whole family. In 2003, for instance, George Balanchine's production of *The Nutcracker* was staged here. To save money on tickets, take advantage of group rates, matinees, or upper-tier seats.

The Palace Theatre is a fully restored architectural masterpiece with incredible acoustics. Permanent home to the Stamford Symphony Orchestra, the Connecticut Grand Opera, the New England Lyric Operetta Company, the Stamford City Ballet, and the Connecticut Ballet, the Palace offers single-night or short-run performances of music, dance, drama, and other family entertainment such as circuses, magic shows, and musical comedies.

Four productions for young children are performed each academic year on weekdays for school groups. These productions are also open to families; call for reservations and show times. Two children's productions are also usually offered in the summertime. Call to see what the current season offers.

Stamford Theatre Works and the Purple Cow Children's Theatre (ages 3 to 12) ♫

200 Strawberry Hill Avenue; (203) 359–4414; www.stamfordtheatreworks.org. September through May. Tuesday through Saturday evenings and Saturday and Sunday matinees.

Not-for-profit professional productions often lauded as innovative, experimental, thought-provoking, and socially relevant are of primary interest here, in a historic, 150-seat barn theater. Most of the full productions staged here are best for adults and children older than 12. Tickets in 2003–2004 ranged from $16 to $29.

The Purple Cow productions are wonderful for children aged 3 to 8. Affordable and fun, they are offered twice daily at 9:30 A.M. and 11:30 A.M. Saturdays in May, June, and July and during the December holiday season. Typical fare includes puppet shows, magic, fairy tales, and dramatizations of children's literature. Tickets in 2003–2004 were $10.00; groups of four or more pay $8.00; lap-sitters pay $3.00.

Curtain Call Theater at the Sterling Farms Theatre Complex
(ages 8 to 12)

1349 Newfield Avenue; (203) 329–8207; www.CurtainCallinc.com. Open year-round.

Specializing in theater for the lighthearted, Curtain Call does four major comedy productions each year, along with cabaret-style musicals and comedies. Ticket prices may be the best theater bargain in the state; subscriptions are even better deals. Both stages are recently renovated and enlarged, with comfortable seating and improved sightlines. The Dressing Room Theatre, in the 2003–2004 season, staged such family entertainment as *Steel Magnolias* and *The Fantastiks*. Bring your own dinner or snacks and beverages and enjoy the show. In the Kweskin Theatre, the full-scale musical productions of *My Fair Lady* and *South Pacific* were delights. *Arsenic and Old Lace* and *The Odd Couple* attracted mixed audiences of young and older. Ask about the appropriateness of individual shows if you'd like to take the family. Many are just right for young audiences. Curtain Call also offers theater workshops for adults and youth.

United House Wrecking Company (all ages) 🔒

535 Hope Street; (203) 348–5371; www.United-Antiques.com. Open year-round, Monday through Saturday from 9:30 A.M. to 5:30 P.M. and Sunday from noon to 5:00 P.M. Closed on major holidays.

Parents might not plan an all-day excursion here with young children but the merchandise and sheer size of this amazing emporium have combined to place this store irrevocably on Stamford's list of attractions. More than 30,000 square feet of retail space make this a browser's dream-come-true. Architectural salvage—stained-glass windows, mantels, claw-foot bathtubs—is the attraction for renovators, but the fun only begins there. Clocks, weather vanes, telescopes, lanterns, wishing wells, pottery, jewelry, traffic lights, toys, china, books, and furniture fill the space to the brim. Mixed with this "normal" stuff is an ever-changing array of truly odd, absolutely fantastical, and downright weird stuff— gargoyles, moose heads, dentists' chairs, a barbershop pole, jukeboxes, circus posters, wagon wheels—in short, everything under the sun including the kitchen sink. You'll have fun choosing something funky or whimsical for the kids' rooms or the family room.

SoundWaters Eco-Cruises and Community Center for Environmental Education (all ages) 🔺

Schooner: 4 Brewers Yacht Haven Marina, at the foot of Washington Boulevard; Education center: Holly House in Cove Island Park; (203) 323–1978; www.soundwaters.org. Open Tuesday through Saturday, 10:00 A.M. to 5:00 P.M., Sunday noon to 5:00 P.M. Closed Monday. For evening programs, the center opens one-half hour prior to the scheduled program. Cruises cost adults $25; children 12 and under $15; sunset and fireworks cruises $30 per person. Private charters available. Two-hour guided canoe trips ($20 per person) around Holly Pond are on Saturday, June through October, at 10:00 A.M. and 2:30 P.M.

If the smell of the salt breeze draws you toward the water, try to catch a ride on the 80-foot **SoundWaters,** a replica of a three-masted sharpie schooner that offers two-hour eco-cruises from June 1 to mid-October. Led by trained naturalists, the cruises focus on the ecology, history, culture, and future of Long Island Sound. You can help raise the sails, haul in the trawl net, and examine the catch in four stations that focus on various aspects of marine life and ecology.

Public sails on this floating classroom are offered three to five times monthly during the warm season. Special sails, such as a Fireworks Sail in early July, are also open to the public. Call for a schedule or to reserve a place on these very popular cruises. All sails require advance reservation and payment, although you can sometimes get lucky by trying last-minute right at the dock.

The *SoundWaters* **Community Center for Environmental Education** is located at Cove Island Park (see Cove Island Park sidebar) in the restored historic Holly House. History, natural science, and marine and maritime exhibits are among the displays here. A wide variety of day and evening programs, some offered at no charge and others at a small (often $5.00) fee, are on the yearlong calendar of events. Nearly every Saturday, a Family Arts and Ecology program is scheduled. These interactive events are perfect for children aged 4 to 12. Most are **free.** Concerts and canoe trips are frequent; they cost $15 and $20, respectively. Reservations for the former are recommended; for the latter, they are required. From Labor Day to Memorial Day, parking at Cove Island is **free** both to Stamford residents and nonresidents. In season, parking remains **free,** but nonresident visitors must tell the parking attendant that they are visiting Holly House and are pre-registered for a program.

Stamford Museum and Nature Center (all ages)

39 Scofieldtown Road; (203) 322–1646; www.stamfordmuseum.org. Open year-round, Monday through Saturday and holidays, 9:00 A.M. to 5:00 P.M.; Sunday 11:00 A.M. to 5:00 P.M. Closed July 4, Thanksgiving, Christmas, New Year's Day. Planetarium shows on Sunday year-round at 3:00 P.M.; adults $2.00, children $1.00 for the shows, plus museum entrance fee. Observatory hours, weather permitting, are 8:00 to 10:00 P.M. on Friday from September through April; 8:30 to 10:30 P.M. from May 1 to Labor Day; adults $3.00, children $2.00 with no entrance fee. The nonresident entrance fee to the Museum and Nature Center is adults $6.00, children under 14 and seniors $5.00; children 3 and under free.

This 118-acre park has features like no other Connecticut nature center. Heckscher Farm is a working nineteenth-century farm re-creation that includes a 1750 barn on the hillside pastureland. A garden yields a bountiful autumn harvest, and animals such as a cow, pigs, goats, chickens, geese, oxen, sheep, and even a pair of river otters inhabit the enclosure. In its midst is a country store and a tiny gem of an exhibit dedicated to eighteenth- and nineteenth-century farm life and tools.

In addition to 3 miles of woodland trails and a pond habitat with an adjacent picnic area, a streamside boardwalk with benches, handrails, and braille signs and sensory stations complements the Overbrook Natural Science Center, which houses aquatic tanks simulating habitats of creatures that inhabit the woodland and its streams. Various species of reptiles and amphibians currently live in the center. A projection microscope allows visitors to view frog eggs, insects, or other natural materials on an overhead screen. Outside the center a brick walkway edges a garden of native plants. The center's trails also connect to the trails of the adjacent Bartlett Arboretum.

On the hillside nearest the parking area is the Stamford Museum, which houses changing fine art exhibitions, Americana, nature exhibits, and a permanent exhibit on Native American life and history. Several dioramas are the highlight of the Native American gallery; it also includes a birchbark canoe, a huge bison head, and other artifacts from four major North American Indian groups. The museum is also home to a planetarium and an observatory, with the largest telescope west of the Mississippi.

The complex also includes Nature's Playground, a wooded one-acre children's play area. An 8-foot-high hollow log leading to a 3-foot hollow branch opens onto a sandpit where kids can dig for fossil and dinosaur bone replicas. A 6-foot-high hollow stump features copies of insect galleries and honeycombs. Two 7-foot-wide hawks' nests in which to climb, a large-scale chipmunk burrow in which to rest, and a 30-foot-long otters' slide on which, of course, to slide are among other features. A water environment area includes play possibilities such as dam construction or boat racing. A tree house, a beaver lodge replica, and a rope spider's web complete the scene.

Among all these areas, the staff conducts workshops, lectures, festivals, and summer camps. Summer folk concerts, an autumn Harvest Fair, an Astronomy Day, and other annual events such as maple sugaring, ice harvesting, and apple cidering are all on the calendar.

Bartlett Arboretum (all ages)

151 Brookdale Road; (203) 322–6971. Open year-round, daily, 8:30 A.M. to sunset. The Visitor Center is open 8:30 A.M. to 4:00 P.M. Monday through Friday, except on holidays. The greenhouse is open daily from 9:30 to 11:00 A.M. Free.

Just down the road from the Stamford Nature Center is this sanctuary of natural-growth oak, maple, and hickory trees interspersed with evergreens, ash, birch, beech, and yellow poplar. Perennial borders, a conifer garden, a native wildflower garden, and a nut tree collection are among the major areas of this gorgeous state-owned arboretum.

Five miles of trails lead through the gardens, woodlands, and wetlands. A shallow reflecting pond at the end of the Woodland Trail is a perfect destination for young children, as is the boardwalk that leads through the red maple Swamp Trail. The self-guided Ecology Trail combines portions of each of these trails. Pick up a guidebook at the Visitor Center so you can enjoy the descriptions of twenty-seven stations along the trail. The arboretum's trails also connect to the Stamford Nature Center's trails, so visits to both areas can be combined.

If your group includes children under twelve, you may be able to borrow a nature activity backpack from the Visitor Center before you set out on a walk. Crayons, scratch pads, a magnifying glass, and a wonderful set of cards with games, questions, activity suggestions, and educational information enhance the experience for the whole family.

Take a stroll through the greenhouse for a look at the incredible cacti and succulents among the tropical and temperate plants in the collection. Lastly, stop again at the Visitor Center, which contains an exhibition hall, an ecology research laboratory, and a lending library of excellent horticultural materials. Used books are often for sale in the lobby, and plants are available at the annual plant sale and Garden Fair in early May.

The arboretum offers **free** guided walks for the whole family throughout the year. **Free** public concerts are held approximately every other Sunday in the months of July and August (call for schedule). Pack a picnic supper to enjoy on the lawn as you listen.

Cove Island **Park**

Located at Cove Road and Weed Street on the eastern end of Stamford, Cove Island Park is an eighty-three-acre recreation area right on the Sound. The largest public park in the city, it is open year-round and offers a wide beach with a pavilion and concessions, picnic areas, horseshoe pits, tennis courts, basketball courts, a softball field, a playground, a path for walkers and joggers, a separate path for in-line skaters and bicyclists, a marina (no dedicated transient slips), and an ice rink.

From Memorial Day weekend through Labor Day, nonresidents can use the park on Monday through Friday only. Visitors can purchase a one-day pass for $30 per vehicle; call the Stamford Parks and Recreation Department (203–977–4692) or the Terry Connors Ice Rink (203–977–4514) for details on purchasing the passes. You can also check the Web site www.cityofstamford. org/ParksandRecreation. Even in season, nonresident walkers or bikers can enter the park at any time at no charge. Nonresident visitors to the SoundWaters Environmental Center may enter in season at no charge if they let the attendant know they are headed there. Off-season, nonresident vehicles can enter daily at no charge.

Try to stay for one of the guided beach walks sponsored by Save the Sound, Inc. throughout the summer. Midday and evening walks offer a study of the shoreline animals and plants. Ask the park attendant for a schedule.

Public sessions (roughly two hours long) are offered at the skating rink year-round. Summer sessions are Friday night and Saturday and Sunday afternoon. Winter sessions are more frequent. Call for the current schedule. Skating costs nonresident adults $10.00 and children $7.00. Skate rentals are $4.00 a pair.

Where to Eat

City Limits Diner. 135 Harvard Avenue; (203) 348–7000. Delightfully retro and refreshingly contemporary choices are on the huge menu at this absolutely sparkling 1950s-style establishment attached to the Fairfield Inn. Perfect for families, it seats 200 for casual snacks, breakfasts, lunches, and dinners at typically modest diner prices. Open 7:00 A.M. to 11:00 P.M. Monday through Friday and until midnight on weekends. $–$$$

Paradise Bar and Grille. 78 Southfield Avenue; (203) 323–1116. This very popular casual eatery at Stamford Landing is a tropical treat in summer and a cozy retreat for watching the gulls in the wintertime. Chef Jimmy Myers is a dad himself; he knows how to adapt his eclectic menu of pastas, pizzas, seafood, sandwiches, and salads to young tastes. Shipwreck chowder is great; crisp salads and American comfort foods are on the menu in all seasons. Open for lunch and dinner daily from noon to 10:00 P.M. $$–$$$

Quattro Pazzi. 245 Hope Street; (203) 964–1801. Cozy, convenient, and confusing—how can we choose between thirty-two different but equally wonderful pasta dishes? Lunch Tuesday to Friday only. Dinner Tuesday through Sunday from 5:00 P.M. $$

Tat's on Summer. 184 Summer Street; (203) 325–2222. This busy, cheerful all-you-can-eat Chinese buffet right downtown provides lunch for $7.37 Monday through Friday from 11:30 A.M. to 3:30 P.M. and dinner for $11.61 Monday through Sunday from 4:30 P.M. Children's meals are discounted 25 to 50 percent, depending on their age. $

Where to Stay

Fairfield Inn by Marriott. 135 Harvard Avenue; (203) 357–7100. 158 units, including 70 suites. Restaurant, health club, indoor pool. Continental breakfast. $$$$

Holiday Inn Select. 700 Main Street (203) 358–8400. 383 rooms, 3 suites, restaurant, coffee shop, fitness center, sauna, indoor pool. Coffeemakers, hair dryers, irons. $$$$

Stamford Marriott. 2 Stamford Forum (203) 357–9555. 506 units, 6 suites, revolving rooftop restaurant, health club, sauna, jogging track, indoor and outdoor pools, sports court, game room. Lower weekend rates. $$$$

Stamford Suites Hotel. 720 Bedford Street; (203) 359–7300. 45 units with full kitchen, health club privileges with indoor and outdoor pools, tennis, continental breakfast. $$$$

Stamford Super 8 Motel. 32 Grenhart Road; (203) 324–8887 or (800) 800–8000. 99 units, with 1 suite. Basic amenities plus TVs. Clean. Continental breakfast. $$$

New Canaan

Exquisite in nearly every way is the gracious and affluent suburb of New Canaan, just 8 miles northeast of downtown Stamford via Route 137 or 106. Its busy village center is chock-full of boutiques, restaurants, bakeries, and bookstores (such as the excellent **New Canaan Book Shop** on Elm Street), many of which are specially designed to fulfill the whims of children. If you hate malls but love to shop, spend a day in New Canaan. Before you drop, though, put away the checkbook and visit two of Fairfield County's treasures.

New Canaan Nature Center (all ages)

144 Oenoke Ridge; (203) 966–9577; www.newcanaannature.org. Discovery Center open year-round, Monday through Saturday from 9:00 A.M. to 4:00 P.M. Closed on major holidays. Trails and grounds open daily, dawn to dusk. Free; donations accepted; memberships encouraged.

A respite from the thrust and parry of lower Fairfield County's version of civilization, the Nature Center's forty acres of diverse habitats include 2 miles of trails and boardwalk through meadow, woods, and marsh. Its compact size makes the center accessible to small children while remaining of interest to older visitors.

A bird-watching platform, two ponds, a wildflower garden, a butterfly field, a maple syrup shed, an orchard, a cider house, and an herb garden are all on the property. The excellent Discovery Center, located in the Visitor Center, houses exhibits and activities in the natural sciences. See a living bee colony, crawl through a "burrow," make leaf rubbings, handle animal homes and hides, or make animal tracks with rubber stamps and ink. Learn about soil, seeds, minerals, geology, migration, and animal defense mechanisms. Check out snakes, newts, turtles, and fish in several habitat tanks, and stop by the gift shop.

Back outside is the wildlife rehabilitation area for injured creatures. Next door is the solar greenhouse—its pretty goldfish pond has a really neat fountain. The Nature Center offers walks, day camps, live animal demonstrations, and canoeing, hiking, and bicycle trips. They also offer natural science birthday parties, parent-child programs, and annual events such as the Halloween Haunting Trail Walk, Fall Fair, and Christmas Market.

New Canaan Historical Society (ages 7 to 12)

13 Oenoke Ridge; (203) 966–1776. The Town House is open to the public year-round, Tuesday through Saturday from 9:30 A.M. to 12:30 P.M. and from 2:00 to 4:30 P.M. The other buildings are open during July and August on Tuesday, Wednesday, Thursday, Friday, and Sunday from 2:00 to 4:00 P.M., and from September through June on Wednesday, Thursday, and Sunday from 2:00 to 4:00 P.M. Donation.

This complex includes five buildings housing seven museums and a library. The 1764 Hanford-Silliman House is furnished in the style of its eighteenth- and nineteenth-century inhabitants. It includes a beautiful collection of dolls, toys, and quilts. The Tool Museum houses the tools of the housewright, cabinetmaker, wheelwright, wainwright, tanner, farmer, cooper, farrier, and shoemaker. The fully operational New Canaan Hand Press is a re-creation of a nineteenth-century printing office with a rare Smith-Hoe Acorn iron press. The 1878 John Rogers Studio and Museum, dedicated to the famed "people's sculptor" of the same name, houses a fine collection of Rogers's work actually sculpted in the studio. The 1799 Rock School is an original New Canaan one-room schoolhouse, with benches, desks, woodstove, and more.

The Town House includes the library and exhibition room, the Costume Museum, and the Cody Drug Store. Changing exhibitions in the Costume Museum are arranged to span the 200 years of American life the collection represents. The Cody Drug Store contains fixtures, salves, ointments, scrip books, patent medicines, and even the ice cream parlor from the original 1845 store, once on New Canaan's Main Street.

The society offers living-history programs and demonstrations to school groups and sponsors special event days (such as an Annual Ice Cream Social) when all buildings are open to the public. Call ahead to arrange a family tour of all the buildings.

Where to Eat

Garelick and Herbs. 97 Main Street; (203) 972–8200. Great eat-here or take-out sandwiches, soups, baked goods, salads, ice cream cart. Open Monday through Saturday, 8:00 A.M. to 7:00 P.M.; 9:00 A.M. to 5:00 P.M. on Sunday. $

Gates. 10 Forest Street; (203) 966–8666. Just outside the village, this place is colorful and noisy, the food is excellent and original, and a children's menu keeps youngsters happy. Open for lunch and dinner daily. $$

Taste of Asia. 73 Elm Street; (203) 966–8830. This spotless eatery offers Szechuan-style cuisine, a handmade noodle bar, and usually on weekends only, Shanghai dim sum. Open daily for lunch and dinner. $–$$. If it's SRO here, try **Plum Tree** (70 Main Street) or **Ching's Table** (64 Main Street); both are great.

Cherry Street East. 45 East Avenue; (203) 966–2100. Open for lunch and dinner, daily from 11:30 A.M. and for breakfast from 7:00 to 10:00 A.M. on Saturday, this casual pub-style eatery offers chili, plus excellent salads, soups, fish and chips, burgers, and sandwiches. $

Where to Stay

Village Inn of New Canaan. 122 Park Street; (203) 966–8413 or (800) 370–2224. Operated by the same family since 1918. 32 country-styled rooms with private baths; 3 are suites, 5 are efficiencies. Deluxe rooms large enough to comfortably sleep a family of four range from $155 to $185. Continental breakfast. $$$–$$$$

Norwalk

Even were it not chock-full of terrific attractions, Norwalk's interesting history and its charming coastline would make it a perfect family destination. As it is jampacked with all these qualities, however, there is no doubt that Norwalk is one of Connecticut's most popular cities with tourists. This guide includes only the top ten attractions and events in town. The city's center is 7 miles east of downtown Stamford and 5 miles south of the center of New Canaan.

The Maritime Aquarium at Norwalk (all ages)

10 North Water Street; (203) 852–0700; www.maritimeaquarium.org. Open daily except Thanksgiving and Christmas Day. Regular hours are 10:00 A.M. to 5:00 P.M.; from July 1 to Labor Day 6:00 P.M. Seal feedings at 11:45 A.M., 1:45 and 3:45 P.M.; shark feeding at 1:00 P.M. The IMAX runs hourly from 11:00 A.M. to 3:00 or 4:00 P.M. depending on aquarium hours; it also offers Friday and Saturday evening shows. Admission charged to the aquarium alone, to the IMAX alone, or to both together. Adults, $9.25, $7.00, or $14.00, respectively; children 2 to 12, $7.50, $5.25, or $10.50; under 2 are free. Parking available at adjacent municipal lots at additional cost. Admission is not required to enter the gift shop or cafeteria.

The flagship of the artsy SoNo neighborhood, this aquarium/theater/maritime museum is a celebration of life near, on, and under Long Island Sound. Overlooking Norwalk Harbor, this attraction includes twenty-two aquariums with sharks, jellyfish, seals, river otters, and 125 other species of marine life.

Stroll from one habitat re-creation to another, beginning at the salt marsh and culminating at a 110,000-gallon tank with 9-foot sharks, stingrays, and other creatures of the open ocean. Watch harbor seals swim in a pool and river otters tumble and slide in a simulated woodland and shoreline habitat with underwater viewing windows. View the underwater ballet of two gentle giants: loggerhead sea turtles that share a 15,000-gallon tank. Handle sea stars, horseshoe crabs, and other tidal pool inhabitants in a touch tank. Throughout the aquarium, learn the secrets of the fragile ecosystems of Long Island Sound and its estuaries.

In the maritime museum area, watch crafters build wooden boats in the centuries-old tradition of New England boatbuilders. Discover the names and uses of boats such as the dory, sandbagger, and sharpie as you learn about marine navigation and Norwalk's oyster industry.

All Aboard the *Oceanic*

If the displays at the aquarium spark your interest in the sea, consider a two-and-a-half-hour cruise on its research vessel, the 40-foot trawler *Oceanic*. Public cruises are daily at 1:00 P.M. from July 1 through Labor Day and on Saturday and Sunday only in May, June, and September. On winter weekends from December through March, see the seals that inhabit the Sound during the coldest months. In summer, onboard educators explain the ecology of the Sound as participants collect water samples at different depths, haul a trawl net, and examine the catch in the shipboard touch tank. Adults and children pay $17.50 for both summer and winter cruises. Reservations are recommended. The *Oceanic* leaves from the Maritime Aquarium Dock on the Norwalk River near the IMAX theater entrance. Call (203) 852–0700, extension 2206.

Before you go home, watch an IMAX film in the six-story-high theater. You might experience the secrets of the coral reef or Egypt, or take a *STOMP* odyssey in whatever film is currently scheduled. An 80-foot-wide screen creates a you-are-there effect, and the 24,000-watt sound system keeps you on the edge of your seat.

Changing exhibitions are frequent and wonderful. Even the aquarium itself has changed in the past few years with the opening of a new Environmental Education Center, a cafeteria, and an expanded museum store.

Special events, lectures, camps, and workshops are commonplace at the aquarium, and many are tailored to children of specific or all ages. The Maritime Aquarium should be on everyone's list of places to go with the family in Connecticut.

Seaport Islander Cruises to Sheffield Island (all ages)

Seaport Dock, just south of the Maritime Aquarium at the corner of Washington and Water Streets; (203) 838–9444 for schedule and information; (203) 334–9166 for special charters; www.soundnavigation.com or www.seaport.org. Weekends and holidays only from early May until the second week of June, with cruises at 10:00 A.M., 1:00 and 4:00 P.M. From mid-June through Labor Day, cruises depart at 11:00 A.M. and 3:00 P.M. on weekdays; weekend and holiday cruises are at 10:00 A.M., 1:00 and 4:00 P.M. Two-hour sunset cruises, in summer only, at 7:00 P.M. on Saturday. Seating is first come, first served for daily cruises, but reservations are required for sunset cruises. Arrive a half-hour early to allow time for parking in a nearby lot. Adults $15.00; children under 12 $12.00; children under 3 $5.00.

This clean, comfortable, forty-four-passenger vessel offers a thirty-minute cruise to the outermost of the Norwalk Islands, where one can disembark for an hour, an afternoon, or a whole day of beachcombing, birdwatching, picnicking, or touring the 1868 stone lighthouse.

The knowledgeable *Seaport Islander* crew and captain offer a lively narration on the trip to the island. Stories about the wildlife areas of Norwalk Harbor are mixed with explanations of various buoys, historical details on landmark structures, and legends of the islands.

Once on dry land at Sheffield Island, passengers can spend time as they choose. Most folks take the tour of the lighthouse. Several of its ten rooms are open to the public, and four flights of stairs lead to the lovely black-capped light tower. Decommissioned in 1902, when a new light was built a quarter-mile inshore, the original light is no longer in the tower. If you have time to spare, bring a picnic along and spread a blanket in the three-acre picnic grove for a leisurely lunch or brunch. No concessions are on the island, so bring your own snacks. Wear bathing suits and sunscreen so you can swim or comb the beach. An environmentally friendly bathroom is on the island.

The sixty-acre island also includes the **Stewart B. McKinney National Wildlife Refuge.** Within its boundaries is a 2,000-foot nature trail with observation deck, or you can encircle the refuge by walking the perimeter of the island. Don't forget to note the time if you set out on such an excursion: The last cruise departs the island at 5:15 P.M. on weekdays and 6:15 P.M. on weekends and holidays. The seating area on the *Seaport Islander* is covered to protect you from sun, wind, or inclement weather. A bathroom and a snack-and-drinks bar add to your comfort.

SoNo Historic District and
SoNo Arts Celebration

Like the Sheffield Island lighthouse, this waterfront area is listed on the National Register of Historic Places, and its comeback from decay is a tribute to the city of Norwalk. Centered on Washington, Water, and South Main Streets, SoNo is a picturesque neighborhood of boutiques, restaurants, galleries, and interesting attractions. The **Railroad Switchtower Museum,** on Washington Street tucked high above the roadway at the railroad overpass, is an interesting slice of history. For more information on this historic structure, call its Visitor Center at (203) 246–6958. It is open on weekends from noon to 5:00 P.M., May through October. Their Web site is www.westctnrhs.org/tower.

If you like the arts, come to SoNo during August for the three-day **SoNo Arts Celebration.** Hundreds of juried fine artists exhibit their work in a sidewalk show spanning several blocks. Live-music performances, an antique auto parade, storytelling, dance exhibitions, a film fest, and a giant puppet parade are all part of the festivities. In the Kinetic Sculpture Race artists move their weird and wonderful contraptions over a 1-mile course through SoNo streets, using any human-powered means they choose. The Children's Area has hands-on projects designed for young artists. Food is abundant, and area attractions and merchants plan special events. Similar events and festivities occur at the Splash! Festival held annually in June; a real treat among the many water-related harborfront activities is the Hong Kong-style dragon boat race. For information on the neighborhood and its events, call (203) 866–7916 or visit www.southnorwalk.com.

Lockwood-Mathews Mansion Museum (ages 5 to 12)

295 West Avenue, just north of SoNo and I–95; (203) 838–9799; www.lockwoodmathews.org. Open mid-March through December, Wednesday through Sunday from noon to 5:00 P.M. Closed on major holidays. Last tour an hour prior to closing. Adults $8.00; students $5.00; children under 12 free.

If any child in your family would like to see a castle, come here. A National Historic Landmark, this remarkable four-story stone chateau redefines splendor and elegance. Originally built in 1864 for Legrand Lockwood, Wall Street investment banker and railroad magnate, the lavish Victorian mansion features the craftsmanship of the finest American and European artisans of the time. Incredibly fine inlaid woodwork, marble floors, frescoed walls, gold-leafed ceilings, crystal chandeliers, and fine decorative arts are found throughout the fifty rooms that surround the mansion's magnificent skylit octagonal rotunda. A beautiful collection of music boxes is displayed on the second floor.

Hour-long guided tours are preceded by a short film describing the painstaking—and ongoing—restoration of the house. A gift shop and lovely grounds are available for browsing and strolling. Annual events include a Victorian Ice Cream Social in early summer and a crafts fair in mid-July. Other special exhibitions and festivals are held each year.

Stepping Stones Museum for Children (ages 1 to 10)

303 West Avenue, in Mathews Park, near the junction of I–95 (exit 14 North or exit 15 South) and Route 7; (203) 899–0606; www.steppingstonesmuseum.org. Open year-round 10:00 A.M. to 5:00 P.M. Tuesday through Sunday. Also open on Monday from 10:00 A.M. to 5:00 P.M. in the summer and on Monday holidays. Open until 8:00 P.M. on Thursday in July and August. Closed on January 1, Easter, Thanksgiving, and Christmas. Adults and children $7.00; children under age one are free.

One of the most popular attractions for families with young children in Fairfield County is this marvelous, interactive learning center. Designed to meet the intellectual, physical, and emotional needs of young children and based on the idea that children learn best through hands-on investigation and discovery, this museum is a "Please touch" fantasyland. It is located on its own five-acre space in **Norwalk's Mathews Park,** which is also home to the **Lockwood-Mathews Mansion Museum.** Firmly rooted in down-to-earth philosophies regarding a child's sense of wonder and curiosity, Stepping Stones branches upward and outward from the point of view that kids love to and need to use all their senses as they learn.

In diverse exhibits that explore the arts, science and technology, and culture and heritage, children can immerse themselves in sensory-rich environments guaranteed to educate as well as entertain. The museum's only permanent exhibit is its entrancing Color Coaster, a 27-foot-tall kinetic sculpture in constant motion near the entrance to this wonderland. Beyond it, in a variety of learning labs, galleries, theaters, and outdoor areas, are such exhibits as Toddler Terrain, Waterscape, I Spy Connecticut, Express Yourself!, In the Works, and Rainforest Adventure.

The youngest visitors entering the tot-friendly Toddler Terrain can crawl into a giant tree or cross a carpeted "pond"—on stepping stones, of course. Or they might check out the Busy Wall, composed of mirrors, gears, doors, and noisemakers. There's even an Infant Oasis for truly tiny patrons. In Waterscape, children enter the gallery under a giant see-through umbrella that protects them from an overhead rainstorm, the run-off from which is channeled into model streambeds, dams, and waterwheels. Here children learn such concepts as flotation and current as they play in the interactive greenhouse environment. I Spy Connecticut invites kids to take simulated helicopter, train, and submarine "rides" to see the state by air, land, and sea. Through such props as mechanical devices, mazes, musical instruments, and puzzles, Express Yourself! and In the Works encourage experimentation, problem solving, and development of varied verbal and nonverbal communications skills. Rainforest Adventure focuses on tropical forests around the world and the ways people can ensure their survival. Children use binoculars, magnifying lenses, field guides, and more to make discoveries in this 1,500-square-foot environment.

Theater performances, workshops by artists and educators, a parent-teacher resource center, and a year-round calendar of indoor and outdoor activities are among the unique aspects of this museum. A real lifesaver here is the Stepping Stones Cafe, which provides inexpensive, child-friendly snacks and light meals for hungry visitors. One of the best such learning environments in the country, Stepping Stones is definitely a sure bet for families.

Aw, Shucks! **Oysters!**

Another of Norwalk's famed festivals is the **Norwalk Oyster Festival,** held annually on the weekend after Labor Day. Celebrating Long Island Sound and its seafaring past, the waterfront events include an arts and crafts show, tall ship tours, an oyster shucking contest, and the typical foods and hoopla of summer festivals. Call (203) 838–9444.

The Norwalk Museum (ages 8 and up)
41 North Main Street at Marshall; (203) 866–0202. Open year-round Wednesday through Sunday (closed Monday and holidays) from 1:00 to 5:00 P.M. Free.

The small but innovative Norwalk Museum seeks to educate and entertain visitors by presenting the last hundred or so years of Norwalk history from a commercial and artistic point of view. Located in a historic building just a block from the Maritime Aquarium, the Museum celebrates the great number of goods invented or manufactured in Norwalk. The Merchants' Court gallery includes items that added to the economy of the city. From hats to scales to high-powered binoculars to light fixtures, each display brings to mind the glory days of authentic local artisans and industries.

The Lockwood gallery of changing exhibitions has more of an artistic focus, typically with Norwalk or Connecticut themes. Past exhibitions, for instance, have featured Connecticut-made chairs, the work of Civil War photographer E. T. Whitney, and items related to Connecticut-born radical abolitionist John Brown. A small gift shop completes the scene for tourists; a reference library is available to researchers.

Stew Leonard's Dairy Store (all ages)
100 Westport Avenue; (203) 847–7213. Open daily year-round from 7:00 A.M. to 11:00 P.M.

The world's largest dairy store/bakery/supermarket is in Norwalk on Route 1, known here as Westport Avenue. Baked goods, dairy products, fine seafood, meats, produce, and a huge take-out buffet are the main attraction for the huge crowds who shop here, but we're sending you here for the rock 'n' roll dairy band, the strolling 6-foot cows that shake hands with toddlers, the horse and dog that croon tunes from velvet-draped stages overhead, the choir of singing lettuces and eggplants, and the barnyard animals in the minifarm out front. You may have to drag children out of here—or you can entice them to the door by buying the ice cream or frozen yogurt sold at the main entrance.

Where to Eat

Brewhouse Restaurant. 13 Marshall Street; (203) 853–9110. This large, bi-level pub-style establishment is an extension of the New England Brewing Company, housed in a 1920s factory building right near the aquarium. Battered fish, chowders, burgers, salads, pizzas, pasta, chicken and veal dishes, and all kinds of kid-friendly appetizers are offered here. Open daily for lunch and dinner. $–$$

New York Pizzaria and Trattoria. 58–60 North Main Street; (203) 866–9068. The best, most authentic New York-style pizza is made here by Jack and Nick Chiaramonte, daily for lunch and dinner; grinders, pasta, wraps, salads, calzones, much more. Very good and very affordable. $–$$

Silvermine Tavern. 194 Perry Avenue; (203) 847–4558. For a special, old-fashioned treat, dine in a colonial inn overlooking a waterfall and pond. Families are warmly welcomed for New England–style country cuisine. $$$

Lime. 168 Main Avenue; (203) 846–9240. If you have had your fill of pizza, pasta, and burgers, come here for delicious natural foods and vegetarian specials from the simple to the gourmet. Soups, salads, excellent breads, and Middle Eastern and Mediterranean specialties, but plenty of seafood, steak, chicken, and grilled cheese and nachos to boot. Open for lunch and dinner daily, except dinner only on Sunday. Nonsmoking. $–$$$

Where to Stay

Courtyard By Marriott-Norwalk. 474 Main Avenue; (203) 849–9111 or (800) 647–7578. 145 units, restaurant, health club, indoor pool. $$$–$$$$

DoubleTree Club Hotel. 789 Connecticut Avenue; (203) 853–3477. 268 rooms, restaurant, fitness room, indoor pool. $$$

Norwalk Inn & Conference Center. 99 East Avenue; (203) 838–5531 or (800) 303–0808. 71 units, restaurant, fitness center, coffee shop, outdoor pool. Full breakfast. $$$$

Silvermine Tavern. 194 Perry Avenue; (203) 847–4558. 11 rooms in 1785 country inn in sylvan setting. Antiques and fireplaces add to the old-fashioned ambience. Continental breakfast. $$$

Westport

Bordering Norwalk on the west and Fairfield on the east, shore-hugging Westport usually needs no introduction. Long famous as a haven for writers, actors, artists, and other glitterati, it is well known as the suburb of suburbs with a dash of panache rivaled only by its imitators. Families are attracted to the beaches and the woodlands as much as to the entertainment, the shops, and the restaurants. Year-round and seasonal activities ensure that there's always fun for the family in Westport.

Earthplace: The Nature Discovery Center (all ages)

10 Woodside Lane; (203) 227–7253; www.earthplace.org. Open year-round. Grounds, 7:00 A.M. to dusk daily. Building, Monday through Saturday from 9:00 A.M. to 5:00 P.M. and Sunday from 1:00 to 4:00 P.M. Closed on major holidays. Adult donation $2.00; children $1.00.

Open 365 days a year from dawn to dusk, the sixty-two-acre wildlife sanctuary at this unique facility includes 2 miles of trails for all ages, especially the very young. A Swamp Loop Trail, an open field habitat, and a trail for the blind are among the five trail options outside. A universal-access nature trail welcomes all visitors, especially those with special challenges. A lovely wildflower courtyard and a bird and butterfly garden showcase both native and introduced plants. An outdoor Birds of Prey area features a bald eagle, several owls, hawks, vultures, and other species.

Inside Earthplace's 20,000-square-foot museum, a large live-animal hall with many species of indigenous creatures is often the site of special demonstrations. Changing displays on ecology, animal biology, a native plant court, a working water-quality lab, a wildlife rehab center, and a great gift shop are all here. Plans are well under way to re-create the Exhibit Hall with interactive areas such as the Tiny Treehouse and the Explorer's Clubhouse.

Best of all, though, are the workshops, guided walks, outdoor classes, and summer camp programs. Beachwalks, family campfires, maple sugaring, birdbanding, a holiday fair, and more are open to all visitors. If none of those options appeal, still come to this little slice of wilderness—wild turkeys, pheasants, red foxes, deer, hawks, songbirds, and more await you.

Sherwood Island State Park (all ages)

Off I–95 exit 18. Turn south at the end of the ramp to enter the park; (203) 226–6983. Open daily year-round, 8:00 A.M. to sunset. Admission per vehicle, $7.00 for Connecticut plates, $10.00 for out-of-state plates from Memorial Day to Labor Day on weekdays. On weekends and holidays from Memorial Day to Labor Day these respective rates are $9.00 and $14.00. Off-season parking is free, except on weekends in May and September, when the charge is $7.00 and $10.00 for Connecticut and out-of-state vehicles, respectively. (Note: The nature trail and nature center mentioned on page 25 were closed in the summer of 2003. The Friends of Sherwood Island State Park are developing plans for a new nature center and improved trail, slated to open in 2004.)

This park's 1½-mile beach is preceded by 234 acres of open space, two large picnic groves, and several drives, footpaths, and walkways. Swimming, fishing, and scuba diving or snorkeling are permitted in the Sound (scuba divers must register with the rangers). Lifeguards are on duty from Memorial Day to Labor Day.

Come here for kite flying, volleyball, badminton, horseshoes, bocce, and bicycling. A softball field is provided and can be used on a first-come/first-play basis. Bring your own equipment for all of the above.

The park's appeal to families is enhanced by a self-guided interpretive nature trail that points out flora, fauna, and special areas of importance to Long Island Sound and its estuaries. Just ½ mile long, it is perfect for families with young children and informative for all ages. A nature center celebrating the marine environment includes a touch tank, exhibits of native reptiles and amphibians, and shorebird specimens; it is linked by a handicapped-accessible foot path to one of the park's two bathhouses, located at the eastern and western ends of the beach. These stone structures house the lifeguard stations, first aid offices, and outdoor showers. Outdoors, a bird observation deck provides an overview of the shore habitat; bird-watchers are welcome year-round. Interpretive naturalist-guided walks and talks are scheduled each season.

The park provides public rest rooms, changing rooms, and showers. Only the rest rooms function in the winter. A concession stand offers food, drink, and souvenirs. Folks are welcome to picnic or barbecue.

Westport Country Playhouse (all ages)

25 Powers Court, off Route 1; (203) 226–0153 or (203) 227–4177; www.westportplayhouse. org. (Note: The playhouse itself closed temporarily in 2004 for renovation, but the Kids' Playhouse series and a limited number of other productions will be staged at another Westport venue. In spring 2004, call or check the Web site.)

For nearly seventy-five years, this wonderful, old-time summer-stock playhouse has offered professional productions starring such legends as Henry Fonda, Helen Hayes, Jessica Tandy, Gene Kelly, Liza Minelli, Cicely Tyson, and many others. Located in a cow barn-turned-tanning factory and then a rustic theater with post-and-beam construction and bench-style seating, the playhouse is currently closed for extensive renovations during 2004, with plans for a gala grand opening in 2005 to celebrate its seventy-fifth season.

Its artistic director, Joanne Woodward, and executive director, Alison Harris, are working to refurbish and redirect the theater on toward new heights, with intentions of developing into a year-round venue with state-of-the-art technology paired to its traditional country-roots charm. Theater lovers can look forward to the usual bill of fare when the lights go up again: musicals, comedies, and dramas, and a full schedule of the theater's second-most famous productions—its Kids' Playhouse series. For nine weeks every summer, a new show is produced each week on Friday at 11:00 A.M. and 2:00 P.M. Fairy-tale productions, a minicircus, puppet theaters, magic shows, and concerts are often among those entertainments. Prices are $9.00 or $12.00 (depending on your seats) per ticket for children and adults. Subscriptions as well as single tickets are sold for all performances, including for the children's shows. Reserve tickets early for the grand reopening in 2005.

Levitt Pavilion for the Performing Arts (all ages)

Jesup Road, behind the Westport Public Library; (203) 226–7600 for a calendar or (203) 221–4422 for recorded information on the concert hotline; www.levittpavilion.com. Free.

If theater ticket prices are too high for your budget (and even if they are not), don't miss the festival atmosphere at the Levitt. Another sort of summer theater, it is one of the most ambitious undertakings of its kind.

On the banks of the Saugatuck River, this open-air series offers approximately sixty evenings of entertainment from late June through late August. Bring a blanket, chairs, and a picnic to the lawn in front of the band shell and enjoy the **free** performances suitable for the whole family.

Tuesday is Potpourri night—maybe swing, maybe the community band, maybe stories for children. Wednesday is Family Night (mime, puppetry, magic, storytelling). Thursday is Classical/Cabaret/Theater, Friday is Party Time (folk, reggae, bluegrass, or rock 'n' roll), Saturday is Pop/Rock/Blues, and Sunday is Big Band/Blues/Jazz. On Mondays there is no show. Occasional special events—one or two—do have an admission charge. Call for a calendar. Showtimes vary slightly, but Wednesday and Sunday performances are usually at 7:00 P.M. and most others are at 8:00 P.M. Fridays and Saturdays are designated as alcohol-free evenings. A food or ice cream concession operates on some nights, but most folks bring pizza or other picnic fare.

Park in the municipal lots in back of the public library on Jesup Road off the Post Road East (Route 1) and walk up the gravel path toward the band shell at the side of the river.

Where to Eat

Bertucci's. 833 Post Road East; (203) 454–1559. Tasty pasta, fresh salads, and crusty rolls, among other family-pleasing dishes and pizzas of all sorts. Open Monday through Saturday from 11:00 A.M. to 11:00 P.M. and Sunday from noon to 11:00 P.M. $–$$

DeRosa's Brick Oven Pizza at the Firehouse. 6 Wilton Road; (203) 221–1769. Superb pizza, great folks here. Maybe they'll make you a Mickey Mouse–shaped pie—fun and delicious. Open daily from 11:00 A.M. for lunch and dinner. $

The Peppermill. 1700 Post Road East; (203) 259–8155. A fixture in Westport for more than thirty years, this casually elegant steak house offers excellent seafood, salad bar, and Sunday brunch. Reasonably priced appetizers, early-bird specials, and a children's menu make it perfect for families who favor a more refined ambience than a pizzeria or cafe. Open Monday through Friday for lunch and for brunch on Sunday. Open for dinner daily. $$–$$$

Where to Stay

The Inn at Longshore. 260 Compo Road South; (203) 226–3316. 12 rooms (3 suites) in this lovely country inn overlooking the Sound. Playground, pool, tennis, golf, boating, beach swimming. Complimentary breakfast buffet. $$$$

The Westport Inn. 1595 Post Road East; (203) 259–5236 or (800) 446–8997. Full-service hotel with 116 units, indoor pool, sauna, whirlpool, fitness center, restaurant. Complimentary continental breakfast. Weekend packages. $$$–$$$$

Fairfield

Settled in 1639, Fairfield is one of Connecticut's oldest towns, so it's not surprising to find beautiful historical homes and still-quaint village centers within its boundaries. Populated mostly by farmers, tradespeople, sailors, and shipbuilders through much of the eighteenth century, the town was burned by the British in 1779. Rebuilding was slow but determined, and soon the community had rallied as Southport and Black Rock Harbors helped to reestablish Fairfield's place as an important port of entry. Two centuries later, Fairfield's shoreline location still influences life in this thriving, comfortable community.

Ogden House and Gardens (ages 7 to 12)

1520 Bronson Road; (203) 259–6356 or (203) 259–1598; www.fairfieldhistoricalsociety.org.
Public tours from May through mid-October on Saturday and Sunday from 1:00 to 4:30 P.M.
Adults $3.00; children $1.00.

A meticulously restored historical site for those interested in pre-Revolution life, Ogden House is a 1750 saltbox farmhouse furnished to portray the lives of its first inhabitants, Jane and David Ogden. An eighteenth-century kitchen garden and a native wildflower garden are also on the picturesque property overlooking Brown's Brook near Mill River.

In addition to annual events celebrating the gardens and the seasons, Ogden House offers special activities of interest to families. A Hands-On History Camp for children aged 8 to 11 is held annually during the second week in July. Designed to take children back to the time of Jane Ogden, the program offers cooking, tin lantern piercing, taffy pulling, and eighteenth-century games. Birthday parties include a guided tour with a docent portraying Mrs. Ogden, hoop rolling lessons, and a choice of crafts such as candle dipping, wood carving, or corn-husk doll making. High school students can make reservations to participate in the archaeological dig taking place on the property and an ongoing schedule of hands-on workshops for children has included teddy bear repair, gravestone study, and principles of archaeology.

Fairfield Historical Society (ages 7 to 12)

636 Old Post Road; (203) 259–1598; www.fairfieldhistoricalsociety.org. Open from 10:00 A.M. to 4:30 P.M. Tuesday through Saturday and from 1:00 to 4:30 P.M. on Sunday. Closed on Monday and major holidays. Suggested donation, adults $3.00; children $1.00.

In its Georgian-style brick home near the town green, this small museum has changing exhibitions, an important permanent collection of pre-Revolutionary to the present artifacts, costumes, furnishings, and decorative arts. A collection of walking sticks includes some made from glass, snakeskin, rhinoceros horn, and tortoiseshell.

A research library is open to those interested in Connecticut history and genealogy. The society sponsors special events such as encampments, reenactments, story hours, craft workshops, lectures, and slide shows.

Birdcraft Museum and Sanctuary (all ages)

314 Unquowa Road; (203) 259–0416; www.ctaudubon.org/centers/birdcraft/birdcraft.htm. Open year-round Tuesday to Friday from 10:00 A.M. to 5:00 P.M. and Saturday and Sunday from noon to 4:00 P.M. Adults $2.00; children under 14 $1.00.

Just south of I–95, this six-acre enclave was founded in 1914 as the first songbird sanctuary in the United States. More than 120 species of birds have been documented here. Huge maples hung with vines, century-old rhododendrons, sassafras, and highbush cranberry are along the trail through the woodlands and across a beautiful wooden boardwalk above a shallow pond. Sit awhile at the gazebo and listen to the birds and frogs. Look for the nesting night herons.

Inside the turn-of-the-twentieth-century museum, designated a National Historic Landmark, browse through four galleries featuring birds and mammals of New England, grouped in diorama displays by habitat and seasons. The murals here are exceptional, as is the gallery of African animals. The venerable history of the museum is preserved in these classic exhibit areas, but there are also many hands-on opportunities for children to touch, listen, and observe.

These exhibits fulfill the dream of Mabel Osgood Wright, founder of the Connecticut Audubon Society and founding member of the American Conservation Movement. It is in the property's vintage cottage, which has taken on a recent incarnation as a visitor center, that guests are introduced to Ms. Wright's important contributions to conservation and are oriented to the varied attractions. The cottage's Nature Observatory space includes a hands-on classroom for activities and workshops, a library, an observation deck, and a nature gift shop and bookstore.

A growing variety of children's programs, story hours, summer camps, and natural history and crafts workshops fill the needs of young naturalists.

You can stroll around on your own or take a one-hour guided tour, arranged by appointment. Come the second Saturday of May for International Migrating Bird Day, a festival of birdwatching, crafts, a book sale, and lessons on how to attract birds to your own yard.

Beachin' It

Long attractive for its 8 miles of shoreline, Fairfield has five public beaches that allow residents and visitors to enjoy the Sound. Call the Fairfield Parks and Recreation department at (203) 256–3144 for current parking policies and prices.

Penfield Beach (Fairfield Beach Road) and **Jennings Beach** (South Benson Road) have the most facilities for families: pavilions, concessions, rest rooms and showers, playgrounds, and convenient parking. **Southport Beach** (Pequot Avenue) is quieter, less crowded, has great sandbars for young children, rest rooms, and a small concession. It's also just past the historic village center of Southport—a pleasant place to stroll and pick up some picnic goodies or grab breakfast or lunch at the **Five Corner Deli** (203–259–9843), also on Pequot Avenue.

Roy and Margot Larsen Bird Sanctuary and
Connecticut Audubon Center at Fairfield (all ages)

2325 Burr Street; (203) 259–6305. The nature center is open year-round, Tuesday through Saturday, from 9:00 A.M. to 4:30 P.M. and on Sunday in the spring and fall only from noon to 4:30 P.M. Closed on major holidays. Admission to the center is free. The sanctuary is open daily, year-round, from dawn to dusk. Admission for adults is $2.00; children under 12, 50 cents.

Located in the Greenfield Hill neighborhood in the north end of town, this beautiful 160-acre tract of New England woodland was created on reclaimed farm property. Built as a model wildlife sanctuary juxtaposing habitats and trails to allow people maximum opportunity to experience the diversity without disturbing the refuge, its 6 miles of trails, including a Walk for the Disabled, lead visitors to marshes, ponds, streams, vernal pools, meadows, and coniferous and hardwood forests.

In addition you can visit the Connecticut Audubon Center at Fairfield (with natural science exhibits, a discovery room, live animal displays, and a gift shop/bookstore) and the Educational Animal Compound of nonreleasable animals the Connecticut Audubon Society has rehabilitated. See a peregrine falcon, a red-tailed hawk, and several owls.

Summer camps, workshops, naturalist-guided walks, junior naturalist programs, and field trips are frequent. You can even have your birthday party here.

The Dogwood **Festival**

Graced by beautiful vintage homes as well as modern mansions, the winding roads of northern Fairfield take you through lightly populated residential enclaves and into a perfect antique village center punctuated by one of the nation's most stately and classic Congregational churches. Known as Greenfield Hill, the area is heavily planted with dogwoods and is famed for its annual **Dogwood Festival** in mid-May. A great outing for Mother's Day or any other reason, it provides opportunities to enjoy the beauty of springtime in Connecticut.

To celebrate the gorgeous pink-and-white blossoms of more than 30,000 dogwoods, the Greenfield Hill Congregational Church (1045 Old Academy Road) plans a four-day schedule of festivities that includes an arts-and-crafts show, a plant sale, walking tours and luncheons, musical programs, children's games, and a white elephant sale. Buy food here or bring a picnic. Bring along a camera to capture the day forever. For information, call the Fairfield Town Hall and ask for the Festival Committee telephone number. Admission and parking are free.

Where to Eat

Firehouse Deli. 22 Reef Road; (203) 255–5527. Open daily, Monday through Saturday 7:00 A.M. to 6:00 P.M. and Sunday 8:00 A.M. to 5:00 P.M. Sandwiches, tacos, salads. Take-out or sit-down self-service. Outside seating in warm weather. $

Centro Ristorante. 1435 Post Road; (203) 255–1210. Right downtown near the Sherman Green gazebo is this casually but elegantly appointed Italian restaurant with a bit of panache and yet plenty down-home enough for families. Homemade pastas, great caesar salad, good seafood, thin-crust pizzas, and much more. Patio in warm weather. Open daily for lunch and dinner. $$–$$$

Southport Brewing Company. 2600 Post Road; (203) 256–2337. Views of the microbrewery, which also operates in this location, are clear from every table in the house, but you are here for the terrific soups, sandwiches, salads, thin-crust pizzas, and chicken, seafood, and pasta dishes. Smoke-free. Patio in season. Open for lunch daily 11:30 A.M. to 4:30 P.M. and dinner from 5:30 P.M. $$

Where to Stay

Fairfield Inn. 417 Post Road; (203) 255–0491 or (800) 347–0414. Convenient, clean, cream-of-the-crop motor inn. 80 units, outdoor pool. Continental breakfast. $$$.

Merritt Parkway Motor Inn. 4180 Black Rock Turnpike; (203) 259–5264 or (888) 242–4742. Perched atop a hill at the north end of town. 40 units, restaurant. Continental breakfast. $$–$$$

Seagrape Inn at Fairfield Beach. 1160 Reef Road; (203) 255–6808. 14 suites with kitchenettes in immaculately renovated Fairfield landmark near Penfield Point. Daily, weekly, and monthly rates. Rooms are stocked with coffee, tea, fresh cream, and paper products. Open year-round. $$$$

Bridgeport

The wealth of activities offered to tourists in Bridgeport is suited to no one better than children. In recent years each of the best attractions has expanded or improved in some way, and the blue street signs help usher visitors to the good, clean fun that can still be found here despite the political scandal that has tarnished this shoreline city.

Unknown to most folks who skirt the city on I–95 and the Merritt Parkway are the facts that Bridgeport has the longest public waterfront in the state, more protected historic districts than any other Connecticut municipality, and two expansive parks designed by famed landscape artist Frederick Law Olmsted. It's not too early to celebrate the renaissance of Bridgeport as its devoted entrepreneurs and investors and its diverse ethnic communities infuse the culture of the city with energy and vitality. The center of the city is a mere 4 miles from downtown Fairfield.

Discovery Museum (all ages)

4450 Park Avenue, exit 47, Merritt Parkway; (203) 372–3521; www.discoverymuseum.org. Open year-round Tuesday to Saturday 10:00 A.M. to 5:00 P.M. and Sunday noon to 5:00 P.M.; also Monday 10:00 A.M. to 5:00 P.M. in July and August. Closed on major holidays. Adults $7.00; children ages 3 to 18 $5.50. Challenger missions extra.

Hands-on in nearly every way, this museum contains interactive exhibits in the areas of art, science, and a smattering of industry, all specially designed so that children aged 4 to 12 can learn about the interrelationship of art and science.

Upper-level galleries explore the physical sciences. The first floor's Interactive Art Gallery, for instance, teaches kids about color, line, and perspective—"paint" with a computer, spin color wheels to create new colors, shift stained "glass" puzzle pieces to create mood changes, or duck into a cavelike structure that plays "red," "blue," and "yellow" music. Recent exhibitions in the museum's main fine arts gallery were the Amistad quilts created to honor the story of the schooner *Amistad,* a toy and game exhibition, and a Hubble Space Telescope exhibit developed by the Smithsonian.

In other areas, children can make discoveries about space science, nuclear energy, electronics, electricity, magnetism, and light. Take a simulated bumper car ride to test your reaction time, hear Alexander Graham Bell's first telephone transmission, measure your height electronically under the giant Stanley Powerlock measuring tape, create a swirling wall of color in the Pepsico Light Gallery, or play Virtual Basketball.

The lowest floor includes Discovery House, a learning space for kids under five, with simplified hands-on science and art for the youngest visitors. It is also home to the **Henry B. DuPont III Planetarium.** Daily shows offer a dramatic look at the heavens; programs change throughout the year. The museum is also the site of one of the nation's sixteen **Challenger Learning Centers,** a computer-simulated mission control and space station where participants perform experiments and collect data as astronauts would. Afternoon mini-missions are offered to the public on weekends; call for reservations.

The museum includes a gift shop and nature trails; special children's programs, curriculum-related Wonder Workshops, and camps are offered frequently.

Harbor Yard **Ballpark and Arena**

Thousands of kids have already cheered through the first few seasons of baseball in Bridgeport's **Harbor Yard ballpark,** constructed near the water-front for the city's Class A, Atlantic League team, the **Bluefish.** The 5,300-seat stadium features box seats, club seats, and skyboxes, a supervised play area, a barbecue picnic area, food concessions, rest rooms, and on-site parking. Here too is the home park of the major league lacrosse team the **Bridgeport Barrage,** playing from June through August.

Also in this sports complex is the **Arena at Harbor Yard,** where the **Bridgeport Sound Tigers** of the American Hockey League take to the ice as the premier affiliate of the New York Islanders. Their forty-game season runs from October through April. Call the Bluefish Ticket Office at (203) 345–4800; for lacrosse games, call the Bridgeport Barrage at the same number; for hockey tickets, call the Sound Tigers box office at (203) 334–GOAL. The sports complex is located at 500 Main Street, off exit 27 on I–95.

The Beardsley Zoological Gardens (all ages)

1875 Noble Avenue; (203) 394–6565; www.beardsleyzoo.org. Open from 9:00 A.M. to 4:00 P.M. daily, except for Thanksgiving, Christmas, and New Year's Day. Tropics building open 10:30 A.M. to 3:30 P.M. Adults $7.00; children aged 3 to 11 $5.00; under 3 free. Zoo-only visitors do not have to pay the parking fee ($3.00 for Connecticut vehicles, $6.00 for out-of-state vehicles) charged to users of Beardsley Park.

This facility has wonderful new exhibits throughout its fifty-two-acre site inside Beardsley Park. Dedicated to wildlife research, conservation, and education, Connecticut's only zoo participates in an international program called the Species Survival Plan. Rare or endangered species such as Siberian tigers, red wolves, scarlet ibises, and sandhill cranes live here with 120 other species. Inside the New World Tropics building, for instance, is an outstanding South American rain forest re-creation. Toucans, woolly monkeys, tortoises, ocelots, golden lion tamarins, and adorable marmosets live with tropical birds in this open-aviary exhibit.

Elsewhere on the site, explore the Wetlands to see river otters, alligators, and other water-loving animals; the Predator Walk that features hunter species; and the Hoofstock Trail that borders the habitat of llamas, bison, deer, and antelope. A New England farmyard enclosure is a petting zoo that features bunnies, goats, geese, and sheep.

Pony rides, a children's stage, a gift shop, a snack bar, and a large picnic grove are on the grounds. A marvelous pavilion houses exhibits from the beautiful antique **Pleasure Beach carousel** as well as its operating modern replica. Admire magnificently restored examples of the graceful animals of the original ride, saved from the wrecking ball, then hop onto the reproduction for a wonderful whirl. It is open seasonally from 10:30 A.M. to 4:00 P.M. Rides cost $1.00.

Be sure to visit more than once. Plans are also under way for such new exhibit themes as an Asian plateau and an Arctic tundra. You can sign up for e-mail delivery of the CTZOOTIMES, a monthly newsletter that will let you know the latest zoo news.

Barnum Museum (all ages)

820 Main Street; (203) 331–1104; www.barnum-museum.org. Open year-round 10:00 A.M. to 4:30 P.M. Tuesday through Saturday and noon to 4:30 P.M. on Sunday. Also open Monday in July and August from 11:00 A.M. to 4:30 P.M. Adults $5.00; children 4 to 18 $3.00; under 4 free.

Prepare to enter the "Greatest Show on Earth" and one of New England's best themed museums. If you only have one day to spend in Bridgeport, make sure you make this museum one of your stops. Refueled by the energy of a new executive director, the Barnum is designed to immerse the visitor in the experience of its exhibits, creating the effect of a journey back in time.

Dedicated to the life and times of P. T. (Phineas Taylor) Barnum, the museum also celebrates the remarkable industrial heritage of Bridgeport and the culture of the circus in general. The first floor concentrates on Barnum the showman, entrepreneur, politician, and journalist. The successful juggler of half a dozen careers during his eighty-one years, Barnum started the circus when he was sixty! According to Barnum, his circus was "the most expensive and marvellous *(sic)* combination of the world's wonders ever brought together." You'll be easily drawn in to his magic from the minute you step inside the museum.

The Barnum Festival

If you are charmed by Barnum's hoopla, return to the city for its annual **Barnum Festival,** a multifaceted celebration that includes the Great Street Parade on or near each Fourth of July. Among parades held across the nation, this event has historically been second in size only to Macy's Thanksgiving Day extravaganza. Road races, a fabulous marching band competition called Champions on Parade, a Jenny Lind voice competition, a children's Wing-Ding carnival, fireworks, and much more are on the monthlong slate of events. For information, call the Barnum Festival Society at (203) 367–8495.

A real elephant right in the lobby sets the tone, and it only gets better from there. Make sure the kids watch the excellent short clip from the movie *Barnum* so they get a fix on who Barnum was.

On the second floor you'll get a sense of the once-great city of Bridgeport in its heyday. A fabulous exhibit of all the products invented here will surprise visitors of all ages.

On the third floor, enter the circus. See Barnum's Fejee Mermaid, a real Egyptian mummy, Tom Thumb and Lavinia Warren's clothing and furniture, memorabilia of Jenny Lind, and the incredible Brinley's circus, a hand-carved five-ring extravaganza, done completely to scale and massive even in miniature.

Downstairs again, a gorgeous changing exhibition gallery offers major traveling shows of interest to the whole family, usually in keeping with Barnum's fascination with popular culture.

Renovations and new interactive displays are slated for the next couple of years. Be sure to step right up and see them.

Downtown Cabaret Theater (all ages)

263 Golden Hill Street; (203) 576–1636; www.dtcab.com. Open year-round, Friday through Sunday; children's series October to May. Performances Saturday and Sunday at noon and 2:30 P.M.

This theater produces award-winning shows from Broadway hits to musical revues nearly every weekend of the year. Matinee and evening performances are given cabaret-style; patrons sit at tables and bring their own picnics and refreshments. Many performances are suitable for children older than 8.

An enormously successful slate of musical matinees for children aged 4 to 12 is offered nearly every weekend from October through May. Single tickets are $12.50; subscriptions to the whole five-show series are $59.25.

Secure parking is available ($2.00) in the City Hall lot across from the Cabaret.

Playhouse on the Green (all ages)

177 State Street; tickets: (203) 345–4800, ext. 150; check www.playhouseonthegreen.org. for program of current season.

Located in an amazingly revitalized historic district in the heart of downtown, the Playhouse on the Green is a 225-seat theater created inside a 1911 bank building across from the beautiful McLevy Green. Led by Executive Director Janet Granger-Hopp, the Playhouse is a year-round venue, offering affordably priced dramas and comedies suitable for adults and teens. The 2003–2004 season, for instance, brought Tom Dudzick's *Over the Tavern* and D. L. Coburn's *The Gin Game* to the stage. Tickets for these shows are $25 to $35. Subscriptions are available. In addition, performances specifically aimed at families with young children are offered once a month from October through May. Folktales, musical revues, jugglers, magic, and seasonal and holiday shows are among these. Tickets for these Polka Dot Kids productions are $12; the shows are at 10:00 A.M. and noon on selected Saturdays.

Lights Up **at the Klein**

Artsport, the management company for the Playhouse on the Green, also manages Bridgeport's beautifully restored Art Deco-style **Klein Memorial Auditorium** (910 Fairfield Avenue; 203–366–4647). Long the home of the Bridgeport Symphony Orchestra, the theater is enjoying a jubilant renaissance. Single-night or short-run performances such as Arlo Guthrie, hypnotist James Mapes, and *Cats* entertained full houses in 2003 and 2004. Order tickets through Artsport now and enjoy the revival of this landmark theater.

The Bridgeport to Port Jefferson
Steamboat Company (all ages) ⬙

Water Street Dock; (203) 335–2040; or 102 West Broadway, Port Jefferson; (631) 473–0286; www.pagelinx.com/bpjferry. Operates daily year-round. Call for reservations, rates, and schedules.

The huge white boats at the pier just a block from the downtown transportation terminal offer ferry service across Long Island Sound. Still more an excursion boat than commuter transportation, the ferry is used as a pleasure cruiser or as a means of getting by car to the prettier parts of Long Island more quickly than you'd go via New York City or the Throgs Neck Bridge. Now there are three car ferries in the fleet that run thirty-two round-trip rides between Bridgeport and Port Jefferson each day. From Bridgeport, the boats usually depart every hour on the half-hour between 6:30 A.M. and 9:30 P.M. The ferries have enclosed passenger decks plus topside sun decks, rest rooms, lounges, and food service in onboard restaurants and bars.

You can go on foot, with bicycles, or with your car to **Port Jefferson,** a small village of shops and restaurants that cater to daytripping crowds from the ferry. Call the numbers above to obtain a brochure describing the Port Jeff attractions. **Theatre Three** (516–928–9100) in Port Jefferson presents reasonably priced, well-known hits suitable for the whole family. Special children's matinee productions are offered in July and August. Go for the day, shop and stroll, have some dinner, see a show, and sail home by starlight. It makes a sensational day trip.

The sailing time on the ferry is about an hour and fifteen minutes each way. Charters, moonlight cruises, and dance cruises are available.

Seaside Park

At Bridgeport's southernmost tip lies **Seaside Park,** a 325-acre expanse designed by Frederick Law Olmsted and Calvert Vaux and donated to the city by P. T. Barnum. The park is reached through the magnificent Perry Memorial Arch over Park Avenue. Designed by Henry Bacon in the same year (1916) he designed the Lincoln Memorial in Washington, the arch is the gateway to the 2½-mile peninsula that features a shoreline drive, a wide, white-sand beach, playing fields, concessions, walking paths, and rest areas. Nonresidents wishing to drive through or spend a day at the park and beach must stop at a checkpoint to purchase a day-use pass; Connecticut vehicles are charged $10.00, out-of-state vehicles are charged $20.00, from Memorial Day weekend through Labor Day weekend. Be sure to find the beautifully restored bronze P. T. Barnum statue along the shoreline drive. The park is widely used year-round and is open from dawn to sunset. Call the Bridgeport Parks Department (203–576–7233) for more information.

Where to Eat

Ash Creek Saloon. 93 Post Road; (203) 255–5131. Just over the Fairfield line; Southwestern decor; tasty American cuisine not too fancy or spicy for kids. $–$$

Take Time Cafe. 211 State Street; (203) 335–7255. Open from 6:30 A.M. to 3:30 P.M on weekdays, this downtown coffeehouse/bakery is close to the museums, theaters, and ballpark. Its nautical decor is a great backdrop for its outstanding bagels, sandwiches, muffins, and other kid-friendly fare, perfect for breakfast, lunch, and picnics. $

Vazzy's. 513 Broadbridge Road; (203) 371–8046. This down-home, family-owned Bridgeport fixture has some of the city's best pasta and hands-down best pizza. Try the delicious mozzarella and garlic pizza-dough sticks—so very good. Open for lunch and dinner Monday through Saturday from 11:00 A.M. and Sunday from 1:00 P.M. $$

Where to Stay

Bridgeport Holiday Inn. 1070 Main Street; (203) 334–1234 or (800) HOLIDAY. Convenient downtown location. 230 rooms, 2 suites, health club, indoor pool, restaurant, coffee shop. Kids **free;** weekend packages with tickets to attractions. $$$

Trumbull Marriott. 180 Hawley Lane, Trumbull; (203) 378–1400. Convenient to parkway, Route 8, and Bridgeport attractions. Health club, indoor and outdoor pools, 320 rooms; kids **free; free** meals for kids under 5 and half-price meals for kids 5 to 12. $$$ midweek; weekend packages.

Stratford

This small municipality on the easternmost border of Fairfield County often gets lost in the shuffle as travelers rush past it on I–95 in an effort to beat the traffic in or out of New Haven and Bridgeport. Despite its long history as one of Connecticut's oldest shoreline communities, it has no reputation as a hot spot for tourism. Nevertheless, it does have some interesting destinations families can enjoy.

Children's Garbage Museum (ages 5 to 12)

1410 Honeyspot Road Extension, I–95 exit 30; (203) 381–9571 or (800) 455–9571; www.crra. org/education. Open to school groups daily in the academic year; open to families from noon to 4:00 P.M. Wednesday through Friday from September through June and 10:00 A.M. to 4:00 P.M. Tuesday through Friday in July and August. Call for Saturday openings. Admission is free.

This museum features twenty-two interactive exhibits that teach children about the importance of recycling and the responsible treatment of garbage. One of the exhibits is a soft-sculpture compost pile in which children can crawl into a simulated worm tunnel to see how organic matter decomposes into soil. The museum's mascot is Trash-o-saurus, a 24-foot-long dinosaur constructed from trash.

Visitors generally spend about an hour at the hands-on exhibit area, then take a tour of the next-door Southwest Connecticut Regional Recycling Plant, where locally collected recyclables are sorted and prepared for sale to remanufacturers. Most visitors then return to the museum to create a craft or buy a gift made from recycled or reusable material.

Boothe Memorial Park and Museum (all ages)

134 Main Street, in the Putney section of town; (203) 381–2046 for tours and museum information, or (203) 381–2068 for parks department. Park grounds open year-round daily from approximately 8:00 A.M. to dusk. Buildings open for guided or self-guided tours May 1 through November 1; Tuesday through Friday 11:00 A.M. to 1:00 P.M. and on weekends from 1:00 to 4:00 P.M. Free.

This thirty-two–acre park overlooking the Housatonic River was once the site of an estate owned by two wealthy, and apparently eccentric, brothers whose family had successfully farmed the site for more than 300 years. Today this National Historic Landmark includes two of the original Boothe homesteads, plus a trolley station, a tollbooth plaza, a model lighthouse, a miniature windmill, an icehouse, an outdoor basilica with an organ house, an 1844 chapel, a barn with a weaving loom and other objects related to nineteenth-century farm life, a working blacksmith shop, a clocktower museum, and an amazing redwood monument called the Technocratic Cathedral!

Surrounding this intriguing conglomeration are acres of parkland offering gardens, walking paths, picnic groves with tables, barbecue grills, and shelters, a playground, ballplaying areas, and rest rooms. The buildings and rest rooms close in November, but ice skating and sledding are allowed in the winter, weather permitting.

Stratford's **Best-Kept Secrets**

The sand spit at **Long Beach** offers one of Fairfield County's best beachcombing opportunities. Park at the base of Washington Parkway among the restaurants near Marnick's Motel and walk from Point No Point, at the eastern end of the seawall, toward the west, where Stratford's Long Beach stretches toward Bridgeport's Pleasure Beach. Except for the occasional interruption of an airplane returning to or leaving the nearby airport, you'll be alone with the wind, the surf, and the wildlife in this beautifully secluded spot.

As you return from a weekend beach walk, the music from **Long Beach Skateland** (Washington Parkway; 203–378–9033) may tempt visitors both young and old to add wheels to your feet and take a few turns around this old-fashioned roller skating rink. To protect their specially coated wooden floor, the owners allow only traditional quad skates, which are available for you to borrow at no extra charge. Most skate sessions feature contemporary Top Forty hits that kids and teens seem to love, but Sunday evenings offer the charming lilts of organ music. Take your pick: year-round, sessions are Friday 7:00 to 9:30 P.M., Saturday 2:00 to 4:00 P.M. and 7:30 to 10:00 P.M., and Sunday 2:00 to 4:00 P.M. and 7:00 to 9:00 P.M. Admission is $4.50 per person regardless of age.

On the east-facing cove that cups the mouth of the Housatonic River, Stratford's **Short Beach Park** (Park and Recreation Department: 203–385–4052) offers families the best daytripping bargain of all the public beaches along the Connecticut shore. Nonresidents pay a $5.00 day fee per vehicle to use the beach and the park's ballfields, tennis courts, basketball courts, and playground. Picnic tables and grills are also available for everyone's use, and a concession operates in the summer months for those who don't care to cook on their days off. For an extra charge, visitors can use the park's nine-hole golf course or its miniature golf course. The park is open year-round, dawn to dusk. Lifeguards are on duty mid-May through Labor Day; during this time the rest rooms and outdoor showers are also operational.

National Helicopter Museum (all ages)

On Main Street at the eastbound side of the tracks at the old Stratford Railroad Depot; (203) 375–5766. Open Memorial Day through October 15, Wednesday through Saturday, 1:00 to 4:00 P.M. Donation requested.

If you have aircraft buffs in your clan, an hour at this small museum, located in the old red Stratford Railroad Depot, will be enjoyable if you can't make it up to the New England Air Museum in Windsor Locks. Exhibits trace the development of the helicopter and the life of aviation pioneer Igor Sikorsky, founder of Stratford's famed Sikorsky Aircraft industries. Museum displays include the cockpit of the V-22 Osprey (an airplane that hovers like a helicopter), several helicopter engines, and miniature models of Sikorsky's helicopters. Also on display are drawings of early helicopter prototypes (such as da Vinci's *Helix*) and photographs of helicopters used in various military operations.

Where to Eat

Marnick's Restaurant. 10 Washington Parkway; (203) 377–6288. In Marnick's Motel on the water; perfect family fare, reasonably priced from steaks and seafood to sandwiches, salads, and burgers. Ask for a window table overlooking the Sound. Open daily. $–$$

Plouf! Le Bistro de la Mer. 14 Beach Drive; (203) 386–1477. This casual waterfront cafe has a French flair for fun decor and excellent bistro-style cuisine. Very authentic, so if you and the children are in the mood for something Parisian, do stop in. Open for lunch Monday through Friday and dinner daily. $$$

Knapp's Landing. 520 Sniffens Lane; (203) 378–5999. At the mouth of the Housatonic River at Sniffens Point, just north of Short Beach, this establishment offers continental

cuisine year-round for lunch and dinner. Seafood, pasta, chicken, and steaks, plus soups, sandwiches, and salads. Open-air deck in warm weather. Open Tuesday through Sunday. $$

Where to Stay

Marnick's Motel. 10 Washington Parkway; (203) 377–6288. Family-owned, recently renovated waterfront motel on the Sound. 29 rooms, beach, restaurant. Waterfront rooms have balconies, microwaves, and refrigerators. Guests welcome to use the motel's private beach for swimming and shore fishing. $$

Ramada Inn Stratford. 225 Lordship Boulevard; (203) 375–8866 or (800) 2RAMADA. 145 rooms, restaurant, indoor pool. Continental breakfast. $$$

Easton/Redding/Weston

The area between Fairfield in the south and Danbury in the north is sliced vertically in two by Route 58, a great road through lovely countryside. Routes 53 and 57 north from Westport also lead you toward the quiet pleasures of life north of the rat race. If you have spent a few days in the cities on the Sound, give yourselves a break and head for the farthest reaches of the county. Meander awhile—along green-canopied lanes in summer, beside snow-capped fences and stone walls in winter.

Going north from Fairfield on Route 58, you'll pass through the stately conifer forests surrounding the Hemlock and Aspetuck reservoirs. Stop in Easton at the casual **Bluebird Inn Restaurant** (203–452–0697) at the junction of Route 58 and Route 136 for some home-cooked vittles. If you start out early, have one of their great breakfasts; they open at 7:00 A.M. and close at 2:00 P.M. Once you're back in the car, pause again just a hair up the road at the aeration fountain spouting high into the air at the edge of the Hemlock reservoir. Let its music soothe your soul, then return to the car and stop just a few miles onward at the **Aspetuck Valley Orchards** (203–268–9033) produce stand. In nearly every season, there's something special here—fresh fruits and vegetables, locally made honey, maple sugar candies—in case someone needs just a little something. Pick up some trail food for later.

Continue north on Route 58 until you reach the junction of Route 107 at Redding Ridge. Take a left and drive east on 107—so, so pretty. Continue on Route 107 (about 5 miles) until you reach Route 57, then go south on Route 57. Drive 2.7 miles and take a left on Godfrey Road, then another left on Pent Road for a walk through southwestern Connecticut's largest nature preserve.

Down on **Silverman's Farm**

Young children may especially enjoy a visit to **Silverman's Farm** in Easton, where an animal farm, a seasonal cider mill, and acres of pick-your-own fruit await those who favor fun in the outdoors. Located at 451 Sport Hill Road (Route 59), 2.5 miles north of exit 46 of the Merritt Parkway, the farm is open daily year-round, except for Thanksgiving, Christmas, and New Year's Day. Come here to pick apples, peaches, plums, nectarines, and sunflowers, or to choose pumpkins, gourds, and Christmas trees. At the animal farm, see goats, sheep, pigs, fallow deer, buffalo, llamas, long-horned cattle, emus, and other exotic birds. Picnic tables, washing stations, and rest rooms are available in this area; admission is $2.00 for children and $3.00 for adults. From early September to mid-November, see fresh apple cider pressed right before your eyes. In the fall, take a tractor-drawn wagon ride through the fields and orchards. Shop for fresh produce, pies, cookies, jams, honey, and syrup in the farm market; check out the florist shop for fresh flowers, mums, wreaths, roping, and poinsettias in season. Call ahead (203–261–3306) for the pick-your-own schedule or to arrange birthday parties here.

The Nature Conservancy's Devil's Den Nature Preserve (all ages) 🚻
33 Pent Road, Weston; (203) 226–4991. Trails open dawn to dusk daily; preserve office open 9:00 A.M. to 5:00 P.M. Monday to Friday. Free.

This beautiful refuge includes 1,746 acres of woodlands, wetlands, and rock ledges separated by valleys with swamps and streams that sustain nearly 200 species of birds and mammals and nearly 500 species of trees and wildflowers. The site of prehistoric native encampments and a seventeenth-century colonial settlement, the preserve has a mill pond, a lovely ravine with a tumbling cascade, and 21 miles of trails, including loop routes for every age, fitness level, and time schedule. **Free** guided walks are offered (call for the schedule), but if you are here at other times or prefer to walk unescorted, pick up a trail map in the parking lot at the registration center. Rangers ask that you register before entering the trails. No pets, bicycles, or mechanized vehicles are permitted here. There are no rest rooms, and no camping is allowed.

Wilton

First settled by Europeans in 1651 and later established as a parish of Norwalk in 1726 by a group of forty families, Wilton remains, in the twenty-first century, a small town of twenty-seven square miles in the Norwalk River Valley. Mostly residential, it is a generally quiet place with some quintessentially New England features that visiting families may enjoy. Two such attractions are described in some detail in the following paragraphs, but for those who may spend a weekend or more in this vicinity, mentions are due the **Wilton Historical Society's Heritage Museum** (224 Danbury Road; 203–762–7257) and the village at **Cannondale Crossing** (30 Cannon Road; 203–762–8617; www.culinarymenus. com/cannondale). At the former site are two historic homes that showcase an extensive collection of decorative arts and domestic implements from 1740 through 1900. Between them, the 1757 Raymond-Fitch House and the 1735 Betts-Sturges-Blackmar House contain twelve period rooms furnished to show the passage of time through Wilton's early history. Locally made stoneware and redware plus an extensive collection of costumes, textiles, dolls, toys, and dollhouses are also displayed. Both homes host special events and exhibitions throughout the year. At the latter site is a charming retail center clustered around the railroad station at Cannon Crossing. In addition to the still-functional railroad depot, there are restored pre–Civil War farm buildings and an 1871 schoolhouse, which house gift and craft shops, a children's clothing store, a purveyor of British goods and comestibles, an antique store, and a restaurant. Visitors can also explore the banks of the Norwalk River and watch the trains go by. Cannondale Village is open year-round.

Weir Farm National Historic Site (ages 5 to 12)

735 Nod Hill Road; (203) 834–1896; www.nps.gov/wefa. Except for Thanksgiving, Christmas, and New Year's Day, the grounds are open daily year-round dawn to dusk. Visitor center open Wednesday through Sunday from 8:30 A.M. to 5:00 P.M. Studio tours Wednesday through Saturday at 11:00 A.M.,1:00 and 3:00 P.M. and on Sunday at 1:00 and 3:00 P.M. Free.

The first and only national park in Connecticut and the only one in the country dedicated to a painter, Weir Farm is the former home of noted American Impressionist J. Alden Weir (1852–1919). One of the foremost painters of his time, Weir acquired the farm in 1882 in the area known as Branchville between Wilton and Ridgefield. His summer retreat from New York City, Weir Farm is the subject of many of his paintings.

On fifty-seven acres straddling the Wilton/Ridgefield border, the secluded site includes Weir's farmhouses, studios, and barns, all among the rocky meadows and rolling woodlands of the lower Danbury Hills. If you need a place to restore the soul, please do come here to visit the place where Weir also raised his three little girls.

A video introduction to Weir Farm's history and importance is offered at the Burlingham House visitor center, which also includes historic photographs of the farm and changing exhibitions of the work of visiting artists. Be sure to pick up a copy of **Passport to Weir Farm,** a kids' activity booklet designed especially for visitors aged 8 to 12, or ask for a *Junior Ranger* booklet that helps youngsters earn a National Park Service junior ranger badge during a two-hour visit here.

The property is open daily from dawn to dusk for strolling and bird-watching. Professional and amateur artists are welcome to bring easels and paints, for sketching on the public portions of the property. The Weir Farm Historic Painting Sites Trail features twelve sites identified as the original inspiration for works of art done at the farm. The self-guided trail is easy walking through woods, fields, and wetlands, past gardens and historic structures, and along old stone walls and fences. A trail guide with color reproductions of the paintings is available for $2.00 at the visitor's center.

You can also sign up in advance for the very popular Stone Walls Walking Tours, given on Sundays at 11:00 A.M. While exploring the farm's landscape, you also learn about the various kinds of walls laid here between 1775 and the 1930s. These tours are **free.**

Life tenancy of two resident artists, Doris and Sperry Andrews, adds significantly to the ambience of an artist's retreat. The Andrews graciously allow the public to take **free** guided one-hour tours of their studios Wednesday through Sunday.

Bring a picnic if you want to spend the day. Wear socks and walking shoes and bring insect repellent. The socks may be a must for some of you—we encountered poison ivy in many places. If you arrive without art supplies, and your children are inspired to draw, ask at the visitor center for the loan of a sketch pad and crayons. They keep them on hand to encourage young artists. You might also ask about art classes offered for children and adults periodically throughout the year.

Woodcock Nature Center (all ages)

56 Deer Run Road, Wilton; (203) 762–7280. Trails open dawn to dusk daily. Visitor center open Monday through Friday from 9:30 A.M. to 4:30 P.M. year-round. Donation requested.

Located in both Ridgefield and Wilton, this small preserve is great for young children. It has 2 miles of trail and swamp boardwalk, a pond, an interpretive center with exhibit areas, and a store with nature-related books, gifts, and supplies. Botany walks, birdwatching, geology and wildlife talks, and similar programs are among the usual activities. A junior naturalist program and summer day camp are offered for children.

Where to Eat

Olde Schoolhouse Grill. 34 Cannon Road at Cannondale Village; (203) 762–8810. Once a one-room schoolhouse built in 1871, this little place on the Norwalk River serves traditional American favorites like crab cakes, tuna melts, chicken-in-a-basket, ribs, club sandwiches, and Oreo milkshakes—delicious. Patio dining in warm weather. Open for lunch Monday through Saturday; dinner Thursday through Saturday; Sunday brunch. $–$$

Soup Alley. 239 Danbury Road; (203) 761–9885. Soup is the word here, Monday through Friday, 10:00 A.M. to 7:00 P.M., and Saturday until 4:00 P.M. Along with nearly a dozen soups daily, you can buy salads, an entree or two, a sandwich or two, beverages, and desserts to take-out or to eat in. Summer hours may be shorter, not longer. $

Where to Stay

Four Points Hotel by Sheraton. 426 Main Avenue, which is Route 7, in Norwalk; (203) 849–9828 or (800) 325–3535. Located near exit 40 of the Merritt Parkway, this hotel has 127 units, including 5 suites. Restaurant, exercise room. $$$$

Ridgefield

While the northern sections of Fairfield County's coastal cities and towns become more rural as you leave the Route 1/I–95 corridor, it's not until you're inland 10 miles or so that you notice Fairfield County's split personality. From points north, Fairfield County is downright bucolic except for the city of Danbury. Small towns with pretty greens and white clapboard churches dot the countryside. The pace slows. The air is clean. You might even forget you are in the most densely populated county of the state. Ridgefield is one such town.

Visitors with children will enjoy the pedestrian-friendly nature and size of its pretty town center, where most of its attractions, shops, and restaurants are clustered. Its Aldrich Museum enjoys national renown for its art as well as for its exceptional family education programs; its historic **Keeler Tavern Museum** is especially welcoming and accessible to children; and its many boutiques and restaurants, both sophisticated and simple, have friendly proprietors who clearly cater to a family-oriented clientele. Spend the day just strolling here on the lovely town green or in pretty **Ballard Park,** right in the center of the village. Have lunch, check out the toy store or even the terrific library, and be sure to leave time for both museums.

The Aldrich Contemporary Art Museum (ages 6 to 12)
258 Main Street, (Route 35); (203) 438–4519; www.aldrichart.org. Open year-round, Tuesday through Sunday, from noon to 5:00 P.M. Adult admission is $5.00; students $2.00; children under 12 free. Gallery tour, Sunday at 2:00 P.M. Late closing on Friday at 8:00 P.M.

Surprising to find in a residential suburb like Ridgefield is this sophisticated museum founded in 1964 by Larry Aldrich, an innovative connoisseur of fine art. Right in the center of town, the internationally renowned Aldrich focuses its attention on new talents and currents in art and culture. Originally located in a historic building, the Aldrich reorganized in spring 2004, moving its exhibitions into a magnificent new addition linked to the renovated older structure. Twelve new galleries, a hundred-seat performance space, an education center, a screening room, a 22-foot-high project space, and a redesigned outdoor sculpture garden are among the new features.

In addition to exhibitions of the work of emerging and mid-career artists, the Aldrich is dedicated to contemporary video artists and performing artists. These focuses are all beautifully accommodated in the redesigned complex. Also enhanced is the museum's capacity for educational space for visitors. World-class concerts, performances, readings, and films are offered on a regular schedule. Children's art days, studio visits, and interactive family tours add to the museum's appeal to visitors of all ages.

Keeler Tavern Museum (ages 5 to 12)

132 Main Street; (203) 438–5485; www.keelertavernmuseum.org. Tours by costumed guides from February 1 through December. Open Wednesday, Saturday, and Sunday from 1:00 to 4:00 P.M. Closed on Easter Sunday, July 4, Thanksgiving, Christmas and in January. Last tour at 3:30 P.M. Adults $5.00; students $3.00; children under 12 $2.00.

Reputed as the most hospitable stop on the coach route between New York and Boston, Ridgefield's historic tavern was built about 1713 and operated as one of the most important inns in Connecticut for 130 years. A hub of community life in Ridgefield and a meeting place for Patriots in Revolutionary War days, the tavern was fired upon by British troops during the Battle of Ridgefield. A small cannonball remains imbedded in a corner post of the house.

The tavern's taproom is a cheerful reminder of the comforts the inn offered to weary eighteenth-century travelers. Although the tavern was modified several times in its history (once by famed architect and former owner Cass Gilbert), its main rooms are furnished according to the period closest to its early days. Visitors can also see the ladies' parlor, the dining room, the bedchambers, and the kitchen. Woodenware, cooking implements, and other domestic utensils illustrate the colonial lifestyle. Be sure to stroll through the lovely walled garden Gilbert designed for his wife.

Where to Eat

Mr. Shane's Homemade Ice Cream. 409 Main Street; (203) 431–8020. Located in a tiny shop at the rear of Main Street's Prudential building, this independent ice cream emporium is an epicurean treasure. Sixty flavors, with sixteen offered daily, freshly made on site. Gotta try the Mud—trust me. Or the Mango. $

Gail's Station House. 378 Main Street; (203) 438–9775. Open daily for breakfast and lunch from 8:00 A.M.; dinner on Thursday, Friday, and Saturday from 5:30 P.M. Sunday brunch served until 5:00 P.M. Come here for award-winning pancakes, omelets, skillet specials, soups, salads, sandwiches, and more. Sit at the counter for a quick bite or settle down at a table and enjoy a bottomless cuppa while the kids enjoy silver-dollar pancakes filled with blueberries or apples and real Vermont maple syrup. Yum! Outdoor seating in warm weather. $–$$

Where to Stay

West Lane Inn. 22 West Lane, Route 35; (203) 438–7323. Elegant 4-Diamond inn, 16 rooms, (3 efficiencies) with private baths. In-season, $150, double; continental breakfast. $$$$

Ridgefield Motor Inn. 296 Ethan Allen Highway; (203) 438–3781. Convenient to I–84, 36 units, restaurant. $$

Bethel

If you have spent the night in Ridgefield on the way toward the top of the county, you might want to take Route 102 south from Ridgefield's center to Route 7 in the village of Branchville, then take Route 107 north again to Route 58. Go north about 3 miles on 58, and you'll soon be in Bethel, a smallish community with an agricultural and manufacturing past. Before you reach town, though, visit Connecticut's Valley Forge.

Putnam Memorial State Park (ages 7 to 12)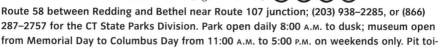
Route 58 between Redding and Bethel near Route 107 junction; (203) 938–2285, or (866) 287–2757 for the CT State Parks Division. Park open daily 8:00 A.M. to dusk; museum open from Memorial Day to Columbus Day from 11:00 A.M. to 5:00 P.M. on weekends only. Pit toilets; picnic tables. Free.

Site of the 1778–79 winter encampment of General Israel Putnam's Northern Brigades of the Continental Army, the park includes a small museum built upon the original picket post from which the sentries guarded the barracks and magazine. The museum contains exhibits related to the Revolutionary War and the encampment.

On a self-guided tour of the area, you can also see the remains of the gunpowder magazine, a reconstruction of the officers' barracks, a guardhouse reproduction, and the remains of the soldiers' huts.

Reenactments of the Revolutionary War encampment, with artillery demonstrations and cavalry and infantry camp life activities, are presented during the annual Patriots' Weekend, usually in July. The rest of the park's 183 acres attract summer visitors for fishing, hiking, and picnicking. Winter brings cross-country skiers.

Israel Putnam Statue

A magnificent bronze statue of "Old Put" shaking his fist at the British while atop his trusty steed stands at the entrance to the park. Not surprisingly, the sculptor is notable herself. Anne Hyatt Huntington created the statue at the age of 94.

Blue Jay Orchards (all ages)

125 Plumtrees Road; (pick-your-own information: (203) 748–0119; www.bluejayorchards. com. Open daily from August through late December from 9:30 A.M. to 5:30 P.M. Free, except for whatever you buy.

Chockablock with good, better, and best New England farm foods, this farm grows apples, pears, and pumpkins. These plus freshly made jams, jellies, maple syrup, honey, sweet cider pressed in its mill, excellent cinnamon cider doughnuts, and home-baked pies fill their roadside market.

A calendar of special events includes an Apple Festival in late September, hayrides to the pumpkins in October, and a Christmas tree sale in December. Let me be fair, though. Sometimes the joint is jumping—hayrides, painted pumpkins, hundreds of red-cheeked kids having a ball. Sometimes it's as sleepy as a dog in August, and the only thing moving is the dust on the road. You might like it better one way or the other—you be the judge. Either way, the apples are crisp and the pies are delicious.

Where to Eat

Emerald City Cafe. 269 Greenwood Avenue; (203) 778–4100. The perfect setting for family dining with restaurant-savvy kids. Amiable chef-owner will make helpful suggestions from extensive and delicious menu of soups, salads, sandwiches, pastas, burgers, many entrees, and house-made desserts, all affordably priced. Open for dinner and Sunday brunch. $–$$

Dr. Mike's Ice Cream. 158 Greenwood Avenue; (203) 792–4388. Stop here for what the doctor recommends—Dr. Mike, that is—ice cream extraordinaire. If you love rich, creamy, coat-your-throat ice cream, you're going to love Dr. Mike's. The long list of flavors is sure to please everyone. The chocolate is superb; the peach, in summer, is sublime. Open from noon to 11:00 P.M. daily in summer. Winter hours are shorter.

Sage Cafe. 153 Greenwood Avenue; (203) 794–9394. For quick middle-of-the-day pick-me-ups, come to this juice bar/cafe specializing in natural, fresh, wholesome foods that nevertheless go down like candy. Fruit smoothies, excellent baked goods, vegetarian sandwiches, much more. Eat in or out, in season. Open Tuesday through Sunday from 11:00 A.M. $–$$

Pick-Your-Own Pleasures

Blue Jay Orchards is one of the largest farms open to the public, but others in Fairfield County also offer pick-your-own crops:

Warrups Farm. 51 John Read Road, West Redding; (203) 938–9403. Vegetables, flowers, pumpkins, maple syrup (demonstrations 10:00 A.M. to 5:00 P.M. the first three weekends in March), beautiful country lane, free-range poultry, and barnyard animals. Hayrides in pumpkin season. Farmstand open Tuesday through Sunday, July through October.

Taylor Family Farm. 57 Great Plain Road, Danbury; (203) 744–1798. Pick your own pumpkins. Hayrides Thursday through Sunday in season. Farm stand with cider, corn, more.

Maple Row Tree Farm. 538 North Park Avenue, Easton; (203) 261–9577; www.mrfarm.com. Christmas trees, wreaths, garlands, oxen- or tractor-drawn wagon rides, hot cider. Open daily from the day after Thanksgiving to Christmas, it's the perfect setting for finding the perfect tree.

Free CT Farm Maps offer complete lists of berry farms, orchards, vegetable farms, tree farms, and sugarhouses. Call (860) 566–3671 or send an SASE with 87 cents postage to the Connecticut Department of Agriculture, 765 Asylum Avenue, Hartford, CT 06105.

Where to Stay

Best Western Stony Hill Inn. 46 Stony Hill Road; (203) 743–5533 or (800) 528–1234. 36 units. Restaurant, outdoor pool, continental breakfast; forty acres with pond. $$$

Danbury

Take Route 53 out of Bethel for about 3 miles to Danbury, a small city famous for its nearly 200-year history of hat manufacturing. Now better recognized for the corporate headquarters that were drawn here by low real estate prices and a convenient location on Interstate 84, Danbury has some family destinations that reflect its interesting past.

Danbury Museum and Historical Society (ages 7 to 12)

43 Main Street; (203) 743–5200; www.danburyhistorical.org. Open year-round Wednesday through Friday, 2:00 to 5:00 P.M. and Saturday and Sunday 2:00 to 4:00 P.M. Donation.

This interesting collection of buildings includes the 1785 John and Mary Rider House with seventeenth- and eighteenth-century furnishings and costumes and the John Dodd Hat Shop with terrific exhibits explaining Danbury's world-famous hat-making industry, the impact hat-making had on the growth of related industries, and the history of hats from a fashionable point of view. A Revolutionary War exhibit includes facts you never knew about the Daughters of the American Revolution, and a fascinating woodworking exhibit of carpentry and joinery tools offers interesting lessons about time-honored handcrafts.

You may also tour (by appointment only) the birthplace of Charles Ives at 5 Mountainville Avenue. The house was built around 1790 and purchased by Ives's ancestors in 1829; Charles was born here in 1874. The house contains Ives family furniture, memorabilia from Charles Ives's youth, his music stand, and a piano he may have played before becoming a Pulitzer-Prize winner.

Danbury Railway Museum (all ages)

120 White Street; (203) 778–8337; www.danbury.org/drm. From April through December, open Tuesday through Saturday 10:00 A.M. to 5:00 P.M. and Sunday noon to 5:00 P.M. From January through March, open Wednesday through Saturday 10:00 A.M. to 4:00 P.M. and Sunday noon to 4:00 P.M. Hours expand somewhat in midsummer; call for exact schedule. Adults $5.00; children $3.00; 4 and under free.

Who doesn't love trains? Whatever magic they have, it is something very attractive to most children and quite a few mature adults. Here in Danbury you can explore the restored Union Station, totally face-lifted with the help of $1.5 million to just about what it looked like when it was built in 1903. Now listed on the National Register of Historic Places, the station is in business again.

Check out the nifty memorabilia in the station, and operate three model railroad layouts. Then, tour the railroad yard filled with vintage railcars, boxcars, a locomotive, and other artifacts. A sleeping car and an observation car from the 20th Century Limited that ran between New York and Chicago are part of the collection. Train rides range from short rides in the yard, hour-long excursions out of the yard, and daylong trips that head for the

Trackin' It Down in Danbury

Kids and kids-at-heart who are hooked on trains may enjoy a visit to **Railworks** at 5 Padanarum Road in Danbury. New and antique model train sets are for sale here by the thousands. From electric models made in the 1920s to modern sets with digital sound systems, these trains are great fun for buyers and browsers alike. The store is open September through April, Tuesday through Sunday and Wednesday through Sunday the rest of the year. Call (203) 797–8386 for hours.

Hudson River Valley. Thomas the Tank Engine rides, Easter Bunny rides, haunted railyard and Halloween train rides, and Santa trains decorated in the railyard are part of the special family fun here. Call or check the Web site for the current schedule of events.

Ives Concert Park (all ages)
Mill Plain Road, Westside Campus, Route 6; (203) 837–9226; www.ivesconcertpark.com.
Spread over thirty-nine acres of the campus of Western Connecticut State University, the center offers top-drawer entertainment in an open-air gazebo–covered stage throughout the summer months. Named in honor of the Pulitzer Prize–winning composer considered the father of American music, the center hosts symphonies, jazz, folk, blues, theater, dance, and popular artists on its summer stage. Ticket prices and performers vary, but you can always count on exceptional quality and value. Lawn tickets for children, for instance, are $11; children 2 and under are **free;** adult lawn tickets are $26. You can bring lawn chairs and picnics, but no pets or grills. Check the Web site for the current season.

Where to Eat

Oregano's. 35 Lake Avenue Extension, Westside Plaza; (203) 778–1580. Pizzas, pastas, salads, calzones, strombolis—whatever they make, they know what they're doing. Great anisette cookies and other house-made desserts. Perfect for families. Open 11:00 A.M. to 10:00 P.M. daily. $–$$

Ethan Allen Hotel. 21 Lake Avenue, Danbury Extension; (800) 742–1776. 195 rooms and suites, restaurant, health club, sauna, outdoor pool. $$$$

Holiday Inn. 80 Newtown Road; (203) 792–4000. 114 units, including 11 suites. Restaurant, outdoor pool. Kids stay **free.** $$$$

Where to Stay

Best Inns and Suites. 78 Federal Road; (203) 743–6701 or (800) BESTINN. 72 units, restaurant, indoor pool, exercise room, continental breakfast. $$$

Brookfield and New Fairfield/Sherman

Six miles north of Danbury (taking Route 7 north), Brookfield town center has developed rapidly in the past five years, especially along the Route 7 corridor. Still, however, the Brookfield countryside remains rural, or at least suburban, in character, and the beauty of Candlewood Lake and Lake Lillinonah adds to the town's charm. Farther to the west and north are the two small towns of New Fairfield and Sherman. Although their centers, linked by the quasi-elliptical path of Routes 37 and 39, have charms of their own, there is no doubt that their greatest attractions are Candlewood Lake and Squantz Pond State Park.

The Brookfield Craft Center (ages 8 and up)

286 Whisconier Road (Route 25) near its junction with Route 7; (203) 775–4526. Monday through Saturday, 10:00 A.M. to 5:00 P.M., Sunday noon to 5:00 P.M. Free.

This nationally known school for fine crafts with classes for children and adults has a gallery and a book and gift shop that are open to visitors. Those interested in classes can pick up a copy of the center's extensive brochure or call ahead and ask them to mail one. Here's a sneak preview. For its summer youth program: papermaking, bead weaving, drawing and painting, Native American pottery, and outdoor sculptures. For adults: print-making, jewelry making, metalsmithing, boatbuilding, photography, weaving, and bas-ketry. The center is housed in four nineteenth-century buildings overlooking Halfway Falls at a truly pretty turn in the road.

Mother Earth Gallery and Mining Company (ages 6 to 12)

806 Federal Road, which is Route 7; (203) 775–6272; www.motherearthcrystals.com. Open Monday and Wednesday through Saturday from 10:00 A.M. to 6:00 P.M.; and Sunday noon to 5:00 P.M. Closed Tuesday. The mine closes at 4:30 P.M. on Sunday and at 5:30 P.M. on the other days.

This looks like an ordinary storefront with an inventory of pretty neat stuff—crystals, minerals, shells, candles, wind chimes, nature-related toys, and environmentally friendly merchandise with a New Age touch. It's also something more.

It has a mine in it. Full of crystals and minerals and semiprecious stones. And you can go prospecting with a bucket and a miner's hard hat complete with headlamp. A birthday party here for $22 per guest buys you a game of Rocko in the Miner's Shack party room, a video trip around the world to teach you about real mines and gem production, a chance to go prospecting for up to a pound per child of amethysts, obsidian, calcites, fossil shark teeth, or whatever else you might find, plus a Planet Earth cake and paper goods and juice included.

Not your birthday? Go prospecting anyway—that by itself is $13.00 per person during regular store hours. Serious collectors and beginners alike will love the exceptional miner-als and gemstones sold here, and, if you are tempted to really go prospecting in the Con-necticut hills, Mother Earth also sells the materials you'd need to find or polish your own gems.

Candlewood Lake (all ages)

Built in 1926 to provide hydroelectric power to the region, Candlewood is the largest artifi-cial lake in Connecticut. Now bordered by private residences, it's pretty as a picture in every season and popular with vacationers and daytrippers even in the quiet of winter. Use Route 39 to travel the length of the western side of the lake; smaller side roads branch off Route 7/202 on the eastern side.

Candlewood's **Story**

Nearly 1,400 men created the lake in the woodlands and farmlands nestled between the rolling hills of Brookfield and New Fairfield. Five hundred lumberjacks hand-felled 4,500 acres of trees, burning the lumber in massive bonfires. Dams were constructed, and in 1928 the first pumping operation began bringing water from the Housatonic River. Soon the Connecticut Light and Power Company was able to generate electricity by letting the water pour down an enormous pipe called a penstock and into an immense turbine.

Almost immediately the incredible beauty of the newly formed lake lapping the wooded shoreline caused land prices to skyrocket. Development escalated rapidly as the area began drawing homeowners as well as vacationers to the pretty coves of the 60-plus miles of shoreline along the 11-mile-long lake. This valuable new landmark was christened **Candlewood** after the native candlewood trees whose sapling branches had sometimes been used as candles by early settlers.

Much of the lakefront is held in private hands, although house, cottage, and cabin rentals are common. Families interested in renting by the week or month can check local newspaper listings or contact the Danbury Board of Realtors at (203) 744–7255. You can also check out www.candlewoodlake.org.

The five towns (Danbury, New Milford, and Brookfield also touch the lakeshore) bordering the lake also have town beaches. Some of these are opened to out-of-town visitors at a daily rate. Public boat launches are also available at some of the town beaches on the perimeter, and docks are on the east shore at Down the Hatch Restaurant and near the Candlewood Inn caterers.

Squantz Pond State Park (all ages)
Route 39; (203) 797–4165; http://dep.state.ct.us/cgnhs/lakes/squantz.

This pretty area of low hills and woodlands surrounds Squantz Pond, a 5-mile arm of Candlewood Lake. The park offers a public boat launch from which boaters can gain access to Candlewood by passing under the Route 39 causeway that crosses the narrowest connection of the two bodies of water. Other wonderful summer fun here includes jet-skiing, waterskiing, fishing, swimming, scuba diving, hiking, and picnicking. In winter the park is perfect for ice-skating, ice fishing, and cross-country skiing. The main entrance to the park is off Route 39 in the town of New Fairfield. From the southern junction of Routes 37 and 39, take 39 north about 4 miles to the entrance. If you're at the north end of the loop, in Sherman, take 39 south about 6 miles.

Along the shore are picnic groves, barbecue areas, a guarded swimming area, and a bathhouse with changing rooms and rest rooms (but no showers). A special pier allows handicapped visitors to fish. Hiking trails start at the north end of the picnic area on the pond's western shore.

A food concession provides typical fare like burgers, dogs, and fries in the summer. They often stock barbecueing necessities like foil and charcoal for those who want to grill a lunch or dinner with their own groceries.

Pedalboats and canoes rent for $10 an hour; canoes can also be rented for the day for $30. Squantz Pond is actually better for canoeists than is Candlewood. The high-speed powerboats on the larger lake create so much wake that canoeists have a safer, saner day with the smaller numbers of boats that remain on Squantz.

Fishing at Squantz Pond and Candlewood Lake

Some fishers say you can't have a bad day fishing in the lakes in this neck of the woods. It's not unusual to land a ten-pound trout, so anglers young and old come to try their luck for one of these trophy fish. Bass also love these waters, and bass tournaments are common summer events as hundreds of boats crowd this vast waterway for both the sport and the great dinners that result from fishing in it. Pickerel, carp, catfish, bluegills, and white and yellow perch proliferate as well. Fish from your boat, the shoreline, or public piers and docks. Remember that Squantz Pond has a special pier for handicapped anglers.

Call the Housatonic Valley Tourism District (800–841–4488) for a map of the lake, which includes suggestions for places to purchase bait and tackle. Ask also for a list of the state boat-launch sites and the marinas that provide fuel, boating goods, boat rentals, and boat services.

Sherman Playhouse (age 8 and up)
Junction of Routes 37 and 39; (860) 354–3622; www.geocities.com/~shermanplayers.

From April through December this community theater presents new and classic plays and musicals. Tickets are typically affordable ($15 or so), and student tickets are even less expensive. Curtain time is 8:00 P.M. on Fridays and Saturdays. Sunday matinees are at 3:00 P.M.

Where to Eat

Down the Hatch. 292 Candlewood Lake Road; (203) 775–6635. In northern Brookfield, this place offers great views of the lake and great food. Fresh fish, big burgers, and perfectly grilled chicken. Outside deck, often packed with families. Open daily for lunch and dinner in season. Closed Monday and Tuesday in early fall. Closed entirely November through March. $–$$

Fiddler's Restaurant. 189 Federal Road, Brookfield; (203) 775–7072. For folks who'd prefer a slightly less casual ambience, this longtime favorite is best described as a country-style pub with excellent seafood, pastas, chicken, steak, and veal dishes, plus an affordable children's menu and plenty of kid-friendly appetizers. Open daily for lunch and dinner. $$–$$$

Rickyl's Brookfield Luncheonette. 800 Federal Road; (203) 775–6042. Freshly prepared and cooked-to-order American cuisine, including omelets, fresh-fruit pancakes, homemade soups, creative sandwiches, salads, and much more. Open Tuesday through Sunday for breakfast, Sunday brunch, and lunch. $

The American Pie Company. Junction of Routes 37 and 39 in Sherman; (860) 350–0662. In the same building as the post office, this eatery has everything kids love at breakfast, lunch, and dinner. Chicken pot pie, shepherd's pie, homemade soups, salads, sandwiches, great desserts. Open daily from 7:00 A.M., no dinner on Monday. $–$$

Where to Stay

Twin Tree Inn. 1030 Federal Road, which is at Routes 7 and 202 in Brookfield; (203) 775–0220; www.twintreeinn.com. 46 units, some with Jacuzzis or private patios; continental breakfast. $$$

General Information

Coastal Fairfield County Convention and Visitors Bureau. 20 Marshall Street, South Norwalk 06854; (203) 840–0770 or (800) 866–7925; www.coastalct.com.

Housatonic Valley Tourism District. P.O. Box 406, Danbury 06813; (203) 743–0546 or (800) 841–4488; fax (203) 790–6124; www.housatonic.org.

Connecticut Welcome Centers in Fairfield County are located at I–84 Danbury (eastbound), I–95 Darien (northbound), Merritt Parkway Greenwich (northbound).

Litchfield County

Artful Pleasures and Historic Treasures

From its northwest corner where it meets the Berkshire Mountains of Massachusetts to the fertile valleys formed by the Housatonic and Farmington Rivers as they dissect the foothills, Litchfield County is famed for its beauty, history, and tranquillity. Punctuated by charming colonial towns, picturesque lakes, and thousands upon thousands of acres of farms, forests, and parks, it is an intriguing mix of rural and affluent culture. Resorts, restaurants, antiques shops, and country inns draw visitors from all over to share in the wealth, while farm markets, country fairs, and nature preserves draw visitors eager to taste the salt of the earth.

Families have much to gain by exploring the Litchfield Hills. Leave behind your health clubs and home-based gymnasium equipment, and come here instead to keep fit and trim

TopPicks for fun in Litchfield County

1. Appalachian Trail

2. Kent Falls State Park

3. Mohawk Mountain Ski Area

4. Mount Tom State Park

5. Canoeing the Housatonic—Clarke Outdoors

6. Fishing at Twin Lakes—O'Hara's Landing

7. Norfolk Summer Music Festival

8. Lee's Riding Stable

9. Tubing the Farmington River—Satan's Kingdom Recreation Area

10. Institute for American Indian Studies

LITCHFIELD COUNTY

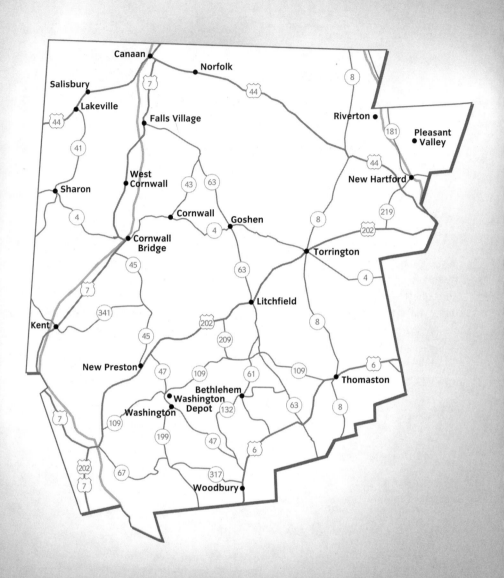

in the fresh air. Outdoor recreation opportunities abound in every pristine corner of the county. Hiking, bicycling, canoeing, fishing, kayaking, whitewater rafting, tubing, downhill and cross-country skiing, horseback riding, swimming, and camping are the lures that entice health-minded families to the Litchfield Hills.

Other families may be drawn to the spark of creative and spiritual energy that seems to reside in the nooks and crannies of the county. Fine artists, country crafters, writers, musicians, actors, and other folks driven by the Spirit and the Muses—even gardeners, vintners, chefs, and Benedictine sisters—have made their homes in these woodlands and have set up shop so that visitors might have the pleasure of enjoying their artistry. Potteries, stained-glass studios, woodcarving shops, glassworks, and galleries and boutiques showcasing all of their creations proliferate side by side with playhouses, concert halls, cooking schools, wineries, arboretums, and ornamental gardens. If your aim is to inspire the budding talents within your family, you will find no lack of opportunity to encourage one another to believe in the importance of creative careers and vocations. If you have no ulterior motive except to enjoy the displays and performances, a grand tour of the county's theaters, ateliers, and galleries will leave you awestruck.

Those of you excited by history, especially Native American lifeways, colonial settlement, and the American Revolution, will love Litchfield County. Historic homes, ruins and archaeological sites, excellent museums, and festivals celebrating the past are ubiquitous here. This book will cover only a select number of these sites and events. This volume's selection is intended to be what the author considers the best sites for families.

Lastly, Litchfield is the perfect place for wanderers. Dress in the casual garb of the vagabond and meander down the scenic highways and waterways that lead to places only more lovely at each bend in the road or river. The Litchfield Hills Tourism District has created an entire booklet of tours suitable for car, foot, boat, and bike. On each of these scenic adventures both body and soul are renewed. Do yourselves a favor and journey here.

Woodbury

Using Routes 25, 34, or 8 to get to I–84, you might make Woodbury your first stop in Litchfield County. Larger and more populated than many Litchfield County towns, Woodbury was settled in 1673 and was once known for its agriculture and its production of cutlery and cloth. Daytripping families will discover that the town is now famed as the place to go for antiques.

Woodbury's Famous Antiques and Flea Market (all ages)
Held at the junction of Routes 6 and 64; (203) 263–2841; www.woodburyfleamarket.com. Open every Saturday mid-March through mid-December, weather permitting, (most vendors come from April through mid-December) from 7:00 A.M. to 3:00 P.M. Free admission and parking.

Families wary of entering crowded shops full of expensive goods may enjoy a trip to this child-friendly outdoor market. Go early for the best selection or late for the best bargains.

Antiques are well mixed with junk; new stuff is well mixed with authentic collectibles. Last time we came, we bought only a $2.00 skillet for our campfire, but we passed by lots of great goods displayed by up to 150 vendors. Two food vendors make it easy for you to come for breakfast or stay for lunch.

The Glebe House Museum and Gertrude Jekyll Garden

(ages 6 and up)

Hollow Road off Route 6; (203) 263–2855; www.woodburyct.org/woodburyglebehouse. Open from 1:00 to 4:00 p.m. Wednesday through Sunday from April through October. Expanded hours on Saturday from 10:00 a.m. to 4:00 p.m. June through August. Open weekends only in November from 1:00 to 4:00 p.m. Open by appointment in December through March. Adults, $5.00; children (6 to 16) $2.00.

This 1745 minister's farmhouse, or glebe, is an exceptional example of eighteenth-century architecture and is especially welcoming to children. The mood inside the house is warm and inviting. Artifacts are laid out in positions of use, and children are enthusiastically addressed on tours tailored to the interests and schedules of visitors. Historically important as the site of the first election of an American bishop of the Episcopal Church in 1783, the house has many fine (and simple) furnishings and a charming gift shop/bookstore. Its beautiful perennial garden is the only one in the United States designed by renowned English landscape designer Gertrude Jekyll.

Most important for interested families, a History Camp for children aged 8 to 12 is offered each summer. A weeklong program of colonial activities, it is an eye-opening experience of eighteenth-century daily life. Several sessions are often offered.

Woodbury Ski and Racquet Area (ages 3 and up)

785 Washington Road, Route 47; (203) 263–2203; woodburyskiarea.com. Open weekdays from 10:30 a.m. to 10:00 p.m., Saturday from 9:00 a.m. to 10:00 p.m., and Sunday from 9:00 a.m. to 4:30 p.m.

This year-round recreational facility attracts thousands of outdoor sports enthusiasts each year. In winter its fourteen alpine downhill trails are especially popular with children and with beginner and intermediate skiers. Lessons, rentals, and night skiing specials are offered, and a double chairlift, two rope tows, a new handle tow, and snowmaking equipment keep the pace active all season long. Two major halfpipes provide excitement for snowboarders, and a quarter pipe has been added recently. A new base lodge and ski shop flesh out the amenities that keep Woodbury on a par with other Connecticut ski areas. Ask about the Winter Carnival in January—a weeklong extreme extravaganza.

Three tubing and sledding courses with a dedicated lift are also available, from a gentle glide for beginners to a two-lane, bobsled-like run for thrill-seekers. Tickets are $20 for three hours. Seven kilometers of groomed cross-country trails are also on the property; recently improved, these trails are lighted and have snowmaking, tracking, and tilling. Trail fee is $15.

A newly resurfaced and expanded year-round skateboarding park and an in-line skate course are also here. In the warm seasons, you can also camp, swim, picnic, and play tennis and paddle tennis. Concerts, from rock to reggae, are also offered from time to time in the summer. Check the Web site to see what's on the calendar.

Flanders Nature Center (all ages)

Church Hill and Flanders Road, off Route 6; (203) 263–3711. Trails open daily year-round, dawn to dusk. Free.

Nature lovers will enjoy this center's two sanctuaries at Van Vleck Farm and Whittemore, where trails lead through 1,000 acres of woodland, bog, a nut tree arboretum, and more. Bird and wildflower walks, a fall festival, and a variety of programs such as maple sugaring in March are among the opportunities for discovery. The Trail House offers a nature shop and some small exhibits; it's open Saturday from 9:00 A.M. to 5:00 P.M.

Highwire Deer and Animal Farm (all ages)

68 Park Road; (203) 263–7500. Open May through August, Wednesday through Sunday, 11:00 A.M. to 4:00 P.M. and in September on Saturday and Sunday only, 11:00 A.M. to 4:00 P.M. Admission is $4.50; children under 2 are free.

Not far from the intersection of Routes 64 and 6 in Woodbury is this privately owned exotic animal farm. About eighty animals are here, including fallow deer, llamas, sheep, a camel, and a zebra. Signs at the enclosures teach about each species. You can pet and feed the animals, and then have your own picnic at one of the picnic tables.

Geppetto's Distinguished Toys (ages 2 to 12)

682 Main Street South in the Sherman Village Shopping Center; (203) 266–4686. Open 10:00 A.M. to 5:00 P.M. Monday through Thursday and Saturday, on Friday from 10:00 A.M. to 8:00 P.M., and noon to 4:00 P.M. on Sunday.

If you have a toy lover in your group, don't head out of town until you stop here. The shop contains an impressive inventory of the world's finest games, dolls, puzzles, train sets, construction toys, books, art supplies, science and crafts project kits, and so on. The brands on hand are largely the same as the stock in other top-of-the-line toy shops, but the kids won't mind if you begin your holiday shopping here.

The Merry Go Round of Fine Crafts (ages 4 and up)

319 Main Street South; (203) 263–2920. Open Monday and Wednesday through Saturday from 10:00 A.M. to 5:00 P.M. and Sunday from 11:00 A.M. to 5:00 P.M. Closed Tuesday.

This seven-room 1837 homestead is a gallery offering the work of Connecticut artisans only. Birdhouses, floorcloths, candles, quilts, paintings, holiday ornaments, and much more are displayed here in themed rooms. A children's room includes a giant dollhouse and a lovely selection of books, wooden toys, dolls, rocking horses, stuffed bears, children's furniture, and clothing. Proud of the quality, originality, and wide price range, the hosts here confidently boast that this is the state's best showcase of Connecticut handcrafts.

Every weekend you can meet some of the artists who exhibit their wares here. Demonstrations of their creative processes help observers to enjoy the commitment each of the artists has made to his or her craft. You and the kids may be inspired by the work of weavers, potters, or painters as they share their stories and their skills. Two special celebrations each year (one outside on the fourth Sunday in June; one in a holiday workshop in the lowest level of the house on the Sunday before Thanksgiving) provide a festival atmosphere with displays of new crafts, demonstrations by artists, and a buffet of refreshments.

Where to Eat

Carmen Anthony Fishhouse. 757 Main Street South; (203) 266–0011. As perfect for families as for discerning adult diners, this casually elegant establishment is open for lunch and dinner daily year-round. Fresh fish is the specialty here, but soups, salads, pastas, and a special selection of kids' favorites are also available. $$–$$$

Elenni's. 40 Sherman Hill Road, Route 64 at Route 6 junction; (203) 263–2566. Greek pizza, pasta, chicken, salads, grinders, calzones. Open daily; Tuesday through Friday, lunch and dinner; weekends, breakfast, lunch, and dinner. $

Where to Stay

Curtis House. 506 Main Street; (203) 263–2101. One of Connecticut's oldest hostelries, this rambling 1754 colonial inn and carriage house in the heart of Woodbury offers guest rooms that range from small with shared bath to huge or linked with private bath. Restaurant. $$–$$$$

Longwood Country Inn. 1204 Main Street South; (203) 266–0800; www.longwood countryinn.com. Small families with children over age 10 looking for deluxe accommodations in a truly refined setting might ask for guest room number five in this lovely restored 1789 Colonial. Full country breakfasts. $$$$

Kent

I don't believe there's a family alive who won't find something to please every member in the beautiful town of Kent. About 12 miles north of New Milford on Route 7, the village center was once little more than a bump in the road, but it hums now with the activities generated by the shops, galleries, restaurants, bakeries, and natural and historical attractions that line Route 7 as it passes through one of northwest Connecticut's most interesting villages.

Bull's Bridge (all ages)
Officially in Gaylordsville, 3.8 miles south of Kent's center; just off Route 7 on Bull's Bridge Road.

Originally built in 1760 by Isaac Bull to carry iron ore and charcoal over the Housatonic, the current covered bridge is one of the two remaining covered bridges open to traffic in Connecticut. The view of the river and its beautiful whitewater cascades and ravines is perfect from the bridge. A small scenic loop trail leads to other views of the woodlands, the rapids, the still water, and the wildlife in the area. A parking area on the western side of the bridge allows you to stop here safely and walk to several clearly marked sites and trails. A second hiker parking area is located a bit farther along Bull's Bridge Road at the entrance to the Appalachian Trail section (see sidebar), which is marked with white blazes.

It's **Revolutionary**

Historically important because of the integral role it played in the Revolutionary War, Kent supplied the Continental Army with iron ore, goods, and soldiers. It also offered a strategic location on a main waterway to Long Island Sound and on the marching road between Lebanon, the army's supply depot, and Washington's headquarters in New York. Now, nearby and along this same route, lies a sizable stretch of the **Appalachian Trail,** including the longest river walk on the whole 2,144-mile hiking path. You can enter this easy-to-moderate 7.8-mile portion of the trail near Bull's Bridge. You'll find the trailhead off of Route 341 west. Go to Skiff Mountain Road, bear right at the fork to the Appalachian National Scenic Trail. The trail is marked with white blazes, and the area closes at sunset.

Kent Village Center 🔒

On Route 7, also called Main Street, mostly north of the Route 341 intersection.

In the center of Kent, stroll through the shops and galleries. All lovely, some are especially suited to families. **Toys Galore and More** (860–927–4091) is self-explanatory. Sometimes they put bubble solution and giant bubble wands outside in the brick plaza—so fine for fun. Other favorites are **Foreign Cargo** (860–927–3900), which has great funky and exotic import clothing, unusual jewelry, and an upstairs gallery of American antiques and Asian, African, and Pacific Island art. If the kids enjoy them or can allow you to enjoy them, at least peek into the art galleries. Housed in an authentic nineteenth-century railroad caboose, the outstanding **Paris–New York–Kent Gallery** (860–927–3357) in Kent Station Square is the most famed. Our favorite is the **Heron American Craft Gallery** (860–927–4804), which offers top-quality handcrafts in all price ranges. When the gallery gazing and boutique hopping leave you weary, head for the restaurants.

Which Way Did He Go, **George?**

Local lore documents that George Washington may have nearly lost a trusty steed as he crossed Bull's Bridge one day in March of 1781. It's uncertain how the accident happened or whether the horse was Washington's own mount, but it is clear that one of his horses fell into the roiling waters under the bridge as his company made the passage on the way to meet with the French to make plans for naval support against the British. Washington's diary for the day records that the cost of retrieving the horse from Bull's Bridge Falls was $215. The time spent on this rescue and the cost incurred lead some historians to guess that the animal may not have been just any ordinary horse.

Sloane-Stanley Museum (ages 5 and up)

Route 7, north of Kent center; (860) 927–3849. The museum itself is open Wednesday through Sunday from 10:00 A.M. to 4:00 P.M. mid-May to October 31. The grounds remain open until 4:30 P.M. during that time. Adults $3.00; children $1.50. *(Note: This museum is one of the state-owned properties whose hours and staff have been reduced due to state budget cuts. Call ahead to be sure the museum reopened for its usual hours in 2004.)*

Just north of the village on the left side of the road where the railroad tracks border Route 7, stop for a look at one of the most surprisingly moving exhibits we've seen in the state. Gathered through the efforts of the late author/artist Eric Sloane, the collection includes tools made by colonial Americans as early as the seventeenth century.

Revealing much about the early settlers' experiences and their adaptation to their new home, the tools are fascinating in their diversity, their ingenuity, and in their beauty. Each object has been finely crafted, mostly by hand, primarily from the hardwoods of the Eastern Woodlands. The presence of each cabinetmaker, each farmer, each cook seems to fill the post-and-beam barn in which the collection is housed. A videotape featuring Sloane himself explains the philosophies behind the artist, his work, and the museum collection.

The museum also includes a complete re-creation of Eric Sloane's art studio along with some of his original works. Outside the museum is a small cabin built by Sloane in 1974 with the use of notations found in a young boy's 1805 diary. The simple realities of frontier life are made obvious throughout the austere interior of this display.

A visit to the ruins of the Kent Iron Furnace (also on the property) may have some interest. Long important as a producer of pig iron, the blast furnace is partially restored. A diorama inside the museum explains the process of smelting pig iron and shows how the blast furnace would have worked.

Connecticut Antique Machinery Association Museum

(ages 5 and up)

Route 7, north of Kent center; enter property at Sloane Stanley Museum; take driveway to right; (860) 927–0050; www.ctmachinery.com. Museum and grounds are open mid-May through October 31, Wednesday through Sunday 10:00 A.M. to 4:00 P.M. A donation of $2.00 is gratefully accepted.

One of Connecticut's newest museums is a tiny village of sorts constructed on eight acres of wooded property adjacent to the Sloane-Stanley Museum. Visitors can tour the eight new and/or restored buildings of the Connecticut Antique Machinery Association. The complex houses the state's largest display of steam and gas engines and tractors, as well as other antique agricultural and industrial machinery and mining equipment. Arranged on the site are such buildings as the Agricultural Hall (a tractor barn housing fifty tractors from the late 1800s to the 1950s), the Cream Hill Agricultural School (the state's first such school, moved here from Cornwall with its original desks, kitchen implements, library, and natural science and curiosities collection), and the Connecticut Museum of Mining and Mineral Science (the largest permanent display in the state of native minerals and rocks, historical bricks, and mining equipment). The last-mentioned includes amazing small dioramas depicting gold mining, brick making, and iron smelting, complete with miniature figures and signage that tells the story of the nation's mining heritage and industry. Among the other buildings are engine halls, an engine house for the museum's operating narrow-gauge railway, and an oil pumping station from Pennsylvania, complete with actual workman's overalls found at the abandoned site.

Most displays are labeled and educational signage is in place in some areas, but be sure to take the guided tours offered here. They generally last an hour, but volunteers will take into account the ages of your party and your areas of interest. Despite its apparent potential for lots of bells and whistles, this tends to be a quiet place. Demonstrations are given only on special-events days, such as the **Fall Festival** (see sidebar). Like the Sloane-Stanley, however, it is pretty fascinating. Check the Web site for upcoming events.

Fall **Festival**

If you're ever in Kent the last weekend in September, stay for the annual **Antique Machinery Association's Fall Festival.** Sounds awful, right? It's not—there's cider making, threshing, wood splitting, blacksmithing, broom making, shingle making, draft animals, antique cars and trucks, homestead displays, and working exhibits of steam and gas engines, farm equipment, steam launches, and motor canoes, plus food, crafts, and fun. Call (860) 927–0050.

Kent Falls State Park (all ages)

Route 7 about 5 miles north of Kent's center; (860) 927–3238. Open year-round. A $5.00 parking fee is charged on weekends and holidays only from Memorial Day weekend through Labor Day weekend.

Wander northward from the Sloane-Stanley Museum until you reach this park on the right side of the road. Leave your car at the parking lot right off Route 7 at the base of the wide meadow that slopes down from the hills above. Beyond the meadow are the beautiful cascading waterfalls known as Kent Falls. Beginning in the town of Warren, the mountain stream known as Falls Brook reaches Kent through a series of drops, about 200 feet in total. Each drop is as pretty as the last as the falls descend through a dense forest of hemlocks, creating pools and potholes that openly invite visitors to dip a toe or two or even more into the cold, clear (but not potable) water.

Two trails to take you to the top of the falls are cut through the forest on either side of the stream. We suggest you climb up the one-quarter mile south trail directly to the right of the falls as you face them from the meadow and descend on the north trail, which you reach by crossing the bridge at the top of the south trail. The trails are fairly steep at points, but not strenuous. Small children will manage well if they rest from time to time. Stairs and railings on the south trail will help those who haven't had a workout in a while. The slightly longer north trail angles off into the woods a bit away from the falls. You'll miss a pretty walk through the New England woodlands if you don't come down this way.

"Swimming" in the strictest sense is prohibited here, but wading or bathing (in bathing suits, please) in designated areas is absolutely allowed. Where else can you cavort directly under a waterfall? The deepest pool, depending on the water level in a particular year, will be waist or even chest high for adults, so don't take your eyes off small children if you're not going in with them. Wading, for them, may be very close to swimming in at least two of the pools in which wading is allowed.

After you cool off, try some fishing in the stream as it nears the meadow. The stream is stocked with trout, and no license is necessary for children under 16. Picnic tables are scattered throughout the meadow and under the trees near the parking lot. Grills and toilets are also available. You have to pack out your own trash, so be prepared. The falls tend to be most dramatic in the spring, by the way, when melting winter snow raises the water level; the forest, however, is most dramatic in fall. In winters when the water freezes, the falls form giant icicles. Maybe you'll just have to return in every season.

Macedonia State Park (all ages)

Four miles northwest of the village off Route 341; park office: (860) 927–3238; campground office: (860) 927–4100. Open year-round; seasonal camping. No day-use charge.

With 2,300 acres, this park has excellent trails offering spectacular views of the Catskill and Taconic Mountains. Camping (eighty sites; mid-April to September 30; $9.00), hiking, stream fishing, picnicking, and cross-country skiing are all available here. Take the loop trail to Cobble Mountain (1,380 feet at the summit) for a view you won't forget. It's just a half-mile to the top, then a mile down on another trail, or you can retrace the way you came. Ask a ranger for a map.

Where to Eat

The Villager. Route 7; (860) 927–3945. Delicious soups, club sandwiches, and entrees like vegetarian lasagna or meatball Parmesan on a very complete menu in the tradition of New England roadside diners. Open for breakfast, lunch, and (sometimes) dinner; 6:00 A.M. to 4:00 P.M. Monday and Tuesday; 6:00 A.M. to 8:00 P.M. on Wednesday through Friday; 7:00 A.M. to 3:00 P.M. on Saturday; and 8:00 A.M. to 2:00 P.M. on Sunday. $

Stroble Baking Company. Route 7; (860) 927–4073. Breads, pastries, cakes, cookies, and coffee are the highly rated specialties here; soups, sandwiches, and salads are the bonus. All are perfect take-out picnic choices. Open daily year-round 8:00 A.M. to 6:00 P.M. $

Fife 'n Drum Restaurant and Inn. Route 7; (860) 927–3509. Three-star restaurant in the style of an elegant but homey tavern, wonderful New England classic cuisine at lunch, dinner, and Sunday brunch. Piano music in the evening, played by the well-known owner/host, who has accompanied Peggy Lee, Frank Sinatra, and other great crooners. Adjacent inn offers lodging, and a lovely shop offers tempting gifts. Closed Tuesday. $$–$$$

Stosh's New England's Own Ice Cream. Route 7, near the soldiers' monument; (860) 927–4495. The best ice cream in Litchfield County. Each day sixteen of 130 flavors of ice cream, yogurts, and sorbets are made up for your pleasure. You can also buy sandwiches, cookies, muffins, drinks, and Dazzle Dogs—all-beef franks served on home-baked, toasted, buttered buns. Open April through October. $

Belgique Patisserie. 1 Bridge Street at the junction of Routes 7 and 341; (860) 927–3631. The best place for tarts, Belgian pralines, chocolates, ice cream, hot chocolate, and coffees. Open year-round, Wednesday to Sunday. $

Where to Stay

Fife 'n Drum Inn. 59 North Main Street in the center of the village; (860) 927–3509. 8 large rooms with private baths, restaurant (see above). $$$

Rosewood Meadow B & B. 230 Kent Cornwall Road; (860) 927–4334 or (800) 600–4334. This 1860 Greek Revival B & B offers a charming "cottage" suite, attached to the main house but with a private entrance to a sweet little apartment with a kitchen, bath, living room, and bedroom. Full breakfast. Nonsmoking. Two-and-one-half-acre property to play in. $$$

Sharon

If your last stop in Kent was Macedonia State Park, you might consider continuing north along Route 341 into New York State, then eastward again on Route 41 back to Connecticut and the town of Sharon. (As the crow flies, Sharon is about 10 miles north of Kent; the surface route is about 15 miles.) Charming and barely there, Sharon existed in the eighteenth century and has not developed much since. That's a tribute, not a criticism, but there's really just one special place here for families. If your kids are old enough, the show is appropriate, and the time of your visit is summer-stock time, you might also enjoy a second treat: a performance at the **Sharon Stage** on Route 343 (860–364–1500).

Sharon Audubon Center (all ages)
Route 4; (860) 364–0520; www.audubon.org/local/sanctuary/Sharon. Access to the trails: adults $3.00, seniors and children $1.50. No charge for center's main building. Trails open dawn to dusk daily year-round; building open year-round from Tuesday through Saturday from 9:00 A.M. to 5:00 P.M. and on Sunday from 1:00 to 5:00 P.M. Closed major holidays.

Like all of the Audubon Society's facilities, the 684-acre Sharon Audubon Center is exceptionally well done, with 11 miles of carefully tended trails and boardwalks throughout several habitats. Pond, swamp, marsh, and woodland areas have clearly marked, self-guided interpretive nature walks. Naturalist-guided tours highlighting such topics as birds, trees, or mammals are also offered for families or groups.

The center's main building includes natural science exhibits, a noncirculating library, and an excellent gift and book shop. The children's Adventure Center has a feature we've not seen anywhere else: listening boxes to sit inside. Tapes triggered by the weight of children play sounds of whales, rainstorms, and more. Kids can crawl through a simulated beaver's den, identify skulls, look at a real honeybee hive, and more.

Outdoors is a wildlife rehabilitation center, providing temporary shelter for injured animals; turtles, snakes, and birds are the most common species found here. If you come in spring or summer near evening or early morning, you may see the beavers at Ford or Bog Meadow Ponds. Warblers tend to stop here on their annual fall and spring migrations, so bird-watchers (and listeners) might enjoy a visit at those times.

The center maintains an herb garden, a wildflower garden, and a butterfly and hummingbird garden. The colorful and fragrant flowers attract these wild and beautiful visitors all summer long. Check the Web site for the dates of the wonderful annual Sharon Audubon Festival, featuring hands-on crafts for children, demonstrations, workshops, music, pony rides, and food. It is held rain or shine. You might return in late October for the Audubon Kids Day. A costume parade, hayrides and a haybale maze, nature activities, and pumpkin carving are among the events. Look, too, on the Web site for the naturalist-led educational programs for parents and children, offered throughout the year.

Where to Eat

Little Brick House Pizza. 29 West Main Street; (860) 364–1321. Open Monday through Saturday, this terrific little spot makes great pizza. Grinders and salads, too. Cash only. Lunch and dinner. $

Country Corner. (860–364–0070); open daily year-round for breakfast and lunch, and dinner on Wednesday through Friday; simple American diner-style cuisine; no fuss, but no muss; outside seating in warm weather. $–$$

Where to Stay

Sharon Motor Lodge. Route 41 (860–364–0036). Twenty-two large rooms with air-conditioning, cable TV, coffeemakers. Nonsmoking rooms. Outdoor pool. Small restaurant across the street. AAA and Mobil approved. Nice grounds, set back from the main road. $$$

Cornwall Bridge

In a roughly elliptical shape drawn by Routes 7, 128S and 4, you'll find the separate villages of Cornwall Bridge, Cornwall, and West Cornwall, with one of the three nearby state parks or forests shouldering each of them. Together this trio comprises the town of Cornwall. Traveling north from Kent on Route 7, Cornwall Bridge is the first of the three. One of those villages you can easily pass through before you know you have reached it, Cornwall Bridge is a beautiful area with a couple of sites of interest to families. As you explore, look along the roadside for a merry landmark called "Lizard Rock."

Cornwall Bridge Pottery (ages 5 and up)

Route 7; (860) 672–6545 or (800) 501–6545. Open daily from 9:00 A.M. to 5:00 P.M. year-round. Call ahead if you want to make sure someone is there to show you around, or feel free to poke around on your own—respectfully. Free.

On the east side of Route 7 a mile north of the Route 45 junction and a mile south of the junction with Route 4, visit the pottery workshop and see the potters and the 35-foot-long wood-fired kiln at work. I suspect you'll love to see this process and so will the family.

Todd Piker is owner, potter, philosopher, and excellent businessman. His pots (and plates, bowls, et cetera) are exceptionally beautiful and eminently useful. Browse here or at the pottery's store (discussed in the West Cornwall section) for the pots you might find most usable for the needs of your family. Still-beautiful and useful seconds are available here; perfect pots are at the store.

Housatonic River Outfitters, Inc.

24 Kent Road at junction of Routes 4 and 7; (860) 672–1010; www.dryflies.com. Open Monday through Saturday from 9:00 A.M. to 5:00 P.M., Sunday from 9:00 A.M. to 4:00 P.M. Longer hours from May through fall.

Come here for top-quality fishing equipment, fly-tying materials, outerwear, fishing vests and other outdoor clothing, maps and books, camping equipment, and luggage. An amazing inventory of anglers' flies includes more than 50,000 in all. They will provide guide services for spin- or fly-fishing the river. All-day guided float trips in comfortable inflatable rafts can be arranged, complete with customized lunches. Licenses are available here. The staff can also arrange lodging and dinner reservations or point you toward activities in the Litchfield Hills.

Housatonic Meadows State Park (all ages) 🕊️ 🔺 🎿 🅰️

One mile north of Cornwall Bridge on Route 7; park office: (860) 927–3238; camp office: (860) 672–6772. Open year-round; seasonal camping. Day use 8:00 A.M. to sunset. No day-use charge. Alcohol prohibited.

One of the state's best and most scenic campgrounds is right on the river and offers plenty of opportunities for hiking, fishing, and canoeing. Along one 2-mile stretch only fly-fishers are allowed. You can watch them or be one of them (the latter only with a license). Cross-country skiing is popular here in winter. In warmer weather, ninety-five campsites are available from mid-April through December; they currently cost $13 per campsite per night. Hikers may like knowing that the park's Pine Knob Loop Trail connects to the Appalachian Trail and passes lovely cascading waterfalls.

Sweets for the Sweet

If someone in your party is in the mood for "a little something," head straight to **Matthews 1812 House** (860–672–0149), 2.5 miles south of Cornwall Bridge at 250 Kent Road (Route 7). There, Deanna and Blaine Matthews have been creating the most delicious little-somethings for nearly a quarter century. Toffees, truffles, tortes, and trail mixes are just the tip of the icing, so to speak. Brownies, cookies, nuts, fudge, syrups, marzipan, jellies, caramels, and incredible cakes await any candy monsters in your group. Everything is made here in small batches, with no preservatives. Stop by Monday through Friday from 9:00 A.M. to 5:00 P.M. year-round. It's so delicious.

Housatonic Meadows Fly Shop and Tightline Adventures Guide Service (ages 8 and up) 🕊️

13 Route 7; (860) 672–6064; www.flyfishct.com. Open from 8:00 A.M. Monday through Thursday and from 7:00 A.M. on Friday and weekends. Closings vary with the day and season.

The folks who run this shop say "There's no tonic like the Housatonic," and they are more than happy to help you find out how to enjoy yourselves on the river. Located right across from the state park entrance and picnic area, the store carries a full line of Orvis tackle, clothing, and gifts, including a bizillion flies and everything else you'd need for a lifetime of fishing. Equipment rentals are also available, along with licenses. Daytrippers in need of instruction or a guide will find all their needs met here. Full- and half-day float trips in drift rafts are expensive for most families, but if you have the do-re-mi, the guides here can sure sing that tune. Lunches are included on the full-day trips. Call well in advance to make your arrangements; you can't just show up at the door.

Cornwall

In the area closest to the village center called Cornwall is one of Connecticut's best sites for family fun in winter as well as in warmer weather.

Mohawk Mountain State Park and Mohawk Mountain Ski Area

(all ages) 🚶 🍴 ⛷️ 🏕️

48 Great Hollow Road, Route 4; (for ski area: (860) 672–6100 or (800) 895–5222; for park: (860) 424–3200; ski area, www.mohawkmtn.com; park, www.dep.state.ct.us. Open for skiing from Thanksgiving Day to early April. Summer parking fee, $5.00, weekends only.

Connecticut's largest and oldest ski area, Mohawk has twenty-three trails and slopes, five lifts, and snowmaking equipment for 98 percent of the slopes. Families can enjoy day and night skiing, snowboarding, and 5 miles of cross-country ski trails in the Mohawk State Forest. Snowmobiling is allowed in designated areas of the park. Rental ski equipment is available, as are services like waxing and repairs. The PSIA Mohawk Learning Center provides lessons for all ages and skill levels; young children can participate in the SKIwee program.

The historic, newly renovated Pine Lodge offers skiers a place to rest and get warm; it has a ski-to restaurant and a sundeck. The base lodge has a retail ski shop and headquarters for rentals, lessons, and food services.

In summer and fall, hiking, mountain biking, and picnicking draw thousands of visitors each year. Famous for its rare and fragile black spruce bog, Mohawk State Park and Forest are laced with trails, including a portion of the Mattatuck Trail and original segments of the Appalachian Trail. A climb to the wooden observation tower at Mohawk Mountain's 1,683-foot summit will leave you speechless, not from the exercise but from the view. The summer park rangers will give you a map and directions to the trailhead. A food concession, toilets, picnic tables, and a nature trail area make for great daytripping.

West Cornwall

You have to visit West Cornwall if only to see Connecticut's finest and largest covered bridge. Built by Ithiel Town in 1837 of native oak, the **West Cornwall Bridge** is a beauty beyond a shadow of a doubt, and I don't think anyone is too jaded to feel its magic as it leads you across the river and back in time. I wish I could have heard the clip-clop of horses' hooves instead of the rumble of my car wheels as we made our crossings.

The village at West Cornwall is picturesque and very tiny, and for many travelers the bridge is in fact the main attraction. If you'd like to linger awhile, however, there's Barbara Farnsworth's used- and rare-book store, a post office for you to drop a pretty picture postcard in the mail, the workshop of famed Shaker furniture maker Ian Ingersoll, some wonderful gift and craft shops, great country deli/markets, and a few lovely restaurants. Here are some of the best places for families:

Clarke Outdoors

The beautiful river that flows through the countryside and the Housatonic State Forest may appeal to your sense of adventure. If so, **Clarke Outdoors** can help you enjoy a 10-mile stretch through quiet water and easy whitewater that is perfect for both knowledgeable and novice paddlers. Drivers take you to the put-in point in Falls Village. You can choose to canoe, kayak, or raft. The halfway point is at the West Cornwall Bridge, where you can take out for a picnic on the banks. The pick-up and take-out point is at the Housatonic Meadows State Park. Hot showers are available back at the Clarke shop.

Available from mid-March through early December, canoe rentals are $52 per canoe on the weekends and $47 on weekdays. No more than three people are allowed in each canoe, and the minimum age allowed is 7. Single-paddler kayaks are $40 per person; sit-yaks are $30 per person. Inflated rafts that can hold four, six, or eight paddlers and passengers are $27 per adult on weekends, $24 on weekdays, and $17 per child 15 and under on weekends and $14 on weekdays. The minimum age allowed on the rafts is 3. All rates include life vests and shuttle service that takes you to the put-in and picks you up at the take-out.

Offering one of the largest selections of canoe and kayak equipment in the Northeast, Clarke's retail store (860–672–6365; www.clarkeoutdoors.com) just south of West Cornwall on Route 7 is also the registration point where you begin this journey. Reservations are a must on weekends and many weekdays. Call at least a week in advance. American Canoe Association–certified instructors, including former national canoe champion Mark Clarke, provide lessons and guided trips. A kayaking school offers weekend lessons for adults and special groups for children 10 to 17. Call (860) 672–6365 for information.

The Cornwall Bridge Pottery Store

Route 128; (860) 672–6545; www.cbpots.com. Open January 1 through May 15 Thursday through Sunday from noon to 5:00 P.M. on weekdays and 10:30 A.M. to 5:30 P.M. on weekends; from May 16 through December 31 on Monday and Wednesday through Sunday at the same hours. Closed on Thanksgiving and Christmas.

This spacious store sells the beautiful, lead-free stoneware crafted by its owner, Todd Piker, and other local artisans. Plates, mugs, bowls, lamps, tiles, and other pottery pieces are the focus, but an interesting array of handblown glassware, woodenware, leather goods, silver and amber jewelry, furniture, some clothing, and other quality crafts are also sold on the two floors of selling space here.

The Wish House

413 Main Street (Route 128), near the covered bridge; (860) 672–2969. Open Wednesday through Sunday 11:00 A.M. to 6:00 P.M. Extended hours in the holiday season.

Just a skip across the railroad tracks is a yellow house with a small second-story porch on the side and hanging geraniums in the summertime. Teddy bears, children's clothing and jewelry, tea sets, wooden toys, kitchenware, linens and towels, hats, handbags, ceramics, and much more should help fulfill a little someone's wishes. Local artists exhibit their paintings or other artworks in this homey space so you can easily imagine how a piece might look in your place.

Where to Eat

The Wandering Moose Cafe. 421 Sharon Goshen Turnpike (Route 128 or Main Street); (860) 672–0178. Casual, diner-style cuisine perfect for families. Breakfast and lunch, Monday through Friday from 7:00 A.M. and weekends from 8:00 A.M. Dinner Wednesday through Sunday from 5:00 P.M. $–$$

Where to Stay

Cornwall Inn. 270 Kent Road (Route 7), in Cornwall Bridge; (860) 786–6884 or (800) 786–6884. The main building of this recently refurbished eighteenth-century inn has two options for families, including adjoining rooms connected by a private bath. Three rooms with two double beds in each are in the annexed motel-style building. Outdoor pool and hot tub. Continental breakfast included. The adjacent restaurant called **Tavern at the Inn** (860–672– 2825) serves New American cuisine at dinners from 5:00 P.M. Wednesday through Sunday. Informal pub menu also available. Seasonal rates. Great for those hiking or skiing at Mohawk for the weekend. $$$

Salisbury/Lakeville

If you can continue north on Route 7, swing left when you reach Route 112, following the signs for Salisbury, Lime Rock, and Lakeville. Route 112 leads to Route 44, where you'll take a right. Connecticut doesn't have a prettier town than Salisbury. They should place signs at the edge of the town that say "Please do not disturb." A quiet corner of pure sanity, Salisbury is home to an interesting variety of attractions that families may enjoy. Here too are some of the loveliest shops in the state. Be sure to explore the village centers.

Sweethaven Farm (ages 5 and up)

Retail store at 7 Academy Street; gardens at Weatogue Road off Route 44; (860) 435–6064. Gardens open to the public on weekends 10:00 A.M. to 4:00 P.M. during the growing season. No charge. Retail shop open year-round Monday through Saturday 10:00 A.M. to 5:00 P.M., Sunday 11:00 A.M. to 3:00 P.M.; closed Tuesday.

The gardens at Sweethaven Farm exemplify what happens when a gentle, knowledgeable, and wholesome soul nurtures the ground and brings forth its goodness in the form of herbs. Owner Noreen Driscoll Breslauer is such a soul. A welcoming enclave of beauty and fragrance, her Sweethaven specializes in organic herbs and flowers. These days, only her lower gardens are open to the public, and you can visit both of them on weekends only in late spring, summer, and early fall.

A favorite of children is the Beatrix Potter–Peter Rabbit garden. Delightfully guarded by scarecrow-style figures of Peter Rabbit and his family, the garden is sowed with the herbs and flowers that appear in the illustrations of Beatrix Potter's stories.

Sweethaven Farm also has a wonderful retail operation in town, selling herbal vinegars, potpourris, wreaths, culinary blends, and topiaries. Local artisans contribute their wares to the inventory, so you will also find baskets, handpainted pots, nature photography, garden antiques, and other handcrafted treasures for home and garden.

Connecticut's **Agricultural Fairs**

Each year more than fifty agricultural fairs are held in the state of Connecticut to celebrate the successful labor of Connecticut's growers and their families. Nearly a score of these are classified as major fairs, and the towns of the Litchfield Hills host some of the state's largest and oldest fairs. Bethlehem, Bridgewater, Harwinton, Riverton, and Terryville are among these. The author's favorite is the Goshen Fair, which is always on Labor Day weekend. For a complete listing of Connecticut's fairs, send a self-addressed stamped business-size envelope with $1.00 in postage to the Association of Connecticut Fairs, P.O. Box 753, Somers 06071. Ask for the complete guide to the fairs, which lists dates, times, events, and other details.

Holley-Williams House Museum and Salisbury Cannon Museum
(ages 7 to 12)

Route 44 in the Lakeville section of Salisbury; (860) 435–2878. Open late June to Labor Day, plus Memorial Day and Columbus Day weekends, from noon to 5:00 P.M. on weekends and holidays or by appointment year-round. Cannon Museum, free. Holley House, adults $5.00; children 5 to 15 $3.00; under 5 free.

Designed especially for children, the Cannon Museum tells the story of the Revolutionary War and the cannon factory that operated in Lakeville in 1776. Using the nearly limitless supply of iron ore discovered in the surrounding hills, the factory made cannon and cannonballs for George Washington's army as well as Connecticut privateers defending the seacoast against British vessels.

The museum describes the unglorified but essential roles of seven historical individuals who contributed to America's fight for independence. Dioramas portray entrepreneur Ethan Allen, blacksmith Samuel Forbes, bookseller Henry Knox, schoolgirl Mariann Wolcott, and three others. The story of each person begins on April 19, 1775, the day the first shot of the war was fired on Lexington Green. Children can also heft real cannonballs made during the Revolution and dress up in a kid-size Revolutionary War uniform.

Other hands-on activities and a twenty-two-point walking tour of historical spots near the Salisbury iron furnace can also be part of an afternoon spent here. Keep in mind that you can also tour the Holley house itself and stroll though its gardens. The house tour focuses on nineteenth-century family life and features a hands-on 1870s kitchen. Don't miss the seven-hole outhouse or the ice house. Both are windows to the past.

Salisbury Farm Fair

The point of taking children to places like **Sweethaven Farm** is to instill in them a respect for and a practical knowledge of the agricultural process and its importance to our survival. Kids need to know that the fruits, veggies, grains, and meats that line our supermarket aisles are brought there through the efforts of Connecticut's growers and others dedicated to land conservation and agriculture.

The annual **Salisbury Farm Fair** is an old-fashioned family affair that offers another way to educate children about farming. Usually held the third Saturday in August, the festivities include themed exhibits that explain various aspects of agriculture and, of course, demonstrations of farming equipment, displays of farm animals, and examples of textile production. You might see someone raising a barn frame, making shingles, carding wool, milking a cow, stitching a quilt, or pressing cider. Cakewalks, three-legged races, hayrides, a penny hunt, and judging of jams, pies, pickles, flowers, and vegetables are also on the schedule of this one-day event. A farmers' market and lots of farm-fresh food heightens the focus on agriculture. For details on this year's fair, call the Salisbury Association at (860) 435–0566.

Lime Rock Park (ages 8 and up)

Route 112 in Lakeville off Route 7; (203) 435–0896 or (800) RACE–LRP; www.limerock.com. Open to the public on Saturday and holidays from April through October. Call for ticket prices, race schedule, and a free racing newspaper. Children under 12 free.

Near the junction of Routes 7 and 112, this famed racetrack has been offering, since 1957, world-class sports car and stock-car racing with celebrity drivers as well as amateurs.

NASCAR racing goes on all summer, and special events are sprinkled liberally throughout the season. Come for the annual Memorial Day Grand Prix, the Formula Ford Festival and Fireworks on the Fourth of July weekend, the BMW Vintage Fall Festival on Labor Day weekend, and the NASCAR season finale. Concessions, rest rooms, and a beautiful setting make this family outing destination as comfortable as it is exciting. Be forewarned that the races are loud.

Bear Mountain and the Appalachian Trail

Parts of Salisbury are traveled exclusively on foot by hikers walking Connecticut's 53 miles of the Appalachian Trail. Near the northernmost piece of the trail as it emerges from Massachusetts lies the peak of Bear Mountain, the highest full peak in the state at 2,316 feet. From its topmost point, you can see lots of Connecticut plus New York State and Massachusetts.

Pack a lunch and some water, and, from the junction of Route 44 with Washnee Street near the Salisbury Town Hall, take Washnee Street west and drive .6 mile to Mount Riga Road. Follow Mount Riga Road 2.6 miles to Mount Washington Road, take a sharp right to the north and continue 2.8 miles to an old woods road on the right. Park carefully on the side of the road and walk onto the woods road, continuing for 1 mile until you reach the white-blazed Appalachian Trail. The ascent from here to the top of Bear Mountain is the easiest of all approaches to it, but young children may still need to take it slow over the rough trail. It can be tricky following wet weather. Proceed to the top of the mountain, where a stone monument rests, and share a lunch while you enjoy the vistas. Watch children carefully, since some overlooks skirt the mountain's sheer face. Some hikers may actually ascend by the toeholds in that vertical trail. Don't let your children attempt that route. Retrace your path to the woods road and your parked car.

You can also access the peak from the longer Undermountain trail off Route 41. Stop in Salisbury's **Village Store** (860–435–9459) on Main Street. The store sells hiking boots, trail gear, and outerwear (not kids' gear, though), and it also rents bicycles and cross-country skis. Ask the folks at the store for suggestions for information on the longer, half-day family hikes. Trail maps are available at the store.

O'Hara's Landing at Twin Lakes (all ages)
254 Twin Lakes Road; (860) 824–7583. Open daily in season.

If you can't resist the idea of a day fishing lazily on a pretty-as-a-picture lake high in the hills, come to O'Hara's Marina on picturesque Twin Lakes. Launch your own boat or rent a canoe, a rowboat, or a small powerboat. Pontoon boats that hold eight to ten passengers are also available. You can fish, water-ski, or water-tube, but you need to bring your own equipment or purchase it here. Twin Lakes has some of the best fishing in the state, so a day on the water is bound to be exciting for young anglers. Bring your own gear or purchase bait and tackle at the tackle shop here. If the trophy trout elude you or the sun gets to you, return to shore and have a bite to eat in the snack bar or cafe-style restaurant. The restaurant serves breakfast and lunch only, but you may not want to leave this pretty place until after sunset.

Where to Eat

The Boathouse at Lakeville. 394 Main Street (Route 44), Lakeville; (860) 435–2111. For lunch or dinner in a real restaurant, this Adirondack-styled establishment is cheerful and welcoming to families. Great sushi and vegetarian dishes, plenty of seafood; soups and sandwiches at lunch. Open daily for lunch noon to 3:00 P.M.; dinner from 5:00 P.M. $$–$$$

Auntie Em's Country Kitchen. 427 Main Street, Lakeville; (860) 435–2090. Open Monday through Saturday 7:00 A.M. to 2:00 P.M., this country charmer is the best place around for breakfast and lunch. Eggs, French toast, excellent chicken salad. You must come—it's just like home. $

Thyme-Enz Harvest. 10 Academy Street, Salisbury; (860) 435–9733. This child-friendly down-home eatery has everything you'd want freshly baked from scratch, excellent veggie lasagna and terrific soups, salads, pastas, and more. Be sure to take home some cinnamon coffeecake muffins. Open Monday through Saturday, 8:30 A.M. to 5:30 P.M. $–$$

The Woodland. Route 41, Lakeville; (860) 435–0578. Hearty American cuisine in a casual, country setting for lunch (noon to 2:30 P.M.) and dinner (from 5:30 P.M.), Tuesday through Saturday. $$–$$$

Where to Stay

The White Hart Inn. On the village green in Salisbury, Routes 41 and 44; (860) 435–0030 or (800) 832–0041; www.white hartinn.com. Elegant country inn in beautifully restored vintage building. Canopy beds, veranda overlooking village. 26 charming rooms with private baths. 2 restaurants including a fun, casual menu in their historic pub. Three meals available daily to guests as well as to the public. $$$$

Interlaken Inn, Resort and Conference Center. 74 Interlaken Road (Route 112), off Route 7, in Lakeville; (860) 435–9878 or (800) 222–2909; www.interlakeninn. On 30 beautiful acres with two lakes, this contemporary building has 82 units, including a century-old B&B and duplexes with fireplaces and kitchens. Restaurant, outdoor pool, sauna, tennis, golf, boating, lake swimming, fitness center. Great weekend packages especially for families—you can even bring the dog! $$$–$$$$

Inn at Iron Masters. 229 Main Street (Route 44), Lakeville; (860) 435–9844; www.innatironmasters.com. 28 spacious rooms with sitting areas, private baths, coffeemakers, hair dryers. Outdoor pool. Continental breakfast. Hearth Room with fireplace. $$$$

Canaan/Falls Village

For those who live near the crowded New York-to-Boston corridor of I–95, visiting Canaan is like visiting another country—a very rural, quiet country. Somehow Canaan and the villages surrounding it soothe the soul, restoring harmony to crowded lives. Fall foliage attracts tourists in droves, but it's pretty here in summer, too. If you live downstate or in the city, you're going to think these pristine hills and woodlands are out of this world. You can smell the green. Drop your plans for anything that smacks of rushing about in the fast lane and come here to the place where "the hills are alive with the sound of music."

Music Mountain (ages 8 and up)

Gordon Hall, off Route 7 or 63; (860) 824–7126 on weekdays 9:00 A.M. to 5:00 P.M. or (860) 364–2084; www.musicmountain.org. Adult tickets $20 at the door, $18 in advance; students (anyone under age 24) $10. They may be purchased by mail in advance, by telephone for credit-card payments, or picked up at the box office on concert days.

This legendary and especially soothing compound in Falls Village (about 4 miles from Lime Rock) is not a place exactly, but a festival. The nation's oldest continuous chamber music festival, it also features jazz, blues, baroque, and folk music on its picturesque grounds just off Route 7 near the Housatonic Valley Regional High School. You can also enter from Route 63 near the junction of Route 126.

Founded in 1930 as the permanent home of the Gordon String Quartet, Music Mountain's intimate and acoustically perfect wooden concert hall seats 335 on its softly cushioned pews; its 132 acres of lawn and grove are idyllic. The site is listed on the National Register of Historic Places. Picnic tables are provided for those who'd like to pack a boxed lunch or dinner to enjoy before the performances.

Offered from early June to mid-September, most of the chamber concerts are on Sunday afternoons at 3:00 P.M. Saturday performances are usually at 8:00 P.M., but some may begin a half hour earlier or later.

Where to Eat

Falls Village Inn. 33 Railroad Street, Falls Village; (860) 824–4910. Off Route 7, this newly renovated German-American, family-friendly restaurant is perfect for children. Warm and inviting at lunch and dinner in all seasons. Delicious potato pancakes. $–$$$

The Cannery. 85 Main Street (Route 44), Canaan; (860) 824–7333. Described as "an American bistro," this stylish yet casual place is welcoming to families, although there is no children's menu. Regional American cuisine presented inventively with good appetizers, pasta, chicken dishes makes it child-appealing. Dinner only, 5:00 P.M. to 10:00 P.M. on Thursday through Monday. $$–$$$

Where to Stay

Lone Oak Campsites. Route 44, East Canaan; (860) 824–7051; www.loneoakcamp sites.com. Open April 15 to October 15, this large family campground has many tent and RV sites, but also rents 40-foot trailers with kitchen, bath, bedroom and a cabin with two rooms and a fridge. $

Inn at White Hollow Farm. 558 Lime Rock Road, Route 112, Lime Rock; (860) 435–8185. 4 "gracefully appointed" rooms, each with private bath, on the upper floor of a lovely white farmhouse. Fully equipped kitchen and dining area and beautiful wrap-around porch on the lower floor. Very private. Coffee and baked goods each morning. On-site hiking and fly-fishing. Corn maze nearby. Smoke-free. $$$$

Norfolk

Norfolk is inarguably beautiful, nestled in the rolling shoulders and knolls of the Berkshire foothills, looking much the same as it might have a hundred years ago. There's not a lot of action here, but a full day or even a weekend, if you plan ahead, can be enjoyed in this sylvan village 7 miles east of Canaan. If you can, bring bicycles.

If ever a New England village could be fairly described as quaint, it is Norfolk. Beyond the few "attractions" described below, there is a lovingly restored "opera hall," which now houses the **Greenwoods Theatre** (860–542–0026), a most exquisite public library well worth a peek inside, the quintessential tall-spired, white Congregational church flanked by an equally lovely fieldstone chapel with beautiful Tiffany windows, and yet another state park, Haystack Mountain, just a mile or so up the road.

The Norfolk Chamber Music Festival (ages 6 and up)

Off the town green at the junction of Route 44 and Route 272 on the Ellen Battell Stoeckel Estate; (860) 542–3000; www.yale.edu/norfolk. Concerts Thursday through Saturday in June, July, and August.

Summer home of the Yale Music School, this magical enclave is the perfectly serene setting for a chamber music festival that invites nationally and internationally famed quartets and quintets of piano, woodwinds, and strings for Friday and Saturday evening concerts throughout July and August. Held rain or shine in the historic redwood and cedar Music

Shed, these 8:30 P.M. concerts are affordable for adults (from $40 in the front orchestra to $15 in the balcony) and, amazingly, completely **free** to children, all summer long, *every* concert. Even young adults (ages 18 to 25) pay just $5.00 for any concert. In addition, on Tuesday and Thursday nights at 7:30 and Saturday mornings at 10:30, Young Artists Recitals feature the Fellows of the Norfolk Summer School playing recognizable favorite standards and an eclectic mix of new and old pieces. Perfect for families, these concerts require no tickets, and the suggested donation is $3.00 per adult. Call or check the Web site for a schedule.

Almost every summer a special family concert is planned especially for children ages 6 to 12. Often, each family concert begins with a "musical conversation," which is an hour-long pre-concert show that previews the featured music and draws children into the theme. No matter which concert you choose to attend, bring along a picnic to enjoy before or after the program. The Pub (see Where to Eat) can provide terrific picnic choices.

Loon Meadow Farm Hayrides and Carriage Rides

What could provide more old-fashioned good fun than a private hayride, carriage ride, or winter sleigh ride, complete with hot cider and antique lap robes? Loon Meadow arranges such outings (by reservation only) on Norfolk's village lanes and woodland trails that lead through Currier and Ives settings in all seasons. Four-person carriages, wagonettes, and haywagons and sleighs are among the vehicles. Rides range from $95 to $160. Call the farm at (860) 542–6085 for the full scoop or check their Web site at www.loonmeadowfarm.com.

Dennis Hill State Park (all ages)
2.5 miles south on Route 272 from center of village. Open year-round. No charge.

Families will enjoy an easy loop-trail hike of 2 miles along an old lumber road through the woodlands to a fieldstone gazebo that provides a place to rest, picnic, and look out over the views of the hills. Along the way you'll pass through stands of oaks, maples, hemlocks, and mountain laurels and see the remains of a colonial hearth and chimney. When you have nearly returned to the same point from which you started, you can walk or drive the paved path to the 1,627-foot summit of Dennis Hill, where an octagonal bungalow with a rooftop observation platform allows you to see, on clear days, three states, views of several towns and villages, and the surrounding mountains—Bear Mountain to the west and Haystack just north of Norfolk, Mount Everett and Mount Greylock in Massachusetts, and the Green Mountains of Vermont.

Both trails are easy to find without maps. The first trail is yellow blazed and begins just beyond a wooden gate; the second is paved, popular, and clearly marked.

Where to Eat

The Pub and Restaurant. Across from the music festival grounds on Route 44; (860) 542–5716. English ambience, but American food, perfect for families. Creative sandwiches, enormous salads, hearty soups, individual pizzas, chili, good bread. Take-out dinners for alfresco dining before the concerts. Open for lunch and dinner Tuesday through Sunday 11:30 A.M. to 10:00 P.M. $–$$

Where to Stay

Blackberry River Inn. (860) 542–5100 or (800) 414–3636. For two and a half centuries this colonial inn has welcomed guests to its 27 acres with hiking trails 4 to 5 miles into the hills, trout fishing in its brook, tennis, outdoor pool, and apple orchard. 20 rooms, including pairs of rooms linked by a private bath, are perfect for families with children. Full country breakfast. $$$$

Angel Hill. 54 Greenwoods Road East; (860) 542–5920; www.angelhill.com. Pristine 1880s Victorian mansion on eleven acres offers families with children 6 and older its separate carriage house, an air-conditioned apartment with a magnificent bedroom, a cozy living room with dining table, a kitchen, a bath with tub and shower, and both nightly and weekly rates for those who can't bear to leave this heavenly second-story retreat. A delightful hostess, gourmet breakfasts, canopy beds, lots of special details to pamper you. $$$$

Goshen

Traveling south from Norfolk on Route 272 toward Torrington will take you through a slice of Goshen, which is a slice of heaven. You can follow 272 south to Route 4, which you'll then take west to the center of Goshen at its junction with Route 63. At this point, the scenery and the clean air may lead you to believe you're at the top of the world. A visit to Goshen's newest attraction may convince you that you've actually stumbled upon Eden.

Action Wildlife Foundation (all ages)

337 Torrington Road, which is Route 4; (860) 482–4465; www.actionwildlife.org. Open April through late October. In April and May, open Wednesday through Sunday 10:00 A.M. to 5:00 P.M. From June 1 to Labor Day, open daily 10:00 A.M. to 5:00 P.M. Call for fall hours. Weekend hayrides, intermittently throughout day, depending on the number of visitors. Pumpkins in the fall. Closed on stormy days. Adults $6.00; children under 12 $4.00; weekend hayrides $3.00.

Located on a 116-acre former dairy farm on Route 4, just west of the Torrington border, this game park is home to more than 200 exotic animals that roam relatively freely over about forty acres currently open to the public. Several fenced or walled compounds averaging about an acre in area provide enclosures for thirty-two species of such creatures as the scimitar oryx, red stags, Scottish Highlander cattle, fainting goats, zebras, fallow deer, pygmy donkeys, aoudads, ostriches, bison, yaks, elks and reindeer, a Russian boar, and many others. Crisscrossed by stonewalls, the park has a petting and feeding barn, a picnic area, and several ponds. Visitors can walk on pathways throughout the complex or, on weekends, take tractor-drawn wagon rides to view the animals.

Also under development here is a museum that is currently paired with the foundation's gift shop. Displayed now are about fifty mounted animal specimens in somewhat limited diorama-style natural environment settings. Park owner James Mazzarelli and other game hunters have collected these big-game, museum-quality mounts from throughout the world. While some animal lovers may take offense at this project, it is intended to educate and inform visitors about endangered habitats and species.

Up, Up, and Away!

Usually held the last weekend in June at the Goshen Fairgrounds is the annual extravaganza called the **Northwest Connecticut Balloon Festival.** Pilots gather at 6:00 A.M. and 6:00 P.M. to launch their colorful crafts, weather permitting, over the beautiful countryside. Come to see the awesome beauty of the balloons and stay for the arts and crafts, carnival, and car show that go on between launches. Food vendors provide sustenance; blues bands and singing quartets provide entertainment. At 9:00 P.M. again, weather permitting, a dazzling display is created through fireworks and a "balloon glow," when the tethered balloons are lit from the ground. Balloon rides ($195 per person) can be reserved in advance; tethered rides up to 150 feet are $10 per person. Admission to the event is $10.00 per person 12 and older; children under 12 are $1.00 or bring a canned good. For more information, check the Web site: www.nwballoonfest.com.

Where to Stay

Mary Stuart House B & B. Route 4, Goshen; (860) 491–2260; www.marystuart house.com. This 1798 country home offers 4 bedrooms, 2 private sitting rooms, and a two-bedroom cottage with kitchen, living room, private bath. Continental or breakfast. Volleyball and badminton in season. Hot tub. Screened porch. Children and pets welcome. $$$–$$$$

Riverton/Pleasant Valley

The Riverton area (east of Route 8 and about 8 miles north of Winsted) is just a plain old nice place to be. Generally described for this book's purposes, the Riverton environs is the roughly rectangular area created by the roads linking Riverton, Pleasant Valley, Barkhamsted, and West Hartland—the perfect spot for a world-weary family to restore some equilibrium.

People's State Forest (all ages)

One mile north of Pleasant Valley on East River Road to the Forest's public entrance and the Stone Museum; park office (860) 379–2469; Stone Museum (860) 379–6118; www.stone museum.org. Open year-round 8:00 A.M. to dusk. Day-use fee on weekends and holidays. Has seasonal hours. Free.

Nearly filling the aforementioned rectangle scribed loosely by Routes 318, 181, and 20 and cut further by the East and West River Roads that flank the sides of the Farmington River's West Branch, this beautiful park is a great stop for families. It provides access to and views of the 14-mile section of the river that has been designated by the National Park Service as an American Wild and Scenic River. The gorgeous Matthies grove overlooks the rushing water as it twists through the 200-year-old pines—be sure to have lunch here if you've packed a picnic. Anglers hip deep in the water during trout season are a pleasant addition to the majestic view.

Open every Sunday in June and every Saturday and Sunday in July and August, the park's Stone Museum has exhibits on native flora and fauna, natural history, and Native American and colonial history and industry. A seasonal series of slide programs is presented here on Saturday evenings at 8:00 in July and August, and hikes are led on varied Saturday mornings throughout the summer and early fall. Call for a schedule.

A blue-and-yellow-blazed trail called the Beaver Swamp Loop follows an old wagon path through the forest, across a bridged brook, and up to a *kame* terrace that was the site of native encampments from 2,000 B.C. to A.D. 600. Remnants of eighteen ancient Indian village sites have put this terrace on the National Register of Historic Places. As you descend the trail, still following the blazes, you can see a colonial house foundation and a meat-smoking chamber as well as other beautiful natural sites. The Beaver Swamp Trail is easy to moderate, takes about two and a half hours to hike, and is 3.5 miles long. A detailed description and map can be obtained through the park office.

Snowmobiling and cross-country skiing are allowed here in winter.

American Legion State Forest (all ages)

West River Road, Pleasant Valley; (860) 379–0922. No day-use charge; $10 per campsite nightly.

On the western bank opposite Peoples State Forest, this quiet camping area has thirty wooded sites along the West Branch of the Farmington River. Clean pine woods, great shower facilities, flat tent sites, and good fishing spots make this a nice family campground. If no ranger is at the park office when you arrive, you just leave your registration in the box with your nightly fee. Open mid-April through December 1, the area has trails to some beautiful sights along the river (watch the steep hillsides as you go along some of the paths).

Something **Fishy**

For nearly fifty years, the village of Riverton has hosted the annual **Riverton Fishing Derby,** held traditionally on opening day of fishing in Connecticut (always the third Saturday in April). The West Branch of the Farmington River is well stocked with rainbow, brown, and brook trout, and each year 500 or more anglers come out to try to catch the biggest of them all.

Free to all participants and spectators as well, the derby starts at 6:00 A.M. and ends at 10:00 A.M. regardless of the weather. No registration or fee is required, but anyone over the age of 16 must have a Connecticut fishing license. If you arrive without a license, you can buy one at the General Store for $20.

Children under the age of 12 have their own area slightly upriver from the rest of the crowd. Anyone old enough to handle a pole can join the Kid Derby and share in the good wholesome fun. Prizes are awarded in adult and youth divisions of this classic event. For information, call (860) 263–2841.

Riverton General Store (ages 4 and up)
Route 20; (860) 379–0811. Open seven days a week from 6:00 A.M. to 8:00 P.M.

Up in Riverton proper, stop the car and smell the roses. Figuratively speaking, that is. The General Store is a good place to begin a walk through the village. Besides basic deli goods, handy camping supplies, and icy-cold root beer, they have everything else under the sun, including stuff manufactured before the turn of the century, settin' and hangin' left, right, and center. I never did ask if the great old stuff was for sale or just for display, but I do know that kids love this place.

Armed with your picnic goods, you might have a look in some of Riverton's other small gift and craft shops as well as its large retail outlet for Hitchcock chairs and other furniture made right here since the 1800s in Lambert Hitchcock's original manufactory. If you are here in summer, catch a performance at the Riverton Theatre (860–738–0377), held under a tent at the Riverton Fairgrounds.

Where to Eat

Old Riverton Inn. See below. Breakfast for guests only. Lunch and dinner Wednesday through Sunday open to the public; reservations highly recommended. $$

Riverton General Store. See previous page. Deli sandwiches and salads, pickles and such, perfect for picnic fare. $

Village Sweet Shop. Route 20; (860) 379–7250. Superior ice cream, chocolate-dipped waffle cones, and hand-decorated chocolates will appease any kids traumatized by overly boring visits to the furniture store. Open year-round from 11:00 A.M. to 5:00 P.M. daily. $

Sweet Pea. 6 Riverton Road (Route 20); (860) 379–7020. Old-fashioned charm spills from every pore of this 1880 house, and the food is even more delightful than the ambience. It's a little fancy, but not so much that children are not warmly welcomed—in fact, they have their own menu. Come here for lunch and dinner, Tuesday through Sunday; brunch on Sunday. $$–$$$

Where to Stay

Old Riverton Inn. Route 20; (860) 379–8678 or (800) EST–1796. Doing business for 200 years, this inn, listed on the National Register, has 12 rooms with private baths; some rooms have canopy beds and fireplaces. Open year-round, it enjoys a front-row seat on the rushing river and has an award-winning dining room. Full breakfast. $$$

New Hartford

This tiny community has put itself on the map as one of the state's most popular sports and recreation destinations. From tubing in summer to skiing in winter, it's a town few families miss in a search for fun in the Great Outdoors.

Farmington River Tubing—Satan's Kingdom State Recreation Area
(ages 10 and up)

Route 44; (860–) 693–6465; www.FarmingtonRiverTubing.com. Open every day in July and August and on weekends and weekday afternoons only from Memorial Day through June from 10:00 A.M. to approximately 6:00 P.M. Call for hours on Labor Day weekend. $15 per person on weekends and holidays; $14 per person on weekdays; $10.60 per person if you're in a group of ten or more who have called at least forty-eight hours ahead for reservations on weekday trips only.

This adventure is certainly on our top-ten list of best family summer activities in Connecticut—that is, if you're ten years or older, four feet five inches tall, and can swim alone without a doubt no matter what your age. We came a few years ago on the Fourth of July, and the river was chock-full of other tubing enthusiasts; we came midweek in June and were alone except for the dragonflies.

When you arrive at Satan's Kingdom, park in the large lot right next to the river and the **North American Canoe Tours, Inc.** outpost. Wear cut-offs and a T-shirt or change in one of the poorly lit changing huts provided at the lot. Put on some sunscreen and old sneakers, preferably your own. If you arrive barefoot, NACT makes you put on one of their spare pairs of soggy previously owned sneaks. Put on a life vest (mandatory equipment for everyone). Pay your money, then walk down to the river with your tube and put your warm body into the cold water, bottom first, as you sit down in the hole of your tube with your feet up over the side. Sound like fun yet? It is, really—I promise. Now all you have to do is float and soak up the Vitamin D rays for two and a half miles in about equally as many hours. The segment lies within the nationally designated Wild and Scenic River portion of the Farmington River.

The best parts for some are the mild rapids—three sets, with NACT lifeguards on duty in kayaks at the largest set only; others like the placid stretches where mergansers nest and the living is easy. This outfitter won't allow you to bring food on the river, so don't arrive hungry. When your ride is over (at a clearly marked take-out point), haul out with your tube. A shuttle bus takes you back to the starting point.

Ski Sundown (ages 3 and up)

126 Ratlum Road, 2 miles northeast of New Hartford on Route 219 off Route 44; (860) 379–9851; www.skisundown.com. Open every day and night during the ski season, usually from early December to late March from 9:00 A.M. to 10:00 P.M. Sunday through Thursday and until 11:00 P.M. on Friday and Saturday. For current lift rates and special packages, call or check their Web site.

For winter fun just a half hour from Hartford and an hour from Danbury and New Haven, Ski Sundown is a convenient alternative to out-of-state skiing. Special trails, FlexTix (which start any time you arrive), and a First-Time package for novice and beginner skiers and snowboarders make Sundown perfect for families new to the sport or with young children. Other programs are geared especially to children of moderate and advanced skills. Even accomplished skiers can enjoy the challenges of the three most difficult trails out of the total fifteen. Four chairlifts keep lines moving quickly and efficiently to the top of the beautiful sixty-five-acre property.

Proud of their well-groomed runs and friendly professional staff, the operators also like to crow about their rental shop, which provides top-drawer skis, boots, bindings, and snowboards, and their Ski Shop, which offers similar goods and clothing for sale. A cafeteria adds a convenient and casual approach to keeping hungry skiers happy and headed back to the slopes with renewed energy. A newly expanded lodge and lounge gives weary skiers a place to rest and relax with fellow skiers.

All-day, after-school, twilight, and evening sessions include reasonable rates for adults, juniors, preschoolers, and seniors. Bring Grampa and the baby, too, and enjoy the winter in the Berkshire foothills.

Where to Eat

Chatterly's. Two Bridge Street; (860) 379–2428. After skiing or tubing, replace carbohydrates in this landmark eatery in the old New Hartford Hotel in the center of the village. Light fare for kids—soup, salads, sandwiches, burgers—or full dinners—steaks, roast pork, seafood—for adults. Open daily for lunch and dinner. $–$$

Where to Stay

Alcove Motel. 87 Main Street, which is Route 44; (860) 693–8577. 15 units, outdoor pool. $

Litchfield

From the Pleasant Valley and New Hartford areas, families may want to head south on Route 8 through Winsted and Torrington and then take Route 118 west about 5 miles to Litchfield. Settled in 1719, Litchfield remains one of the prettiest towns in the state, attracting visitors in droves to its meticulously preserved colonial architecture, its boutiques, and its restaurants. Antiques shops, elegant inns, and vineyards lure travelers looking for pastoral pleasures of a sophisticated nature. Judging these elements alone, it seems an area more suited to adults than to families, but we discovered a few places everyone should visit.

White Memorial Foundation and Conservation Center Museum
(all ages) 🚶 🐦 🚫 🍂

80 Whitehall Road, 2 miles west of Litchfield Center off Route 202; (860) 567– 0857; www.whitememorialcc.org. Grounds open daily, year-round, from dawn to dusk. Free admission. Museum open daily 9:00 A.M. to 5:00 P.M. Monday through Saturday and Sunday noon to 5:00 P.M. Winter hours slightly reduced. Adult admission to the museum $4.00; children 6 to 12 $2.00.

The state's largest nature preserve, with 4,000 acres and 35 miles of trails, White Memorial is a wonderful place to hike, ride horses, cross-country ski, fish, and picnic. Two family campgrounds offer lakeside or woodland sites, and a public boat launch provides access to Bantam Lake. A bird observatory overlooks a specially landscaped area attractive to many bird species. Thirty viewing stations have been created for bird-watchers and photographers. The Trail of the Senses is an especially lovely interpretive walk that invites youngsters to touch, smell, and listen as they traverse the quarter-mile pathway.

You might also want to sign up for a special program, take one of the many guided walks, or visit on the annual Family Nature Day in late September. Bird banding, tree identification, old-time outdoor games, a pond life study, and much more are offered at this very popular event.

Make certain that you go to the Conservation Center Museum. Housed in the former Whitehall mansion, this excellent hands-on nature center artistically arranges dioramas and interactive exhibits on birds, bees, soil, seeds, woodland animals, and much more in a bright, open atmosphere. Upstairs, an outstanding natural science library is open even to daytripping visitors, with a children's section so comfortable it practically invites you to sit down and read the wonderful materials here.

Bantam Lake and Sandy Beach (all ages)

East Shore Road, Morris; (860) 567–7550. Open to the public on weekends only from Memorial Day through the end of June, daily from late June through Labor Day from 9:00 A.M. to 7:00 P.M. The cost per car or boat is $5.00 per visit; the cost for each bicycler or walker is $1.00. Nonresident season passes $65 per family.

If you want to take a dip in pretty Bantam Lake, leave Litchfield center on Route 202 West, take a left on White's Woods Road, and another right on East Shore Road. Just before the bend in the road, you'll find the entrance to Sandy Beach. Actually in the town of Morris, the secluded beach provides 800 feet of clean sand on the shore of Connecticut's largest natural lake.

Lifeguards, bathrooms and bathhouses, and a snack bar are among the amenities. A canoe launch, a volleyball "court," and a picnic area with tables and fire pits make this a great place to spend the day. If you're a good swimmer, aim for the raft; it has a terrific slide that sweeps you right into the cool, clear water. Return in winter to see the ice boaters clip across the frozen lake or to try your luck at ice fishing.

Lee's Riding Stable (ages 4 and up)

57 East Litchfield Road (Route 118); (860) 567–0785. One-hour guided trail; rides $25 per person (riders 7 years and older only). Open 364 days per year.

If you love horses, horseback riding, and truly decent people, go directly to Lee's. Only positive things happen here for kids at this peaceful horse farm. Visitors are welcome any time; reservations for trail rides are preferred but not absolutely necessary. Trail ride groups are normally limited to six to eight riders, so you don't get that mule-train feeling, and the attitude of the staff is friendly and enthusiastic. No one has a hint of reluctance to take you over the same trails they've seen time and time again—a pleasant change from the bored demeanor of staff at other stables. The trails take you through some 5 miles of exceptionally pretty country in and adjacent to Topsmead State Forest.

Pony rides in an outdoor ring are $5.00 for twice-around-the ring or $35.00 for a half-hour. A miniature petting zoo with goats, chickens, geese, sheep, rabbits, a cow, a donkey, and an adorable Shetland pony is a hands-on operation. Buy a bag of feed or bring your stale crackers, and the penned animals will adore you.

If the staff is not too busy, they'll give you a tour of the stables and pastures. Riding lessons are also offered. An indoor ring is used in bad weather; it is also the home of the Litchfield Little Britches program offering therapeutic riding for the handicapped (call for information). Birthday parties, longer outings, and custom group rides can all be arranged.

The registered Morgan horses are gorgeous, and Lee Lyons, the special angel who runs the whole show, has a down-to-earth approach that makes everyone feel comfortable and wanting to come back.

Mount Tom State Park (all ages)

Route 202, southwest of Litchfield Center, in Bantam; (860) 868–2592. Open April 1 to October 15, daily dawn to dusk. Parking fee on in-season weekends, $5.00.

A small lake offers fishing, swimming, scuba diving, and non-motor boating in summer; ice fishing and ice-skating are possible in winter. A beach and picnic area with a snack bar concession, lifeguard, picnic tables, grills, rest rooms, and changing houses (but no showers) make this a good family-fun destination.

Those who want more vigorous recreation can take the short hike to the top of the 1,325-foot mountain. The yellow-blazed trail is little more than a mile, but it's a pretty steady climb; older kids may do it in fifteen to twenty minutes, youngers may need a half hour. The extra 30-foot climb up the wooden interior staircase of the black granite tower at the top is very well worth it. The view over the treetops is spectacular—you'll be glad you did it. Hold hands with kids under 6.

Litchfield History Museum and Tapping Reeve House and Law School (ages 8 and up) 🏛

7 South Street and 82 South Street; (860) 567–4501; www.litchfieldhistoricalsociety.org. Open mid-April through November, Tuesday through Saturday 11:00 A.M. to 5:00 P.M. and Sunday from 1:00 to 5:00 P.M. Adults $5.00 for both museums; children under 14 free.

If history lessons intrigue your children, have a brief look at the collections in the historical museum for some insight into the culture and community of the town, then stop at the Tapping Reeve House and Law School if you want to inspire future attorneys to emulate the 130 members of Congress who graduated from this first law school in the nation, open to the public as an historical exhibit.

Where to Eat

Aspen Garden. 51 West Street near the Green in Litchfield center; (860) 567–9477. Omelets, salads, innovative pizzas, Greek specialties, pasta, seafood, reasonably priced and friendly to families. Terrace dining outdoors in nice weather. Open daily at 11:00 A.M. for lunch and dinner. $$–$$$

Ming's. Route 202; (860) 567–0809. Dependably good Chinese cuisine in a relaxed setting in the Federal Square shopping center. Open daily for lunch and dinner. $–$$

Chuck's Steak House. Route 202; (860) 567–1414. Inviting to families, this steak house also has an excellent salad bar, chicken and seafood dishes, and good light-fare choices for kids. Open daily for dinner, early-bird specials from 4:30 to 6:00 P.M. $$–$$$

Where to Stay

The Litchfield Inn. Route 202; (860) 567–4503. Set back from the road, this large inn offers 32 rooms with private baths, continental breakfast, and lovely common areas for your comfort. On-site restaurant (**Bistro East;** 860–567–9040; lunch and dinner daily; weekend entertainment). $$$$

Washington/Washington Depot/ New Preston

Often called unspoiled and compared to the alpine lake regions of Austria and Switzerland, New Preston and its most famous attraction, Lake Waramaug, are perhaps Connecticut's most popular daytripping destinations. If you can't get to Europe to check out whether the comparison works, come here and enjoy the four-season beauty of this delightful area just about 10 miles southwest of Litch- field. The town of New Preston is chockablock with antiques shops; the kids will probably want to move right along to other attractions.

When Lake Waramaug loosens its grip on your soul, take Route 47 south from Route 202 to Washington. Don't blink or you'll miss this town hidden in the twists and turns of these lovely hills. The fourth town in the colonies to be named for George, the pretty little village is a true New England gem. As beautiful as the village is, however, the special treasures here are the natural envi- ronment and the legacy of the native Algonkian people, whose civilization preceded that of the colonists by several thousand years.

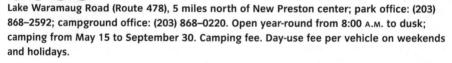

Lake Waramaug State Park (all ages)

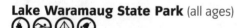

Lake Waramaug Road (Route 478), 5 miles north of New Preston center; park office: (203) 868–2592; campground office: (203) 868–0220. Open year-round from 8:00 A.M. to dusk; camping from May 15 to September 30. Camping fee. Day-use fee per vehicle on weekends and holidays.

To start with the basics, *Waramaug* is the Indian word for "good fishing place." If you're so inclined, this sounds like the best fishing tip I've ever heard. In addition to this most popular sport, the park offers opportunities for picnicking, swimming, scuba diving, and sailing (you bring your own gear), and it provides paddleboats (which you rent). Trails for hiking and seventy-eight very nice sites for camping are also available. Nightly camper nature pro- grams are scheduled in summer, and ice-skating, cross-country skiing, and ice fishing are possible in winter.

Gunn Historical Museum (ages 6 and up)

5 Wykeham Road; (860) 868–7756; www.biblio.org/gunn. Museum open Thursday through Saturday 10:00 A.M. to 4:00 P.M. and Sunday noon to 4:00 P.M. Closed major holidays. Free. Family Fun programs (860–868–2310) on Tuesday evenings at 6:30 P.M. in summer, in the Junior Library.

If you fall in love with the village, a visit to the museum at the Gunn Memorial Library on the town green will flesh out the colonial history and lifeways of the area. Within the lovely 1908 fieldstone building is a collection of quilts, needlework, kitchenware, spinning wheels, furniture, and other household decorative and utilitarian items. A children's room includes dolls, dollhouses, toys, children's clothes, and other objects of interest to youngsters. Here, too, you can see original signatures of George Washington and Thomas Jefferson. Be sure to look up—a magnificent ceiling mural decorates the lobby of the original library building.

Institute for American Indian Studies (ages 4 and up)

38 Curtis Road off Route 199; (860) 868–0518; www.birdstone.org. Open Monday through Saturday from 10:00 A.M. to 5:00 P.M. and Sunday from noon to 5:00 P.M.; closed on Monday and Tuesday from January through March. Adults $4.00; seniors $3.50; children 6 to 16 $2.00.

Magnificently displayed in a discreet building smack dab in the woodlands near Steep Rock Nature Preserve, the exhibits here are interpretations of the institute's research on the history and culture of Indian America. The permanent exhibit, entitled *As We Tell Our Stories: Living Tradition and the Algonkian Peoples of New England,* includes the taped stories of Algonkian people and an extensive collection of Native American tools, baskets, implements, and art. A furnished reproduction longhouse is built inside the museum and is filled with artifacts used in everyday life. An excellent gift shop and two galleries of art are also inside.

Outside, an authentically constructed seventeenth-century settlement with three wigwams, a longhouse, a rock shelter, native plant trails, and a garden planted each season with corn, beans, and squash provides a peek into the proud 10,000-year history of these people. A simulated archaeological site offers intriguing insights into their moving story.

Craft workshops, dances, films, storytelling, and more are on the annual events calendar. Children's summer camps are also on the schedule.

Steep Rock Reservation (all ages)

(860) 868–9131. Open dawn to dusk year-round. Small parking area off River Road. No facilities. No charge.

After a morning at the Indian studies institute, you might want to stay in the great outdoors to reflect on all you've learned about the fragile, life-sustaining ecology of the Eastern Woodlands. Linked to the institute property by a common border, this 700-acre natural preserve is one section of a two-parcel land trust owned and maintained by the Steep Rock Association. Dedicated to preserving and protecting, for the good of future generations, the beauty and integrity of this important ecosystem and all of its flora and fauna, the association has opened its trails to hikers. With pathways that hug the Shepaug River and climb to Steep Rock, the sanctuary offers incredible vistas that should keep families mindful of their integral role in conservation of our remaining wild places. Come here to the cool woods to hear the whispering wind in summer, enjoy the glorious blaze of the foliage in autumn, linger as the snows fall silently in winter, and walk softly beside the wildflowers as the new leaves open in the springtime. The association fears that overuse of these lovely footpaths may force them to close to the public, so please remember to walk respectfully only on cleared trails, pack out every scrap of what you carry in, and take nothing but memories with you as you leave.

Where to Eat

Doc's Trattoria and Pizzeria. Lake Waramaug South Shore Road (Route 45), New Preston; (860) 868–9415; www.docstrattoria. com. Housed in a charming cottage overlooking the lake, Doc's offers the best pizza in Litchfield County, plus other delicious Italian favorites in a casually sophisticated setting. Lunch is served Tuesday through Sunday from noon to 3:00 P.M. Dinner, served Tuesday through Sunday, starts at 5:00 P.M. Innovative salads, pastas, chicken, and seafood keep the place popular with parents; kids love the imaginative pizzas and half-orders that help them leave room for dessert. Reservations are a good idea. $$–$$$

G.W. Tavern. 20 Bee Brook Road (Route 47), Washington Depot; (860) 868–6633. Traditional favorites like meatloaf, chicken pot pie, steaks, pastas, soups, salads, and a cheerful staff and adaptable chef who welcome children. No special children's menu, but lots of side dishes to make choosing easy. Lunch and dinner daily; brunch Saturday and Sunday. $–$$

The Pantry. 5 Titus Road, Washington Depot; (860) 868–0258. Gourmet fare in a simple setting often used by adults with fancy tastes and deep pockets. Good for families needing picnic fare. Muffins, croissants, and other delicious bakery treats, salads, and sandwiches. Open 10:00 A.M. to 6:00 P.M. Tuesday through Saturday. Table service from 11:00 A.M. to 5:00 P.M. $

Bethlehem

About 6 miles east of Washington as the crow flies (14 miles by Route 109 east to Route 61 south), Bethlehem is Litchfield County at its best—gorgeous hills, pretty village, quiet byways of unsurpassed serenity. Its evocative name conjures images of peace and sentiment that its residents play upon in a few special ways. In the months before Christmas folks deluge the Bethlehem Post Office with holiday cards they would like to bear the Bethlehem postmark. A Christmas festival celebrates the spirit of the season, and an annual country fair in late summer celebrates the bounty of Bethlehem's fields and orchards. And, as in most towns in this state, there's a historical society museum and an ancient homestead that spans two and a half centuries of history in its furniture, art, and gardens.

Together these features portray a part of the magic of Bethlehem. The village is so tiny that you can easily find the shops, the post office, the fairs, and the historic homes. The town Web site (www.ci.bethlehem. ct.us) can lead you to the facts about these attractions. The information below will help you out if you wish to call for details before you visit. Following those are the details on a very quiet but special place just a bit off the gently worn paths in Bethlehem.

- **Bethlehem Post Office.** 34 East Street; (203) 266–7910.

- **Bethlehem Fair.** (203) 266–5350. Often the second full weekend in September.

- **Old Bethlehem Historical Society Museum.** Corner of Routes 132 and 61; (203) 266–5188. Open Sunday 1:00 to 4:00 P.M. from June through August.

- **Bellamy-Ferriday House and Garden.** 9 Main Street North (Route 61); (203) 266–7596. Open May through October on Wednesday, Friday, and weekends from 11:00 A.M. to 4:00 P.M. Adults $5.00; children $1.00. Exquisite house and glorious gardens with property linked to the nature trails of a nearby land trust.

The Abbey of Regina Laudis and the Monastic Art Shop
(ages 6 and up) 🎵

273 Flanders Road between Route 6 and Route 61; (203) 266–7637; www.abbeyofregina laudis.com. Abbey church open year-round for daily Mass (8:00 A.M.) and vespers (5:00 P.M., except Sunday 4:30 P.M.). Art shop open daily except Wednesday from 10:00 A.M. to noon and 1:30 to 4:00 P.M. Creche open daily 10:00 A.M. to 5:00 P.M. from the day after Easter through January 6. Call ahead to confirm these hours.

A treasured presence just a jog off Route 61 is Bethlehem's beautiful abbey. No wonder that the inspiring Benedictine nuns chose this place to build their wonderful community— it is on a magnificent hillside overlooking the glory of Creation. Traditionally, each summer in early August, the sisters opened the gates of the abbey and welcomed visitors to share in the festivities of their Abbey Fair. Sadly for us, this splendid outpouring of spirit and celebration grew too large for the sisters to manage, as thousands of guests showed up for a taste of their remarkable experience. Today a simple theater production for the whole family replaces the old tradition with a new one.

Though there is no guarantee that a production will be performed every year in August, the show has gone on every year since the fair ended. Staged in the abbey's open-air covered theater, the productions are often the first weekend in August, with three performances on Friday and Saturday. The suggested donation for the show is $10.00 for adults and $5.00 for children under 12.

At other times of the year, you can come to hear daily Mass and evening vespers at the church on Robert Leathers Road. The voices of the sisters at vespers are especially moving. You can also browse in the abbey's Monastic Art Shop, which has an art gallery as well as books, crafts, and comestibles made by the sisters.

The best family attraction here is the abbey's magnificent Neapolitan creche, which illustrates the Nativity in a starlit scene of more than a hundred eighteenth-century figures beautifully dressed in silks and brocades and placed against the backdrop of an Italian hillside landscape. Displayed in one of the abbey's barns, it is a fascinating and intricate work of art that families of every faith can appreciate.

Where to Eat

Painted Pony. Route 61; (203) 266–5771; www.paintedponyrestaurant.com. Best known for juicy prime rib up to a whopping forty ounces, this place is also great for salads, pastas, chicken, and seafood. Special menu for children. Open daily from 11:00 A.M. to 11:00 P.M. on weekends and to 10:00 P.M. on weekdays. $$

Theo's Pizza. South Main Street; (203) 266–5558. Great pizza, salads, lasagna, stuffed shells, manicotti—you get the picture. Theo says, "If you want it, we're going to try to make it!" Greek specialties, simple desserts; casual, friendly atmosphere. $

Where to Stay

The Dutch Moccasin. 51 Still Hill Road; (203) 266–7364. This rambling post-and-beam Dutch-style colonial built in the wooded hills in the eighteenth century by settlers and Native Americans is a treasure for traveling families. Year-round nightly, weekly, and monthly arrangements can be made for idyllic respites in this beautiful

country bed-and-breakfast set on a forest-lined dirt road.

Five spacious, comfortable rooms with wide chestnut floors and handcrafted decorations are easily adaptable to families. One room has a Jacuzzi; three have private baths. Full family-style breakfasts might include pancakes, French toast, and other hearty, healthy fare. Inquire about special family rates and arrangements.

In summer your host, John Georgette, may arrange a picnic or a campfire that might draw you outdoors to the hiking trails or the old swimming hole down by the creek; in the fall, you might plan to be here for the Halloween party. In winter John turns a portion of his closed road into a toboggan run and shares his collection of sleds with you. Hot cocoa, hot cider, and even hot apple pie may be offered after a day in the winter woods. A piano in the cafe room provides a perfect excuse for a sing-along.

Close to public tennis courts, cross-country skiing, ice fishing, historic sites, and Mother Nature's finest scenery, this is a great place for counting the stars and listening to the whispering wind. No pets. $$–$$$$

Thomaston

East of Bethlehem (take Route 61 south, then Route 6 east through Watertown and onward to Route 8) is the town of Thomaston, named for clockmaker Seth Thomas. Thomas's clocks were made right in Thomaston with brass gears manufactured in the mills of Waterbury. Today those two communities are linked in other ways. One of these links is a railway: the original Naugatuck Railroad that opened in 1849 to connect Bridgeport with all the towns north to Winsted. Located in the beautiful and still rugged Naugatuck Valley, Thomaston welcomes families to its historic downtown (where one can see the famed Seth Thomas clocktower), its Victorian railroad station, and the vintage train that offers travelers splendid views of the scenic Naugatuck River, its wildlife, and the communities along its banks.

Railroad Museum of New England/
Naugatuck Railroad Scenic Excursion (all ages)

242 East Main Street; (860) 283–7245; www.rmne.org. Operates May through October, Saturday and Sunday at 1:00 and 3:00 P.M.; Tuesday, 10:00 A.M. Adults $10.00; children 3 to 12 $7.00; children 2 and under, **free.**

This moving museum is actually a scenic railroad excursion that resulted from the signing of a thirty-year lease of the 19.5-mile Waterbury to Torrington Line, which gives the Naugatuck Railroad Company operating rights over the 150-year-old track. The new "Naugy" now operates between the 1881 Thomaston Passenger Station in downtown Thomaston and the Waterville Station in Waterbury. Sunday afternoon trips in July and August run from Thomaston to Torrington.

Grab the kids and jump aboard for the great sights and sounds of this grandly exciting adventure. What is it about train rides that is so appealing? Maybe it's the bells and whistles or the clackety-clack, maybe the huge sighs and shudders of the enormous locomotives, maybe just the heart-tingling joy of heading off to new horizons on a beast so mighty it can scale mountains. Ride this baby with your eyes and ears wide open to all the fabulous wonders around you—from inside one of the factory complexes near the historic Brass Mills of Waterbury to the Mattatuck State Forest's cool green canopy in summer or blazing patchwork of scarlet and bronze in autumn, past small towns with charming old houses and tiny depots, and onward across—yes, right across the face of—the spectacular Thomaston Dam.

The train consists of restored historic New England passenger and freight cars pulled by historic New Haven and Maine Central locomotives. The usual hour-and-a-quarter excursions are 18-mile round-trip rides. No reservations are required.

I could give you a whole history lesson on the economic importance of this line in the olden golden days of industry in the Naugatuck Valley, but you'll hear some of that on the train. For now, just pull on your pin-striped OshKosh overalls, buy your ticket, and have a ball.

General Information

Litchfield Hills Visitors Bureau. P.O. Box 968, U.S. 202, Litchfield 06759; (860) 567–4506; www.litchfieldhills.com. Call or write for the tours booklet, which provides itineraries for walking, hiking, driving, and boating tours of the area. Also ask for guide called *Unwind in the Litchfield Hills.*

Litchfield Web site: www.litchfieldct.com.

Connecticut Angler's Guide. Published by the State Department of Environmental Protection Bureau of Natural Resources Fisheries Division, this booklet describes everything you'd need to know about fishing in the state of Connecticut. Call (860) 424–FISH to request a copy.

Covered Bridge Bed-and-Breakfast Reservation Service. (860) 542–5944. This organization can help families find appropriate inns and bed-and-breakfast facilities for children.

Hartford County

Capital Ideas in the Heart of Connecticut

Sliced into unequal parts by the Connecticut River, the north-central region of Connecticut is a region of diversity including farming communities, towns with a long history of industry, and a city of pre-Revolutionary importance as a seat of government. This diversity makes for perfect touring conditions, as it offers something for all tastes, interests, and ages.

Hartford itself offers a full slate of attractions typical of an urban cultural center. The arts, sciences, history, and industries of the city, its suburbs, and the nation are well represented on its long list of museums and exhibits. Traveling families should try to plan at least a day in the state's capital city, keeping in mind that even if you were only to visit the most important museums and family-fun sites, you could easily spend three days here.

TopPicks for fun in Hartford County

1. Lake Compounce Theme Park and Entertainment Complex
2. Huck Finn Adventures
3. Pickin' Patch
4. Talcott Mountain State Park and Heublein Tower
5. Old New-Gate Prison and Copper Mine
6. Old State House
7. Mark Twain House
8. Science Center of Connecticut
9. New Britain Museum of American Art
10. Dinosaur State Park

HARTFORD COUNTY

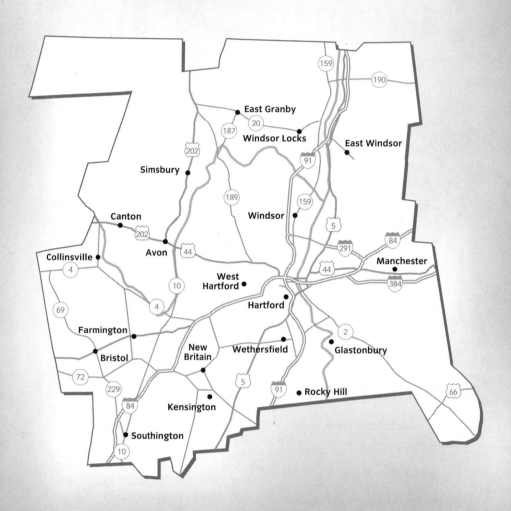

East Granby

Windsor Locks

East Windsor

Simsbury

Canton

Collinsville

Avon

Windsor

West Hartford

Manchester

Hartford

Farmington

Bristol

New Britain

Wethersfield

Glastonbury

Kensington

Southington

Rocky Hill

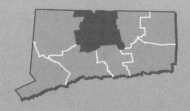

In the towns surrounding Hartford, you will find attractions that reflect each community's unique history and importance. Defined by such tourist district names as Tobacco Valley or Olde Towne, every area of this county provides opportunities for family fun.

Southington

The town of Southington lies halfway between New York and Boston just east of I–84, a location that even in prehighway days helped it become an important industrial community, producing cement, tinware, and carriage hardware in the nineteenth century and aircraft parts, electronic equipment, and medical instruments in the twentieth. With all the work folks do in these parts, there needs to be a time and place for play. Southington offers both.

Nuts about **Apples**

Every October, Southington's population swells by many thousands as the annual **Apple Harvest Festival** attracts an estimated 300,000 revelers. For more than thirty years, this street festival has celebrated the Southington apple crop in every way possible—a parade, a carnival, a road race, a variety talent show, apple foods and ethnic foods, music, arts and crafts, and dancing. Admission is **free.** Follow the crowds to the town green on Route 10. It's usually the first weekend in October, plus Thursday, Friday, and the following weekend.

The festivities extend to the orchards themselves. Two orchards in Southington have apples to pick or buy, plus cider, candies, other produce, and gifts. Call Roger's Orchards (860–229–4240) or Karabin Farms (860–621–6363). For information on the festival, check the official Web site: www.apple harvestfestival.com.

Mount Southington Ski Area (ages 4 and up)
Off I–84 exit 30; follow signs to 396 Mt. Vernon Road; business office: (860) 628–0954 or (800) 982–6828; snow phone: (860) 628–SNOW; www.mountsouthington.com. Open from November through April for skiing.

If hiking in summer or skiing in winter appeals to your family, Mount Southington is a good place to start. Fourteen downhill trails with five surface lifts and two chairlifts provide a convenient and state-of-the-art alternative to out-of-state facilities for young families who don't want to travel too far to ski.

Night skiing, snowboarding, and ski parties are all part of the business here. More than 100 professional instructors give group and private lessons, including the SKIwee program for 4- to 12-year-olds and learn-to-race programs on four electronically timed race courses for ages 8 to adult. Snowmaking machines keep the slopes active from November through much of early spring. A snack bar/cafeteria and the Mountain Room restaurant give you a chance to refuel, and a ski shop and a rental shop help you get the equipment you need. Come to their annual Ski Swap in late October for great deals on equipment.

Where to Eat

Brannigan's. 176 Laning Street; (860) 621–9311. Irish theme, cheerful staff, well-known ribs, good steaks, pastas, chicken, salads, sandwiches, children's menu. Open from 11:30 A.M. for lunch and dinner daily. Lunch $–$$ Dinner $$

Krys's Italian Restaurant and Pizzeria. 83 West Main Street in Plantsville section; (860) 628–4321. This place has won awards for its pizza, and its pasta is not bad either. Open daily from 11:00 A.M. $

Serafino's Luncheonette. 36 North Main Street; (860) 628–7979. A friend swears by this place for breakfast and lunch daily year-round. Like an old-fashioned five-and-dime lunch counter, it's a busy throwback to earlier days. Open 7:30 A.M. to 7:00 P.M. $

Where to Stay

Holiday Inn Express. 120 Laning Street; (860) 276–0736 or (800) 221–2222. 122 units, outdoor pool, continental breakfast. $$$

Residence Inn by Marriott. 778 West Street; (860) 621–4440. 94 suites with full kitchens. Pets welcome. Exercise room, outdoor pool. Buffet breakfast. $$$$

Bristol

Though firmly in Hartford County, the small industrial city of Bristol is classified by the State Tourism Commission as part of the Litchfield Hills. The city's history as a center of venerable Yankee industries, however, gives it a distinctive character much more in line with Hartford than Litchfield. To arrive here from Southington, take Route 10 north to Route 229, and you'll reach Bristol about 8 miles from that junction.

American Clock and Watch Museum (ages 4 and up)

100 Maple Street; (860) 583–6070. Open daily from March 1 through November 30 from 10:00 A.M. to 5:00 P.M. except for Thanksgiving Day. A guided tour takes about one hour. Adults $5.00; children 8 through 15 $2.00; children under 8 free.

In honor of those industrious craftsmen, you might start a day in Bristol here. More than 3,000 clocks and watches are beautifully displayed in a nineteenth-century colonial home with two modern wings filled with the largest of the ticking, striking, and chiming clocks.

A forest of grandfather clocks shares one wing with a marvelous representation of an eighteenth-century wooden-works clock workshop that displays ledger books, manuals, and clocks in various stages of finishing. Back in the main house, a charming clock shop is re-created with hundreds of clocks that would have been sold in the 1890s, including the original fixtures from an actual 1890s shop in Plymouth, Connecticut.

The collection is magnificent and very appealing to children. We found clocks shaped like Old King Cole, a bumblebee, a frying pan, a pumpkin, a violin, a town crier . . . the list could go on and on. The museum also contains the largest collection of Hickory Dickory Dock clocks held anywhere. Children may enjoy finding familiar figures such as Mickey Mouse, Bugs Bunny, Barbie, and other licensed characters among the antique cabinet clocks, pocket watches, wristwatches, and much more.

The New England Carousel Museum (ages 4 and up)

95 Riverside Avenue (Route 72); (860) 585–5411; www.thecarouselmuseum.com. Open April through November, Monday through Saturday 10:00 A.M. to 5:00 P.M. and Sunday, noon to 5:00 P.M., and December through March, Thursday through Saturday 10:00 A.M. to 5:00 P.M. and Sunday noon to 5:00 P.M. Closed on New Year's Day, Easter Sunday, Memorial Day, Independence Day, Labor Day, Thanksgiving, and Christmas. Adults $5.00; children 4 to 14 $2.50.

One of the nation's largest displays of antique carousel pieces has its home in Bristol. The golden age of the carousel from 1880 through the 1930s is portrayed in the restored hosiery mill—the "Stockingnet Factory"—that houses both the museum and the restoration workshop of carousel expert Bill Finkenstein. The main hall contains a changing

Connecticut **Carousels**

The carousel museum may make you ache for a ride, but you can't do it on their site. Luckily, you're in a great state for carousels. Although by the end of the nineteenth century more than 3,000 carousels operated in the United States, fewer than 100 still exist. Connecticut is home to three antiques, plus a few more recent and brand new ones like the one in the Danbury Fair Mall, the one at Lake Compounce (see next page), and the one at Lake Quassapaug (see Middlebury section of New Haven County chapter). Of the three antique carousels, two are currently operating, and we test-rode them for you in New Haven and Hartford (see Lighthouse Point Park and Bushnell Park, respectively). The third, the restored Pleasure Beach carousel, is partly displayed in Bridgeport at Beardsley Park, next to the operating reproduction that twirls in the specially constructed Carousel House on the Zoo grounds (see Beardsley Zoological Gardens). There's also a 1925 kiddie-sized carousel at Sound View Beach in Old Lyme and a full-sized wonder in the Mystic County Fair amusement arcade in Mystic.

parade of Coney Island, Philadelphia, and Country Fair–style figures so colorful and stately that one cannot help but be drawn into their magic. Many horses have been rescued from demolition, restored here, and kept on long-term loan from private collectors, a situation that infuses the museum with new life each time an exhibit is brought in.

The simplicity of the hall underscores the grandeur of the horses, chariots, band organs, and rounding boards. You can't help but smile and you might even feel like dancing when you hear the beautiful band organ music that fills the hall.

Guides tailor their tours to the age and interests of the visitors. Children are invited to feel a horsehair tail and to guess at details of carousel construction. A re-creation of a carver's workshop reveals the secrets of the craft; the particular details of master carvers such as Illions, Stein and Goldstein, Denzel, and Looff are pointed out.

Call for information on the museum's Painted Pony Pajama Parties, evening or sleepover programs that include crafts, games, and storytelling. Also stop for a look at the **Bristol Center for Arts and Culture,** a gallery now located on the first floor of the building along with local artist Glo Session's gallery.

Lake Compounce Theme Park and Entertainment Complex
(all ages) 🎢 🏊

822 Lake Avenue (Route 229 North), 2 miles from I–84 exit 31; (860) 583–3300; www.lake compounce.com. Open most days from Memorial Day to late August, then weekends and holidays only until late September. Call for specific hours and days of operation. Ride-all-day rates: adults $29.95; children under 52 inches $20.95; children 3 and under free. **Season passes good for unlimited visits, $69.95. Evening rates and group rates also. Parking $5.00.**

Lake Compounce upholds its record as the oldest continually operating amusement park in the United States. After recent $50 million face-lifts, its more than thirty rides and other amusements have charmed the crowds back to its 325 acres of merriment.

Besides the old-fashioned fun in the sun encouraged by its twenty-eight-acre lake and its sandy beach, the park still operates its 1911 carousel with Wurlitzer organ, a 1927 white wooden Wildcat roller coaster, and its nearly century-old open-air sky trolley. Along with those are new temptations for thrill-seekers. Boulder Dash is the East Coast's longest and fastest roller coaster. The Zoomerang roller coaster whips passengers through corkscrews at 50 mph; the Splash Harbor wave pool and water slides, the Thunder Rapids raft ride, and Mammoth Falls, a fiberglass flume ride, ensure fun of a wet nature; and the Top Spin takes riders for an upside-down whirl-and-wash of sorts.

A 100-foot Ferris wheel attempts to compete with the 750-foot ascent of the Southington Mountain Sky Ride, while a Shoreline Trolley car shuttles passengers to the new 2,400-seat picnic pavilion. Young visitors will enjoy the Kiddieland Circus World with ten rides for children under 48 inches, plus a magic show, a puppet show, and much more. A miniature golf course and paddleboats (both an extra charge) add to the entertainments.

Bring along a bathing suit or a change of clothes and a towel so you can enjoy a ride on the water slide or a dip in the lake. Lockers and changing rooms are provided. Several food concessions and a large full-service restaurant provide lots of choices for snacks, meals, and beverages. Groups of twenty-five or more can request special rates, so visitors might consider the reduced price a good excuse for a neighborhood outing, a family reunion, or a birthday bash.

Where to Eat

On Route 10 you'll find national chain restaurants such as Ruby Tuesdays, Chilis, and Bertucci's, offering affordable sit-down fare for families. On Route 6, try **Angellino's** (650 Farmington Avenue; 860–589–0669) for pizza, pasta, salads, and much more for lunch and dinner daily. $–$$

Where to Stay

Radisson Inn Bristol. 42 Century Drive; (860) 589–7766 or (800) 333–3333. 120 units, including 2 suites. Health club, sauna, indoor pool. Complimentary full breakfast at **Jilian's Restaurant** on premises. Special packages. $$$

Canton/Collinsville

Fishing and antiquing are probably the most popular tourist activities in the Canton/ Collinsville area near Route 179 north of Burlington and west of Avon, but they are not likely to sustain the long-term attention of everyone in the family. Luckily some other options make the area a crowd-pleaser anyway.

Huck Finn Adventures (all ages)

(860) 693–0385; members.aol.com/hucfinadvn/Start.html. Open in spring, summer, and fall. Call for reservations and directions. Mini solo kayaks, catamaran canoes, a wooden raft, and an inflatable raft are also available.

First of all, this operation is run by an easygoing fellow with a great appreciation for the beauty and adventure to be enjoyed in the outdoors. An all-around nice guy, John Kulick offers leisurely trips specially designed for families with young children or beginner canoeists. You choose from 3-, 5-, or 9-mile trips in flat water about waist high over a sandy bottom along a quiet section of the Farmington River between Avon and Simsbury.

Everything you need for the self-guided outing is provided, except for the picnic or snacks you bring along. The outfitter sets you up with stable 17-foot canoes, paddles, life vests and so on. The charge per canoe is $45. The canoes have seats in the middle for the kids, so two adults and two young children are usually comfortable in one canoe. Instruction on paddling, put-in, and take-out is offered at the outset for novices, but this is gentle enough for little risk to true beginners.

You'll paddle past King Philip's Cave high up on the Talcott Mountain Ridge. On the ride back to your put-in spot, the driver of your shuttle van will tell you the story of King Philip, or Metacomet, chief of the Wampanoags. A bloody three-year war began in 1675, when Metacomet began to massacre the settlers he feared would destroy his people. When Simsbury, among other towns, was burned by the Wampanoags in 1676, their notorious leader supposedly watched from the cave. You might want to stop in the small park near the old iron bridge along the way for a picnic at the Pinchot Sycamore, the largest tree in Connecticut. Actually located in Simsbury in the Weatogue section on Route 185, its circumference is 25 feet 8 inches; its height is 93 feet; its branches spread 138 feet. A picnic area with tables is there for your use.

Two adults paddling at a leisurely pace can do these trips in two to three hours (paddling time), but you're welcome to spend the day picnicking and exploring, or drifting like Huckleberry himself. Twilight and moonlight trips can also be arranged. Whitewater instruction is usually done in May and June as water conditions allow.

Collinsville Canoe and Kayak (all ages with some limits)

41 Bridge Street (Route 179); (860) 693–6977; www.cckstore.com. Seasonal hours, depending on weather and water conditions; call to inquire. Canoe rentals $15 hourly, $40 daily on-site, $45 daily off-site. Kayak rentals at similar prices for solo and tandem kayakers.

This outfitter offers guided and self-guided canoe trips and kayak trips on flat water, whitewater, and the Sound. Self-guided trips on flat water are commonly taken from the put-in points near the Collinsville Canoe store on Route 179. Guided tours are offered on the Farmington River as well as Bantam Lake in Bantam, Lake McDonough in Barkhamsted, and White Memorial in Litchfield, plus Selden Neck, Great Island, Fishers Island Sound, the Mystic Seaport, the Thimble Islands, the Norwalk Islands, and other areas. Reservations are necessary for all guided tours and are highly recommended, especially for weekends, even for the self-guided Farmington River flat water trips.

Canoe Cruises under the City

Perhaps the most amazing of all discoveries the author made while researching this book was the incredible underground canoe trip offered by **Huck Finn Adventures** through the flood control tunnels under the city of Hartford. Limited to eight to twelve people aged 9 years or older, these guided tours enter the tunnels after a shuttle ride that leaves from Charter Oak Landing. For about two hours (with a trip total of about three and a half hours), you explore the buried Park River, which flows through a fascinating system of tunnels. In water of about bathtub depth, you'll glide in the dim underworld, doing some sound and light experiments and even drifting in the total darkness for three to seven minutes when you all turn off your headlamps. John Kulick provides a narration explaining the mechanics of the system and pointing out sites of interest. What an experience! Adults pay $45; children 9 to 15 pay $35. Call (860) 693–0385 for more details.

The age minimum for kayaks and canoes is up to parental discretion, but the child must be able to fit snugly into a life vest. They also offer instruction in beginning canoeing and kayaking for whitewater, flat water, and the sea.

Canton Historical Museum (ages 6 and up)

11 Front Street; (860) 693–2793; www.cantonmuseum.org. Open April through November, Wednesday through Sunday from 1:00 to 4:00 P.M.; open until 8:00 P.M. Thursday. December through March Saturday and Sunday from 1:00 to 4:00 P.M. Adults $3.00; children 6 to 15 $1.00; children under 6 **free.**

If you're intrigued by the history of the area after a day on the river, visit this marvelous museum. A complete, original post office, a general store re-creation, a blacksmith area, a barbershop area, a Victorian bride's parlor with wedding dresses, a late-nineteenth-century kitchen setting, and tons of farming equipment, medical equipment, household implements like looms and spinning wheels, and much more awaits your perusal on the one-hour guided tour. A special children's area includes dolls, toys, and other items of interest, and a true highlight is an operational model train diorama of the whole Collinsville village and countryside as it appeared about 1900.

Roaring Brook Nature Center (all ages)

70 Gracey Road; (860) 693–0263; www.sciencecenterct.org/rbncpage/home.html or www.roaringbrook.org. Open year-round Tuesday through Saturday 10:00 A.M. to 5:00 P.M. (Mondays also July through August) and Sunday 1:00 to 5:00 P.M. Adults $3.00; children 12 and under $2.00. Hiking trails open daily, dawn to dusk.

Canton's sanctuary is perfect for families. An excellent longhouse typical of the Wampanoag people is part of their indoor exhibits. Small dioramas, a wild animal attraction area, a live-animal area with native creatures, and a small gift shop are also indoors. Six miles of trails through exceptionally pretty country are on the sanctuary. A wildflower trail is especially lovely in spring and summer. Ask at the nature center for wildlife and flora guides and checklists before you venture into the beautiful Werner's Woods property. Indoor programs as well as guided walks are offered throughout the season for families. A full slate of concerts, some especially designed for young children, is one of the best and most unique features of this nature center. Tickets range from $5.00 to $17.00.

Where to Eat

La Salle Market and Deli. 104 Main Street, Collinsville; (860) 693–8010. Open daily year-round from 6:00 A.M. to 8:00 P.M. Monday through Saturday and Sunday until 7:00 P.M., this village market has five eat-in tables or take-out service if you need picnic food for a canoe or road trip. Bagels, muffins, breakfast sandwiches, deli sandwiches and salads, hot dogs, burgers, meatballs, and much more. Pizza is served in the evenings, and open-mike entertainment is offered Thursday through Sunday. A friendly throwback to the good old days, it's great for families. $

A Trifle More than Truffles. 220 Albany Turnpike , which is Route 44, Canton; (860) 693–3799. In the Canton Village Shopping

Center, this bakery/cafe serves breakfast and lunch every day and can also help you pack a pretty nice picnic. Soups, sandwiches, salads, quiches, wraps, French toast, focaccia, burgers, plus a full line of baked goods for here or to go. Open from 6:00 A.M. $

Avon

Named for the river in Stratford, England, Avon originated in 1645 as a section of Farmington. First known as Nod, for North District, it grew substantially in the following century when the new stagecoach route from Boston to Albany came through town. Along with the Albany Turnpike came prosperity for the farmers and traders of the region, who capitalized on the needs of the travelers passing through town. Inn and tavern keepers, blacksmiths and harness makers, merchants and even bandits—all benefited from the construction of the road we now call Route 44.

Avon has retained all signs of the affluence it achieved in its past. Now a bedroom community populated largely by commuting Hartford executives and professionals, it is plump with restaurants and shops catering to a comfortable clientele. For tourists, of course, this means wonderful food and great places for shopping. Unfortunately, the kids might lose interest after awhile. No worry—Avon is home to a few places the kids might really enjoy, albeit with one caveat: It's best to be here in summer or fall.

Avon Cider Mill (all ages)

57 Waterville Road (Route 10); (860) 677-0343. The mill's market is open daily, mid-September to October 31 from 9:00 A.M. to 6:00 P.M.; November 1 to December 25, they close at 5:00 P.M.

When the trees show signs of turning, come here. From apples trucked in from upstate New York, the Lattizori brothers make 35,000 to 40,000 gallons of cider every year, starting in mid-September. You can actually watch them make the cider in the press their grandfather bought in 1919, but you'd have to get up pretty early in the morning. Cider-making begins at 2:00 A.M. and is usually done by 7:00 A.M. Set the alarm if you want to see the press in action. If you like to sleep a little longer, just plan on tasting the wonderfully sweet cider—the ultimate chaser for the melt-in-your-mouth cider doughnuts sold here as well.

The market also offers local produce and crafts, pumpkins, and fall accoutrements like Indian corn, gourds, mums, and more. Later in the season, they truck in the Christmas trees. After Christmas, the Lattizoris rest a bit; they close shop until spring, when they bring out plants for your gardens. In midsummer, local produce like sweet corn tempts the tourists right off the road.

Pickin' Patch (all ages)

276 Nod Road, off Route 44; (860) 677–9552. Open daily in season from 8:00 A.M. to 6:00 P.M.

In the same vein, only more so, you might like to stop by the Pickin' Patch, just a mile and a half up Nod Road, which begins at the Avon Old Farms Inn at the corner of Routes 10 and 44. Owned by Janet and Don Carville, the farm has been in the Carville family since 1666 when their ancestors came from Hartford after accompanying Thomas Hooker to Connecticut.

This farm is a fountain of riches, namely nearly everything growing under the sun from asparagus to zucchini. As the name suggests, this is a pick-your-own place from roughly mid-April onward to December until the Christmas trees are gone and they turn the lights out on Christmas Eve. The tenth oldest family farm in Connecticut, the farm grows the largest variety of berries, vegetables, and flowers in the state. Strawberries, blackberries, blueberries, squash, spinach, collards, peas, cucumbers, tomatoes, peppers, and much more are sold at half the cost of retail if you pick them yourself.

The joint really starts hopping when pumpkin season and the **free** hayrides begin. On Saturday and Sunday in October from 10:00 A.M. to 5:00 P.M., you can ride the tractor-driven hay wagons out to the fields to pick your own pumpkin.

Farmington Valley Arts Center (ages 6 and up)

25 Arts Center Lane, just under a half-mile west of the junction of Routes 44 and 10 North, in Avon Park North office/industrial complex. Turn from Route 44 into Ensign Drive, then left onto Arts Center Lane. The second and third buildings slightly askew at your left are the Art Center buildings, numbers 25 and 27; (860) 678–1867; www.fvac.net. Studios open year-round (see below) by chance or by appointment; store open year-round Wednesday through Saturday from 11:00 A.M. through 5:00 P.M. and on Sunday from noon to 4:00 P.M. Open Monday through Saturday 10:00 A.M. to 5:00 P.M., Thursday until 8:00 P.M., and Sunday noon to 5:00 P.M. in November and December.

Historically important as former factory buildings, these century-old brownstone structures now house the twenty studios of the forty working artists who comprise the center. Painting, ceramics, weaving, and sculpture are just a few of the media explored here by professional artists and their students. Classes are offered for children and adults at every level—beginners as well as advanced. Artists work on individual schedules, but someone is almost always here to watch, and you are welcome to stroll from studio to studio throughout the year, especially on Wednesday through Sunday from February through October or seven days a week in November and December. Open Arts Day in early June is a festival event with demonstrations, classes, musicians, dancers, a theater performance, and other experiences related to the arts.

From the first Saturday in November until Christmas Eve, the annual holiday exhibit, called the *Art of Giving/The Giving of Art*, features strolling musicians, luminaria, and other festivities on opening night, plus sales of contemporary American crafts thereafter in the Fisher Gallery and in the Visitors' Gallery, which is the FVAC store. This shop offers a varied collection of pottery, jewelry, toys, prints, clothing, and other exceptional crafts made by U.S. crafters only. As you pass the FVAC office on your way to the gallery, stop and ask for a course catalog. The teen and children's summer classes at the Learning Center Annex are wonderful.

First Company Governor's Horse Guards (all ages)

Military Reservation, 232 West Avon Road (Route 167); (860) 673– 3525; www.govhorse guards.org. Public viewing of drills on horseback every Thursday evening, usually shortly after 7:30 P.M. throughout the year. Open horse shows in June and September. Call for schedule or check the Web site. Visitors welcome at other times to view horses, daily.

If you are in Avon at a time that coordinates with the activities of the Governor's Horse Guards, stop for a look. The nation's first cavalry unit organized in 1658 as the mounted guards of Connecticut Colony, the original thirty or so riders and horses served both as ceremonial escorts and in active duty in the War of 1812, World War I, and World War II. The company's current responsibilities are mostly decorative. Their choreographed maneuvers are amazingly intricate "dances" performed at such events as presidential and gubernatorial inaugurations. You can watch them practice their astounding routines at the compound on Route 167 between Routes 4 and 44.

Where to Eat

Max a Mia Ristorante and Cantinetta. 70 East Main Street (Route 44); (860) 677–MAXX. Northern Italian contemporary cuisine is what they call it; we call it delicious. Fresh focaccia, excellent salads and pastas galore, thin-crust pizza made in wood-fired oven. Open for lunch, dinner, and Sunday brunch. $$

Avon Old Farms Inn. 1 Nod Road, at the junction of Routes 44 and 10; (860) 677–2818; www.avonoldfarmsinn.com. A splurge for many families, this classic is one of the ten oldest restaurants in the country and one of the best in the state. New American cuisine freshly prepared and presented in a beautiful setting. Open year-round daily. $$$$ To spend a bit less, try the **Tavern Room,** which offers a wonderful lunch buffet for $9.95.

Bakers Dozen Bagel Company. 315 West Main Street; (860) 676–2245. This spic-and-span family-owned bakery has made thirty-five varieties of bagels on-site for the past twenty-five years. Bagel sandwiches, stuffed bagel pockets, soups in winter, more. Eat in or out for breakfast, lunch, and beyond. Open daily from 6:30 A.M.; closings vary (earliest is 2:00 P.M. on Sunday). $

Where to Stay

Avon Old Farms Hotel. 279 Avon Mountain Road, at the junction of Routes 44 and 10; (860) 677–1651; www.avonoldfarms hotel.com. Across the street from the Avon Old Farms Inn, which is a restaurant, is this cream-of-the-crop, 160-unit hotel with standard and luxury rooms and 3 suites. Luxury amenities, from the soap to the chocolates, from towels to apples. Continental breakfast. Outdoor pool, sauna, health club. Seasons Restaurant and Pub. $$$$

Simsbury

Six miles north of Avon, Simsbury is an appealing suburb of 22,000 people, many of whom work in Hartford, just twenty minutes south. Established in 1670 by English colonists, Simsbury was built on land long populated by the Wampanoag Indians, who had no understanding of the English concept of land claims when they began to share local tribal lands with the newcomers. Their misapprehension of the situation led to some turbulence that culminated in the burning of Simsbury by the Wampanoags on March 26, 1676. Sad to say, the Wampanoag people underestimated the tenacity of the settlers and were nearly eradicated in the bloody King Philip's war that ensued. Reconstruction of colonial Simsbury commenced in 1677 when it was clear that no further resistance was possible. The settlers of Simsbury soon had a community that flourished, as did industries of copper mining, smelting, steel production, copper coinage, silver plating, and safety fuse manufacturing. Now largely residential, Simsbury offers to the public one of the best historical settlements in the state.

The Phelps Tavern Museum and Phelps Homestead
(ages 6 and up)
800 Hopmeadow Street (Route 10); (860) 658–2500; www.simsburyhistory.org. Open year-round, Tuesday through Saturday from noon to 4:00 P.M. Last full tour at 2:30 P.M. Closed holidays. Adults $6.00; children 2 to 17 $3.50.

Once called Massacoh Plantation, this property has eight structures—some reproduction, some original, and some transported here for the purpose of creating a museum. A tour of the property usually begins at the replica 1683 meetinghouse wherein the Simsbury founding fathers decided matters of church and state and from which supposed witch Goody Griffin is said to have departed by flying through its keyhole.

The 1771 Elisha Phelps House, occupied by the Phelps family for nearly 200 years, is restored to the period of 1830–40 when it served as a hotel/tavern for travelers on the New Haven–Northhampton Canal. The site also includes a Victorian carriage house with an authentic tin peddler's cart, a 1740 one-room schoolhouse, a barn, an icehouse, a 1795 cottage also owned by the Phelps family, and a re-creation of the safety fuse manufactory with fixtures, records, and furnishings of the original factory.

Tours by (usually) costumed docents of the Simsbury Historical Society are thorough and excellent, though a full tour for children under 8 may be longer than they can bear. Feel free to ask for a short version if you are the only folks in the group. You can stroll the grounds unguided, but you cannot tour the buildings without a docent. Called Three Centuries by Candlelight, the museum's holiday festivity in late November or early December is a living history reenactment of scenes from Simsbury's past. Like Charles Dickens's Scrooge, you watch the scenes unfold as the costumed actors go about their drama as if you were not there. All this happens by candlelight, of course, since the houses are not electrified. This very impressive event is marvelous for children and adults.

Talcott Mountain State Park (all ages)

Route 185; (860) 242–1158. Park open year-round dawn to dusk. Heublein Tower open mid-April to late August Thursday through Sunday 10:00 A.M. to 5:00 P.M. and, for foliage season, from early September through October, open daily at same hours. Free.

If the excellent history lessons at Massacoh Plantation overwhelm some in your party, refresh yourselves with a brisk hike. A popular family area because of the amazing Heublein Tower at the 1,000-foot summit of the Talcott Mountain Ridge, it has moderate trails, benches, picnic sites, and, on clear days, views of four states from the tower. Some, including Mark Twain, who used to walk this ridge, say it's the finest view in all of Connecticut. The park overlooks many of the fertile Farmington Valley farms and pretty towns like Avon. From Route 10 between Simsbury and Avon, you can't miss seeing the white 165-foot-tall tower built in 1914 by businessman Gilbert Heublein.

Once you're in the park, you hike the 1.5-mile King Philip's Trail to the tower and then climb up the tower. The observation deck, at the top of several fights of stairs, provides a 50-mile view on clear days. A local history exhibit is also at the tower base, with interesting facts about the park and tower.

International Ice Skating Center (ages 3 and up)

1375 Hopmeadow Street (Route 10); (860) 651–5400; www.isecskate.com. Public skating Sunday through Friday from noon to 1:20 P.M., Saturday at 2:00 to 3:20 P.M. and 7:00 to 8:20 P.M., and Friday evenings from 8:30 to midnight. Added sessions on some holidays or during school breaks. $6.00 per person; group discounts available. Skate rental $3.00. Visitors welcome daily 6:00 A.M. to midnight. Great Beginnings program for parents and tots, Monday, Wednesday, and Thursday from 1:30 to 2:20 P.M. $4.00. Tours of the facility available at no charge; call ahead.

You want to skate, and you'd love to see the example of Ekaterina Gordeeva, Oksana Baiul, Viktor Petrenko, Scott Davis, and other skating champions. Come here to the world-class twin facility that is their home rink. An Olympic-sized and an NHL-sized rink are both linked to the Sk8ters Cafe, a restaurant and coffee shop that allow diners a view of both rinks. Two thousand seats allow spectators to watch figure skating and hockey events and practices. Small classes for beginners to pros are offered here, and the instruction programs and scholarships bring young skaters from all over the world. Parent and toddler programs include games and activities and popular children's music to make learning to skate easy and fun. Skate rentals, purchases, and sharpening and repair services are all available to the public. Private birthday parties can be arranged.

Flamig Farm (ages 2 to 10)

West Mountain Road; (860) 658–5070; www.flamigfarm.com. Open daily 9:00 A.M. to 6:00 P.M. or dusk, April 22 (Earth Day) to late November. Pony rides weekends only 11:00 A.M. to 3:00 P.M., $5.00 for children up to 75 pounds. Other rides offered, weather permitting. Zoo admission $3.00 for folks over 1 and under 80.

A petting zoo of farm animals is the big ticket at this farm most of the season. See Belgian draft horses and miniature horses, llamas, pigs, goats, sheep, chickens, rabbits, turkeys, geese, ducks, and even a pair of Texas longhorns named Strawberry and Oreo. You can buy a cupful or a handful of grain if you'd like to give the animals a snack, and you can pet them all, of course. You might also like to visit the barns and bring your own meal to their picnic area.

Pony rides are given on weekends only; occasionally a draft horse is saddled as well for larger riders. In pumpkin season, public hayrides to the pumpkin fields are given on weekends only on the half-hour from 11:00 A.M. to 4:00 P.M. Horsedrawn rides are $5.00 per person; tractor-drawn rides are $1.00. Private tractor hayrides (about $95 an hour), horsedrawn hayrides (about $150 per hour), sleigh rides (snow permitting, about $125 an hour), and two-person carriage and sleigh rides (about $100 an hour) are also frequently arranged. Pony-ride birthday parties at their place or yours are also frequent. Check the Web site for news of the farm's seasonal plans. In the fall, haunted hayrides are often scheduled. Call or check the Web for times and prices. A Christmas village complete with decorated barns, elves, reindeer, a holiday trolley, Santa's workshop, and more, opens every day from December 1, usually, until December 23. Come for breakfast with Santa. Adult admission is $10.00; children under 12 pay $5.00. Tots 2 years old and younger are **free.**

Where to Eat

Sakimura. 10 Wilcox Street; (860) 651–7929. For a delicious and cultural food adventure, try lunch or dinner at this excellent Japanese establishment. A sushi/sashimi bar, more than two dozen appetizer dishes, teriyaki, tempura, and American favorites made Japanese style are among the many choices. Open Tuesday through Sunday. $–$$$

Mario's. 244 Farms Village Road; (860) 658–9556. Excellent traditional Italian pasta dishes, seafood, chicken, veal. Pizza, too. Open for lunch and dinner Tuesday through Saturday; dinner only on Sunday. $–$$

Pettibone Tavern. 4 Hartford Road; (860) 658–1118. For Sunday brunch, children under 5 are **free;** children 5 to 12 pay $7.95, and parents pay $19.95—a good value for good American fare in a historic setting. Dinner daily as well. Steaks, seafood, simple choices for children, such as grilled cheese and spaghetti. $$–$$$$

Where to Stay

The Simsbury Inn. 397 Hopmeadow Street; (860) 651–5700. 100 "luxury rooms with a country inn ambience" is the way the inn describes itself. They're right. Indoor pool, three restaurants, health club, sauna, tennis, jogging paths, and continental breakfast make this a special place for families. $$$$

East Granby

This little town 4 miles east of Granby (north of Simsbury by means of Route 10/202) is downright bucolic, and it's a pleasure merely to explore the gentle twists and hills of its rural roadways. Just a handful of miles from the Massachusetts border, its village center is a quiet place of refuge from the busy hub that grows in an ever-widening circle around Hartford.

Old New-Gate Prison and Copper Mine (ages 4 and up)

Newgate Road off Route 20; (860) 653–3563. Open from mid-May through October, Wednesday through Sunday from 10:00 A.M. to 4:30 P.M. Adult admission is $4.00; children 6 to 17 $2.00, children under 6 free. *(Note: This museum has been closed for some time due to state budget cuts. Call ahead to be sure it has reopened, as was hoped for in spring 2004.)*

Amid the beautiful hills of East Granby is a National Historic Landmark. The first North American copper mine chartered by the British monarchy in 1707, New-Gate is also Connecticut's first prison, named after London's notorious New-Gate Prison. When copper mining ceased in the facility in 1773, the subterranean tunnels and chambers were designated as a perfect place to confine the burglars, horse thieves, and counterfeiters who had broken the laws of the English colonies. Soon, however, English sympathizers were imprisoned here as the American Patriots revolted against the monarchy and took New-Gate as their own. During the Revolution, George Washington sent captured Tories here along with American deserters. Just to make sure no one was having any fun underground, prisoners were forced to mine the tunnels and to make nails and shoes.

Now the old brick rooms and ruins of the prison and much of the mine are open to the public. A self-guided tour of the 65-foot-deep mine takes about thirty minutes. I recommend *highly* that you call ahead and ask for a guided tour, which the staff is happy to provide to those who ask. All the guides are wonderfully educated as to the facts and fictions of this remarkable site.

The view from the prison grounds is one of the finest views in the state. The fall foliage here is glorious. You can picnic on the lawn or on tables. A great wildlife nature trail designed to demonstrate wildlife habitat management practices homeowners can use on their own property is accessible from the parking lot. Pick up a trail guide inside the prison.

Windsor

Six miles north of the state capital lies Windsor, which calls itself Connecticut's oldest town, settled in 1633 by Englishmen from Plymouth Colony in Massachusetts. These adventurers camped at the confluence of the Connecticut and Farmington Rivers in a place the native inhabitants called Matianuck. Briefly named Dorchester by the newcomers, the town was renamed Windsor in 1637 and has enjoyed a prosperous history ever since, based on the varied enterprises of brick making, cigar tobacco farming, and the milling of woolens and paper. Now largely suburban in nature, this town of just over 30 square miles on the western bank of the Connecticut River has a variety of attractions that will add to a family's appreciation of the state's north-central Heritage Valley.

In addition to the main attractions listed in the following paragraphs, the town of Windsor offers a pleasant array of places and events where families might enjoy a day or a weekend. Summer concerts on Thursday evenings on the historic town green, a winter carnival, a clown day, and a just-for-fun dog show are the kinds of activities that character-ize this family-oriented town. Other annual events include the one-of-a-kind Shad Derby Festival the third Saturday in May, a Yankee Doodle Fourth of July Celebration, and an early autumn Revolutionary War Encampment (see www.revolutionarywindsor.com). Walking and cycling on the Windsor Center River Trail, ice-skating on the town green, and canoe-ing on the Farmington River are among the town's many outdoor activities; indoors are museums that explore 300 years of history (see sidebar). Consider booking a room at a local hostelry and have an old-fashioned good time.

Northwest Park and Nature Center (all ages)
Luddy/Taylor Connecticut Valley Tobacco Museum (ages 8 and up)
Lang Road; park and nature center: (860) 285–1886; tobacco museum: (860) 285–1888. Park open daily year-round, dawn to dusk. Nature center open daily year-round, Monday through Saturday from 10:00 A.M. to 5:00 P.M. and Sunday noon to 4:00 P.M. Tobacco museum open March to mid-December, Tuesday through Thursday and Saturday from noon to 4:00 P.M., with somewhat longer hours in summer. Call for details or check the Web sites: www.northwestpark.com or www.tobaccohistsoc.org. Admission to the park, nature center, and museum is free**.**

Lovely **Northwest Park** has nearly 475 acres and 10 miles of trails, along with picnic areas and pavilions, community and demonstration gardens, a playground, and much more of appeal to visitors of all ages. Explore the Wetland Forest Trail, the Bog Loop, the Softwood Forest, or the Woody Succession Trail. Check out the Hemlock Trail or the Pond Trail. All of these are open any time of year. Stop at the live-animal exhibits in the Animal Barn and Nature Center. See the demonstration maple sugaring house or linger quietly in the bird and butterfly gardens. Hiking, biking, and picnicking are among the self-guided activities you might pursue here, or take a guided walk or participate in a family nature program or kids' camp. An annual Country Fair offers games, races, hayrides, and entertainment espe-cially for children aged 2 to 10. Call or check the Web site for this year's date.

Snowshoeing and cross-country skiing are possible here during snowy winters; a rental center offers equipment for $10.00 (full-day) or $7.50 (half-day). Throughout the academic year, come in the evening or on occasional afternoons on selected Saturdays for the Northwest Park Coffee House Concert series; tickets for the 7:30 P.M. perform-ances in this alcohol-free, smoke-free venue are $12 per person; all performances are suit-able for families. Check the Web site for the current schedule.

At the **Luddy/Taylor Connecticut Valley Tobacco Museum,** located in Northwest Park, you can explore a restored tobacco curing barn to gain a sense of the venerable his-tory of tobacco farming in this valley. The world's finest cigar wrappers are still grown in this area, although the total acreage is reduced to 2,000 acres from a peak of 30,000 acres in 1921. Learn how the shade-leaf tobacco was grown and cured; see the authentic equipment stored in the barn; peruse the historical displays in the museum building near the barn and gain an appreciation for the ways the tobacco industry contributed to the economy and even the ethnic culture of this region.

History in the Heritage Valley

Windsor is proud of its history as the cradle of European settlement and development in the Connecticut River Valley, and it celebrates that through several museums and events that may be of interest to families. Most of these are located in or not far from the town's historic district, which centers roughly around the Broad Street town green and the Palisado Green, on or near Routes 75 and 159. The marvelous **Windsor Historical Society** (96 Palisado Avenue near the corner of North Meadow Road; 860–688–3813) has three galleries with changing art and artifact exhibitions and a hands-on history learning center that covers three centuries of life in Windsor. Here, for instance, you can try on colonial-style clothing, pretend to attend the one-room schoolhouse, or learn about hearth cooking. The society also operates the adjacent and nearby 1758 **Strong House** and the 1765 **Chaffee House**. The museum is open and tours of these homes are given Tuesday through Saturday, year-round, from 10:00 A.M. to 4:00 P.M. Adults pay $3.00; children pay $1.00. The **Huntington House Museum** (289 Broad Street; 860–688–2004; www.huntingtonmuseum.org) is a breathtaking 6,500 square-foot, neoclassical Colonial Revival mansion that operates as both historic house and fine arts museum; in addition to items from its permanent collection and traveling shows featuring internationally known artists, the changing exhibitions of locally and nationally known working artists are top-notch. The museum's family programs are wonderful, frequent, and inexpensive. Take a docent-led house tour or just enjoy the art and architecture on your own. It is open year-round Thursday through Saturday 10:00 A.M. to 4:00 P.M. and Sunday 1:00 to 4:00 P.M. Adults pay $6.00; students pay $4.00; children under 12 are free. The 1780 **Oliver Ellsworth Homestead** (778 Palisado Avenue; 860–688–8717) re-creates the life of its namesake Revolutionary patriot and statesman through domestic furniture, implements, and ephemera. It is open for tours from noon to 4:30 P.M. May through October on Tuesday, Wednesday, and Saturday; adults pay $2.00; children under 12 are free.

Summerwind Performing Arts Center (all ages) 🎵

40 Griffin Road North; (860) 687–9836; www.swind.org. Season is generally mid-June through mid-September. Most performances at 7:30 P.M.; special family performances may be in the afternoon. Call or check the Web site for the current schedule and tickets.

This venue is a nearly new outdoor performing arts center located on a ten-acre site just a few miles from I-91. Accessed by a pretty bridge over a small lake, it is surrounded by lawns where families feel especially at ease setting out chairs or a blanket and a picnic dinner. Under the tentlike tension structure of the main amphitheater, where the stage is located, 1,500 patrons can be seated on chairs, but families may prefer the lawn space for 4,500 more concertgoers. Classical, jazz, folk, blues, and ethnic and American roots music is performed here in the evening, usually at 7:30 P.M. throughout the summer season; special performances for families may start earlier in the day. The premier 2003 season included such world-class performers as Wynton Marsalis and Dave Brubeck, Celtic and Zydeco groups, and the Hartford Symphony. Children are welcome at all performances.

The venue does not permit smoking, either under the canopy or on the lawn; cooking is also prohibited and pets must stay home. No beer or hard liquor is allowed on the grounds or in the free parking lot; wine is allowed at evening performances, but patrons are asked not to bring alcoholic beverages of any kind to family performances. Food and beverages are available for sale if you have not brought a picnic. Swimming in the lake is strictly limited to fish and ducks.

Where to Eat

Bart's Deli and Restaurant. 85 Palisado Avenue; (860) 688–9035. Within the historic district not far from the center of town is this cozy and down-to-earth place right on the banks of the Farmington. Great breakfasts and, for lunch and early dinner, hearty sandwiches of all kinds, rings and dogs, burgers, and traditional American hot meals. 7:00 A.M. to 8:00 P.M. year-round. Picnic tables by the river if you'd like to eat outdoors. $-$$

Dom's Broad Street Eatery. 330 Broad Street; (860) 298–9758. Try Dom's for cuisine similar to Bart's—hearty traditional American breakfasts, generous sandwiches, soups, and salads and such for lunch. Open year-round from 7:00 A.M. to 2:00 P.M. on weekdays, from 6:00 A.M. on weekends, and breakfast only on Sunday. $

Trout Brook Bissell Tavern. 1530 Palisado Avenue; (860) 285–0878. Overlooking the water, you can eat in or out, in season, at this dependably good steak house open for dinner only from 5:00 P.M. Tuesday through Saturday and from 3:00 P.M. on Sunday. Ribs, steaks, seafood, pot roast, design-your-own pasta specials, hot sandwiches, chowders, salads, much more. $$-$$$

Where to Stay

Residence Inn by Marriott. 100 Dunphy Lane; (860) 688–7474; www.residenceinn. com. 96 suites with fully equipped kitchens. Complimentary continental buffet breakfast; outdoor pool, whirlpool, sports court. Pets welcome. $$$$

Windsor Locks

Best known for its current role as the home of Bradley International Airport, Windsor Locks is on the Connecticut River about a dozen miles from downtown Hartford and has a large concentration of hotels, motels, and restaurants serving travelers. It also has one of the nation's best aviation museums.

New England Air Museum (all ages)
Route 75; (860) 623–3305. Open daily year-round, except on New Year's Day, Christmas, and Thanksgiving, from 10:00 A.M. to 5:00 P.M. Adults $7.00; children 6 to 11 $3.50; under 6 free.

Right within sight of the runways at Bradley International Airport is the largest aviation history museum in the Northeast and one of only four such collections in the United States. From a 1909 wood-and-canvas Bleriot XI monoplane to modern jets, the museum includes eighty aircraft of military and civilian origins. Most are restored and housed inside two hangars, transformed to museum-gallery quality.

Excellent exhibits tell the story of flight from the drawings of Leonardo da Vinci to the space flights of NASA astronauts. The evolution of humankind's mastery of gravity is chronicled at every turn, nowhere more evidently than in the aircraft themselves. The museum owns the oldest aeronautical artifact in the United States—a beautiful wicker balloon basket built by Silas Brooks of Plymouth, Connecticut, in 1870. From that vintage onward, the museum houses biplanes, Piper Cubs, Seabat helicopters, B-25 bombers, Grumman Hellcats and Wildcats, F-4 Phantom jets, hang-gliders, and many other fully and partially restored aircraft.

Lindbergh memorabilia, an outstanding Igor Sikorsky exhibit, and an air-mail display are among the special areas. Films on flight, the space program, and other topics are played continuously in the museum's theater. On Open Cockpit Sundays (offered a few times annually) you can climb inside the cockpits of several restored aircraft. Most of the signage of the exhibits is directed to adults. Parents of young children will have to read or paraphrase most of the excellent information provided by the museum. Despite this problem, the museum is well suited to children, and the museum shop is full of merchandise perfect for kids.

By the way, the road to the museum runs right alongside the airport runway. Pull over and sit there awhile for great views of the coming and goings of local, national, and international aircraft.

Where to Eat

Skyline Restaurant. 106 Ella T. Grasso Turnpike; (860) 623–9296. For good Italian food in a family-friendly place close to views of the air traffic, come here from 11:00 A.M. to midnight for lunch or dinner. One of the most extensive children's menus we've seen in the state, with great choices such as chicken parmigiana and ravioli along with the typical tenders, dogs, and the like. You can't see the planes take off or land, but they are there in the sky. Ask for a window seat. Open daily year-round. $–$$

Where to Stay

Ramada Inn at Bradley. 5 Ella Grasso Turnpike (Route 75); (860) 623–9494 or (800) 2–RAMADA. 148 rooms, indoor/outdoor pool, restaurant, buffet breakfast, weekend packages. $$$$

Doubletree Hotel. 16 Ella Grasso Turnpike (Route 75); (860) 627–5171. 200 rooms, 2 suites, indoor pool, sauna, fitness center, whirlpool, restaurant. $$$

Fairfield Inn by Marriott. 2 Loten Drive; (860) 627–9333 or (800) 228– 2800. 135 rooms, outdoor pool, continental breakfast. $$$

East Windsor

Follow Route 20 East from East Granby and pick up Route 140 East to get to East Windsor. Once the northernmost point that could be reached by steamboats before encountering rapids on the Connecticut River, it became a busy freshwater port with a crowded warehouse area still known as Warehouse Point. Now an interesting mix of suburban and rural areas, East Windsor holds a few treasures for families who look past the fast-food joints and businesses that line the main thoroughfares close to the airport and I–91.

Connecticut Trolley Museum (all ages)

58 North Road (Route 140); (860) 627–6540; www.ceraonline.org. Open Wednesday through Saturday from Memorial Day through Labor Day from 10:00 A.M. to 5:00 P.M. and Sunday, noon to 5:00 P.M.; Labor Day through late November and from April to Memorial Day on Saturday from 10:00 A.M. to 5:00 P.M. and on Sunday from noon to 5:00 P.M.; and from late November through December, Saturday 10:00 A.M. to 4:00 P.M. and Sunday noon to 4:00 P.M. Closed Thanksgiving Day, Christmas Eve, Christmas Day, and from January 1 through March 31. Also open weekday evenings during the Winterfest Light Display, from December 1 through 23. Adults $6.00; children 6 to 18 $3.00; children under 5 **free.** Includes admission to the adjacent fire museum. Festival admission $1.00–$2.00 more per ticket.

If the kids are fans of Mister Rogers Neighborhood, they may enjoy a ride on the real live trolleys that make 3.5-mile round-trip excursions through the East Windsor woodlands. The museum owns nearly eighty trolleys collected from all over the world. Half of these are housed in five storage barns; the remainder sit on the side of the tracks, waiting for restoration. Of the dozen or so that have been restored, two to eight may be out on the tracks on any given day. The cars run every fifteen minutes; your admission ticket buys you unlimited rides and a tour of the visitor center, which houses several restored cars, a steam locomotive (for Thomas the Tank Engine fans), and a large model trolley collection.

Come in October and December for special festivities. From mid-October to just before Halloween, come for the Pumpkin Patch ride on the weekends. Planned especially for children ages 3 to 10, it features games, treats, prizes, and rides to a nearby pumpkin field, where each rider chooses a pumpkin to take home. In December, the Winterfest features decorated cars and a canopy of colorful lights along the track through the woods. This evenings-only festival often begins shortly after Thanksgiving and goes on through December 30.

The museum has a Trolley Stop Snack Shop with a small outdoor seating area, rest rooms, and a trolley-car gift shop. Birthday parties and group outings can also be arranged here.

Connecticut Fire Museum (all ages)

58 North Road; (860) 623–4732; www.ctfiremuseum.org. Open in May and June on Saturday from 10:00 A.M. to 5:00 P.M. and Sunday noon to 5:00 P.M.; in July and August on Wednesday through Saturday and on Sunday at those same hours; and in September and October on weekends only, noon to 5:00 P.M. Adults $6.00; children 6 to 12 $3.00; children 5 and under free. Includes admission to the adjacent trolley museum.

This museum next door to the Connecticut Trolley Museum houses an amazing collection of vintage fire-fighting vehicles and equipment. An original 1904 switchboard alarm system, which still operates, is preserved exactly as it would have been used in decades past. The main hall contains twenty-one trucks, from a turn-of-the-century horse-drawn sleigh to a 1955 Zabek pumper. Other memorabilia, tools, and model fire trucks are also displayed. This museum is crowded and quite grimy, but if you love fire engines, this is the place to come.

Where to Eat

Maine Fish and Seafood Restaurant. Bridge Street (Route 140); (860) 623–2281. Seafood, sandwiches, burgers, and more. Open Monday through Saturday at 10:30 A.M. and Sunday at noon for lunch and dinner. $–$$

Where to Stay

Best Western Colonial Inn. 161 Bridge Street; (860) 623–9411. 120 rooms, outdoor pool, patio, and gardens, whirlpool, steam bath, restaurant, continental breakfast. $$$

Holiday Inn Express–Bradley Airport. 260 Main Street; (860) 627–6585. 115 rooms, continental breakfast, exercise room. $$$$

Manchester

First the summer camping ground of the Podunk Indians and later called "Silktown" because of its fabrics and paper mills, Manchester is now a mostly residential area just 9 miles to the east of Hartford. It seems that shopping mall developers like the open farmlands around Manchester, a fact that has forever altered the rural landscape outside of the historic town center. Visiting families may want to shop till they drop—or just drop in to one of Connecticut's children's museums and a few other attractions instead.

Lutz Children's Museum (ages 2 to 10)

247 South Main Street; (860) 643–0949; www.lutzmuseum.org. Open Tuesday and Wednesday noon to 5:00 P.M., Thursday and Friday 9:30 A.M. to 5:00 P.M., and Saturday and Sunday noon to 5:00 P.M. Admission $4.00.

Devoted to making interesting concepts in art, history, science, and nature accessible to children, the Lutz offers hands-on experiences for children from toddlerhood to 10. Special activities, experiments, and workshops lead to discoveries that are reinforced by the opportunity to participate. Live domestic, native, and exotic animals engage the youngest visitors most dramatically. Other do-touch exhibits on natural history and science capture the attention of older siblings. A large playground on the grounds provides an outlet for energy. Another outdoor portion of the museum is the **Oak Grove Nature Center** on Oak Grove Street. Its nature trails are open daily from dawn to dusk at no charge.

Connecticut Fire Museum (all ages)

Connecticut Firemen's Historical Society, 230 Pine Street; (860) 649–9436 or (860) 875–5002. Open mid-April through mid-November Friday and Saturday from 10:00 A.M. to 5:00 P.M. and Sunday from noon to 5:00 P.M. Adults $4.00; children $1.00; under 5 free.

If the trucks at the Connecticut Fire Museum in East Windsor weren't enough to please you, come here to see more. Located in a turn-of-the-century firehouse, the collection includes hand-pulled, horse-drawn, and motorized trucks and other fire-fighting equipment such as buckets, hats, helmets, tools, lanterns, and much more.

New England **Hobby Center**

Even if you have no hobbies, stop to see the sights in this amazing store, located at 71 Hilliard Street. Open year-round (but closed on Mondays), its customers come in search of its huge inventory of model railroad equipment and layout materials and its wonderful dollhouse furnishings and building materials. The big draws for tourists, however, are the twice-monthly Sunday afternoon (2:30 to 4:00 P.M. on the first and third weekends) shows put on by the **Silk City Model Railroad Club.** Watch the trains circle their marvelously detailed and extensive layouts, complete with lights, whistles, and other wonders. Call (860) 646–0610 for details.

Wickham Park (all ages)

1329 West Middle Turnpike; (860) 528–0856. Open April through October daily from 9:30 A.M. to dusk. Parking fee Monday through Thursday $1.00, Wednesday to Friday $2.00, weekends and holidays $3.00.

This former estate has a breathtaking spread of more than ten acres of formal ornamental gardens. Panoramic views of the woodlands, ponds, and brooks of the 215 acres of the park provide incentive to play and picnic here. Walking trails, a playground, an aviary, a log cabin, a snack bar, and sports facilities encourage daytripping families to stop for a break from the museums.

Where to Eat

Romanos Macaroni Grill. 170 Slater Street; (860) 648–8819. Primarily Italian food plus steaks, chops, chicken, for lunch and dinner from 11:30 A.M. daily. Kids' menu. Not exactly picturesque, but convenient, especially if you went to the mall. $–$$

Where to Stay

Clarion Suites Inn. 191 Spencer Street; (860) 643–5811 or (800) 992–4004. 104 suites with kitchen, dining area, living room, fireplace. Outdoor pool, sports court, exercise room. Pets welcome. Full breakfast. $$$$

Hartford

The hub of the county is, of course, the state's capitol city of Hartford. Connecticut's oldest city, it holds a wealth of historical, cultural, and educational attractions. Founded in 1636 by Thomas Hooker and his Puritan followers, Hartford evolved from a peaceful agrarian community to a bustling industrial metropolis by 1900. The first city in the United States to be fully electrified, Hartford was by that time reputedly the wealthiest city in the nation. Well-established as the center of the insurance industry, it was also a center for the production of firearms, machine tools, typewriters, and bicycles.

Hartford's neighborhoods grow more diverse with each wave of immigrants, and the people within the city limits invested their talents in building a city of "firsts." Bushnell Park was the first public park in the United States to be conceived, built, and paid for by its citizens through popular vote. Elizabeth Park Rose Garden was the first municipal rose garden in the country. The Wadsworth Atheneum was the nation's first public art museum. These and other important fixtures of the city provide ample incentive to explore Hartford time and time again. This guide contains only the best sites for families. Try to get your hands on a Greater Hartford tourism pamphlet for thumbnail descriptions of all of Hartford's excellent museums, parks, and historic sites.

Old State House (ages 4 and up)

800 Main Street; (860) 522–6766; www.ctosh.org. Open year-round, (except for major holidays), Monday through Friday from 10:00 A.M. to 4:00 P.M. and Saturday from 11:00 A.M. to 4:00 P.M. Free.

Many tourists begin a trip to Hartford here. Having recently undergone a complete restoration, the state house is the perfect place in which families can orient themselves to the city and gain some perspective on its laudable history. Designed by Charles Bulfinch and constructed in 1796, on the site of the founding of the colony in 1636 by Thomas Hooker, the building is the oldest state house in the nation, established in service of the American people and their new Constitution.

The site on which George Washington greeted French General Rochambeau in 1780 when he arrived to assist the Patriot cause, the halls of the Old State House have also echoed with the footsteps of Lafayette, Andrew Jackson, and many other principal players of American history. Both the *Amistad* and the Prudence Crandall trials took place here. If you are thinking that this must be, therefore, a dusty, stodgy relic that expects quiet awe from whispering students on class trips, you've made a terrible mistake.

The beautifully restored Old State House is anything but stodgy. With public rest rooms, total handicapped (and stroller) accessibility, public telephones, and signage in five languages plus Braille, the building is bright, sparkling, and airy in spite of its hallowed halls reputation. It invites—yes, *invites*—children to touch, to run, to cheer, to ask questions. Costumed guides working in character bring history to life in every area of every floor. You may meet some of Connecticut's most famous citizens here—each of them a real blast from the past.

In addition to a museum store (which specializes in Connecticut-made crafts), concert halls, and gallery exhibits of art and history, a visitor center directs you to the city's best places to be. Bring a sturdy bag if you want to add to your supply of brochures. On the second floor is Steward's Museum, a re-creation of the state's first museum, founded by Joseph Steward, collector of everything extraordinary, impossible, and downright fraudulent. A smorgasbord of delights Barnumesque in nature, the museum has among its many wonders a unicorn's horn, an elephant's molar, a whole Bengal tiger, and an ostrich egg, just to name a few.

Wadsworth Atheneum (ages 4 and up)

600 Main Street; (860) 278–2670; www.wadsworthatheneum.org. Open daily year-round except on Monday and major holidays. From 11:00 A.M. to 5:00 P.M. Tuesday through Sunday; open until 8:00 P.M. on first Thursday. Adults $9.00; students 13 through college $5.00; children 12 and under free. Free **to all on Thursday and before noon on Saturday.**

Just two blocks from the Old State House is the Wadsworth Atheneum, a midsized museum housing more than 45,000 works from ancient to modern times. The nation's oldest continuously operating public art museum, the atheneum has a well-deserved reputation as one of the finest museums of its kind in the United States. An excellent collection of nineteenth-century French and American Impressionist masters, major works from the Hudson River School, Old Master paintings, American and European decorative arts, a costume and textile gallery, several rooms from important architectural periods, the *Amistad* collection of African-American art, a gallery of contemporary art, and much more are part of the attraction here.

The museum offers a wonderful service to children—ask the folks at the main desk for

"art cards," which make the museum appealing to and manageable for kids. Each of the fifteen or more colorful cards has a game, a search, or an idea for exploring the galleries with young children.

The museum's cafeteria has a children's menu, the exceptional gift shop is a place in which you could do all your holiday shopping, and the calendar of events includes films, workshops, concerts, and tours for families with young children. Special family activities and gallery tours directed to children are offered on Shawmut First Thursdays, each first Thursday of the month. An annual festival of holiday trees is staged each December.

Bushnell Park and Carousel (all ages)

Elm Street and Jewell Street; (860) 987–5900; www.bushnellpark.org. Park open daily year-round, dawn to dusk; free. Carousel open mid-April to mid-May and in September on weekends only from 11:00 A.M. to 5:00 P.M. Also open from mid-May through August on Tuesday through Sunday from 11:00 A.M. to 5:00 P.M.; 50 cents per ride.

Just west of Hartford's Ancient Burying Ground Cemetery on Main Street, pass under the Soldiers and Sailors Memorial Arch on Jewell Street at the entrance to the park.

Spend some time exploring the park, which is America's oldest public park, established in 1854. Landscaped as an arboretum, its plantings, monuments, fountains, and bridges are pointed out in the wonderful free pamphlet called *Bushnell Park Tree Walks,* available in the Old State House, the Capitol Building, or from the DEP office at 165 Capitol Avenue. Guided tours of the park can also be arranged; call (860) 232–6710 or visit the Web site. An art gallery showing works by local artists is in the park's pumphouse, which is an actual working pump station for the city's flood control authority. Throughout the park are statues of famous Connecticut citizens, such as Israel Putnam, and monuments honoring veterans of foreign wars. The memorial arch, for instance, is dedicated to the 4,000 Hartford citizens who served in the Civil War. This huge sandstone arch depicts scenes from the war on its terra-cotta frieze. After you pass through the arch, immediately look to your left and you'll find the Bushnell Park Carousel in a low, brown pavilion with stained-glass windows encircling its upper walls.

Managed for the City of Hartford by the New England Carousel Museum in Bristol, this gorgeous 1914 carousel was hand carved by master craftsmen Stein and Goldstein; its band organ is a 1924 Wurlitzer. Charming murals, lit by 800 lights, portray the seasons of the year. Forty-eight exceptionally well-restored prancing horses on gleaming brass poles provide the best carousel ride we had in the state. Thirty-six of the steeds are jumpers, which go up and down; the rest are stationary. Two ornate chariots complete the set. Compared to other carousels we rode, this carousel is *fast.* Hold onto toddlers, parents, and don't be fooled by the slower warm-up of the first pass. You'll pay 50 cents per ride, so bring a pocketful of change. I think you'll ride this one more than once. If you're in the city on December 31, come for the carousel's First Night celebration, a great way to hail the New Year. You might also enjoy the Haunted Carousel festivities in late October, of course, for Halloween.

Hartford **Extras**

If you are on a whirlwind tour of Hartford, visit the above-described attractions first. If your schedule allows other pleasures, choose from among the following sites.

- **Connecticut Historical Society.** 1 Elizabeth Street; (860) 236–5621; www.chs.org. A beautiful facility with hundreds of products, furnishings, artifacts, and portraits related to Connecticut history. Open noon to 5:00 P.M. Tuesday through Sunday. Adults $6.00; children $3.00. Excellent multimedia exhibit on the *Amistad* incident. Great library, great bookstore, family events throughout year. Look for new Connecticut History Center in 2008.

- **Charter Oak Landing.** Riverfront Plaza; follow signs from Brainard Road exit off I–91; (860) 722–6505. Thankfully rescued from decay as part of the work of an organization called Riverfront Recapture (860–293–0131; www.riverfront.org), the plaza has a playground, gazebo, benches, walkways, a boat launch, and tons of activities from the arts to sports. It is now linked to Great River Park across the river. Riverside Park is also right nearby. Check the Web site or call either phone number to get schedule of events, or just grab a picnic and have a good time here.

- **Travelers Tower.** 1 Tower Square; (860) 277–4208. If it's a clear day, this is a great place to have a look at the lay of the land. Elevator ride, then 100 stairs. Year-round, but **free** tours mid-May to late October. Check out the Website: hartford.omaxfield.com/travelers.html.

- **Museum of American Political Life.** University of Hartford, 200 Bloomfield Avenue, West Hartford; (860) 768–4090. Exhibits on the right to vote, the political party system, the history of American presidential campaigns, the influence of media on elections, the processes of reform and protest, and more. Interesting folk art, posters, buttons, and other memorabilia. Tuesday through Friday 11:00 A.M. to 4:00 P.M. Donation.

- **Menczer Historical Museum of Medicine and Dentistry.** The Hartford Medical Society, 230 Scarborough Street; (860) 236–5613. Nine rooms of instruments, equipment, furnishings, medications, and portraits related to medicine and dentistry from the eighteenth through twentieth centuries. Recreation of a 1920s dental office and special focus on Horace Wells, the Hartford dentist who pioneered use of dental anesthesia.

- **Bushnell Memorial Hall.** 166 Capitol Avenue; (860) 246–6807. Designed in the 1930s by the architects of New York City's Radio City Music Hall, this National Historic Landmark has a year-round slate of top-billed performing arts, including a family matinee series. Home of Connecticut Opera, Hartford Ballet, Hartford Symphony. Promenade Gallery features works of area artists. Visitors are welcome to see the theater; forty-five-minute backstage tours are available year-round on Wednesday and Thursday from 11:00 A.M. to 3:00 P.M. Call (860) 987–6087.

State Capitol Building (ages 6 and up)

210 Capitol Avenue; (860) 240–0222; www.cga.state.ct.us/capitoltours. Free one-hour tours of the capitol and the Legislative Office Building year-round on weekdays on the quarter hours between 9:15 A.M. and 1:15 P.M. and on Saturday from April through October between 10:15 A.M. and 2:15 P.M. In July and August, a 2:15 P.M. tour is added on the weekdays. Closed on state holidays.

When you escape the enchanting music of the Wurlitzer, you might notice the gleaming gold dome of the state capitol building high on the hill to the right (or west) of the carousel. You can't miss it, actually. It's the icing on a rather overstated piece of cake, so to speak. Opened in 1879, the Connecticut State Capitol Building's architecture has been the subject of much commentary. Words like "monstrosity" have been used to describe this remarkable structure, but few families will be offended by its departures from architectural purism. To a child, this behemoth is just grand.

You can take a guided tour or stroll here yourselves. Pick up a self-guided tour brochure in Room 101 (to your left and toward the back of the lobby if you've entered from the front vestibule). The tour includes visits to the public galleries of the assembly rooms, explanations of the functions of major offices, and information on how a bill becomes law.

If you are touring on your own, your first stop might be the main rotunda from which you can look up at the magnificent dome. The first floor also includes several pieces of sculpture—some huge, some graceful, like the young Nathan Hale. A large collection of Civil War memorabilia in the west wing is impressive; it includes uniforms, many former U.S. flags, and the equipment of important personages.

Museum of Connecticut History (ages 8 and up)

231 Capitol Avenue; (860) 566–3056; www.cslib.org/museum.htm. Open year-round, Monday through Friday from 9:00 A.M. to 4:00 P.M., Saturday from 9:00 A.M. to 3:00 P.M. Closed on Sunday and state holidays. Free.

This beautiful collection is housed in the same magnificent building as the Connecticut Supreme Court and the Connecticut State Library, opposite the capitol building. Check out the library's incredible main reading room while you are here. The museum exhibits include all aspects of Connecticut history from all periods, with examples of Connecticut products such as Colt firearms, clocks, hats, furniture, and much more. See the table on which Lincoln signed the Emancipation Proclamation. See the 1622 Royal Charter of the Colony of Connecticut. Have a look at the portraits of Connecticut's governors.

Changing exhibitions, special tours, and events of interest to families are on the calendar. This museum is well worth a second day in the city—if your kids are old enough to appreciate it, move this to day one.

Silver Star and *Mark Twain* **Riverboat Rides** (all ages)

Deep River Navigation Company, Charter Oak Landing and Riverfront Plaza; (860) 526–4954 or (877) MKTWAIN; www.marktwaincruises.com. Tuesday through Sunday, May 10 to September 30; Wednesday through Sunday, October 1 to 26. Mark Cruises vary from forty-five minutes to three hours and cost approximately $8.00 to $35.00 per adult, depending on length of cruise, entertainment, and food service. Children 3 to 11 pay typically half-fare (unless lunch is provided); children under 3 are free.

Get a Connecticut River view of the city from the deck of a real riverboat. On the *NV Silver Star,* the lunchtime and afternoon cruises give folks a chance to remember that the great river still flows in this once-neglected, now-recovering area. Go to Wethersfield Cove downriver or to the riverside parks upriver or to the ferry landing at Rocky Hill.

For the *Mark Twain's* lunchtime tours, you can choose from the forty-five-minute Grab and Go Cruise or the ninety-minute Riverboat Lunch cruise. You can also take the Tequila Sunset Music Cruise (7:30 to 10:00 P.M.) complete with DJ, or the ninety-minute cocktail cruise, which is very popular with families. Bring a picnic basket or buy hot dogs, pizzas, snacks, and beverages on board.

These cruises have somewhat less of a historical/ environmental air than those on the *Silver Star* and more the feel of a hospitality/party excursion. The *NV Mark Twain* has two dining rooms and an open sundeck. Among other popular choices for families are its Wednesday night Clambake Cruise and its Sunday Family Ice Cream Cruise (3:00 P.M.) and Sunday Supper Cruise (5:00 P.M.). All include food service and are often sellouts, so reserve early. Call for current hours and prices.

Elizabeth Park and Rose Gardens (all ages)

Prospect and Asylum Avenues; (860) 722–6514 or (860) 231–9443; www.elizabethpark.org. Open daily year-round, dawn to dusk. Greenhouses open Monday through Friday, except holidays, from 8:00 A.M. to 3:00 P.M. Free.

The first municipal rose garden in the country, this beautiful park has 15,000 rose bushes of 800 varieties. With lanes, arbors, and gazebos that bring *The Secret Garden* to mind, the formal garden is most glorious in late spring and throughout summer. Truly a haven within the bustle of the city, Elizabeth Park's rock gardens, ornamental grasses, perennial and herb beds, and a trail through its forest of specimen trees make it a lovely spot to play.

Special events such as concerts, poetry readings, or storytellings are sometimes on the calendar here. Check the Web site calendar for events that might interest your family. In mid-June come to the park's gala celebration of peak rose season. Called Rose Weekend, the event features music, food, art, tours, and activities for the whole family.

The park extends across Prospect Avenue to acres of athletic fields and a children's play area with swings, tennis courts, and a picnic grove. The Elizabeth Park Overlook provides a panoramic view of the city as well as a gorgeous spot to watch the sun rise. Frisbee players, kite flyers, joggers, rollerbladers, bicyclers, and brides and grooms regularly inhabit this space in spring, summer, and fall. In winter you can sled on the huge hill near the Overlook or skate (conditions permitting) on the pond. The **Pond House Cafe** (860–231–8823) is open from Tuesday through Saturday for lunch from 11:00 A.M. to 2:30 P.M. and for dinner from 5:00 to 9:00 P.M. or for Sunday brunch from 10:00 A.M. to 2:30 P.M.

Mark Twain House and Museum Center (ages 6 and up)

351 Farmington Avenue, at Woodland Street; (860) 247–0998; www.MarkTwainHouse.org. Open year-round, daily May through October and the month of December on Monday through Saturday from 9:30 A.M. to 4:00 P.M. and on Sunday from noon to 4:00 P.M., and January through April and in November at same hours but closed on Tuesday. Closed January 1, Easter Sunday, Thanksgiving, and December 24 and 25. Adults $16.00; youth 13 to 18 $12.00; children 6 to 12 $8.00; children under 6 free. Last tour 4:00 P.M. daily.

Next on a must-do tour of Hartford is the home of novelist Samuel Langhorne Clemens, who gained fame as Mark Twain. It is located on a property known as Nook Farm, once the site of a lively community of artists, writers, and other literate folk. Quite bucolic in the last decades of the nineteenth century, Nook Farm is now nearly eclipsed by the sprawl of Hartford and its suburb of West Hartford. Nevertheless, the homes and grounds give visitors a sense of the area's former air of gentility and simplicity.

Of course, simplicity is nowhere to be found in the Twain house. The Gilded Age with all its splendid cacophony of detail is apparent in every inch of this remarkable home. Guided tours here are among the most excellent tours we have taken in the state. You will hear marvelous tales of the family's life and a generous sampling of the sardonic wit and wisdom of its owner. While living here from 1874 to 1891 with his wife, Olivia, and their three daughters, Samuel Clemens wrote *Tom Sawyer, Huckleberry Finn, The Prince and the Pauper, A Connecticut Yankee in King Arthur's Court,* and *Life on the Mississippi.*

The nineteen rooms of the house are restored to reflect its appearance in 1881, when the house was redecorated by a guild of artisans including Louis Comfort Tiffany. The tour includes the family living quarters and Twain's private study (where he did much of his writing). Nearly half the decorations and furnishings in the house were owned by the family, including many photographs, a feature that gives the suggestion that Twain himself might appear in a doorway at any moment.

Brand-new in 2003 is a magnificent three-story Museum Center with exhibit spaces, a lecture hall, classrooms, a museum store, and a 75-seat cafe with an outdoor terrace.

Harriet Beecher Stowe Center (ages 6 and up)

77 Forest Street at Farmington Avenue; (860) 522–9258; www.harrietbeecherstowecenter. org. Open year-round Tuesday through Saturday from 9:30 A.M. to 4:30 P.M. and Sunday noon to 4:30 P.M. Open on Monday also from Memorial Day through Columbus Day and in December. Closed major holidays. Adults $6.50; children 6 to 16 $2.75. Children 5 and under are free.

Just across the lawn from the Twain House is the 1871 cottage built for Mrs. Stowe and her family. The house is austere compared to its gaudy neighbor, but it is in itself a serenely beautiful Victorian dwelling that has been restored in every detail. The last residence of Harriet Beecher Stowe, whose *Uncle Tom's Cabin* can be said to have changed the course of U.S. history, this house is furnished mostly with items belonging to the Stowe family. The kitchen is patterned closely after the model kitchen described by Stowe and her sister Catherine in their book *The American Woman's Home*. In this home, too, one fairly expects its owner to step into the room and continue the grand tour.

Docents here present the center's renewed emphasis on family-friendly tours. When you visit, you can expect tours tailored to the interests of any children present. The house is filled with many decorative artworks done by Stowe herself. An accomplished painter, she often painted the flowers she loved to grow in her gardens. Outside, the gardens have been replanted with the many exotic and native perennials that Stowe grew here before her death in 1896.

Tours of the Stowe house include a trip to her niece's house on the corner of the Nook Farm property at Farmington Avenue and Forest Street. The Katherine Seymour Day House contains personal belongings of Harriet Beecher Stowe and excellent historical exhibits that explain the effect of *Uncle Tom's Cabin* on the abolitionist movement and the Civil War. It also includes exhibits on nineteenth-century architecture, decorative arts, history, and literature. An extensive research library on these subjects as well as social reform, the women's suffrage movement, and women's studies in general is also open by appointment. Children are welcome to use the library. A letter of recommendation from a teacher or librarian is necessary to gain access.

Tour tickets are purchased in the Carriage House Visitors Center, which houses an introductory exhibit on the Beecher family as well as an excellent gift shop. The Stowe Center hosts a few annual events designed especially for children. A celebration of Mrs. Stowe's birthday is among these; it is typically in mid-June. Check the center's Web site for the dates this year and for other events.

Where to Eat

Black-Eyed Sallys. 350 Asylum Street; (860) 278–RIBS. Award-winning cajun, creole, and barbecue, gumbo, grits, collard greens—all the real, down-home Southern cooking you can eat. Come for po' boy sandwiches or pulled pork or chicken or chicken-fried steak, at lunch or at dinner. Absolutely delicious. The joint hops after 9:00 P.M. with the best blues open-mike jam anywhere around; come early with the kids. $–$$$

In the city's South End is Franklin Avenue, also known as Hartford's Little Italy. Stroll the sidewalks between Elliot and Eaton Streets and search for your own favorite eatery among the espresso cafes, bakeries, grocers, and full-service restaurants. Our favorite is **Carbone's** (860–296–9646; 588 Franklin Avenue). Pricey but delicious. Children very welcome among adult diners. $$$

Where to Stay

The Goodwin. 1 Hayes Street, at Goodwin Square, opposite the Civic Center; (860) 246–7500 or (800) 777–7803. 124 units, including 11 suites, restaurant, health facilities. $$$$

Hilton Hartford Hotel. 315 Trumbull Street at the Civic Center; (860) 728–5151 or (800) 325–3535. 390 units including 6 suites, restaurant, health club, sauna, indoor pool. $$$$

Crown Plaza Hartford–Downtown. 50 Morgan Street; (860) 549–2400. 350 units, restaurant, exercise room, outdoor pool. $$$

Ramada Inn by Marriott Hartford Downtown. 942 Main Street, near Market Street; (860) 524–5550 or (800) 331–3131. 120 rooms, studios, and suites. In-room kitchens, complimentary hot breakfast buffet. Restaurant. $$$$

West Hartford

West Hartford sashays outward from the left of Hartford just as smoothly as Fred Astaire and with just as much debonair grace. In its upscale downtown less than 5 miles from downtown Hartford you'll find terrific shops and restaurants and a couple of attractions great for a family day trip. Peruse the boutiques, visit the Noah Webster House, spend some time at the Science Center of Connecticut, and have dinner at one of nearly thirty restaurants.

Noah Webster House/Museum of West Hartford History
(ages 6 and up) 🏛

227 South Main Street; (860) 521–5362; www.noahwebsterhouse.org. Open for tours September through June, Monday and Thursday through Sunday from 1:00 to 4:00 P.M., and July through August on Monday, Thursday, and Friday from 11:00 A.M. to 4:00 P.M. and on Saturday and Sunday from 1:00 to 4:00 P.M. Last tour 3:00 P.M. Call for extended summer hours and holiday closings. Adults $5.00; children 13 to 18 $3.00; children 6 to 12 $1.00; under 6 free.

The birthplace and childhood home of the author of the first American dictionary, Noah Webster House is one of the best colonial restorations in the state, not least of all because it was the home of one of America's finest citizens. An excellent short film introduces visitors to Noah's story and the history of the house, and guided tours by costumed docents fill in the gaps of the tale.

The house has an active calendar of family and children's events—genealogy workshops, open-hearth cooking, colonial dancing and games, and more. Children going into grades four, five, and six can participate in the Colonial Child Summer Camp, a week of activities typical of an eighteenth-century childhood.

Even if you come only for the day, you'll see Noah Webster's desk and clocks and 200 original editions of his books, including his *Blue-Backed Speller* and the dictionary he spent nearly twenty-seven years writing.

The Science Center of Connecticut (all ages)

950 Trout Brook Drive; (860) 231–2824; www.sciencecenterct.org. Open year-round, Monday through Saturday 10:00 A.M. to 5:00 P.M. and Sunday from noon to 5:00 P.M. Closed on Easter, Thanksgiving, and Christmas. Adults $7.00; children 3 to 11 $5.00; children under 3 free. Planetarium and laser shows are an additional charge, which varies according to program.

One of the best interactive science and technology museums in the state, this center has made huge strides recently toward becoming one of the best in the nation. The newest areas of the facility have at their heart the Science Center's guiding philosophy that scientific principles are best learned through experience as well as explanation. The marvelously engaging exhibits are interactive, allowing children and adults to discover a range of scientific facts or truths and to conduct experiments that reinforce those findings.

In the main exhibition hall, major changing exhibitions run approximately two months. The live animal center has a diverse collection of birds, reptiles, and mammals from around the world. In the Idea Zone, play with bubbles, learn about gears and motion, or race a car on the LEGO racetrack. In the Kids Factory, young visitors (ages 4 to 7, especially) explore light, color, water, and communications. In the Zoom Zone, conduct experiments and find solutions with hands-on science and math activities. The Long Island Sound touch tank offers a chance to learn about marine ecology, and the outdoor paleo-pit simulates an archaeological dig. The world's largest walk-in kaleidoscope, a model of the Hubble Space telescope, and an outdoor full-scale walk-in model of Connecticut's state animal, the sperm whale, are all part of the current museum.

The Gengras Planetarium explores the sun, stars, and galaxy along with daily laser light shows. Evening laser shows feature rock, country, classical, and jazz programs. Many shows are accompanied by environmental or mythical narratives.

Where to Eat

Back Porch Bistro. 971 Farmington Avenue (rear); (860) 231–1922. Friendly service, cheerful decor, tasty American fare. Outside dining in season. Open from 11:30 A.M. Monday through Friday for lunch, and from 5:00 P.M. Monday through Saturday for dinner. $$

A. C. Petersen Farms Restaurant. 240 Park Road; (860) 233–8483. Open for breakfast, lunch, and dinner from 7:00 A.M. to 11:00 P.M., this landmark is newly renovated but still old-fashioned at heart. Great traditional American meals and terrific ice cream, perfect for families. $–$$

Where to Stay

West Hartford Inn. 900 Farmington Avenue; (860) 236–3221. 50 units, exercise room, restaurant, continental breakfast. $$$

Farmington

From West Hartford take Route 4 south to the pristinely restored seventeenth-, eighteenth-, and nineteenth-century homes that line the main street of affluent and elegant Farmington. From these homes to the prestigious Miss Porter's School to the upscale shops and restaurants, Farmington presents the polished side of Hartford County. Having played a principal role in the *Amistad* story, Farmington also was a principal station on the Underground Railroad, contributing to its importance in the history of the state and the nation.

Farmington Historical Society Tours of the *Amistad* Sites
(ages 8 and up)

Main Street; (860) 678–1645. Tours arranged by appointment only. The fee is $3.00 per person with a $24.00 minimum.

This organization has created a guided tour of the nine Farmington sites associated with the Africans of the *Amistad*. Visit the places where the Africans lived and studied while in Farmington; see the gravesite of one who lost his life. Tour the hall where abolitionists met and the homes and churches of citizens who spoke out against slavery and in support of the *Amistad* group. Most of the sites are in private hands today, so a tour provides the best and easiest access.

Hill-Stead Museum (ages 8 and up)

35 Mountain Road; (860) 677–9064 or (860) 677–4787. Open May through October, Tuesday through Sunday 10:00 A.M. to 5:00 P.M. and November through April, Tuesday through Sunday 11:00 A.M. to 4:00 P.M. One-hour guided tour; last tour an hour before closing. Adults $9.00; students $7.00; children 6 to 12 $4.00; under 6 free.

This Colonial Revival home is not the place to come with small, squirmy folk who'd rather be chasing the butterflies on the gorgeous front lawn of this 150-acre country estate. It is, however, a fine place to come if you and the children would like to see the magnificent artworks that hang in the mansion designed by Stanford White and owner Theodate Pope Riddle, herself an architect. The house is beyond reproach in its taste and gentility as well as its elegant design, and its outstanding art collection is unparalleled by other house museums. Cassatt, Degas, Manet, Monet, and other French and American Impressionists are on the walls of this beautiful home. The decorative arts are of the caliber that make docents turn ashen at the sight of toddlers. School tours are common here, however, and the docents are warmly welcoming and comfortable with youngsters.

Be sure to stroll the wonderfully restored sunken garden and walk the wooded paths through the naturalized bulbs and wildflowers.

Stanley-Whitman House (ages 6 and up)

37 High Street; (860) 677–9222. Open year-round, May through October from Wednesday through Sunday from noon to 4:00 P.M. and on Saturday and Sunday only at the same times from November through April. Adults $5.00; children 6 to 18 $2.00.

An impeccable restoration of this 1720 house brings the period alive again in this amazingly well-curated site. Tours include a peek behind the scenes through windowlike panels that offer a look at early-eighteenth-century construction methods. Some programs here are directed toward children. Call to ask for details, because those events will be of the most value to families. Among the other inside points of interest are a gift shop and an exhibit of archaeological artifacts and discoveries. Outside is a kitchen herb garden.

The *Amistad* Story

From Havana, Cuba, on June 28, 1839, the Spanish ship *Amistad* set sail with fifty-three Africans who had been taken from their homeland to be sold as slaves. On their way to another part of Cuba for what they knew would be a lifetime of enslavement and hard labor, the captives, led by Joseph Cinque, seized control of the ship and forced its owners to set a course for Africa. Under cover of night, however, the navigators charted a northward course, hoping to reach an American slave state before their plot was discovered. Instead, the boat sailed into Long Island Sound, where it was apprehended by the U.S. Navy and taken into custody in New Haven. A two-year trial in which the Africans were defended by John Quincy Adams centered on the question of whether the captives were to be considered slave or free. Eventually declared free, the *Amistad* Africans were sent to Farmington to live while funds were raised to return them to the area in Africa now called Sierra Leone. Thirty-seven survivors from the original group set sail for home as free people again in November 1841, reaching their home shores in January 1842. Nine sites linked to the case and to the lives of the Africans during the waiting period remain in Farmington.

Day-Lewis Museum (ages 6 and up)
158 Main Street; (860) 678–1645. Open only on Wednesday from 2:00 to 4:00 P.M., except in August and December through February. Call ahead to be sure of hours. Adults $2.00; children $1.00.

This small museum, owned by Yale University, is in a colonial post-and-beam house on a piece of property discovered to be the site of human habitation 10,000 years ago. The Native American artifacts unearthed at the site during an archaeological dig are on display here.

Winding Trails Cross-Country Ski Center (ages 4 and up)

50 Winding Trails Drive, off Route 4; (860) 678–9582. Open daily 9:00 A.M. to 4:30 P.M., weather permitting. Weekend and holiday trail fees are posted each season for adults and children 5 to 12. Children under 5 are always free. Weekdays are less expensive than weekends. Rentals of skis also have adults and children's prices. Sleds are rented for two-hour periods. Call for the current rates.

For more than twenty years, this pretty 350-acre property has been the site of a 20-kilometer trail system for cross-country skiers. Skaters will love the eight-acre natural ice rink on picturesque Walton Pond. Through woodland and past brooks and other spring-fed ponds, the trails are groomed daily and are clearly mapped and posted with signs noting degrees of difficulty.

Rental skis are available here, as are wooden toddler sleds so the whole family can enjoy a healthy day in the crisp air. You can also try out demo equipment and purchase equipment of your own in the retail shop. Waxes, gloves, and hats are among the other goods you can buy in the shop.

The Winding Trails Lodge offers a place for you to warm your toes by the fireplace and wrap your cold fingers around a warm mug of cocoa. If you prefer, remain outside at the tables near the snow-draped pines.

Instruction is offered to beginners on weekends at 9:30 and 11:00 A.M., 1:00 and 2:30 P.M., and 10:00 A.M. and 1:00 P.M. on weekdays.

Balloons over the Farmington Valley

Although not in the budget for most families, one of central Connecticut's most famous activities is hot-air ballooning. I've heard that these excursions are incredibly beautiful, incredibly quiet, incredibly wonderful. If you can spare $200 or more per person to sail skyward over the Farmington Valley for about an hour, call these companies, which, weather permitting, will cruise over the Farmington Valley year-round seven days a week usually just after sunrise or a few hours before sunset. Apparently there is no better way to see Connecticut's countryside.

- Airvertising & Airventures, West Simsbury (860) 651–4441
- Berkshire Balloons, Southington (203) 250–8441
- Emerald City Balloons, Manchester (860) 647–8581
- Kat Balloons, Inc., Farmington (860) 678–7921
- Livingston Balloon Company, Simsbury (860) 651–1110
- Sky Endeavors, Bloomfield (860) 242–0228
- Steppin' Up Balloons, Southbury (203) 264–0013

Where to Eat

TGIFridays. On Route 4; (860) 561–4930. Enormous menu, fast service, and affordable prices make mealtime happy. $–$$

Chuck's Steak House. 788 Farmington Avenue at intersection of Routes 4 and 10; (860) 677–7677. Open for dinner from 4:00 P.M. Monday through Sunday; lunch only on Sunday from noon. Steaks, chicken, salad bar 24 feet long! $$–$$$

Where to Stay

Centennial Inn Suites. 5 Spring Lane; (860) 677–4647 or (800) 852–2052. Elegant country inn with 112 suites with kitchen, living room, fireplace, and one or two bedrooms. Outdoor pool, whirlpool, continental breakfast. Pets welcome. $$$$

Hartford Marriott Hotel–Farmington. 15 Farm Springs Road; (860) 678–1000. 381 units, restaurant, health club, indoor and outdoor pools, tennis, game room, jogging trail. $$$$

The Farmington Inn. 827 Farmington Avenue; (860) 677–2821 or (800) 648–9804. 72 units, with 13 suites, restaurant, passes to health club, continental breakfast. $$$$

New Britain/Kensington

Ten miles southeast of Hartford is the small city of New Britain, once nicknamed "Hardware City" with an ethnic population that included every major European nation and most of the minor ones. The steady pace at the Stanley tool works has slowed in recent years, and the immigrant groups have mixed and changed, but the city is much the same—a modest metropolis with a low-key reputation that keeps it well out of the limelight. It has some special treasures, though, inside its city limits and in nearby Kensington. Less than 5 miles southeast of downtown New Britain on Route 372, the small town of Kensington is home to Hungerford Park and the Youth Museum's nature center.

New Britain Youth Museum (ages 2 to 12)

30 High Street; (860) 225–3020; www.newbritainyouthmuseum.org. Open year-round, Tuesday through Friday from 1:00 to 5:00 P.M. and on Saturday from 10:00 A.M. to 4:00 P.M. Free.

The New Britain Youth Museum is not new, it's not big, it's not slick or sleek or sophisticated. Some days it's downright sleepy, and on most days there are just a few activities in its mere two rooms of exhibits. Still, it is a two-thumbs-up terrific place for kids. At this little wonder you may see, like we have, some of the best exhibitions you've seen anywhere.

You also may participate in some of the best and least expensive children's workshops offered anywhere.

Curated by its ever-creative director, Deborah Pfeiffenberger, the museum has an extensive permanent collection of dolls and toys, and a continuing focus on historical and cultural artifacts of childhood. An exhibit called *Journey Through Time* presents the prehistory of Connecticut. Explore geology, dinosaurs, and the native human history of the state here. It also has a terrific puppet theater area and a wonderful outdoor play area called Garden Tales, where children learn about botany and fairy tales all in the same space. Share a storybook or find such native plants as goat's beard in this charming area. For information on the museum's natural history exhibits at Hungerford Park in Kensington, see the separate entry on the next page.

New Britain Museum of American Art (all ages)

56 Lexington Street; (860) 229–0257; www.nbmaa.org. Open year-round, Tuesday, Thursday, Friday, and Sunday noon to 5:00 P.M.; Saturday 10:00 A.M. to 5:00 P.M., Wednesday noon to 7:00 P.M. Closed Monday and holidays. Adults $6.00; students $4.00; children under 12 free. Saturday from 10:00 A.M. to noon is free for everyone.

If you have never taken the children to an art museum, begin here. Perfect for young families because of its manageable size, this attraction is in every way a gem. Housed in a beautiful early-twentieth-century mansion built by William Hart, founder of the Stanley Works tool company, the museum has an unusually welcoming ambience and excellent tour materials. A poster perched on an easel in the foyer captures the essence of the museum's philosophy: "Whenever you visit the New Britain Museum of American Art, we want you to feel free to laugh, talk, take the kids, hold hands, ask questions, voice an opinion, bring a date, gawk, express yourself, learn something new, stay as long as you like, come back again."

Walnut Hill Park

The New Britain Museum of American Art overlooks **Walnut Hill Park,** designed by Frederick Law Olmsted, who also designed New York City's Central Park. Its sweeping lawns and towering oak trees make it a perfect place to play or picnic. A children's playground, playing fields, and bicycle paths make the park a family destination. A summer music festival at the Miller Bandshell is held in July and August on Monday and Wednesday evenings at 7:30 P.M. at no charge. An annual American Arts and Crafts Fair in mid-September includes admission to the nearby museum for the $6.00 entrance fee.

Visitors are invited to touch the woodwork and sit in the furniture, and the tour book adds, "By the way, do not feel anxious if your children are a bit noisy or active. We are delighted to have visitors of all ages." In fact, they have created an exceptionally good tour book called *Looking at Art* just for the children. Also for children are special programs such as the Creativity Hour, held after school the first Thursday of every month in the school year. Come sketch and learn along with a museum educator and special guest artists and poets.

The museum's 5,000 holdings from the early eighteenth century to the present include some of the greatest treasures of American art. Gilbert Stuart, Asher Durand, Thomas Cole, Frederic Church, Winslow Homer, Maxfield Parrish, John Singer Sargent, Mary Cassatt, Childe Hassam, Georgia O'Keeffe, N. C. Wyeth, Andrew Wyeth, Norman Rockwell, and Thomas Hart Benton are just some of the artists represented here.

Copernican Space Science Observatory and Planetarium
(ages 4 and up)

1615 Stanley Street, Central Connecticut State University; (860) 832–3399 or (860) 832–2950. Planetarium shows year-round on Friday and Saturday 8:30 P.M.; special children's shows 7:00 P.M. on Friday, 1:30 P.M. on Saturday. Adults pay $3.50; children 5 to 12 $2.50. Closed on state holidays.

This observatory boasts one of the largest public telescopes in the United States. Special programs on a variety of fascinating themes related to the stars and space science are offered throughout the year for both children and adults. Exhibits on flight and the American space program are adjacent to the observatory and planetarium.

New Britain Youth Museum at Hungerford Park (ages 2 to 10)

191 Farmington Avenue (Route 372); (860) 827–9064; www.newbritainyouthmuseum.org. Trails open dawn to dusk; free of charge. Exhibit Hall admission $2.00 adults; $1.00 children 2 to 17; under 2 free. Live-animal programs on Saturday at 11:00 A.M., 1:30 P.M., and 3:30 P.M. year-round; open to those who have paid admission. Open year-round, Tuesday through Friday 1:00 to 5:00 P.M. and Saturday 10:00 A.M. to 5:00 P.M. Closed on Sunday and Monday.

Located on twenty-seven acres of wooded park, swamp, pond, and wetland habitats, the New Britain Youth Museum at Hungerford Park represents the natural history collection of the museum. Indoor exhibits are housed in a restored 1920s show-horse stable. Long-term exhibits are stimulating and detailed, changing sometimes in just a season or lasting a year or two. We have observed outstanding exhibits here, curated by the remarkable Ann Peabody.

A weather station, aquariums, terrariums, an iguana rain forest habitat complete with waterfall, and a small variety of animals are also indoors. Outside the main exhibit hall are extensive and wonderful gardens, designed as sensory experiences for the visitors who are welcomed to taste, feel, look, smell, and touch the plants.

A pig, goat, steer, sheep, and turkeys, ducks, and geese are among the animals in the Hungerford Barnyard; among the animals you might see inside in the Exotic Animal Room are lizards, turtles, snakes, and a leopard tortoise. A trail system and a pond with observation stations are all part of the complex. Picnic tables and trash containers are provided.

Frequent programs are open to members and visitors. Some are intended for children only; others are whole-family events. Check the Web site.

Where to Eat

Fatherland. 450 South Main Street; (860) 224–3345. Delicious, authentic Polish food in a low-key setting friendly to families. Excellent house-made soups, several kinds of pierogies, traditional stuffed cabbage, and perfect potato pancakes, including sweet potato ones. Half-sized servings for kids. Open for lunch and dinner, Monday through Thursday noon to 9:00 P.M., Friday and Saturday until 10:00 P.M. and Sunday to 7:00 P.M. $

Where to Stay

Days Inn and Conference Center. 65 Columbus Boulevard; (860) 224–9161. 73 rooms, fitness room, continental breakfast. $$

Rocky Hill/Glastonbury

If your children have been attracted to dinosaur research, they'll love Rocky Hill, about 8 miles south of Hartford off I-91. The hills and valleys just west of the Connecticut River are relatively new, you see. The area commonly called "Rockie Hill" in its colonial days was far different 185 million years ago. Then it was a bona fide Jurassic Park—a wide mudflat on the edge of a broad, shallow lake that filled a basin carved by glaciers a few million years before that. The lake was densely populated with vegetation, fish, and small reptiles of a roughly crocodilian description. The dinosaurs roaming nearby liked the menu, so they stayed until their luck ran out in the next ecological disaster.

Now only their tracks remain, a fact discovered during excavations in the 1960s for a modern ecological disaster called an office building. Bulldozer operator Ed McCarthy recognized something unusual about the ground he was clearing, and soon the place was crawling with paleontologists. Now families are the most frequent pilgrims to this ancient site.

Dinosaur State Park (all ages)

400 West Street; (860) 529–8423 or (860) 529–5816; www.dinosaurstatepark.org. Exhibit center open Tuesday through Sunday 9:00 A.M. to 4:30 P.M. year-round, except holidays. Adults $5.00; children 6 to 17 $2.00; under 6 **free.** Casting area open May 1 to October 31 from 9:00 A.M. to 3:30 P.M. at no charge. Park open daily year-round (except on holidays) from 9:00 A.M. to 4:30 P.M. at no charge.

Many of the 2,000 Jurassic period tracks uncovered have been recovered to preserve them, but about 500 are exposed to public view in this amazing park. A giant geodesic dome protects the mostly three-toed impressions from the elements. A walkway around the tracks provides a good view, and a full-scale reproduction of the sort of dinosaur most likely to have made the tracks stands in a running pose on the platform above the pit. The exhibit center also has exhibits on geology, history, and dinosaurs, and a mural showing how the region may have looked in the Jurassic period. An auditorium shows related films throughout the summer. A book shop and rest rooms complete the indoor facility.

In the warm months, visitors are invited to make plaster casts of some of the tracks in the outdoor casting area. Signs provide the instructions, but you must provide the supplies necessary to complete the project. Bring a quarter-cup of vegetable oil, ten pounds of plaster of paris, a five-gallon plastic container, and clean up rags and paper towels. If you decide to do this, you have to be finished by 3:30.

Outside the dome there is no evidence (except in the casting area) of prehistoric animal life, but the park offers sixty acres of nature preserve with more than 2 miles of hiking trails and a picnic area. The Dinosaur Park Arboretum is home to more than 250 species of conifers, plus gingkoes, redwoods, magnolias, and other plants that originated in prehistoric times.

Connecticut Audubon Holland Brook Center at Glastonbury (all ages) 🧑 🐘

1361 Main Street; (860) 633–8402; www.ctaudubon.org/centers/glastonbury. Open Tuesday through Friday 1:00 to 5:00 P.M., Saturday 10:00 A.M. to 5:00 P.M., and Sunday 1:00 to 4:00 P.M. Closed major holidays. Free, except for $1.00 for Discovery Room in nature center.

Explore native flora and fauna in person along the trails of forty-eight-acre Earle Park, then inside at the exhibits of the nature center. Other exhibits examine the ecosystem of the Connecticut River. A hands-on Discovery Room has natural objects to touch, smell, and see as you discover interesting facts about the birds, the bees, the trees, and so much more. A nature shop and bookstore provide great materials for continuing your learning at home and in the field. Year-round programs for families include guided walks, animal observation, and much more.

Ferry 'Cross The River

Another way to examine the ecosystem of the Connecticut River is aboard the *Hollister III*, the latest boat in the 300-year-old ferry service that crosses from Rocky Hill to Glastonbury. Four minutes from one side to the other, the ferry ride is accessible from the Rocky Hill Landing on Route 160 off the Silas Deane Highway or the Glastonbury Landing on Route 160 off Route 17. It runs weekdays only from 7:00 A.M. to 1:00 P.M. You can pay 75 cents per person to walk on; pay a bit more for ice cream at the Pilot House at the riverside in Rocky Hill.

Where to Eat

Max Amore. 140 Glastonbury Boulevard in the Somerset Square Shopping Area; (860) 659–2819. You can't miss here—the pizza is wonderful, the toppings are creative, the pasta dishes are on par with the pizza for innovation. Seafood, poultry, and vegetarian choices are here, too, as are special dishes for children under 10. $–$$

Rose's Berry Farm. 295 Matson Hill Road, South Glastonbury; (860) 633– 7467. On Sundays in season, have breakfast on Rose's deck overlooking the picking fields of strawberries, blueberries, raspberries, pumpkins, mums, and Christmas trees. When you are full, pick fruit for a home-cooked breakfast tomorrow. Buy fresh-baked muffins, pies, cider, and picnic goodies. $

Where to Stay

Udderly Woolly Acres B&B. 581 Thompson Street, Glastonbury; (860) 633–4503. Open year-round, this small, certified-organic working farm offers families a two-room suite that includes a sitting room and a roomy bedroom with two twin beds, one child-size trundle bed, and a rollaway bed upon request. A private bath, private entrance, a small refrigerator, and a hearty breakfast make this a cozy place for families to rest their heads. $$$

Hartford Marriott Rocky Hill. 100 Capital Boulevard; (860) 257–6000 or (800) 228–9290. 250 rooms and suites, restaurant, fitness center, whirlpool, indoor pool. $$$

Wethersfield

Preserved a mere 5 miles south of the modern hub of Hartford, the historical center of Wethersfield is in itself a miniature museum. Its pretty Main and Broad Streets are chock-full of seventeenth- and eighteenth-century homes that reflect Wethersfield's past. The first permanent settlement in the colony and the most northerly trading post on the Connecticut River, the town has the largest authentic historic district in the state. It is easy to enjoy the fantasy that one has stepped back in time in Wethersfield.

The Wethersfield Historical Society (ages 6 and up)

150 Main Street; (860) 529–7656. **Old Academy and Cultural Center open year-round Tuesday through Saturday from 10:00 A.M. to 4:00 P.M. and on Sunday, 1:00 to 4:00 P.M. The Francis and Hurlbut-Dunham Houses are open March through December, Thursday through Saturday from 10:00 A.M. to 4:00 P.M. and Sunday from 1:00 to 4:00 P.M. Cove Warehouse open mid-May to mid-October from Thursday to Sunday. Combo ticket for all sites is $5.00 for adults.**

The Wethersfield Historical Society owns and maintains five historical buildings, four of which are open to the public. The 1790 Hurlbut-Dunham House (separate tour, adults $3.00) at 212 Main Street is an elegant late Georgian brick beauty updated in the mid-1800s in the Italianate style. The Cove Warehouse (separate tour, adults $1.00), at the end of Main Street at Cove Park on the river, is the only warehouse to have survived the flood of 1692 that created the cove; it has exhibits on local maritime industry and history. A research archive and a library of local and state history, genealogy, and architecture are in the 1804 Old Academy. A museum shop, exhibits on Wethersfield's history, and a gallery of changing exhibitions are housed in the Keeney Memorial Cultural Center (860–529–7161; separate tour, adults $2.00) at 200 Main.

Webb-Deane-Stevens Museum (ages 6 and up)

211 Main Street; (860) 529–0612. **Tours every hour from May 1 to October 31 on Wednesday through Monday from 10:00 A.M. to 4:00 P.M. (last tour at 3:00 P.M.) and from November 1 to April 30 on Saturday and Sunday from 10:00 A.M. to 4:00 P.M. Combo ticket for this and Buttolph-Williams, adults $8.00; students $4.00; children under 5 free.**

This wonderful museum is composed of three eighteenth-century homes, each restored and furnished to provide a glimpse into distinct periods of American life. Each house, respectively, offers a look at the family lifestyle of a merchant, a diplomat, and a tradesman spanning the years from 1690 to 1840. The terrific tours take one hour; they can also include a twenty-minute additional tour of the Buttolph-Williams House. The gardens behind the three houses are extraordinary, featuring flowers and herbs of the eighteenth century.

Buttolph-Williams House (ages 6 and up)

249 Broad Street; (860) 529–0460 or (860) 529–0612. **Open from May 1 to October 31 from 10:00 A.M. to 4:00 P.M., Wednesday through Monday. Adults $3.00; children $1.00.**

This beauty reflects the medieval architecture of a turn-of-the-eighteenth-century "mansion" house. Furnished to provide a sense of an affluent family within a Puritan community, the 1700 house is the site of many fine family events, workshops, and celebrations. You can take the twenty-minute tour of this house alone for $3.00, or get a combo tour of this plus the Webb-Deane-Stevens house for $8.00.

Comstock, Ferre and Company (ages 4 and up)

263 Main Street; (860) 571–6590. **Open daily year-round from 9:00 A.M. to 6:00 P.M. (Sunday 10:00 A.M. to 5:00 P.M.) with some seasonal changes.**

The oldest continuously operating seed company in the United States, this famous establishment has sold seeds, plants, and gifts from its eighteenth-century post-and-beam warehouses since 1840. A National Historic Landmark as well as a national treasure for families who love to garden, this is a great place for families to buy some wonderful heirloom seeds or bulbs for home gardens.

Wethersfield Nature Center (all ages)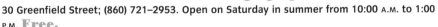

30 Greenfield Street; (860) 721–2953. **Open on Saturday in summer from 10:00 A.M. to 1:00 P.M. Free.**

This 120-acre environmental education center has live animals, including native mammals, reptiles, and birds, plus hands-on science displays, a log cabin, a wildlife and botanical library, and a gift shop. Used frequently throughout the week by local scout and school groups, it is also a nice place for day-tripping families to rest, relax, and explore. Bring lunch and have a picnic.

Where to Eat

Vito's. 673 Silas Deane Highway; (860) 563–3333. This Wethersfield classic welcomes families to share their creative Italian cuisine, including specialty pizzas, terrific pasta dishes, wonderful pesto, and a Marsala sauce second to none. Special affection is shown to children. Open daily year-round for lunch and dinner from 11:00 A.M. to 10:00 P.M. on weekdays, until midnight on Friday and Saturday and opening at noon on Sunday. $–$$

Where to Stay

Motel 6. 1341 Silas Deane Highway; (860) 563–5900. 145 units, clean and basic for families. $

Best Western Camelot. 1330 Silas Deane Highway; (860) 563–2311. Remodeled recently, 110 units, whirlpool, exercise room, sauna, extensive continental breakfast. Non-smoking rooms. $$$

General Information

North Central Tourism District. 111 Hazard Avenue, Enfield 06082; (860) 763–2578 or (800) 248–8283; www.ctheritagevalley.com.

Greater Hartford Tourism District. 234 Murphy Road, Hartford 06114; (860) 244–8181 or (800) 793–4480; events hotline: (860) 522–6400; www.enjoyhartford.com.

Central Connecticut Tourism District. One Grove Street, Suite 310, New Britain 06053; (860) 225–3901; www.centralct.org.

Farmington Valley Visitors Association. 15 Farm Springs Road, Farmington 06032; (800) 4–WELCOME. Info on special events and attractions in Avon, Simsbury, Canton, Farmington, and West Hartford.

New Haven County

Urban Culture and Country Adventure

S haped sort of loosely like a five-pointed star, this county reaches widely from its historic center in the city of New Haven. The small cities of Meriden and Waterbury in the north are balanced by suburban towns and rural villages to the east and west. Sliced into three parts by the Quinnipiac and Naugatuck Rivers, the county is usually perceived more along those divisions than as a whole.

New Haven is most definitely the cultural center of the county, a situation made difficult by the unfortunate struggle to overcome the public perception that the city might be a dangerous place. In fact, New Haven has much to offer and little to fear. Areas of interest to tourists are well cared for, well lit, and well protected. Both in and outside of its cities, New Haven County is a great place for families.

TopPicks for fun in New Haven County

1. Connecticut Audubon Coastal Center and Silver Sands State Park

2. Yale Peabody Museum of Natural History

3. Eli Whitney Museum

4. Freedom Schooner *Amistad* at Long Wharf

5. Thimble Islands cruises

6. Lake Quonnipaug and Dudley Farm

7. Hammonasset State Park and Meigs Point Nature Center

8. Lake Quassapaug and Quassy Amusement Park

9. Barker Character, Comic, and Cartoon Museum

10. Naugatuck Railroad Scenic Excursion

NEW HAVEN COUNTY

Clogged Arteries in Greater New Haven

The largest roads through and into New Haven are Interstate 95 (running east–west but labeled north–south) and Interstate 91 (running north–south and actually labeled north–south). Both are usually jammed with cars during rush hours, though I–91 tends to run a little more smoothly than I–95. From roughly 7:30 to 9:30 A.M. and again from 4:00 to 6:30 P.M., drivers are likely to encounter slow-moving traffic on both roads. My advice is that families stay put at those hours and avoid the madness. Eat breakfast or an early dinner, or linger at home, in the parks, or at the museums for an extra hour. You are unlikely to get anywhere quickly by trying to exit the highway to find alternate routes. Type A personalities who convince themselves that traffic is an evil opponent they must circumvent at all odds can try Route 1 (an option only for the insane), Route 80 (a viable option but also likely to be crowded single-file with commuters if the interstate is really backed up), or Route 34. Route 10 will take you north or south between I–95 and 15 (called the Wilbur Cross Parkway in this county and the Merritt Parkway in Fairfield County); this is an option for skirting the I–95/I–91 interchange.

Major Routes throughout New Haven County

The Wilbur Cross Parkway (Route 15) sweeps diagonally on a northeast–southwest course through the county, from Milford in the south to Meriden in the north. Traffic can become heavy on this road at rush hour or on summer weekends, but it rarely is so heavily congested that the flow nearly stops. Route 8 runs north–south through the western part of the county, from Derby to Waterbury, then on up to Litchfield County. Often crowded at rush hour in its Fairfield County portion, it is rarely crowded in New Haven County once the northbound traffic passes Ansonia. Interstate 84 passes in an arc right across the northernmost part of the county from Southbury through the northern part of Cheshire. In Cheshire the road splits; I–84 continues to New Britain and Hartford, and I–691 connects to Meriden and I–91.

If you prefer slower or quieter suburban and rural routes, you can travel north–south on Route 69 all the way from the Wilbur Cross Parkway in northern New Haven through Waterbury and on to Hartford County, Route 63 from the Wilbur Cross through Naugatuck and on to Litchfield County, or Route 10 from I–95 or the Wilbur Cross through Cheshire and on to Hartford County. To travel east–west, pretty Route 68 will link Route 8 to Route 15 and on to Durham in Middlesex County. Route 80 meets I–91 in New Haven and travels east-west across North Haven, North Branford, and the northern parts of Guilford and Madison and onward to Middlesex County.

Milford

This community on the western border of the county is Connecticut's sixth oldest town, settled in 1639 by families from New Haven and Wethersfield. It now has enough citizens to qualify it as a small city, but its pretty green, duck ponds, beaches, and residential neighborhoods have helped it retain the charm of a New England shore town. Although busier than most, especially along the Boston Post Road, where few signs of charm are at all apparent, it still draws families to its downtown arts-and-crafts shows, its summer concerts at the gazebo on the green, its coastal attractions, and its famed Oyster Festival.

Connecticut Audubon Coastal Center (all ages)

One Milford Point Road, off Seaview Avenue; (203) 878–7440); www.ctaudubon.org/centers/ coastal/coastal.htm. Open year-round. Outdoor areas open dawn to dusk at no charge. Center open Tuesday through Saturday from 10:00 A.M. to 4:00 p.m and Sunday noon to 4:00 P.M. Adults $2.00; children 2 to 12 $1.00. Craft workshops every Thursday from 1:00 to 4:00 P.M. Free bird walks from 9:00 to 10:00 A.M. every second and fourth Saturday.

This pristine habitat is composed mostly of salt marshes that border the Sound and the mouth of the Housatonic River. It provides families the opportunity to see one of the last surviving unaltered coastal properties in Connecticut. Just a few of the sanctuary's 800 acres of marshland and shore are passable to foot traffic, but these reveal the treasures of the rich ecosystem that flourishes here. A pathway provides access to the area's beach, a serene place for exploring and enjoying the native flora and fauna. Observation platforms help you gain a better view of the shore birds and other wildlife. This is not a park, so no picnic areas or trash receptacles are provided. Simply stroll peacefully through the habitat and learn about this fragile environment through the signage, the guided walks, and the displays and workshops in the coastal environment education center.

Among exhibits on the coastal environment, the center includes a 300-gallon saltwater tank with specimens native to the area. One such denizen is a diamondback terrapin, an endangered creature that inhabits the tidal estuaries. Though this one cannot be returned to the seashore, she serves as a reminder of the beautiful life forms we all have a responsibility to protect. Birthday parties that include beach walks and other nature fun can be arranged here. Inquire about the lecture series, summer camp programs, and family activities.

Historic Wharf Lane Complex (ages 6 and up)

34 High Street; (203) 874–2664 or 874–5789. Open Memorial Day through Labor Day on Saturday and Sunday from 2:00 to 4:00 P.M. Free.

Revisit the past through a visit to the three historic houses maintained by the Milford Historical Society. Featuring the 1700 Eells-Stow House, the 1780 Clark Stockade House, and the circa 1785 Bryan-Downes House, the complex has been curated to portray three centuries of life in New England through the furnishings, artifacts, and tours given in the trio of homes. One of the homes contains the Claude C. Coffin collection of Native American artifacts, touted as one of the finest archaeological records ever gathered in the state of Connecticut. Period flower and herb gardens add a touch of authenticity to the site.

Milford **Beaches**

In addition to the passive recreation possible on the beach at the coastal center, Milford offers families a chance to enjoy its public beaches for fun of a more active nature. The State of Connecticut also owns a stretch of shoreline in Milford, and visitors are welcome at its as-yet-undeveloped beach. For further information, call the Milford Parks and Recreation Department at (203) 783–3280.

Gulf Beach. Gulf Street. Visitor parking $5.00 per vehicle from Memorial Day through Labor Day. Concession, rest rooms, lifeguards, birdwatching/fishing pier.

Walnut Beach. Corner of East Broadway and Viscount Drive. Parking $5.00 or **free** street parking. Small pavilion, rest rooms, picnic tables, lifeguards. Nice, wide-open views of the famed Charles Island, convenient location adjacent to Silver Sands State Park and close to Milford Point CAS Coastal Center. Open daily July 1 through mid-August. Weekends-only earlier and later in the season.

Silver Sands State Park. Off Mayflower Avenue between Robert Treat Drive and Nettleton Avenue; call the Department of Environmental Protection at (860) 485–0226. Approximately 250 acres of shoreline. Lifeguards, portable toilets, and a boardwalk across the top of the beach and into the saltmarsh are the current amenities. Rest rooms, a first-aid station, and a pavilion are on the agenda for phase two of the project. Bring drinking water, picnic foods and beverages, and trash bags. No charge.

Where to Eat

Cafe Atlantique. 33 River Street; (203) 882–1602. This little corner bistro advertises itself as a fine wine and espresso bar, and it is also something much simpler: a great place for families for breakfast, lunch, snacks, and a light dinner. Open Monday through Friday from 8:00 A.M. and from 9:00 A.M. on weekends. Live music on weekends. Great sandwiches, soups, salads, baked goods. $–$$

Paul's Famous Hamburgers. 829 Boston Post Road; (203) 874–7586. This classic drive-in offers the finest in burgers, dogs, grilled chicken, fish sandwiches, fries, rings, and other American fast-fare. Be sure to order a real milkshake so thick your cheeks ache after you finish one of these babies. Eat at tables inside and out, or take it on the road. $

The Gathering. 989 Boston Post Road; (203) 878–6537. Salad bar, steaks, seafood, chicken, grilled and steamed specials, pasta, children's menu. Open for lunch and dinner. $$–$$$

Where to Stay

Comfort Inn. 278 Old Gate Lane, off exit 40, I–95; (203) 877–9411 or (800) 221–2222. 120 units, including 4 suites, sauna, indoor and outdoor hot tubs, continental breakfast. $$$

Hampton Inn-Milford. 129 Plains Road; (203) 874–4400 or (800) HAMPTON. 148 rooms, fitness center, continental breakfast. $

Fairfield Inn by Marriott. 111 Schoolhouse Road; (203) 877–8588. 104 rooms, outdoor pool, fitness center, continental breakfast. $$$

Howard Johnson Hotel. 1052 Boston Post Road, off exit 39A, I–95; (203) 878–4611 or (800) I–GO–HOJO. 165 units with 3 suites, restaurant, coffee shop, in-room refrigerators, health and exercise facilities, sauna, whirlpool, playground, indoor and outdoor pools, miniature golf. $$

Milford **Landing**

At the head of Milford Harbor at the mouth of the Wepawaug River is an all-transient docking facility for visiting boaters. Owned by the city of Milford and located at 37 Helwig Street, the marina features fifty slips for vessels up to 65 feet, a launch ramp, 30- and 50-amp service, concierge service, and trained dock staff to assist at tie-up. Complimentary morning coffee and newspaper are provided for overnight guests. Handicapped access, rest rooms, shower facilities, ice and water, and a laundromat help make families comfortable. Six public tennis courts and basketball courts are also in the immediate area; the marina staff will assist overnight guests in arranging court time. For slip reservations and further information, call Operations Director Dick Hosking at (203) 874–1610.

Landlubbers are also welcome to enjoy the landing's walkways and picnic and barbecue areas on the promenade. Visitors arriving by land can also reserve time on the tennis courts by contacting the park and rec department at (203) 783–3280. Within walking distance of the town green and its shops, restaurants, and historic sites, Milford Landing provides an excellent central location from which travelers can explore Milford.

Milford **Oyster Festival**

Slap on the sunscreen and load your wallet with a wad of cash for the irresistible fun at this annual celebration of the gustatory delights of the homely but delicious oyster and other pure pleasures of summer on the shore. The second full weekend in August is the usual date of the Milford Oyster Festival, which brings tens of thousands of visitors and nationally and regionally known performers to the harbor, the Green, and Fowler Field on New Haven Avenue. An arts-and-crafts show, a classic car show, children's activities, a canoe race, a moonlight music dance party, and a food court featuring oysters, of course, as well as other family-friendly treats are all part of this popular festival. Admission is free; the food, the crafts, and the boat rides will cost you at least a little something. Call (203) 878-5363 for more information.

New Haven

Once the site of a Native American village called *Quinnipiac,* which means "long water land," New Haven was renamed by English settlers who established a colony here in 1640. Since its earliest days an important center of industry, education, and culture, New Haven remains one of the most vital cities in the state. A treasure chest of attractions and historic sites appealing to every generation of visitors, New Haven takes pride in its firsts—fact and folklore support evidence of America's first football, frisbees, burgers, dogs, pizza, and even lollipops being birthed right here in New Haven.

This chapter contains the best family attractions in the city, but by no means does it attempt to consider all the possibilities your family may enjoy. Check the *New Haven Register,* the *New Haven Advocate,* the *Connecticut Post,* or the Connecticut section of the *New York Times* for listings of the events scheduled at New Haven's universities, museums, galleries, parks, and theaters.

West Rock Ridge State Park
Wintergreen Avenue; (203) 789-7498. Open year-round daily from 8:00 A.M. to sunset. In-season entrance fee for cars, $1.00.

If the layout of the city mystifies you, you might want to start a tour of New Haven high above the urban clamor. Overlooking the entire city (and the Sound and other parts of Connecticut on a clear day), West Rock is one of two ridges of basalt forced skyward through volcanic action 200 million years ago. The state park runs along the top of the western ridge and has a variety of recreational areas including hiking trails, a fishing pond called Lake Wintergreen, and a picnic area.

A scenic drive traverses parts of the park. Its southern portion is open to motor vehicles only on a seasonal basis, usually April through November; call for opening dates. The northern section is closed to vehicles but open to hikers, cyclers, and skiers year-round. Folks in cars wishing to hike when the scenic drive is closed can park at the nature center on Wintergreen Avenue or at Lake Wintergreen. The park entrance is about 200 feet south of the nature center entrance, also on Wintergreen Avenue.

The park's blue-blazed main trail, called **Regicides Trail,** is accessible at the top of the ridge via the scenic drive or you can walk in off-season from the nature center (see following paragraphs). This 6.3-mile trail begins near the summit at Judges Cave and follows the crest of the West Rock Ridge range northward, ending at its junction with the Quinnipiac Trail in Hamden. The trail offers some beautiful views of the harbor and, of course, leads through scenic woodlands, as you might expect. The most infamous site on the trail is **Judges Cave,** where in 1661 John Dixwell, Edward Whalley, and William Goffe hid from bounty hunters hoping to claim the £100 reward for their capture as traitors against the Crown, having signed the warrant for the execution of Charles I many years earlier.

Help for **Visitors**

Be certain to call the Greater New Haven Convention and Visitors Bureau (203–777–8550 or 800–332–7829) to ask for their terrific guides to the city and its 'burbs. You can also write to or visit the Bureau at 59 Elm Street, New Haven 06510 and visit their Web site, www.newhavencvb.org.

West Rock Nature Center (all ages)
1020 Wintergreen Avenue, not far from exit 59 off Route 15; (203) 946–8016; cityofnew haven.com/parks/westrock.htm. Open Monday through Friday 10:00 A.M. to 4:00 P.M. Closed holidays. **Free.**

Owned and operated by the city, this separate area just north of the entrance to West Rock Ridge State Park on Wintergreen Avenue covers forty acres. Short nature trails take you past the ravine, a small waterfall, and so on. The center also has a picnic shelter and rest rooms. Come in the wintertime with your sleds and toboggans.

East Rock Park (all ages)
Enter from East Rock Road in New Haven or Davis Road in Hamden; playground, environmental education center, and ranger station in College Woods at corner of Cold Spring and Orange Street; (203) 946–6086; www.newhavenparks.org. Park open daily year-round from sunrise to sunset. Summit Road open daily from April 1 to October 31, 8:00 A.M. to sunset, and at the same time on Friday and weekends only from November 1 through March. Two other roads are closed to vehicles but open to cyclists, in-line skaters, and walkers. Hiking trails are closed to mountain bikes. **Free.**

The twin of West Rock, East Rock, is on the other side of the city, recognizable by its matching sandstone and traprock cliffs. Its 425-acre park is city owned and is most well known for its spectacular views of the city and harbor from its monument-topped summit. Long-range binoculars and benches at the scenic overlook add to your enjoyment of the view as you rest here awhile and get your bearings on the city below you. A large, grassy picnic area with barbecue grills is frequented by visitors who pause here to explore the area around the towering Soldiers and Sailors monument, which honors New Haven veterans, and the Compass Rose, which identifies New Haven points of interest within sight.

An education center called the Trowbridge Environmental Center contains displays about local wildlife and plant life. Guided nature walks, workshops, and talks appropriate for families and children are on the schedule at this center. Visitors can also walk the 10 miles of hiking trails, including the 1,000-foot, 285-step cliffside ascent called the Giant Steps Trail. A bird sanctuary, a self-guided nature trail, playing fields, picnic pavilions, playgrounds, an ice-skating rink, a basketball court, and opportunities for sledding, fishing, and kite flying are also located within park boundaries. Stop at the Trowbridge Center for a map.

Yale University Visitor Information and Walking Tours

Whether you're in a consumer-minded mood or not, Yale is a wonderful university to tour. See the Gothic splendor of the Sterling Memorial Library (where you can peruse newspapers in dozens of languages). Slip into the dimly lit galleries of the Beinecke Rare Book and Manuscript Library (where you can see a Gutenberg Bible among other treasures). Walk through Phelps Gate, listen to the bells in Harkness Tower, stop at the statue of Yale grad Nathan Hale outside the 1750 Connecticut Hall (the oldest building in New Haven and the last remaining structure from Yale's Old Brick Row), where Noah Webster, Nathan Hale, and William Howard Taft perfected their studies.

You can join a free one-hour guided walking tour on Saturday and Sunday at 1:30 P.M. and on Monday through Friday at 10:30 A.M. and 2:00 P.M. It leaves from the Yale Visitor Information Center (203–432–2300) at 149 Elm Street, across from the north side of the New Haven green. No reservations or tickets are necessary. You can also pick up a self-guided tour pamphlet from the visitor center and explore the campus on your own. A second tour option covers important downtown sites near the New Haven green. Those tours are on Thursday at noon; call (203) 432–2302.

Connecticut Children's Museum (ages 2 to 10)

At corner of Orange and Wall Streets; (203) 562–5437; www.childrensbuilding.org. Open most Fridays and Saturdays, noon to 5:00 P.M. Call ahead. Adults and childen 3 to 10 $5.00.

This educational play center/museum is housed in the recently renovated Children's Building, not far from the city green district and the arts district of Audubon Street. While public visiting hours are limited, this center is well worth a visit and is especially cheerful on wet, too-hot, or too-cold weekends when little spirits get dampened by the weather. No one can manage to be cranky in this stimulating play space.

Exhibit areas are carefully shaped to engage the eight intelligences as described by Howard Gardner and others. In the musical intelligence room, for instance, you will find children "Making Music" everywhere. Colorful murals expose children to music through art. A piano, a saxophone, and a guitar invite them to see and touch. A work station has wind chime components, an ocean drum makes rhythm visible, and a steel drum and pipe drum reveal that instruments can be made from found objects. On the guitar stage young musicians can play in the museum band with instruments from around the world. In the bodily/kinesthetic room, mirrors reflect faces and children explore emotions in English, Spanish, and American Sign Language. Sculptures portray the characters from *Frog and Toad Are Friends, Blueberries for Sal*, and *Caps for Sale*. Visitors can read books about their favorite animal and then become a frog, bear, or monkey with props and costumes on a stage with spotlights.

In the mathematical room, kids can adjust their green visors and gather at a kidney bean–shaped table, adding, subtracting, and counting the room's collections. A maze wall has movable slats so children can create pathways for rolling balls; a gear wall allows kids to arrange the gears and turn a crank to rotate them. Tangrams, mosaics, and fraction games are available for quiet problem solving, and a magnetic number wall invites children to do math with giant numbers.

In the space place, you can visit a construction site. Architectural blocks, a chalkboard house, gravity tubes, and a garbage sculpting center provide exercise for spatial intelligence. Another room has beekeeper gear, an observation hive with thousands of live bees, and a sitting space of hexagonal honeycombs where visitors can just nest awhile. Magnifying glasses help young naturalists examine an ant farm and other earthly wonders. There's even a "great, green room" complete with a bunny in a bed and a little red house as well as the famous "comb and a brush and a bowl full of mush." The words of Margaret Wise Brown's beloved classic *Goodnight Moon* are on large magnets in different languages and Braille for children to assemble on the great, green magnetic wall.

On Saturdays at 2:00 P.M., artists and educators engage children with dramatic readings of favorite books. The aim is to engage young readers in a hands-on book experience through creative interpretation of the story. You can't go wrong here with children aged 2 to 7; you might even have trouble getting many 10-year-olds to go home.

Yale University Art Gallery (ages 4 and up)

1111 Chapel Street at York Street; (203) 432–0600. Open Tuesday through Saturday from 10:00 A.M. to 5:00 P.M. and Sunday from 1:00 to 6:00 P.M. Closed Monday and major holidays. Free; donation suggested.

Founded in 1832, the oldest university art museum in the United States, the art gallery's 85,000-piece collection extends from ancient to modern art. Engaging for children, especially in the sense that the scene changes markedly from gallery to gallery, it provides families with an excellent overview of the history of art. Take the kids here to see objects from ancient Egypt, elsewhere in the Middle East and Africa, the Pacific islands, and the Far East. The American paintings and decorative arts are exquisite; O'Keeffe, Kandinsky, and Pollack are among the twentieth-century artists, but earlier treasures abound, including Hudson River School and American Impressionists. The European collection includes van Gogh, Manet, Monet, Picasso, and other artists. The sculpture garden provides an intriguing outdoor respite.

The museum hosts wonderful changing exhibitions of work that may never again be collected in one place in this area, so families should be sure to look for announcements of upcoming shows. The museum also offers tours, programs, and concerts designed to appeal to families.

Yale Center for British Art (ages 4 and up)

1080 Chapel Street at High Street; (203) 432–2800. Open year-round Tuesday through Saturday 10:00 A.M. to 5:00 P.M., Sunday noon to 5:00 P.M. Closed Monday and major holidays. Free.

Home to the largest collection of British art outside Great Britain, the center exhibits paintings, drawings, prints, rare books, decorative arts, and sculpture from the Elizabethan period to the present. Works by Stubbs, Hogarth, Turner, Constable, Blake, Lear, and Reynolds are among the treasures here. Aligned with a research institute, a reference library and photographic archive, and a paper conservation laboratory, the museum has a serene and serious aura, but families are most welcome here. You should aim to enjoy at least some of the collection, even if only for a brief visit with young children. Special exhibitions often include works that you may never again see in the United States. You may want to visit when there is an exhibit of special interest, adding to the excursion a peek into the second- and fourth-floor galleries, which display works from the permanent collection.

Many of the museum's **free** lectures and symposia are best suited to adults and students, but children are welcome to all gallery tours, concerts, and films. Programs especially for children occasionally appear on its calendar of events. The monthly Sunday afternoon concerts are especially wonderful and are offered at no charge, as are the tours and films. The museum gift shop is exceptional and very child-oriented—a great place to shop for the holidays or special occasions.

The Yale Collection of Musical Instruments (ages 8 and up)

15 Hillhouse Avenue, between Trumbull and Grove Streets; (203) 432–0822. Open from September through June, Tuesday through Thursday from 1:00 to 4:00 P.M. Call for the concert schedule.

The public hours scheduled here make it mighty hard to arrange a visit with a school-aged child, but if you have a little someone who really loves music, this awe-inspiring collection is well worth a half day out of school. More than 850 European and American instruments from the sixteenth to twentieth centuries are on display, and an annual concert series is offered from September through March. The museum suggests a donation of $1.00; concert tickets are extra.

Carillon Concerts at Harkness Tower

If you are in New Haven in summertime on Friday night at 7:00 P.M., grab a
blanket and a picnic dinner and head to Harkness Tower,
near the Old Campus between Chapel and Elm Streets.
There in the courtyard, relax awhile and listen to the incredible
music of the carillon. Students of the art as well as international artists play here several times each summer for
about an hour. Don't pack anything crunchy in your picnic
and make sure you close your eyes for the full and unforgettable effect of the glorious classical pieces on each concert's
program. For a schedule of these free performances, call the
Yale Events Hotline (203–432– 9100) or the Yale Guild of Caril-
lonneurs (203–432–2309). In case of rain, the concerts are held
at Phelps Hall at 344 College Street.

Yale Peabody Museum of Natural History (all ages)

170 Whitney Avenue; (203) 432–5050. Open year-round daily, Monday through Saturday
10:00 A.M. to 5:00 P.M. and Sunday noon to 5:00 P.M. Adults $5.00; children 3 to 15 $3.00.

Last in the Yale neighborhood is one of the most popular family destinations in the state.
Everybody has probably already been here, but for those people who have not, just think
dinosaurs, dinosaurs, dinosaurs, plus fossils, birds, insects, seashells, rocks, shrunken
heads, minerals, meteorites, mummies, mastodons, mammals, and much, much more.
Also here is the enormous mural in the Great Hall depicting beautiful (although outdated)
images of how the age of the dinosaurs might have looked. Excellent wildlife and cultural
dioramas from many habitats and periods include studies of Neolithic, Pacific, Mesoameri-
can, ancient Egyptian, and Connecticut Native American peoples. A Discovery Room
designed especially for young visitors meets the need to touch, feel, and smell interesting
natural objects. Changing exhibitions and tons of special events, classes, workshops, and
hands-on activities are offered throughout the year.

New Haven Colony Historical Society (ages 6 and up)

114 Whitney Avenue; (203) 562–4183. Open year-round from Tuesday to Friday 10:00 A.M. to
5:00 P.M. and Saturday and Sunday from 2:00 to 5:00 P.M. (except closed on Sunday in July
and August). Closed major holidays. Adults $4.00; children 6 to 16 $2.00.

This beautiful building designed expressly as the museum of the Colony of New Haven is
alone worth a visit—a Colonial Revival masterpiece built in 1930 in the late Georgian style,
it has a most lovely skylit rotunda, marble staircases, an alluring salmon-colored ballroom,
and magnificent moldings at every doorway. Kids may not appreciate the architecture, but
they may enjoy the exhibits focusing on the inventions and industries begun in New Haven

County. See Eli Whitney's cotton gin, Charles Goodyear's rubber inkwell, an organ made by the New Haven Organ Company, and an original Mysto Magic Erector Set. Enjoy a marvelous three-story dollhouse with a veritable bevy of silent inhabitants and a thousand other details of decoration. Be sure to linger at the exhibit on Sengbe Pieh and the *Amistad*. Along with these are maps, ships' models, and other wonderfully curated, often interactive changing exhibitions.

Historic New Haven **Walking Tours**

The staff at the New Haven Colony Historical Society have designed a walking tour of Historic New Haven's buildings, parks, monuments, and other historical and cultural sites. Begin the self-guided tour near the eighteen-acre green that was planned in 1638 for the common use of New Haven residents. See its three historic churches, its famed Bennett Memorial Drinking Fountain, and the World War I Memorial Flagpole. Check out the finest sites of Yale University, then browse through the Grove Street Cemetery, looking for the graves of Noah Webster, Eli Whitney, Roger Sherman, Lyman Beecher, Timothy Dwight, Charles Goodyear, Roger Sherman, Walter Camp, and other famed Americans. Walk past the mansions of Hillhouse Avenue on your way to the Peabody Museum, then stop at the Historical Society, the New Haven City Hall, and the *Amistad* Memorial.

Amistad Memorial and the Freedom Schooner *Amistad* at Long Wharf Pier (ages 4 and up) 🏛

The Memorial is located in the plaza at 165 Church Street at the New Haven City Hall. Accessible year-round and around the clock at no charge. The Freedom Schooner *Amistad* is berthed, when she is not sailing as an educational ambassador to other ports, at Long Wharf Pier off Long Wharf Drive. For a schedule of *Amistad* homeport tours and voyages, call *Amistad* America at (203) 495–1839 or visit their Web site (www.amistadamerica.org), an excellent source of facts about the *Amistad* incident and the construction of this historic replica.

Lessons of courage, honor, and justice are to be learned at the base of the marvelous bronze sculpture outside New Haven's City Hall and aboard the re-creation of the *Amistad* itself at Long Wharf Pier. Created by Kentucky artist Ed Hamilton, the *Amistad* Memorial reminds visitors of the bravery of Joseph Cinque and the commitment of his American supporters to take a moral stand against the outrage of slavery and the illegal capture of free Africans from their homelands.

The story of the *Amistad* Africans started in the seas off Havana, Cuba, in 1839, when fifty-three Mendi captives seized control of the merchant ship *La Amistad,* which was taking them closer and closer to the unspeakable ordeal of a lifetime of slavery. Days under sail on an eastward course toward Africa were compromised by the slavers' alteration of the course toward the northern United States by night. Eventually apprehended by the U.S. Navy as the ship met the waters of Long Island Sound, the slavers accused their captives of piracy, and the Africans were taken into custody and held in the New Haven jailhouse, then on a site opposite the present city hall. Here the captives awaited trial, as abolitionists and attorneys and former president John Quincy Adams joined the battle to restore the freedom of the Africans.

The heroic acts of the group's leader, Sengbe Pieh, also known as Joseph Cinque, are celebrated on the 14-foot, three-sided bronze sculpture that stands near the site of the jailhouse where the kidnapped Mendi Africans were imprisoned. Although the morally laudable and eventually triumphant teamwork of the principal players in this incident did not lead directly or immediately to the release of other captive Africans, it did contribute greatly to the abolitionist movement and inspired the courage of countless other Africans who sought, fought for, and won their own freedom. This monument reminds all visitors of the importance of pursuing justice, freedom, and equality for all people against all odds. A tour ($2.00 per person or $5.00 per family is the suggested donation) of the re-creation of the schooner itself (usually in port from April through October) is a moving, eye-opening experience that makes the reality of the Mendi ordeal all the clearer. When the schooner is in port, it also does three-hour public sails on Friday and Saturday from 5:00 to 8:00 P.M. Tickets are $30; reservations are necessary.

Connecticut **Freedom Trail**

In recognition of the importance of numerous Connecticut sites associated with the abolition of slavery and the movement toward freedom and equality for African Americans, the Connecticut General Assembly authorized the development of an educational effort to publicize the sites under a unifying umbrella called the Connecticut Freedom Trail. From monuments such as the *Amistad* Memorial to Underground Railroad sites to notable birthplaces, gravesites, and museum exhibits, the Freedom Trail traces the historical importance and contributions of Connecticut's African Americans and their supporters. An excellent informational pamphlet providing a map and details about the thirty-six sites throughout the state is easily obtained at the tourism information centers, individual tourism districts, or the Connecticut Historical Commission, 59 South Prospect Street, Hartford 06106 (860–566–3005).

Theater and Music in New Haven

The arts flourish in New Haven, but it takes some investigation to find the best performances for families. Call these groups and theaters to inquire about single concerts and plays as well as series suitable for children.

New Haven Symphony Orchestra. 33 Whitney Avenue; box office: (203) 776–1444 or (800) 292–NHSO. The fourth oldest orchestra in the United States, this symphony offers an October to June concert season in beautiful Woolsey Hall at the corner of College and Grove, plus a **free** summer series on the Green. In addition to these, they offer the festive and family-friendly annual Holiday Pops! concert, a joyous collaboration of orchestra and choruses singing traditional carols, gospel, and even reggae tunes.

Shubert Performing Arts Center. 247 College Street; (203) 562–5666; shubert@shubert.com; www.shubert.com. This recently refurbished theater offers Broadway shows, ballet, opera, modern dance, comedy, and more in a full season from September through May. Many shows are suitable for or aimed especially at families, and some are offered at special prices as low as $10 per ticket.

Greater New Haven Acoustic Music Society. University of New Haven, 300 Orange Avenue, West Haven; (203) 468–1000. These contemporary folk artists sponsor acoustic concerts and workshops featuring national and regional touring artists and local performers at ten summer performances at the Eli Whitney 1816 Barn across from the Eli Whitney Museum.

Outdoor Summer Concerts on the Green/New Haven Jazz Festival. Presented by New Haven Office of Cultural Affairs, (203) 946–7821. **Free** summer concerts in July and August on selected Saturday evenings. Outstanding jazz artists from around the nation and globe. Bring a blanket and picnic or eat at the food booths set up at the edge of the Green. Dance in the twilight with music all around you.

International Festival of Arts and Ideas. (203) 498–1212 or (888) ART–IDEA; www.artidea.org. Musicians, dancers, puppeteers, storytellers, theater performers, and children's entertainers come from nearly every continent to raise our awareness and our spirits in an outpouring of artistic energy that spans five days late in June each year. Of the scores of indoor and outdoor performances staged on or near the Green and on the Yale Campus, most are **free**; a handful require paid tickets. See classical and modern dance; hear opera, folk, salsa, reggae, jazz, and classical artists; participate in art activities, dances, or mask and puppet pageants.

Lighthouse Point Park and Carousel (all ages)

2 Lighthouse Road, off Woodward Avenue, from I–95 exit 50 northbound, or exit 51, Frontage Road, southbound; follow the signs down Townsend Avenue to Lighthouse Road and the park; park manager: (203) 946–8005; ranger station: (203) 946–8790; cityofnew haven.com/parks/lighthousepoint.htm. Park open daily year-round, 6:00 A.M. to sunset, free of charge except from Memorial Day to Labor Day when each out-of-town carload pays $6.00. Carousel operates from Memorial Day to Labor Day, on Tuesday through Friday from 3:00 to 7:00 P.M. and on Saturday and Sunday from 11:00 A.M. to 7:00 P.M. It is closed on Monday except on the holidays.

New Haven is not often characterized as a city on the sea, but it is a major working port in New England, and some of the best the city has to offer is by the shore or on the Sound. Although it is not known for its fine beaches, the city does have a great seaside park and swimming area.

Now popular mostly with city residents and bird-watchers, Lighthouse Point Park was once the enormously popular last stop on the New Haven trolley line. In those olden days the park had bathhouses, boat rides, and baseball games, with such legends as Babe Ruth and Ty Cobb playing here on Sunday afternoons in the Roaring Twenties. Nearly destroyed in the hurricane of 1938, the park later was home to a small amusement park.

Today only one of its famed rides remains. Housed in a New Haven landmark building listed on the National Register of Historic Places is the Lighthouse Point Carousel, an astonishingly well-restored treasure and a joy to ride. Assembled around 1911 from new and used parts, this sparkling beauty carved mostly by masters Looff and Carmel has seventy-two figures mounted in twenty ranks on a 60-foot platform. Jumping horses that slide on gleaming brass poles stand four abreast, alternating with the steadfast steeds, which stand shoulder to shoulder in rows of three. With these are a beautifully saddled camel and twin dragon chariots, the latter carved by Charles Illions. For 50 cents per ride, you can hop on any one of these gorgeously painted Coney Island–style mounts, with names like Wild Wind, Sweet Sue, City Lights, Sea Dreamer, and Sundance. The names were chosen by the schoolchildren of New Haven at the time of the restoration. The beveled mirrors at the center of the ride reflect the glimmer of hundreds of twinkling light bulbs; the refurbished antique murals on the rounding board at the top of the carousel depict scenes from the history of New Haven; the air-driven Stinson Band Organ makes heavenly music. Group reservations are accepted—what a great place to party.

The eighty-two-acre park also has the pre–Civil War Five Mile Point Lighthouse and a great little nature center at the East Shore Ranger Station. You may learn something about natural history, marine ecology, and maritime history at a program here.

The park's beach is clean and safe; a first-aid station, a snack bar, spotless changing rooms and showers, a small wooden playground, several swing sets, and a picnic grove are here. A public boat launch, a fishing pier, volleyball nets, a nature trail, and several excellent birdwatching areas in the bird sanctuary are also here. Hawk watching during the annual migration, from late August through November, brings birders from all over the state.

In mid-November, look for announcements of the **UI Fantasy of Lights** (203–777–2000) holiday display that is staged each year at the park. Cruise the park's roadways past sixty colorful oversized symbols of Christmas joy. At the entrance to the park, each carload pays $5.00 on weekdays and $7.00 on the weekend. This fee benefits the Easter Seals rehabilitation programs. Each vehicle is loaned a cassette tape (or tape plus tape player) that features a musical program timed for the ride through this animated holiday spectacle.

Fort Nathan Hale and Black Rock Fort (ages 6 and up)

Woodward Avenue; (203) 787–8790. Open daily Memorial Day to Labor Day from 10:00 A.M. to 4:00 P.M. Free.

After you leave Lighthouse Point, you might want to make a historical pit stop as you travel north again on Townsend Avenue. Take a left on Fort Hale Park Road to visit two of New Haven's oldest historic sites. Black Rock Fort was built in 1776 by order of the Connecticut Colony to protect the Port of New Haven from the British. Unfortunately, by the time the British arrived in 1779, only nineteen defenders remained at the fort; they were swiftly captured by the enemy, which then marched on to New Haven.

Fort Nathan Hale was built near the same site in the early 1800s as the British and Americans prepared again to fight. This time, during the War of 1812, the defenders successfully repelled the British invaders. Rebuilt in 1863 with new ramparts, bunkers, a drawbridge, and eighteen guns, the fort was prepared for Civil War action, but it never came.

Now you can make a self-guided tour of both sites. The drawbridge, its moat, the ramparts, bunkers, and other fortifications either still exist or have been restored. It's a neat site with terrific views of the harbor, but it's very low-key. In addition to the remains of the forts, there is a handsome statue of the young Nathan Hale, a colorful flag display, and some signage and self-guided tour brochures at the information booth at the entrance to the site.

Schooner Sound Learning Cruises (ages 4 and up)

60 South Water Street; (203) 865–1737; www.schoonersoundlearning.org. Late May through September. Private charters of varying duration and price, plus public sails. Educational Sea Adventures on Wednesday and Friday from 6:00 to 9:00 P.M. or Sunday from 1:00 to 4:00 P.M. or Sunset Cruises on Sunday from 5:00 to 8:00 P.M. Cruises leave from the Long Wharf.

If you want to see New Haven from the Sound and get a history and ecology lesson and a great boat ride to boot, call this tour operator during the warm months. Weather permitting, they'll take you out on chartered half-day, full-day, and sunset sails aboard the *Quinnipiack*, a 91-foot gaff-rigged wooden schooner. The lively crew offers entertaining and educational stories about the history of New Haven, the ecology of the Sound, and the cultures that affected the present ecosystem. Tickets are $25 for adults, $10 for children. On both types of cruises, passengers are welcome to bring picnics and beverages. Inquire also about weeklong summer day camps for children.

Other New Haven **Parks**

New Haven has a variety of small parks that serve the needs of the families of its many neighborhoods. Among these parks are a few that are notable for special reasons. Call the city Department of Parks, Recreation, and Trees (203–946–8025) for details about each park's hours of operation and special events.

Edgerton Park. On Whitney Avenue and Cliff Street near the Hamden line; enter observatory area at 75 Cliff Street; (203) 777–1886. Listed on the National Register of Historic Places; twenty-two-acre property originally owned by Eli Whitney and later the site of the Edgerton mansion. Planned according to an eighteenth-century English landscape garden to emphasize the importance of open space. Crosby Conservatory of tropical plants with a simulated rainforest path. Greenbrier Greenhouse with culinary herbs and seasonal plants for sale year-round, plus a children's corner with modestly priced plants. Outdoor flower gardens and magnificent trees, walking, biking, and cross-country skiing paths, picnicking areas, community garden center. Seasonal fairs and concerts.

Edgewood Park. 720 Edgewood Avenue between Whalley Avenue and Chapel Street; (203) 946–8028. 120 acres with nature walkways, playground, ranger station with wildlife displays, duck pond, tennis and basketball courts, playing fields, Holocaust memorial, and Spanish-American War monument.

Wooster Square Green. On Chapel Street between Academy and Wooster Place. Near New Haven's Little Italy is a historic district of some of New Haven's prettiest architecture designed in the early 1800s around a central square named for New Haven's Revolutionary War hero David Wooster. Have a look at the monument to Christopher Columbus, sit on benches under flowering cherry trees and breathe deeply—the aromas of olive oil, garlic, and spicy tomato sauces will remind you that you are steps from the city's finest Italian restaurants and the world's best pizza and pastries.

Where to Eat

Louis' Lunch. 263 Crown Street; (203) 562–5507. Louie Lassen opened this landmark luncheon stand in 1895 and claimed responsibility for the first hamburger cooked in America in 1900. Now this famed eatery has its place on the National Register. Fresh-daily burgers and cheeseburgers, served on toast in adult and child-sized portions. Tuna salad served year-round on Friday. Open Tuesday and Wednesday 11:00 A.M. to 4:00 P.M. and Thursday through Saturday from 11:00 A.M. to 2:00 or 3:00 A.M. Closed Sunday and sometimes Monday and for the entire month of August. $

Pepe's Pizzeria Napoletana. 157 Wooster Street; (203) 865–5762. Some would argue that no better pizza has ever been made, even in Italy. Most folks claim Frank Pepe's famous white clam pie is the most delicious item on the menu, but those who eschew clams would swear on their own favorites. Be ready to wait for pizza this perfect—it won't matter how early you get here, other aficionados will have staked a place before you. $–$$

Sally's Pizzeria. 237 Wooster Street; (203) 624–5271. Anyone who loves this place knows that Sally was the late, great Salvatore A. Consiglio and that he learned some of the tricks of his trade from his uncle Frank Pepe down the street. Now his talented descendants still throw the best pies in the neighborhood into the huge 12-by-12-foot coal-fired brick oven that pushes out twenty pies at once. Closed Monday. Sunday, Tuesday, and Thursday are the quietest days. $

Claire's Corner Copia Cafe. Corner of College and Chapel Streets; (203) 562–3888. Close to the Green, the university, and the museums, Claire's offers the best soups made in the city, plus other flavorful vegetarian dishes from lasagnas to pasta salads, sandwiches, chili, quesadillas, great breads, pastries and cakes. Takeout or tables with a semi-self-service, casual flair. Open for breakfast, lunch, and dinner year-round daily from 8:00 A.M. to 10:00 P.M. $

Where to Stay

Quality Inn and Conference Center. 100 Pond Lily Avenue; (203) 387–6651. 123 units, health club, sauna, Jacuzzi, indoor pool, continental breakfast. $$

Holiday Inn New Haven at Yale. 30 Whalley Avenue; (203) 777–6221. 160 units, restaurant, exercise facility, outdoor pool. $$$

Fairfield Inn by Marriott. 400 Sargent Drive; (203) 562–1111 or (800) 243–0059. 152 units, including 55 suites, outdoor pool, health club, sauna, continental breakfast. $$$

Residence Inn by Marriott. 3 Long Wharf Drive; (203) 777–5337. 112 suites with kitchens, outdoor pool, Jacuzzi, continental breakfast. $$$$

East Haven

This shoreline community is a bustling outgrowth of New Haven's sprawl, seen mostly by travelers passing along I-95 through the shopping areas on Frontage Road. If it weren't for the seemingly endless construction on or near the Lake Saltonstall Bridge, few travelers would slow down along this route to see what the town has to offer. Those who exit the highway in East Haven will find one of Connecticut's most popular family attractions.

Shore Line Trolley Museum (all ages)

17 River Street; (203) 467–6927; www.bera.org. Open Memorial Day to Labor Day from 10:00 A.M. to 5:00 P.M. Also in April on Sunday only, and in May on Saturday and Sunday at the same hours. Weekend tours in September and October, plus Columbus Day and in November on Sundays only, prior to Thanksgiving. Call for a special events schedule for

December. Adults $6.00; children 2 to 11 $3.00. Trolleys run at least every thirty minutes; last trolley leaves at 4:30 P.M.

The efforts of the Branford Electric Railway Association have kept alive and well one of Connecticut's oldest tourist attractions—the oldest continually operating trolley line in the United States.

Nearly 100 classic trolley cars are stored on the grounds and in the car barns of the property. Admission buys you unlimited 3-mile round-trip rides on the beautifully restored cars, plus a self-guided tour of the museum's display areas, which include the history of the technology and the local lines, plus some interactive and audio-video exhibits. The trolley rides themselves are great fun, especially for young children, and special days are offered throughout the year, broadening the appeal for older children. Among these are Pumpkin Patch days in October and Santa on the Trolley days in December. Call to ask for a special events schedule or check the Web site.

You can picnic on the grounds, but there is no food concession or snack bar. You can also arrange birthday parties and special charters at a group discount if booked in advance.

Branford/Stony Creek

One of the prettiest and most relaxing family excursions in the state centers in and around Branford's Stony Creek, as quintessential a quaint New England fishing village as can be found in these parts. Only Stonington, in New London County, transports one more thoroughly to the nautical past.

Less than 10 miles from New Haven, Stony Creek has a long and lively history, complete with tales of pirate treasure and other romances of the sea and heart. Once home to farmers, fishers, and quarriers, the village is now famed for its quiet Yankee charm and its sprinkling of pink granite islands just offshore—the Thimbles.

In fact, the village's principal industry, if one can call it that, is the Thimble Islands sightseeing tour business. Three enterprising captains have updated the centuries-old trade of ferrying livestock, groceries, visitors, and even the occasional piano from the Town Dock to the islands. Now, from mid-May through Columbus Day, landlubbers can board ship to enjoy the sea breeze and scenery while listening to the colorful tales of the islands' past and present.

To reach the Stony Creek Dock, take I–95 to exit 56, and go south on Leetes Island Road for two miles. At the stop sign, go straight on Thimble Island Road, and follow the signs to the dock. For more information about this village and its history and attractions, check the Web site www.thimbleislands.com.

Volsunga IV (all ages)
Stony Creek Dock; (203) 488–9978 at the dock; (203) 481–3345 for reservations and information. Cruises every hour on the hour, weather permitting, from 11:00 A.M. to 4:00 P.M. daily except some Mondays July 1 to day before Labor Day. From mid-May through June

and from Labor Day through Columbus Day, the tour times differ somewhat, with fewer cruises daily and no operation on Monday of several weeks at either end of the season. Call ahead or check the Web site www.thimbleislands.com for current schedule. Adults $9.00; children $5.00. Groups of more than twelve should make reservations. Two-hour evening charters ($325 for thirty people) are also available.

From Captain Kidd to General Tom Thumb, the stories told by Stony Creek native Captain Bob Milne aboard the *Volsunga IV* are exceeded in quality only by his sure navigation of the reefs surrounding the 23 inhabited islands of the total 365. Milne's 40-foot vessel is rated for forty-nine passengers.

All seats are great seats for parents and kids alike on its single deck, and Captain Bob's easygoing manner makes for terrific storytelling, easily heard over the *Volsunga IV's* sound system (the engine is soundproofed). Along with views of the islands' ninety-five homes, which range from a palatial Spanish mansion to Victorian cottages to a verita-ble aerie on stilts, you will enjoy the sights of human and winged islanders—kids wearing life jackets in their yards, teens diving from rocks, and seabirds to spare.

Sea Mist II (all ages)

Stony Creek Dock; (203) 488–8905; www.seamistcruises.com. Forty-five-minute cruises every hour on the quarter hour, from 10:15 A.M. to 4:15 P.M. daily except Tuesday, in July and August, and in May and September (including Labor Day) through October on Monday and Friday through Sunday at 12:15, 2:15, and 4:15 P.M. Adults $9.00; children $5.00. Two-hour charters available ($400 for up to thirty-four people). Reservations suggested for large groups. Public seal watches at noon on weekends only in March and April; two hours; adults $20, children 12 and under $15.

Captain Mike Infantino Jr. offers a similar ride on his similar boat, a 45-foot vessel that car-ries forty-six passengers. The navigation is just as sure, the stories are an entertaining mix of myth and fact, and the views of the sea, the birds, the islands, and the islanders are basically identical. All passengers are seated comfortably and can easily hear both the stories and the sounds of the sea. Chartered seal and bird watches can also be planned for groups of ten or more. Call for details. Bird watches are arranged year-round; seal watches are typically December through mid-April.

Islander (all ages) 🔺

Stony Creek Dock; (203) 397–3921. Fifty-minute cruises every hour leaving at twenty min-utes before the hour, from 10:40 A.M. to 4:40 P.M. daily from mid-June through Labor Day. Adults $9.00; children $5.00. Reservations suggested for groups of more than twelve.

The smallest of the three cruise options, Captain Dave Kusterer's 26-foot port launch car-ries about twenty-five passengers on a fifty-minute tour. The size of his boat allows explo-ration of a few spots the larger boats can't reach and also allows Captain Dave to be right there in the middle of the more intimately sized deck. Like Captain Bob's, his stories reflect his personal knowledge of the lifestyles and histories of the islanders.

Stony Creek **Kayak**

Creeker Christopher Hague offers instruction and guided sea kayaking trips for experienced and novice kayakers aged 8 and older. Three-hour day and sunset tours with instruction are $70 per person May 15 through October 15. These tours, usually among the Thimble Islands and on nearby lakes and rivers, can also be scheduled in Branford or Guilford harbors or other sites for a minimum of eight participants. The three-hour trips are wonderful for families. Ideal for beginners or those with limited experience, the first half-hour of the tour is dedicated to on-land orientation and outfitting clients in their kayaks and gear. The next two and a half hours on the water are focused on exploring the area and learning how to kayak properly. All necessary kayaking equipment is provided, but you should bring snacks, drinking water, a change of dry clothes to leave in your car, sunglasses with a string, hat, sunscreen, and sports sandals or old sneakers. Children 8 and older are outfitted with equipment specifically designed for them. Children 13 and younger cannot be accommodated on weekends for three-hour tours. Exceptions are made for private groups. For more information, call (203) 481–6401.

Stony Creek Village (all ages)

On your ride down to the water, you may notice Stony Creek's other attractions. Most notable despite its modest facade is the **Puppet House Theatre** (128 Thimble Island Road; 203–488–5752; www.puppethouse.org), site of a full slate of theater and improv productions each summer and sporadically throughout the year. It is also home to one of Connecticut's most interesting theater productions—the **Sicilian Puppet Theatre.** Brought to life just a few times each year, the puppets themselves are extraordinary 4- to 5-foot hand-carved figures. Beautifully painted and dressed in armors of hand-embossed brass, these 100-year veterans of the stage battle each other furiously in the enactment of tales of the Crusades, Charlemagne and his Paladins, and the Sicilian Knights. You'll be on the edge of your rattan theater seat at one of these remarkable performances. For the full slate of productions, call for a current schedule.

Be sure to have a look at the gallery of fine-art paper-cutter Martha Link Walsh. **Island Tastes,** near the village park and its popular children's playground, offers a funky collection of clothes and gifts for sale. Down the street toward the dock is **Stony Creek Antiques,** the **Stony Creek Market** (203–488– 0145), which is great for breakfast, lunch, dinner (some nights), soft drinks, and picnic fare, and **Creekers: Stony Creek Marine and Cuisine,** which also carries drinks, deli, and snacks, and does summertime-only lunch and dinner under a tent at the waterside. When your appetite is satisfied, stroll the rest of the village.

When you return to your car, you can reach the Branford town green by following Route 146 to its end and continuing straight into the center of town. There are many stores and restaurants in that area plus the beautiful landmark Blackstone Library and the historic Harrison House museum. Then go north on Cedar Street and hop on I–95 heading east (north) and exit at Leetes Island Road. Turn left at the top of the ramp to go north on Leetes Island Road. At Route 1, take a right and visit the **Hilltop Orchards** store for fabulous pies year-round and apples, pumpkins, and mums in season, plus country-style gifts and culinary treats.

Where to Eat

Stony Creek Market. 178 Thimble Island Road; (203) 488–0145. For breakfast, arrive from 8:00 to 11:00 A.M. For lunch, come between 11:00 A.M. and 3:00 P.M. and take their overstuffed sandwiches out on the front deck for a great view of the harbor. For dinner, from 5:00 to 9:00 P.M. Tuesday through Sunday, the market doubles as **Stony Creek Pizza,** serving pizza, salads, and occasional pasta specials. These folks also operate a small bakery with great breads and pastries and to-die-for scones. $

Lenny's Indian Head Inn. 205 South Montowese Street; (203) 488–1500. Come here for a menu of New England seafood, epitomized in Lenny's Famous Shore Dinner of clam chowder, cherrystones, sweet corn on the cob, lobster, steamers, and watermelon. Steaks, burgers, fries and rings, and a children's menu served in the casual ambience of worn wood floors and wooden booths makes this a happy, noisy, thumbs-up place for families. Open daily year-round for lunch and dinner. Indoor seating year-round; patio in warm season. $–$$

Indian Neck Market. 2 Sybil Avenue; (203) 483–8220. Open daily for breakfast, lunch, and simple dinners until 8:00 P.M. and for ice cream in the summer until 9:00 P.M., this spic-and-span market/deli/restaurant has terrific breakfasts, sandwiches, soups, salads, baked goods, daily special hot dishes, and Ashley's Ice Cream. Open from 7:00 A.M. on weekdays, 8:00 A.M. on weekends. $

Where to Stay

Days Inn and Conference Center. 375 East Main Street; (203) 488–8314 or (800) 329–7466. 78 units with 3 suites and 2 mini-suites, outdoor pool and Jacuzzi. Continental breakfast. $$

Branford Motel. 470 East Main Street; (203) 488–5442. 100 units with 20 efficiencies, Jacuzzi. $

Guilford

One of the most exceptional colonial greens in New England is in the center of Guilford, one of the prettiest towns along the New Haven County shoreline. Lying south of the Boston Post Road, as you drive toward the Sound, its twelve acres are crisscrossed by walkways and dotted with benches that make this a popular site to relax and to play. Shops, restaurants, churches, galleries, and beautiful colonial, federal, and Victorian homes surround this classically lovely spot. Bring the kids here for bicycling or in-line skating, to listen to a summer concert, or to browse at one of the frequent fairs or festivals held on the site. Afterward, leave the green to explore other parts of Guilford. Walk or cross-country ski on the wooded trails through an old quarry site. Stroll, snooze, or sift for forgotten treasures on the beach. Visit one of the three historical homes representing life as experienced by the white settlers of the area in the 1600s and 1700s. You'll hardly remember you are just 15 miles east of New Haven.

Guilford Handcraft Center (ages 4 and up)

411 Church Street (Route 77), north of Route 1 and approximately 200 yards north of the I–95 overpass; (203) 453–5947. Studios open year-round for classes and visitors; call for schedule and course catalog. Gallery and shop open year-round Monday through Saturday from 10:00 A.M. to 5:00 P.M. and Sunday from noon to 4:00 P.M. Extended hours for annual Holiday Exhibition and Sale in December. Closed Thanksgiving, Christmas, and New Year's Day. Free.

Composed of a shop, a gallery, and a school, the Handcraft Center was founded in 1962 by the local artists who organized the first of the annual expositions (see sidebar). Still a home away from home for many of those artists, the center has pottery, weaving, painting, and metalsmithing studios, plus multiuse classrooms for instruction in basketry, etching, printmaking, and woodcarving. Visiting artists also travel here to offer workshops for adults and children. A bounty of talented role models offers instruction, guidance, and encouragement as young artists tease from their own minds and fingers the wondrous creations born in these studios. The center is itself a place to visit, but call first to see what's going on. The Mill Gallery hosts small expositions throughout the year, and the shop sells the works of as many as 300 artisans. Craft birthday parties and other special events are also offered here.

Guilford **Handcrafts Exposition**

Surely the most magical of all the events held on the green, this fabulous three-day festival, from Thursday to Saturday in the middle week of July, celebrates American handcrafts created by nearly 150 juried artists from all corners of the nation. Displayed under huge, cheerfully lit tents, the pieces demonstrate an astonishing array of talent in every medium. Basketry, weaving, jewelry, toys, clothing, candles, leather goods, sculpture, pottery, paper crafts, glass, musical instruments, furniture—you name it, it's here.

A Discover GHC tent features hands-on activities and demonstrations by crafters who practice their arts at the Guilford Handcraft Center. Entertainments such as storytellers, face painters, and other live performers help make the event a happy experience for all visitors.

A food concession sells typical fast-food fare. We always pack a picnic to enjoy under the trees. Adult admission $5.00, children under 12 free. Call (203) 453–5947 for more information.

Henry Whitfield State Museum (ages 6 and up)

248 Old Whitfield Street, south of the green at the corner of Stone House Lane; (203) 453–2457 or (860) 566–3005; www.hbgraphics.com/whitfieldmuseum or www.chc.state.ct.us/whitfieldhouse.htm. Open for mostly self-guided tours on Wednesday through Sunday from February 1 to December 14 from 10:00 A.M. to 4:30 P.M. and from December 15 through January by appointment. Adults $3.50; children 6 to 17 $2.00. *(Note: Sadly affected in 2003 by state budget cuts, the Whitfield House was closed for most of that year. Call ahead in 2004 for current news of the reopening.)*

This historic home is the oldest stone house in New England and the oldest house in Connecticut. Built in 1639 by Reverend Henry Whitfield, the post-medieval house has stone walls three feet thick and is the last remaining of four such houses strategically placed in Guilford as strongholds for the citizens during threat of war. No record confirms that the house was ever in fact used for this purpose.

Now restored more as a museum than a period house, the structure contains an outstanding collection of furniture, housekeeping implements, textiles, weapons, and other important Connecticut pieces. The entire house, including the attic, is open to the public, as are the gardens and lawns. Among the large collections displayed in the attic, you can see the 1726 Ebenezer Parmelee steeple clock, the first wooden works tower clock made in the colonies. In the separate, adjacent visitor center is a tourist information center, a reference library, an exhibit gallery with excellent changing displays, and a charming gift shop.

Hyland House (ages 6 and up)

84 Boston Street, which leads east from the south side of the Green; (203) 453–9477; www.hylandhouse.com. Open from early June to early September daily except Monday from 10:00 A.M. to 4:30 P.M. and on weekends from Labor Day to Columbus Day. Adults $2.00; $1.50 for children 12 and older; under 12 free.

This red overhung saltbox frame house was originally the home of the Hyland family. One of the Hyland daughters married Ebenezer Parmelee of clock-making fame; it was through their efforts that the house was expanded from its original two-rooms-over-two size. Though the house was built in 1660, the museum's focus is on the fifty to seventy-five years before the Revolution. Everything that the family might have used during that period is here for your education.

Here visitors step into the eighteenth century, especially in the house's wonderful kitchen in the lean-to addition at the back of the house. How we wish the friendly docents would leave us alone to play here.

The architectural details and the collections in this house are among the finest in the state. Gorgeous paneling, wide-board floors, walk-in fireplaces, and artifacts of every sort are abundant. Outside, the flower and herb garden is lovely in summer and fall.

The house docents are in tune with the interests of children of every age level, making the house come alive with scores of facts and stories. The house is the site of a Historic

Foodways Festival on the last full weekend in September. Hearthside cooking and other activities are among the special events designed for families.

Thomas Griswold House (ages 6 and up)

171 Boston Street; (203) 453–3176 or (203) 453–4666; www.thomasgriswoldhouse.com. Open June through September from Tuesday through Sunday from 11:00 A.M. to 4:00 P.M. October, weekends only at same hours. Adults $2.00; students $1.00. Children under 12 free.

Greatly restored by the Guilford Keeping Society, this 1774 saltbox home has a large number of important architectural details, including an original Guilford cupboard and a 10-foot-wide fireplace. This house also includes period rooms set with furnishings and implements in positions of use. Samplers, coverlets, costumes, dolls and toys, and a whimsical napkin ring collection are among the treasures here.

Special events such as twilight tours, an antiques show, or reenactments are sometimes offered. Check the Web site's calendar of events. On these special days the museum's blacksmith shop and barn are usually open.

Westwoods Trails (all ages)

Trail entrance on Sam Hill Road near its junction with Route 146; (203) 453–8068. Open year-round at no charge from dawn to dusk. Copies of the trail map available at the Guilford Town Hall, the Guilford Free Library, the Guilford police station, the Guilford Parks and Recreation Department on Church Street, or from the Guilford Land Conservation Trust, P.O. Box 200, Guilford 06437. *(Note: Many of the area's trails have been temporarily closed due to safety issues arising from a tree disease that causes rotting limbs. The Orange Circle and White Circle trails remain open and are carefully maintained.)*

For you who are fatigued with art and history, a walk in the woods may be the answer to your prayers. Head, therefore, to Guilford's Westwoods Trails, located less than a mile from the green in an open-space area of more than 1,000 acres. Forty miles of trails lace through forest and marshland.

Take Route 146 west from the green to Sam Hill Road and park in the small lot right near that corner. Follow the white-blazed trail from that point and connect with the other trails that lead to waterfalls, rock cliffs, colonial caves, an Indian cave, rock carvings, and vistas of the Sound and lake. The "G" Trail connects the Westwoods trails to the Stony Creek Quarry Preserve; here you can see the remains of old quarrying operations.

Jacobs Beach (all ages)

Seaside Avenue off Whitfield Street; Guilford Parks and Recreation: (203) 453–8068. Park and playground area open year-round from 8:30 A.M. to 9:00 P.M. Swimming allowed only when lifeguards are present, from Memorial Day to Labor Day, on Monday through Saturday from 9:00 A.M. to 5:00 P.M. and on Sunday from 11:00 A.M. to 5:00 P.M. Out-of-town visitors pay $6.00 per vehicle on weekdays and $8.00 per vehicle on weekends from Memorial Day through Labor Day.

Hikers and bikers may want a refreshing swim or at least a cool wind through their hair after some trail exercise. Head down to the Sound for a rest on the sand at Jacobs Beach.

Comb the beach for treasures swept in on the tide, play on the playground, listen to the rustling marsh reeds. You can swim if the lifeguards are on duty, but you can use the beach and volleyball court even if the guards are off-duty. Rest rooms and a pavilion with picnic tables and nearby grills are also here. The beach is relatively small, but it's a pretty spot, and out-of-towners are more than welcome. Season passes cost families $50.

Lake Quonnipaug (all ages)

Route 77 in North Guilford, about 3 miles north of Route 80. Open Memorial Day through Labor Day; gated during remainder of year. Monday through Saturday 9:30 A.M. to 7:30 P.M., Sunday 11:00 A.M. to 7:30 P.M. Purchase day tickets at the lake for $6.00 per person on weekdays and $8.00 per person on weekends. Best buy for families is a season pass for $20.00 per adult 21 to 59 or $40.00 per adult couple, plus $7.50 per child under 12, and $15.00 per child 12 to 20. The pass allows unlimited visits per season and can be purchased only at the Guilford Parks and Recreation Department (203–453–8068) at 32 Church Street downtown.

If freshwater swimming is pleasing to you, head north to Lake Quonnipaug for salt-free water play, boating, fishing, and picnicking. This pretty lake is in a rural area dotted with barns, pastures, stone walls, and fences—the perfect setting for a New England day trip.

A good-sized beach and grassy area are open to the public there. Bathrooms with two outdoor showers are also provided. Small cartop boats such as inflatables, canoes, kayaks, sailboards, or tubes may be launched from the grassy area, but no snorkeling or scuba diving is allowed. A state-owned public boat launch ramp is at the north end of the lake, outside of the Guilford property.

Dudley Farm (all ages)

2351 Durham Road (Route 77), north of Route 80; (203) 457–0770. Open year-round Monday through Saturday 10:00 A.M. to 2:00 P.M. Farmers' market June through October on Saturday from 9:00 to noon. Suggested donation for a house tour, $3.00.

Settled in the arms of nature, the eight standing buildings and nearly two dozen remnant structures at this peaceful ten-acre farm site are the legacy of the Dudley family, who tilled the soil and tended animals through two centuries in Guilford. Now the Dudley Foundation has as its mission the preservation of the farm and its structures and the restoration of its meadows, fields, and flower gardens. Through this ongoing process, the foundation hopes to inspire present generations to recognize their own connection to the soil. A visit here may rekindle in both children and adults an appreciation for the natural environment and an attitude of stewardship toward the earth. The farm offers an ever-increasing array of guided and self-guided tours, activities, workshops, and demonstrations. A 2-mile loop trail through ninety-five acres of woodland traces the path of eighteenth-century wagon roads.

Tours of the farm and adjoining mill site feature a seventeen-room 1840s farmhouse, with many of those rooms restored to their beginning-of-the-twentieth-century state, an enormous U-shaped barn that evolved through two centuries of farm life, a sugarhouse, a small barn restored for use as a schoolhouse for visiting classes, an herb garden and restored flower gardens, a vegetable field, beehives, and animal enclosures sheltering goats, oxen, sheep, chickens, and geese.

Families may prefer to visit on Saturday, when the farm is often at its busiest. In the morning it offers a market of its own produce as well as that of other local farmers and crafters. Browse among fruits, vegetables, flowers, honey, and other goodies, then see what the farm staff is demonstrating in the house, the barns, or on the grounds. Depending on the weather and season, you may see, or even participate in, sheep-shearing, beekeeping, maple sugaring or syrup making, twig furniture construction, quilting, rag rug weaving, tool repair and maintenance, or barn chores. On the first Saturday of each month, musicians play acoustic instruments under the trees.

Special events throughout the warm season include an Arbor Day celebration, May Day festivities, and a Farm Day. In winter, two weeks or so are spent on the old-fashioned adventure of tapping the running sap of the farm's majestic maples. The foundation produces a newsletter to let folks know what's happening at the farm as its restoration continues. Call to order a copy and a schedule of events.

Anne Conover **Nature Trail**

The National Audubon Society offers a new 1-mile trail through the Guilford Salt Meadows Sanctuary near the East River. Open dawn to dusk year-round, the sanctuary and the trailhead are accessible from Meadowlands Road off Clapboard Hill Road, not far from exit 59 (Goose Lane), on the north side of I–95. Secondary-growth forest and meadow-, river-, and tidal marshland are habitats for herring and eels, eastern box turtles, saltmarsh sparrows and osprey, and many other birds and beasts of the Eastern Woodlands. The trail is easy, short, and quite beautiful. A kiosk at the parking area provides trail guides. Admission is free. For more information, check the Web site: www.audubon.org/local/sanctuary/guilford.

Where to Eat

Anthony's of Guilford. 2392 Boston Post Road; (203) 453–4121. Reasonably priced and well-prepared mostly Italian specialties in a comfortable setting welcoming to families. Open year-round for lunch and dinner. $–$$

Guilford Mooring. 505 Whitfield Street; (203) 458–2921. Burgers, sandwiches, salads, soups, seafood, pasta, and chicken dinners make this a good bet for families. The harbor and marina views make it a seaside respite. Casual and busy, for lunch and dinner daily. $$

The Little Stone House. 514 Whitfield Street at the Guilford Dock; (203) 458–2554. Practically in the water, this great little family-friendly cafe offers gourmet-quality soups, sandwiches, baked goods, and meals-to-go. Eat in or outside on the patio. Open 10:00 A.M. to 6:00 P.M., year-round, Tuesday through Sunday. $–$$

The Place. 901 Boston Post Road; (203) 453–9276. Seasonal dining in the rough at one of Connecticut's most unique eateries. Outside under tents, sit on rough-hewn seats at picnic tables and eat charcoal-grilled steak, pit-roasted corn on the cob, and fresh seafood. Open from May to October from Monday though Thursday from 5:00 to 10:00 P.M., Saturday from 1:00 to 11:00 P.M., and Sunday from noon to 10:00 P.M. $$

Where to Stay

Guilford Suites Hotel. 2300 Boston Post Road; (203) 453–0123 or (800) 626–8604. 32 suites with bedroom, sitting room, bath, and kitchenette. Continental breakfast. $$$

Comfort Inn. 300 Boston Post Road; (203) 453–5600. 45 rooms in brand-new facility. Coffeemaker, refrigerator, complimentary continental breakfast; access to nearby health club. $$$–$$$$

On the same property is the **Tower Suites Motel,** (203) 453–9069, with 15 efficiency suites. Nonsmoking suites available. $$$$

Madison

Perhaps the loveliest town on the New Haven County shoreline, Madison was one of Connecticut's earliest settlements. Once called East Guilford and connected geographically and politically to the town of Guilford, it was incorporated as a separate town in 1826. In previous centuries a fishing and shipbuilding center and later a seaside resort area, Madison is now primarily a comfortable residential suburb whose population increases sizably in the summertime. Despite its limited ethnic diversity, many Madison families love their town because of its safe, community-centered ambience—and its beautiful beaches. In fact, Connecticut's longest stretch of public beach is located here, and all visitors are welcome.

Hammonasset State Park (all ages)
Off the Boston Post Road, exit 62 off I–95; (203) 245–2785. Open daily year-round, 8:00 A.M. to sunset; most planned activities held in summer. Per-vehicle admission charge of $7 for in-state plates and $10 for out-of-state plates on weekdays from Memorial Day to Labor Day; $9 and $14, respectively, on weekends. Also $7 and $10 on weekends only from mid-April to Memorial Day and from Labor Day through mid-October. Weekdays free to all during those weeks. No charge off-season. Alcohol-free. Campsites $15 nightly.

Enormously popular, this park offers a two-mile beach with pavilions and picnic shelters, a 550-site campground, playing fields, a spiffy year-round nature center with a new amphitheater and walking trails, a bike path, and sun, sand, rocks, and salty spray in abundance.

Come here, then, to camp, swim, fish off the jetty, scuba dive, picnic, play ball, hike, sailboard, or boat on Long Island Sound. Day visitors and campers alike must stop at the **Meigs Point Nature Center.** An excellent small facility, it has several fresh- and saltwater aquariums, a marine touch tank, a number of well-executed dioramas, and a variety of live amphibians and reptiles. Outside, the Willard's Island walking trail winds out through the salt meadow and onto Willard's Island, once farmed in colonial times and now home to red cedar and sassafras trees and the mammals and birds of the marshlands. Fourteen stations explain the flora and fauna, including the nesting sites of the beautiful ospreys that soar overhead in spring, summer, and fall.

The nature center rangers provide walks, talks, slide presentations, and craft workshops for children all summer long. The Junior Naturalist program for children 9 to 12 and the Outdoor Explorer program for 6 to 8-year-olds include **free** activities such as fishing, crabbing, tidal pool exploration, and bird and bat house building. Held midweek in July and August, the program is open to drop-in visitors.

The windswept campground is a great seaside vacation spot. Well run, clean, and beautiful in all seasons, it is extremely popular in the summertime. The sites are almost all open, so if you like the hills and woods, you are in the wrong park. Bring a metal tub or fire ring (or rent one here); there are no grills or firepits, and campfires are permitted only in metal containers. Campfire programs, bingo, an occasional dance, and a children's playground with swings and a great wooden ship are part of what you'll enjoy here. Bring bikes and in-line skates—the campground has excellent lanes for both sports.

Downtown Madison

Families may enjoy a stroll through Madison's shops, which provide a marvelous alternative to cookie-cutter mall stores and impersonal outlets. Many of the boutiques, galleries, antiques stores, coffee shops, cafes, delis, and restaurants of Madison are in vintage homes and historic commercial buildings centered mostly on Wall Street, the Boston Post Road, and Samson Rock Road in the village center.

The shops are mostly locally owned, independent enterprises that offer an extra measure of friendliness and service. Many stores offer gifts, toys, jewelry, and clothing for children. Be sure to stop for hot cocoa at the Madison Gourmet Beanery, children's books at R. J. Julia Booksellers (voted the best independent bookstore in the nation), and toys and trinkets at Belles and Beaus. Parents may want to enjoy a cup of tea at the incomparable British Shoppe and Front Parlour Tearoom.

Allis-Bushnell House (ages 6 and up)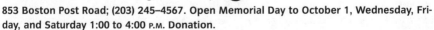
853 Boston Post Road; (203) 245–4567. Open Memorial Day to October 1, Wednesday, Friday, and Saturday 1:00 to 4:00 P.M. Donation.

The 1785 Allis-Bushnell House is notable for its unusual corner fireplaces and cupboards, its stenciled floors, the exceptional collection of tools and fishing and farming equipment in its annex, and its eighteenth-century herbs in its lovely rear garden. Home of Cornelius Bushnell, a founder of the Union Pacific Railway and chief financier of the Civil War iron-clad ship, the USS *Monitor,* it also has a collection of fascinating memorabilia regarding the famed vessel. A small model of that ship and other ships educate visitors about Madison's maritime history.

Junior docents add a charming touch as they greet visitors, answer questions, and perform tasks throughout the house. Senior docents lead the one-hour tours that are willingly tailored to your interests and schedule. Children may particularly enjoy the museum's small collection of toys, dolls, period costumes, and interesting medical implements. Many of those items have been moved to the historic Lee Academy on the Madison green, where a children's museum is located. Inquire at the main house for specific hours of operation.

Deacon John Grave House (ages 6 and up)

581 Boston Post Road; (203) 245–4798. Open Wednesday mid-June through Labor Day Wednesday through Friday noon to 3:00 P.M., Saturday from 10:00 A.M. to 4:30 P.M., and Sunday noon to 4:30 P.M. After Labor Day through Columbus Day, open Saturday and Sunday noon to 3:00 P.M., in winter, by appointment. Adults $2.00; children $1.00.

Just a block east of Madison's town green surrounded by stately period homes and its classically New England white Congregational church is one of Connecticut's oldest homes on a pretty parcel known in the past as Tuxis Farm. Occupied for more than 300 years by descendants of its original owner, Deacon John Grave, the house is a fine example of seventeenth- and eighteenth-century architecture, easily seen through the fine restoration work that has taken place here.

Adapted for use in the past as an ordinary, a school, a wartime infirmary and weapons depot, and even a courtroom, the house also was home to ten children at one time—and that was before its eighteenth-century additions were added! Come here to imagine the life of a farming family in pre-Revolutionary days, see the secret staircase that led to a hidden room used for storing arms during the French and Indian War, hear the ghost stories associated with the house, and sample open-hearth cooking done on special events days. Call to inquire about these special days when the tours include demonstrations or costumed interpreters.

Where to Eat

Red Tomato Pizzeria. 37 Boston Post Road; (203) 245–6948. Order out or eat in at this cheery eatery that makes excellent thin-crust New Haven–style pizza baked right on the bricks. Fresh vegetable and meat toppings—even the clams are freshly shucked. $–$$

Friends and Company. 11 Boston Post Road; (203) 245–0654. The perfect blend of casual and refined, this riverside establishment is a longtime local favorite for healthfully prepared brunch, lunch, and dinner. Seasonal menu; traditional kids' menu. Open year-round, for lunch Wednesday through Saturday, brunch on Sunday, and dinner daily. $$

The Clam Castle. 1324 Boston Post Road; (203) 245–4911. Serving the shoreline since 1967, this classic drive-in seafood shack upholds a long tradition of fresh fish, terrific clam chowder, famed onion rings, plus traditional American sandwiches, breakfast, lobster rolls, soft shell crabs, clam fritters, scrod, shrimp, scallops, calamari, and more. Eat inside or out, March through November, daily. $

Zhang's. 44 Boston Post Road; (203) 245–3300. Open daily for lunch and dinner, this sit-down or take-out restaurant with a Far Eastern flair offers Chinese and Japanese fare at moderate prices. All dishes spiced to your taste; tons of choices. $–$$

Where to Stay

The Madison Beach Hotel. 94 West Wharf Road; (203) 245–1404. Directly on the beach, this restored 1800 hotel offers the best possible views of Madison's shoreline. 35 units with 6 suites; continental breakfast served on porch, in Victorian lobby, or on your balcony. **The Wharf** (203–245–0005) restaurant with deck dining. Beach chairs and towels provided. Open March 1 to January 1. $$$

Madison Post Road B & B. 318 Boston Post Road (203–245–2866). This charming home not far from the main village offers four large rooms with private baths, common areas, beach passes, continental breakfast. Nonsmoking. $$$$

Beech Tree Cottages. 1187 Boston Post Road; (203) 245–2676. Nightly and weekly rentals are available in summertime at this three-acre enclave just steps from Hammonasset Beach. Each clean but simply furnished cottage has a bath and kitchen facilities; some are perfect for couples; others large enough for a small family. Friendly hosts. Lovely grounds with rope swing, volleyball net, walkways. $$$–$$$$

Hamden

The most conspicuous feature of Hamden (north of New Haven) is in fact one of the most conspicuous features of all of Connecticut. Best viewed from a distance for the fullest impact, the rounded hills of Sleeping Giant State Park look exactly like a figure in repose, its head toward the west, its chest and body stretching eastward. (A great view is possible from I–91.) Hamden is also famous for its notable early citizen, inventor Eli Whitney.

Sleeping Giant State Park (all ages)

200 Mount Carmel Avenue off Route 10; ranger station: (203) 789–7498. Open year-round daily from 8:00 A.M. to sunset. Parking fee ($7.00 for Connecticut plates; $10.00 for out-of-state vehicles) charged in-season (usually April 15 to November 1) on weekends and holidays only.

Up close, the park is a great outdoor recreation area. Just off Route 10 a few miles north of Hamden's business center, its fifteen hundred acres of rolling woodland are traversed by hikers and cross-country skiers on 32 miles of trails. You can fish for trout in Mill River or you can hike the Tower Trail, an easy walk on a wide gravel path to the top of the ridge. At the top is a four-story stone building completed in 1939 as a WPA project. Go inside and walk up its ramps (not wheelchair-accessible) for scenic views of the area. The park also offers a pine-canopied picnic grove with tables, an open-air picnic shelter, drinking water, rest rooms, and grills.

A booklet available at the park entrance booth explains the forty-point self-guided nature trail, which takes somewhat over an hour to traverse. You may also join one of the many **free** guided trail walks offered here mostly on Sundays in the spring and fall. Six to eight of these are scheduled during each of these seasons at 1:30 P.M. The hikes are fine for all members of the family. Topics include wildflower identification, hawk watches, Giant lore, and more. For a hike schedule, call the Sleeping Giant Park Association at (203) 272–7841 or check the Web site: www.sgpa.org.

Eli Whitney Museum (ages 4 and up)

915 Whitney Avenue (Route 10); (203) 777–1833; www.eliwhitney.org. Open year-round; Memorial Day to Labor Day daily 11:00 A.M. to 4:00 P.M. During remainder of year, open noon to 5:00 P.M. Wednesday through Friday and on Sunday and from 10:00 A.M. to 3:00 P.M. on Saturday. Closed Thanksgiving, Christmas, and New Year's Day. Adults $3.00; children $2.00.

Back down Route 10 toward the center of town is the Eli Whitney Museum. Not at all another historic home, this child-focused learning museum happens to center around the remaining and restored buildings of Whitneyville, a factory complex founded by Eli Whitney in the nineteenth century, but is entirely a hands-on place for inquiring young minds. On the site is a covered bridge, a wonderful outdoor Water Learning Lab (open May through October, weather permitting), and exhibits and project stations inside the restored armory and gun factory.

The exhibits in the armory focus on the scientific principles used by Whitney in his inventions, including interchangeable gun parts, the cotton gin, and more. A fascinating one-third-scale model of the factory village once centered in this neighborhood is here as well. The museum hosts many special events and activities of interest to children. Visitors can participate in projects such as building a toy boat, a birdhouse, or a pinball or maze game. Each of these walk-in building projects costs approximately $6.00 per person. A marvelous toy train exhibition has been an annual event during the weeks around the winter holidays; call to inquire if it will happen again this year. Summers and school vacation times are the times you are most likely to find wonderful, special hands-on fun provided for children. An extensive summer camp program offers excellent workshops and classes by registration only. An 1816 barn offers a summer theater series, country dances, and numerous folk concerts.

Brooksvale Park (all ages)

Brooksvale Avenue, off Route 10; (Hamden Parks and Recreation: (203) 287–2579. Open 365 days a year from dawn to dusk. Free.

Take a left turn off Route 10 going north to reach Brooksvale Park, a 190-acre recreation area that families flock to for hiking, picnicking, ice-skating, cross-country skiing, sledding, softball, basketball, and good old relaxing in the outdoors. A small petting zoo with domestic animals like peacocks, a horse, oxen, rabbits, geese, ducks, and such are there for the delight of young visitors.

This popular park is a great place to stop if you are using the Farmington Canal Linear Park that spans a nearly 6-mile stretch between Hamden and Cheshire. Brooksvale Park is directly adjacent to the linear walkway and happens to be nearly midway between the southernmost and northernmost end points, so it is a wonderful place for families to lace on their skates or have a rest before or after beginning a trek along the canal.

New Haven County's **Best Ice Cream**

Just north of Sleeping Giant State Park, back out on Route 10, is **Wentworth Old-Fashioned Ice Cream,** which is worth a drive from practically anywhere.

Fifty flavors, twenty-four toppings, freshly made cones, egg creams, root beer floats, fresh-squeezed lemonade, and coffees and baked goods are served up by friendly faces in this cheerfully painted parlor. They are open daily from 10:00 A.M. to 10:00 P.M. Sunday to Thursday and until 11:00 P.M. on Friday and Saturday in the summer; in the spring and fall, they close earlier, depending on the weather and business on the particular day. From late November until roughly late February, they're closed. Call (203) 281–7429.

Farmington Canal Linear Park (all ages)
Parking at Todd Street across from Sleeping Giant Golf Course or at Brooksvale Park on Brooksvale Avenue. Open year-round from dawn to dusk. Free.

This 2.6-mile section of recreational pathway lies along the abandoned railway that previously ran along the old Farmington Canal from Northhampton, MA, to New Haven. Measuring a total of 83 miles, the canal required a 10-foot towpath, a depth of 4 feet, a width of 36 feet, and 25 locks to control the flow of water. All this was constructed using only manpower, horsepower, and simple tools like scoops and dregs. Twenty years later, the canal system was outmoded—replaced by the swifter and less expensive railroad in 1848.

See the Cheshire section (later in this chapter) for other details on this wonderful reuse of land through some of the county's prettiest woodlands. The two sections provide nearly 6 miles of paved and soft-shoulder pathway suitable for walkers, bikers, bladers, joggers, and cross-country skiers. Picnicking is possible along the route on benches made from stone taken from Sleeping Giant State Park. You can also linger at Brooksvale Park in Hamden or Lock 12 Historical Park in Cheshire. This is a great place for a simple family outing on a nice day.

Season Pass for State Parks

Frequent visitors to Connecticut's state parks may want to purchase a season pass that can be used in every state park for the entire Memorial Day through Labor Day season. The pass exempts users from any additional parking fees for individual parks. Unlimited visits to the parks are allowed, and no parks are excluded, except that in Gillette Castle State Park and Dinosaur State Park, the pass covers only the entrance fee to the outdoor areas. Visits to the Castle itself and the Exhibit Dome of Dinosaur Park incur an additional fee.

For information on obtaining passes, contact the State Parks Division at (860) 424–3200.

Where to Eat

Aunt Chilada's Mexican Eatery. 3931 Whitney Avenue; (203) 230–4640. Overlooking the Sleeping Giant Golf Course near one of the entrances to the Linear Park, this establishment invites kids to eat **free** (one child per parent) on Sunday from 4:00 to 8:00 P.M. Clowns and prizes on that night draw in crowds of families. On Tuesday it's taco night—two for $3.00 is a good deal for children. You can also choose salads, enchiladas, fajitas, and much more. Open for lunch and dinner year-round; closed Monday. $–$$

Where to Stay

Days Inn. 3400 Whitney Avenue; (203) 288–2505. 34 units, Jacuzzi. $$$

Howard Johnson Inn. 2260 Whitney Avenue; (203) 288–3831. 90 units, restaurant, outdoor pool. $$$

Cheshire

Centered near the junction of Routes 10 and 70 toward the north of the county, Cheshire was founded in 1690 by families who made their living as farmers, a fact that still influences this eclectic suburb. Close to New Haven, Meriden, Hartford, and Waterbury, Cheshire is a bedroom community for those cities, but it is also a region of nurseries, orchards, dairy and tree farms, and even a vineyard.

Bishop Farm (all ages)

500 South Meriden Road, (Route 70); (203) 272–8243. Open seven days a week year-round from 10:00 A.M. to 5:00 P.M. (sometimes earlier and later in the fall). Free.

Right on Route 70 is one of the oldest and best of Cheshire's farms. The Bishop Farm represents the work of five generations. In business since 1805, Bishop grows and sells six varieties of apples, ten of peaches, four of pears, and five of plums, plus blueberries and raspberries. In the fall they make cider and apple juice at their mill—you can watch them do so on pressing days and then buy some to take home.

In its gift shop and snack bar, you can purchase Vermont cheese, pure honey, ice cream, chicken pot pies, apple crisp, gourmet coffees, and soft drinks. A Christmas Shop is open in season, and Christmas trees are for sale from Thanksgiving through December.

Hayrides, pick-your-own fruits, and a petting barnyard are part of the fun here. In most years more than 70,000 pounds of pumpkins leave these fields. Fall is also a perfect time for walking the trails through the orchards and relaxing near the pond while you have an apple crisp or one of Bishop's apple cider doughnuts.

Call for pick-your-own information and remember that the level of activity varies with the weather and the seasons. If you intend to make this an outing in itself, call to see what's being offered that weekend.

Barker Character, Comic, and Cartoon Museum (all ages)

1188 Highland Avenue, (Route 10); (203) 699–3822 or (800) 995–2357; www.barker animation.com. Open year-round Wednesday through Saturday from 11:00 A.M. to 5:00 P.M. Free.

Want to just smile and smile and smile some more, Mom and Dad? Cheshire is home to another pair of ambitious entrepreneurs who bring a world of pure pleasure to children and parents. Herb and Gloria Barker, who own **Barker's Animation Art Gallery** here, share their love affair with cartoons, comics, advertising characters, TV Westerns, and all the toys and gewgaws that have been manufactured in association with them.

Located on two landscaped acres of converted farm property, the complex includes the Barkers' huge animation art gallery, but it is in the museum and on its grounds that visiting families will begin to grin. This is a baby boomer heaven—at least for trivia nuts and folks who love see- ing wonderful gizmos from childhood. Lone Ranger cereal box rings, Dennis the Menace sling shots, Popeye Pez dispensers, Little Orphan Annie Decoder badges—you name it, it's here.

Special free events are frequent here. On those days strolling "live" characters might greet visitors, famed cartoon- ists might be guests, or kids may be invited to participate in a scavenger hunt or a trivia game.

On weekends especially, the outdoor Storybook Stage show- cases life-sized costumed characters performing Disney versions of classic stories. Also outside, a re-creation of Snow White's wishing well sings in response to your push of a button, and in the children's play- ground, Donald Duck and other characters dance at your child's request.

Inside, a cartoon theater plays cartoon movies from the 1930s on a big screen, and in the museum area, thousands upon thousands of transparen- cies, comic strips, toys, trinkets, lunchboxes, and other memorabilia of the art and industry of cartooning are displayed for your perusal. This is the place to learn the complete stories of Betty Boop, Raggedy Ann and Andy, Sylvester, and hundreds of other characters. You'll learn some of the fascinating details of the technology, art, and history of many classic films from major and minor studios. Make a visit to this happy place and be inspired to take up collecting—or animation—yourself.

Farmington Canal Linear Park (all ages)

Parking areas at Cornwall Avenue, Mount Sanford Road, and Lock 12 at North Brooksvale Road; Cheshire Parks and Recreation Department: (203) 272–2743. Open daily year-round from dawn to dusk. Free.

Cheshire has joined hundreds of other communities across the United States in reclaiming for both recreational and historic preservation purposes the valuable land of abandoned railroad lines and canal routes. Thus far, the town maintains a 2.84-mile section that ends at the Hamden town line. A 2.6-mile Hamden section picks up where this one leaves off (see earlier in this chapter).

This ribbon of land was once on the property of the Farmington Canal, built in 1828 and extending from New Haven Harbor to Northampton, Massachusetts. The longest canal in New England, it was eventually replaced by a railroad along the same corridor. Now a 12-foot-wide pathway has replaced the railway, and the picturesque canal flows beside it (when the rains and snowmelt permit). The wooded pathway is used by joggers, walkers, in-line skaters, and cyclists in the summertime, and whenever there is snow, a swath is left unplowed for cross-country skiers. Mostly paved with asphalt, the path has a stone dust shoulder perfect for joggers. No skateboarding is permitted.

Lock 12 Historical Park (ages 6 and up)

487 North Brooksvale Road; (203) 272–2743. Park open March through December daily from 10:00 A.M. to 5:00 P.M. Museum open for guided tours on weekends only in the spring. Call for a schedule of the tours and special events. Free.

Users of the Farmington Canal Linear Park (as well as other Cheshire visitors) can stop at the park-within-the-park at Lock 12 of the canal. Unfortunately, the museum here is not open all season, but when it is open costumed docents explain the history of the site and the technology of the locks. Engineered by Henry Farnum under the direction of James Hillhouse and Eli Whitney, the canal was an astonishing feat for that period. This site includes the museum building, the lockkeeper's house, a helicoidal bridge, and a picnic area. Of course, access to both the Hamden and Cheshire sections of the linear park is available here.

Where to Eat

Pasta Plus. 1020 South Main Street, (Route 10); (203) 272–1937. Perfect for families, who are drawn in by the aromas of fresh sauces, fresh baked breads and cookies, and fresh pasta. Chef's specials on Monday and Tuesday nights for $7.95; great brick-oven pizza, pastas, chicken, seafood, calzones, and grinders. Open for lunch and dinner 11:30 A.M. to 10:00 P.M. Sunday through Thursday and until 11:00 P.M. on Saturday and Sunday. $–$$

Downey's. 200 South Main Street, (Route 10); (203) 271–1910. Classic American fare and traditional Italian specialties in this casually refined but family-friendly restaurant. Salads, soups, great appetizers, steak, chicken, seafood, and pastas. Open daily year-round for dinner, and for Sunday brunch. Piano entertainment. $$–$$$

Where to Stay

Cheshire Welcome Inn. 1106 South Main Street, (Route 10); (203) 272–3244. 25 units, with 8 efficiencies and 2 apartments in clean, nicely landscaped setting. $$

Waterbury

Known for nearly two centuries as one of the nation's most industrial cities, Waterbury is also one of Connecticut's best embodiments of the term "melting pot." For three centuries its citizenry has been among the most diverse of all Connecticut populations, as wave after wave of immigrants has come here in search of the American Dream.

Though their toil in the factories and mills of Waterbury was often far from idyllic, many of these workers would say their dream did come true. This success is evident in the thriving, busy neighborhoods, the beautiful early-twentieth-century architecture, and the rich variety of cultural entities like the Waterbury Symphony, the nearby Thomaston Opera House, and the newly renovated Mattatuck Museum.

Mattatuck Museum (ages 4 and up)
144 West Main Street; (203) 753–0381; mattatuckmuseum.org. Open Tuesday through Saturday 10:00 A.M. to 5:00 P.M., Sunday noon to 5:00 P.M. Closed on Sunday in July and August and on major holidays. Adults $4.00; children under 16 free.

Excellent for families wishing to expand their appreciation for the unique contributions the little state of Connecticut has made to American culture, the Mattatuck Museum shows off its valuable collection in a recently built facility on the Waterbury green. Elaborately designed to enhance the "museum experience" for children, this engaging museum is the only one in Connecticut that has selected the works in its art galleries entirely from American masters who have been associated with Connecticut. This exclusivity is not at all a drawback. It allows visitors to celebrate both Connecticut artists and Connecticut themes through the work of John Trumbull, Frederic Church, Maurice Prendergast, Alexander Calder, and others.

Fine arts of the nineteenth and twentieth centuries, decorative arts, and furniture are part of the permanent collection, but the period settings are among the best exhibits in the state for children. In the Brass Roots history exhibit, you can examine a re-created seventeenth-century house frame, you can wander through a nineteenth-century board-inghouse re-creation that has the voices of immigrants telling their stories, and you can explore a nineteenth-century brass mill while listening to the voices of workers describing their workdays in the factory. You'll learn what a colonial house looked like, you'll discover the pastimes of wealthy Victorians, and you'll even find out what role a saloon may have played in the lives of the workers who populated this busy industrial city at the end of the nineteenth century.

Cultural Arts in Waterbury

Waterbury and nearby Thomaston also offer other excellent opportunities for family fun. All of the following groups have reputations for presenting arts performances of the highest caliber for audiences of all ages. They are:

- **The Brass City Ballet;** (203) 573–9419. This celebrated company offers performances throughout the year.
- **The Waterbury Symphony Orchestra;** (203) 574–4283. Full season of symphony concerts, special Pops' concerts, and a Discovery series especially for families. Children's tickets for the last are $5.00.
- **The Seven Angels Theatre;** (203) 757–4676; www.sevenangelstheatre.org. Awarded three Connecticut Critic Circle Awards for direction, acting, and design, this Equity venue stages a year-round professional series of Broadway-quality musicals, plays, children's theater, and cabaret concerts.
- **The Thomaston Opera House;** (860) 283–6250. 1884 structure in process of total restoration—can't help but be fabulous when it's done. Musicals suitable for families; the former seasons have included *Godspell*, *The Secret Garden*, and *The Fantastiks*, for instance.

You will also learn of the amazing number of products that originated in the industries of Waterbury and other towns of western Connecticut. Clocks, watches, buttons, cameras, tableware, rubber products, and furniture made the Naugatuck Valley one of the most productive areas of the nation during and after the Industrial Revolution.

One of the best permanent exhibits is the fascinating story of the African-American captive named Fortune, who lived in Waterbury during the 1700s with other free and enslaved Africans. Learn their remarkable stories in this new installation. The Mattatuck has a museum store and a cafe overlooking a courtyard garden. This complex also includes a 300-seat performance center, a research library, and a studio art classroom. Special events such as music festivals, dance performances, children's workshops, and lectures are listed on the Web site calendar.

Where to Eat

Diorio Restaurant. 231 Bank Street; (203) 754–5111. Excellent Italian fare is served at this elegant Waterbury landmark. High-backed booths and an etched-glass mirror across the back of the bar add to the old-time charm, and the great food earned three stars from the *Hartford Courant*. Children are warmly welcomed. Open for lunch and dinner Monday through Friday, dinner only on Saturday. $$$

Domenic's Apizza. 505 Wolcott Street; (203) 753–1989. Apparently it is understood that north of New Haven's Wooster Street there is no finer place for pizza than

Domenic's. Who am I to argue? More than thirty years' practice makes perfect pies. Open Monday and Wednesday from 4:00 to 9:00 P.M. and Thursday through Sunday from 11:30 A.M. to 10:00 P.M. $

Where to Stay

Holiday Inn Express. 88 Union Street; (203) 575–1500, (203) 573–1000, or (800) HOLIDAY. 111 units, fitness center, outdoor pool, continental breakfast. $$$$

Courtyard by Marriott. 63 Grand Street; (203) 596–1000. 200 units, including 11 suites, two restaurants, fitness center, sauna, Jacuzzi, indoor pool. $$$

Middlebury

Way out in the middle of the hills that begin the rise toward Litchfield County and the Berkshires is the pretty community of Middlebury, about 6 miles southwest of Waterbury. And right in the middle of Middlebury is one of the state's most popular family amusement parks.

Quassy Amusement Park (all ages)

Route 64; (800) FOR–PARK or (203) 758–2913; www.quassy.com. Open nearly daily Memorial Day through Labor Day and on April, May, September, and October weekends. Be sure to check the Web site for hours of operation and current pricing before you go. Parking $4.00 per vehicle; regular admission rates are $15.95 per person 42 inches and taller and $12.95 for those under 42 inches for an all-rides/all-day pass. Saturday night after-5:00 carload specials are $10.00 per carload, plus parking. After 5:00 P.M. on any night, a rides pass is $5.50 per person, except on Sunday, when the rate drops to $2.95. Season passes available.

Located on the shores of Lake Quassapaug, Quassy Amusement Park is a sort of old-fashioned affair similar to the Savin Rock park old-timers may remember in West Haven. Not quite as sophisticated as other New England amusement centers like Connecticut's

Lake Compounce or Massachusetts' six Flags New England, Quassy is newly refurbished and a whole lot of fun for families, especially those with young children.

More than twenty-five rides, an eighteen-hole miniature golf course, a narrow-gauge miniature railway, paddleboats, a petting zoo, a lakeside entertainment theater, and a swimming and picnic area at the lake make this a perfectly happy place for a family outing. You can ride the carousel (a beautiful fiberglass repro of the original), two roller coasters, bumper cars, and all kinds of carnival-style rides with names like the Whip, the Monster, and the Himalayas. At the Saturation Station near Lake Quassy's beach, you can find thirty ways to get wet. The Big Flush water coaster is one of the park's newest rides. Take a wild, rubber-raft ride down its 400-foot twisting tube of rushing whitewater. You might also try the new Frog Hopper, a vertical thrill designed for kids 2 to 13. Or climb the catwalk up the *Titanic* and slide 45 feet down the deck to a soft landing.

Along with these features are the usual arcades, games of chance and skill, and a special area for children under 5. The park's food concessions sell typical American fare like hot dogs and barbecued chicken. Special events like a concerts, ethnic festivals, and fireworks add to the seasonal fun.

Where to Eat

Vinny's Pizza. 504 Middlebury Road (Route 64); (203) 758–8846. Strictly pizza is the rule here, with the only exceptions being soda, beer, and wine to help the tasty pie make its way to your happy tummy. Clean, comfortable, and great for families leaving Quassy, this simple place aims to please—and does. Open Wednesday through Sunday from 3:30 P.M., closing at 9:00 on Wednesday, Thursday, and Sunday and at 9:30 on Friday and Saturday. After pizza, stop next door for ice cream at Johnny's Dairy Bar. $

Derby

One of the oldest towns of the Naugatuck Valley, Derby's development has been characterized largely by manufacturing since the Industrial Revolution. Luckily, a small portion of its lush woodlands, once the hunting grounds of the Paugussett Indians, has been preserved for future generations. To reach Derby from New Haven, take Route 34 10 miles west.

Osbornedale State Park/Kellogg Environmental Center/Osborne Homestead Museum (all ages) 🧑‍🤝‍🧑 🦆 🦌 🏛

Park at Chatfield Street; Kellogg Center and Homestead Museum at 500 Hawthorne Avenue; park office: (203) 735–4311; Homestead Museum: (203) 922–7832; Kellogg Center: (203) 734–2513. State park open year-round 8:00 A.M. to dusk daily. Homestead Museum open late April through December 15 on Thursday and Friday from 10:00 A.M. to 3:00 P.M., Saturday from 10:00 A.M. to 4:00 P.M., and Sunday noon to 4:00 P.M. Environmental Center open year-round Tuesday through Saturday from 9:00 A.M. to 4:30 P.M. Free.

This pretty property lies in the hills just north of the confluence of the Housatonic and Naugatuck Rivers. Once the site of a silver mine and a spring water operation, the 400-acre park was for many years the site of a famed breeding farm for prize-winning Osbornedale Holstein cows owned by Frances and Waldo Kellogg.

Activities at the park include hiking and fishing in the summer and skating and cross-country skiing in the winter. However, most activities here center around the Kellogg Environmental Center and the Osborne Homestead Museum, located on the property immediately adjacent to the park. The nationally registered 1850 Colonial Revival homestead is the former residence of Frances Eliza Osborne Kellogg, who willed Osbornedale Park to the State of Connecticut. The house and its formal rose and rock gardens are open for tours (April through December) that focus on the history of its first occupants and the fine art and antiques collection that they amassed here. Please consider offering a small donation if you take one of their hour-long tours. At other times of the year, the grounds of the mansion can be explored daily from 8:30 A.M. to 3:30 P.M.

The Kellogg Environmental Center is a natural science and environmental education facility. Wonderful both in its physical design and in its mission to educate the public, the center includes a solar exhibit area, a water study area, a nature store, a solar greenhouse, and classrooms and labs. Talks, walks, slide presentations, and activity workshops are offered here on a drop-in and registration basis.

General Information

Connecticut River Valley and Shoreline Visitors Council. 393 Main Street, Middletown 06457; (860) 347–0028 or (800) 486–3346; www.ctrivershore.org.

Greater New Haven Convention and Visitors Bureau. 59 Elm Street, New Haven 06510; (203) 777–8550 or (800) 332–STAY; www.newhavencvb.org.

Waterbury Region and Visitors Bureau. 21 Church Street, Waterbury 06702; (203) 597–9527 or (888) 588–7880; www.water buryregion.com.

Middlesex County

Riverside Villages and Shoreline Towns

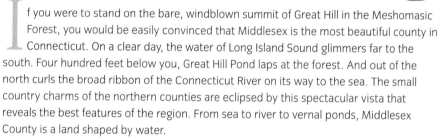

I f you were to stand on the bare, windblown summit of Great Hill in the Meshomasic Forest, you would be easily convinced that Middlesex is the most beautiful county in Connecticut. On a clear day, the water of Long Island Sound glimmers far to the south. Four hundred feet below you, Great Hill Pond laps at the forest. And out of the north curls the broad ribbon of the Connecticut River on its way to the sea. The small country charms of the northern counties are eclipsed by this spectacular vista that reveals the best features of the region. From sea to river to vernal ponds, Middlesex County is a land shaped by water.

Also shaped by the sea and the river have been the lives of the inhabitants of these shores. Many of the attractions families visit in these parts are closely linked to the culture and industries that developed in response to the geography. Come to Middlesex for saltwater taffy, seafood of every sort, steamboat rides, covered bridges, raft races, and riverside rendezvous. Enjoy the bounty of its forests and farms—the water has nourished these well, and the riches they yield are jewels in Connecticut's crown.

TopPicks for fun in Middlesex County

1. Connecticut River Museum and Riverquest Expeditions

2. Essex Steam Train and Riverboat Ride

3. Gillette Castle State Park

4. Devil's Hopyard State Park

5. *Camelot* All-day Greenport, L.I., Cruise

6. Kidcity Children's Museum

7. Amy's Udder Joy Exotic Animal Farm Park

8. Durham Fair

MIDDLESEX COUNTY

Cromwell

East Hampton

Middletown

Middlefield

Durham

Haddam

East Haddam

Chester

Deep River

Killingworth

Ivoryton

Essex

Westbrook

Clinton

Old Saybrook

Essex

North of Old Saybrook on Routes 9 or 154, surely Essex must fall on nearly everyone's list of favorite Connecticut towns. Honored in the past by the accolade, "best small town in America," Essex is most certainly a New England gem, especially at the height of summer and in the stillness of winter. Elegant, gracious, and welcoming to families, Essex is another of Connecticut's windows on the past. Three-masted schooners, whale-oil lamps, scrimshaw, taverns with steaming bowls of chowder, sailors and captains and patient wives waiting at the widow's walks—these are the stuff of Essex's past.

Today, Essex offers a reminder of all of that. Its concentration of eighteenth- and nineteenth-century homes on narrow village lanes, its wharf and marinas, its shops and restaurants—all are evocative of earlier centuries when Essex was one of the busiest ports on the Connecticut River.

RiverQuest Expeditions

If any young sailor in your party is in the mood for a little "expotition," check out the daytime harbor excursions on *RiverQuest*, leaving from the Connecticut River Museum's Steamboat Dock, daily from 10:30 A.M. to 4:30 P.M. The excursion lasts approximately an hour and cruises Essex Harbor and the lower Connecticut River. The twin-hulled, 54-foot *RiverQuest* has a rest room aboard and a fully enclosed cabin; it holds fifty passengers. These narrated cruises of the lower Connecticut River reveal the many reasons this waterway is a designated National Heritage River and has been declared "one of the last great places" by the Nature Conservancy. Learn about the abundant wildlife here and the natural and cultural history of the river itself. Departures are at 10:30 A.M. and noon and at 1:30, 3:00, and 4:30 P.M. Reservations are not required but are strongly encouraged. Tickets for the museum and a harbor excursion cost adults $15; children 5 to 12 pay $10, and children under 5 are free. For a harbor excursion only, adults pay $12 and children 5 to 12 pay $8. For more information on these and other educational excursions, call Connecticut River Expeditions at (860) 662–0577 or (860) 767–8269, check the Web site www.ctriverexpeditions.org, or call the Connecticut River Museum or check its Web site.

Connecticut River Museum (ages 4 and up)

67 Main Street at Steamboat Dock; (860) 767–8269; ctrivermuseum.org. Open year-round, Tuesday through Sunday from 10:00 A.M. to 5:00 P.M. Closed on Monday and major holidays. Adults $5.00; children 6 to 12 $3.00; children under 6 free.

This small, top-notch museum presents the history of the Connecticut River from its geology to its inhabitants, from its industries to the cultures that developed in the area because of the river. New gallery arrangements and exhibits literally explore the river from A to Z in this restored 1878 dockhouse. Among the artifacts and displays are scale models of the river's most famous warships, steamboats, and pleasure crafts as well as shipbuilding tools, marine art, and archaeological treasures unearthed in the area. One gallery focuses on the first submarine, the *American Turtle,* represented by a working replica.

Every year between Thanksgiving and New Year's Day, an exhibition of interest to children is in the changing exhibition gallery. Past exhibits have included dollhouses, snow globes, and model trains. These shows open on the day after Thanksgiving with storytelling and refreshments. Connecticut artist Steven Cryan has crafted several magnificent model train exhibitions. Don't miss this year's show; Steven is often on hand to talk to kids about his work.

In summer, activities are planned especially for families. Usually held on the weekends, past hands-on programs have included such topics as seafaring navigation by the stars, native and colonial knife making and flint knapping, rope making, and knot tying. These workshops are included with admission to the museum, although there may be a higher admission charge than is usual during the week. An interesting lecture series ($5.00) is also on the calendar. Most of these occur on weekdays at 7:30 P.M., but some school-aged children may enjoy the topics if you can arrange the night out.

Essex Steam Train and Riverboat Ride (all ages)

Valley Railroad, 1 Railroad Avenue, off Route 154, about a quarter mile from Route 9 exit 3; (860) 767–0103 or (800) ESSEXTRAIN; www.essexsteamtrain.com. Open early May through December, plus special events throughout the year. Basic rides cost adults $16 for train only, $24 for train and boat; children 3 to 11 $8 train only, $12 train and boat; children under 3 free. Parlor car extra. Special events and combinations are offered regularly and fares vary for each; riverboat combos only in warm season. Call for a brochure and information or check the Web site.

Essex is also home to one of Connecticut's most popular family tourist activities, offered by the Valley Railroad Company. On a typical daily run, these vintage steam locomotives and railcars take passengers on a 12-mile, one-hour, round-trip ride from Essex to Deep River. At Deep River Landing, you can opt to board the triple-decker riverboat for a one-hour cruise upriver, past Gillette Castle to the East Haddam Bridge and the Goodspeed Opera House and then back downriver. The total trip takes about two and a half hours if you take the boat ride.

Special events include an Easter Eggspress in March or April, a Trick or Treat Special in October, and a Santa Special and a Polar Express in December, popularly used for special family celebrations and birthday party–type excursions. Even Thomas the Tank Engine visits here, usually one or two weekends each year.

Come to enjoy the old-fashioned fun and educational elements of these rides. Each segment of the ride includes an entertaining narration about the railroad and the steamship lines. The sights and sounds of the river and countryside—and the trains—are wonderful. Bells, whistles, and the clackety-clack of the railroad track are accompanied by the shouts of blue-capped conductors calling, "All aboard!"

At the trainyard you can visit the station, the car barns, and the gift shop before or after your ride. If you need a bite to eat, a stationary grill car offers burgers, dogs, fries, nuggets, soft drinks, and such ($). If you want a special dining experience, book tickets for the Essex Clipper Dinner Train and dine aboard a 1920s dining car, with a two-hour excursion through the river valley as you feast (May through October).

The Parade **of Lighted Ships**

Early in December (or, rarely, in late November) the Connecticut River Museum sponsors a **free** festival called Trees in the Rigging, which features a lantern-lit community caroling march led by the Cappella Cantorum and the Ancient Mariners' Fife and Drum Corps and a parade of lighted ships on the river. Beginning at the Essex Town Hall at 4:00 P.M. on Sunday evening of the selected weekend, carolers make their way down West Avenue and Main Street to the waterfront park at historic Steamboat Dock to see the colorfully lit garlands and nautical flags on the scores of participating boats. Santa himself arrives on the dock by tugboat, and carolers and children greet him and warm themselves with hot mulled cider at the museum. Among the decorated homes and shops of the village, this charming festivity draws many visitors eager to experience the magic of Essex in winter.

Where to Eat

Griswold Inn. 36 Main Street; (860) 767–1776. Stop here for a meat pie in winter near one of the fireplaces or in summer for fresh seafood in the room with the moving mural of the steamboat on the Connecticut River. A special "young sailor's" menu, bottomless glasses of soda, and helpful suggestions for plate-sharing options make the place nice for young diners. Come for the famed Sunday Hunt Breakfast, served from 11:00 A.M. to 2:30 P.M.; kids under 7 eat for **free.** $$–$$$

Crow's Nest Gourmet Deli. 35 Pratt Street in the Brewers Dauntless Shipyard at the end of Bushnell Street off Main; (860) 767–3288. Perfect for families, this eat-in, take-out, or out-on-the-deck eatery is the best place in town for ice cream and the only restaurant overlooking the water in Essex. Open year-round for breakfast and lunch daily from 7:00 A.M. to 4:00 P.M. from mid-June to Labor Day; closing at 3:00 P.M. in spring and fall; closed on Tuesdays from Columbus Day to Memorial Day. Come for omelets, pancakes, create-your-own sandwiches, fajitas, lobster, chicken, ribs, and chowders. Don't miss the cookies, muffins, scones, cheesecakes, and other treats made fresh every day. $–$$

Oliver's Tavern. 124 Westbrook Road (Route 153), not far south of Valley Railroad, but not in the center village of Essex; (860) 767-2633. Good American fare (steaks, seafood, specialty sandwiches, chowder) in a warm, friendly setting that happily caters to children. Open daily year-round from 11:30 A.M. for lunch and dinner. $–$$

Where to Stay

Griswold Inn (same address and phone; www.griswoldinn.com) is also a very fine hostelry, offering 30 rooms and suites and even a charming guest cottage. Beautiful maritime and river artworks, fireplaces, private baths, and continental breakfast served in the library for all guests make this a cozy place for families. $$$–$$$$

Ivoryton

Officially a section of the town of Essex, this little village just a few miles east of Route 153 gained its name from its production of ivory products, in particular piano keys, in the nineteenth century. First settled in the mid-seventeenth century, Ivoryton's interest in preserving the traditions of the early colonials comes as no surprise in its museum celebrating one of the colonies' oldest traditions.

Ivoryton also boasts a regional reputation in the arts because of the performing companies that share the space of a venerable theater at the village center. The **Ivoryton Playhouse,** which has been home since 1930 to some of Connecticut's best repertory and summer stock theater groups, is now home to companies both amateur and professional. The playhouse hosts a terrific summer series for children.

Museum of Fife and Drum (ages 6 and up)

62 North Main Street; (860) 399–6519 or (860) 767–2237. Usually open in July and August on Sunday from 1:00 to 5:00 P.M. or by appointment year-round. Closed third weekend of July and the fourth weekend in August. Donations: adults $2.00; children under 13 free.

This small museum is dedicated to the history and development of parade music, with a special emphasis on the traditional fife and drum corps that are called ancients. See the uniforms, parade and performance gear, musical instruments, music, and photographs of corps from all over the nation and Europe. Learn about the history of fifing and drumming from the Middle Ages through modern times. Special exhibits focus on Revolutionary War and Civil War corps. Evening performances are offered at the museum on Tuesday at 7:30 P.M. in July and August.

The River Rep Theatre for Children (ages 2 to 10)

At the Ivoryton Playhouse, on Main Street; (860) 767–8348; riverrep.com. Friday at 11:00 A.M. from late June through late August. All seats $8.00.

Perfect for children 2 to 10, this traditional summer series includes hourlong retellings of fairy tales, magic shows, modern classics like *You're a Good Man, Charlie Brown,* and so on.

This company also does excellent adult productions, but families are in for the most enjoyable and affordable theater with this cheer-filled series. Occasional family entertainment is also offered in other seasons. Call the Ivoryton Playhouse Foundation at (860) 767–7318 to get on the mailing list.

Deep River/Chester

These two small towns are two of the most charming country villages in the state, although neither is exactly the family entertainment center of its county. Still, there are some excellent opportunities in both places for families.

Chester is quiet, quaint, and *tiny.* Located on Route 148 and surrounded by the Cockaponset State Forest, Chester was founded in 1692 as Pattaquonk Quarter, the fourth parish of Saybrook. An independent town by 1836, it seems content to remain in that century. Its winding lanes lined with historic buildings are unblemished by purveyors of fast food, slushy red soft drinks, or other atrocities of modern civilization. In Chester you will find lovely shops, great restaurants, and serenity.

When I first heard the name Deep River as a child on a family day trip to Gillette Castle, I thought Tom Sawyer must live in this town. Somewhere, he sits dangling his feet in the water, chewing on a piece of straw and watching the steamboats pass by.

Thirty years later, Deep River is not much different than it was the first time I saw it. Centered on the main thoroughfare of Route 154, it is a quiet town that still has the look

Deep River Muster of Ancient Fife and Drum Corps

Held every third Saturday in July, this great family-style event is a must-see experience for summer travelers. A gathering of up to seventy separate corps from all over the nation and overseas, this famed muster includes a colorful parade up the main street (Route 154) of Deep River. This great parade may be the only one of its kind—or at least the largest. Chairs and blankets line the parade route long before you hear the first salute. Authentic uniforms, unforgettable music, and even bagpipers, pirates, Uncle Sam, and Dan'l Boone are part of the show.

After the parade, which can easily last two hours, walk to Devitt Field (at the bottom of the parade route), where the corps meet for food, drink, and special performances. You can buy fifes, drums, music, tricornered hats, and other related items in the tents lining the perimeter of the field. You can even find out how to join a corps yourself. The parade and admission to the field are **free**, but parking will cost you about $5.00 in one of the many "lots" set up on the front lawns of the townsfolk. For information, call (860) 767-2237.

and feel of a town of the 1950s. Famed in the more-distant past as a steamboat port accepting cargo and passengers to its docks, Deep River was once at the heart of the ivory trade that gave neighboring Ivoryton its name and supported the piano factories that you can still see in Deep River along Route 154. In the late 1800s, three quarters of the ivory taken from Zanzibar was shipped to Deep River. Today piano keys are long forgotten as the principal product of the area, and the tourists arrive mostly just to savor its quaint aspects. Here are a few of the highlights of both towns.

Canfield-Meadow Woods Nature Preserve (all ages)

Access from the east side of 377 South Main Street, Deep River, just south of the Sunoco station. Open daily year-round free, dawn to dusk.

Three hundred acres of woodlands, wetlands, ridges, and valleys are the habitats and terrains in this preserve. Open for passive recreation such as hiking and wildlife watching, the preserve has any easy 3.5 mile trail; maps are usually at the trailhead.

Connecticut River Artisans (ages 6 and up)

5 West Main Street, Chester; (860) 526–5575. Open Wednesday through Sunday from 10:00 A.M. to 5:00 P.M. year-round.

If you can't resist a peek at the shops, I recommend this one in particular. A cooperative that showcases the traditional and contemporary work of about twenty local craftspeople, it has beautiful and original furniture, pottery, clothing, jewelry, sculpture, and more in all media. The prices are fair but upscale; luckily, it costs nothing to enjoy the artistry. You may even get to meet the person who created your favorite piece—the artisans share the work of running the shop. Other shops in the village are equally lovely, but this one is especially creative and inspirational. Browse the others after a stop here before the kids get antsy.

Where to Eat

The Whistle Stop Cafe. 108 Main Street, Deep River; (860) 526–4122. You can't get any more small-town charming than this or serve more basically good food for families. Children are catered to, in fact, by owner Hedy Watrous, who bought the business started by her grandfather in 1928. Children's specials are offered at every meal, and breakfast is served all day, beginning at 7:30 A.M. Lunch begins at 11:00 A.M. and ends at 2:00 P.M., when the cafe closes. You can eat inside or outside. Open Thursday through Monday. $–$$

The Wheatmarket. 4 Water Street, Chester, around the back of the shops on the main village lane; (860) 526–9347. These friendly folks close their place on Sundays, but they serve delicious, out-of-the-ordinary sandwiches, soups, cheeses, and breads all the rest of the week. Vegetarians will find food they can eat here, thank goodness, and families who arrive early can have dinner here or buy to take out. Open Monday through Friday from 9:00 A.M. to 6:00 P.M. and until 4:00 P.M. on Saturday. Closed Sunday. $

Where to Stay

The Inn at Chester. 318 West Main Street; (800) 949–STAY or (860) 526–9541. On Route 148 about 4 miles outside the village, this restored and greatly added-upon farmhouse offers 42 guest rooms with private baths.

Tennis courts, a sauna, a gym, a wonderful restaurant (with special dishes for young diners) and tavern room, and a continental breakfast for all guests help to make this expansive (but expensive) retreat cozy enough for families. $$$$

East Haddam

This so-called river town also spreads far easterly for several miles in the place where Middlesex County pushes itself squarely into the western boundaries of New London County. Though it is famed as the home of Connecticut's castle and its riverside opera house, it is also a rural enclave that few visitors explore past the sight and sound of the river. Adventurous families should spend an extra day near East Haddam just to be sure they've seen all its wonders. Take Route 9 or Route 154 to Route 82 to reach its center.

Gillette Castle State Park (ages 3 and up)
67 River Road; (860) 526–2336. The park is open year-round from 8:00 A.M. to sunset; no entrance fee is charged. The castle is open from 10:00 A.M. to 5:00 P.M. every day from the Saturday of Memorial Day weekend through Columbus Day. Last castle tour at 4:30 P.M. Adults $5.00; children 6 to 17 $3.00; children 5 and under free.

I have yet to find a guidebook that can resist mentioning this medieval-looking wonder. Toured by 100,000 visitors each year, the castle is so popular with families that most of you reading this book have probably already been here. Recent restorations have ensured that many more generations of visitors can enjoy this enchanting structure.

The splendid fieldstone fortress sits on a bluff called the Seventh Sister, high above the eastern bank of the Connecticut River. Completed in 1919 as the retirement home of actor William Gillette (famed for his stage portrayal of Sherlock Holmes in the early part of the twentieth century), the house was built according to the exact specifications of its somewhat eccentric owner. The turrets, terraces, archways, and fountains found outside are awesome enough, but the interior will make you gape. The twenty-four rooms, each more unique or unusual than the last, contain gorgeous stonework, extraordinary hand-carved woodwork, and many of Gillette's original furnishings and possessions. The castle also contains a re-creation of Sherlock Holmes's sitting room at 221B Baker Street, London, and an incredible assemblage of Holmes-related memorabilia, the largest such collection in the world.

During the four weekends between Thanksgiving and the week before Christmas, the castle has an annual Victorian Holiday Celebration. The interior is specially decorated, and musical performances and other entertainments are offered. Call ahead to be sure this tradition is continuing.

The castle grounds are part of the 200-acre **Gillette Castle State Park,** an area of breathtaking views of the river and valley. Three and a half miles of trails allow you to explore safely, and you'll find many spots perfect for fishing, picnicking, napping, or playing knights and ladies.

Ferry 'Cross the River

If you're headed to Gillette Castle or you need to cross the river for any other reason, catch a ride on the **Chester–Hadlyme ferry** (860–443–3856) that docks at the end of Route 148. The ride takes about four minutes and costs $2.25 per car and driver, plus 75 cents for each passenger. The flatboat *Selden III* begins each day's labor on the Hadlyme side at 7:00 A.M.; the last ride of the day leaves Chester at 6:45 P.M. Running daily (with the exception of Thanksgiving Day) from April 1 through November, the Chester–Hadlyme ferry service is one of the oldest in the country; it's been in continuous operation since 1769.

Goodspeed Opera House (ages 6 and up)
Goodspeed Landing on Route 82; box office: (860) 873–8668; tours: (860) 873–8664.

You must have noticed this building as you crossed the river on Route 82. It's huge, it's white, and it looks like someone in 1876 was trying to create the biggest, best Second Empire opera house in the nation.

Evidence suggests that the architect was successful. Restored inside and out, the beautiful Goodspeed presents a three-show season of hit musical productions from April through December. Mostly revivals of Broadway favorites from the 1920s through the 1960s, the shows in this intimate theater are great family entertainment. Except for the youngest members of your family who might have trouble staying settled through these full-length performances, bring the whole family if you can afford the moderately priced (compared to Broadway) tickets.

Real theater buffs may enjoy the thirty-minute tours of the opera house offered in season on Saturday and Monday; call for specific times and reservations. For $2.00 per adult and $1.00 for children under 12, you get to see the dressing rooms and all the inner workings, plus you hear great stories of the Goodspeed's illustrious past.

Nathan Hale Schoolhouse

So-called because the Connecticut patriot taught here, at the age of 18, for six months in 1773 and 1774, this one-room building is at the rear of St. Stephen's Church property on Route 149, just a bit north of the Opera House. We've never stopped to tour it, but it is open on weekends and holidays from 2:00 to 4:00 P.M. in the summertime only, if you have an interest. Admission is 25 cents.

Devil's Hopyard State Park (all ages)

Route 82 to Mount Parnassus Road to Hopyard Road; (860) 873–8566. The park is open year-round from 8:00 A.M. to sunset. Free entrance to park; camping fee. *(Note: Despite the remarks in the following paragraphs, which present the ideal here, state budget cuts have caused a less perfect reality. When you visit, the campground could be closed, some trails may be off-limits, and even some picnic areas and rest rooms may be closed. Call ahead. Park rangers work very hard to keep this lovely area open and safe.)*

Beautiful in all seasons, the moderate trails through the heavily wooded terrain of this lovely park are wonderful for families. Views of the countryside are especially breathtaking in the fall, but the 60-foot cascades of Chapman Falls are most impressive in the spring. Look for the potholes in the rocks at the base of the falls. Legend says that these formations were made by the hot hoofs of the Devil as he hopped from ledge to ledge so as not to get wet.

Leave your own footprints on the footpaths that lead to the many scenic overlooks of the pretty Eight Mile River that threads itself through the woods and farms in the area. Stay overnight (if you dare) in one of the twenty-one wooded campsites with drinking water and outhouses. You can call for reservations or try your luck at the first come, first served game. You can also fish from the streams and picnic wherever you like. A large picnic area with tables is provided near the parking area, but in our opinion the best spots for picnicking are actually at the trailside overlooks. Choose the one that pleases you most. Leave well before dark if you believe the stories that this wood is haunted by the Devil and the ancient hags of Haddam.

Where to Eat

Me and McGee. 40 Saybrook Road (Route 154), across the river in Higganum; (860) 345–3777. Ask anybody in East Haddam how to get here—they'll know. The great food and good company at this friendly, casual eatery keep the locals coming back and the tourists glad they came. Excellent breakfast omelets, fresh-daily homestyle soups, famed fish and chips, specials that reflect the seasonal harvest, and Mom-made bakery treats and breads. Open 6:00 A.M. to 2:30 P.M. every day except Sunday. $–$$

The Cooking Company. 1610 Saybrook Road at Swing Bridge Market Place, Haddam, near junction of Routes 82 and 154; (860) 345–8008. Open from 10:00 A.M. daily except Sunday, this gourmet deli/bakery/coffee-house has excellent hot or cold sandwiches, wraps, salads, soups, and desserts. Eat in or take out. $

Hadlyme Country Store. Near the corner of Routes 82 and 148 (called Ferry Road after the intersection); (860) 526–3188). Open daily from 7:00 A.M. to 6:00 P.M., except 5:00 P.M. on Sunday, this charming little store is run by cheerful folks who sell great picnic/hiking food and supplies—sandwiches, salads, fresh baked goods, soda, ice cream, even charcoal and marshmallows. $

Where to Stay

The Gelston House. At Goodspeed Landing; (860) 873–1411. Children are more than welcome here in this decidedly polished inn frequented most often by adult travelers. If your budget permits it, the lovely suites in this six-guest-room inn will meet all your family's needs. Rollaway beds are cheerfully added for children, but you have to bring your own portacribs for infants and toddlers. $$$$

Sunrise Resort. Route 151; (860) 873–8681. Only open May through October, this family resort/ campground on the Salmon River has 200 guest units, 30 campsites, an outdoor Olympic-sized pool, an on-site restaurant, a playground, tennis, volleyball, shuffleboard and bocce courts, a playground, paddleboats, rowboats, and canoes. Nightly and weekly rates. $$

Wolf's Den Family Campground. 256 Town Street (Route 82); (860) 873–9681. Tent and RV sites for 209 campers. Swimming, fishing, and hiking nearby. Tennis on the property. Game room and laundry facilities, toilets and showers. Nightly and weekly rates. $$

Haddam

The river beckons to visitors once again in Haddam, this time on the west bank. In this town, too, the boundaries far exceed the visitor's concept of the few structures that hug close to the river. The town actually goes westward all the way to the Durham town line, but it is here near the water that the action for families centers.

Camelot Cruises, Inc. (all ages)

1 Marine Park, right off Route 82 at the bridge; (860) 345–8591 or (800) 522–7463; www.camelotcruises.com or www.greenport.com. Cross-Sound cruises in summertime; river cruises from April through December; foliage cruises from late September through November on Tuesday, Thursday, and Sunday. Call for rates and schedules.

This excursion line docks its 500- and 600-passenger triple-decker cruise ships right at the riverside across from the Goodspeed Opera House. *Camelot I* and *II* offer all-day cruises to Greenport, Long Island, from early June to late August. Bring a bicycle along or walk to the many shops, restaurants, museums, beaches, and historic sites of this picturesque former whaling village. A typical trip leaves Haddam at 9:30 A.M. and returns at 6:00 P.M. Adults pay approximately $34.50; children under 12 cost $10.00, and children under 5 ride **free.** These trips are made on Wednesdays only.

Murder mystery dinner cruises and luncheon matinees, fall foliage lunch cruises, Sunday brunch buffet cruises, and New Orleans Jazz and Rock & Roll Oldies dinner cruises are also offered throughout the spring to fall season. Special excursions are also available. Reservations are necessary for those cruises and for groups.

Where to Eat

The Blue Oar River Bank Grille. 16 Snyder Road, off Route 154 in the Midway Marina; (203) 345–2994. For a casual meal outdoors on picnic tables or on the veranda inside, come to this sailor's secret, 1 mile north of the swinging bridge. The views of the Connecticut River are beautiful, the chowder is great, and the sandwich specials or grilled dinners will please yachters and landlubbers alike. Open April through mid-October, for lunch and dinner, Tuesday through Sunday, 11:30 A.M. to 9:00 P.M. Dinner specials start at 5:00 P.M. $–$$

East Hampton

Near the shores of Lake Pocotopaug is the tiny hamlet of East Hampton, the town in which I took my first childhood family vacation, saw my first snapping turtle, and learned both how to canoe and how to capsize a canoe. Whoops!

Hurd State Park (all ages)
South of East Hampton center, on Route 151; (860) 526–2336. No day-use fee.

Hurd State Park is another of the excellent facilities the State of Connecticut maintains for public use. Like other state parks, it is typically beautiful, clean, safe, and fun. It's special, however, because of its location overlooking the Connecticut River and because of its pretty Hurd Brook Gorge. Its 884 acres offer a wide variety of recreational activities, including rock climbing, snowmobiling, cross-country skiing, freshwater fishing, and hiking. The Split Rock trail takes you to some magnificent views of the river valley.

The Bridge of Middlesex County

Over on Route 16, almost at the New London County line, is the **Comstock Covered Bridge,** one of the last remaining authentic covered bridges in Connecticut. Designed by Ithiel Town in the lattice-truss style, it's open only to foot traffic now. Artists and photographers and those who would like to fish in the Salmon River frequent the area. If you happen to be nearby, stop and have a look. The bridge is very large and pretty, a quiet, cool refuge on a sunny day.

Most important, Hurd offers campsites for youth groups and for boaters. Many folks canoe and camp from here to Gillette Castle or to **Selden Neck State Park,** a 528-acre island downriver toward Lyme; accessible only by boat, those parks also have primitive riverside campsites available from May through September. The state has provided toilets and drinking water at Hurd; drinking water, outhouses, and fireplaces are at Selden Neck. No admission fee is charged at any time for day use of Hurd or Selden Neck, but overnight camping fees are charged at all three facilities. Call for information on the varied options open to daytripping or camping canoeists.

Great Hill Overlook

You might recall from the intro to this chapter a mention of Great Hill in the Meshomasic State Forest. It is from the Cobalt section of East Hampton that you will reach it. Drive to the intersection of Routes 151 and 66 in Cobalt and go east on Route 66 just a bit over a mile to Cones Hill Road. Take a left on Cones Hill Road and drive 1 mile to its junction with Clark Hill Road and Great Hill Road. Take the right fork onto Clark Hill Road and drive a little more than a half mile until you see a dirt service road (which may be marked Forest Road) on the left. A tad more than half a mile up the dirt service road, you will come to the Shenipsit Trail, which is marked by blue blazes. Park at that crossing and hike south (toward the left, from where you met the crossing) about 1¾ miles on the trail. At that point, the Shenipsit main trail turns left, and a white-blazed trail toward the south will take you several hundred feet to the summit of Great Hill. You'll retrace your steps to your car. This is a moderate hike of about 4 miles round-trip.

You may also begin at the same intersection of Routes 151 and 66, go north on 151 for ¹⁄₁₀ mile to the first road crossing, bear right at the road crossing, drive ⁹⁄₁₀ of a mile, turn right at the Y intersection, and take this gravel section of Great Hill Road to the trailhead, about ⁴⁄₁₀ mile down the road. Before you attempt the trail, call the Connecticut Forest and Park Association at (860) 346–2372, which produces the wonderful *Connecticut Walk Book.* They can confirm the trail's condition or refer you to the volunteer trail manager.

Middletown

This small city, once the largest and busiest port on the whole Connecticut River, is now best known as the home of Wesleyan University, one of the nation's finest centers of higher education. The city's interesting history and architecture and its position on the river have led entrepreneurs to capitalize on the tourist business that may help to revive the formerly sleepy atmosphere of the recently refurbished downtown area. These efforts as well as some traditional favorite events and sites make Middletown a good destination for families looking for fun in one of Connecticut's funkiest small cities.

Kidcity Children's Museum (all ages especially infant to 10)
119 Washington Street; (860) 347–0495; www.kidcitymuseum.com. Open Sunday through Tuesday from 11:00 A.M. to 5:00 P.M. and Wednesday through Saturday from 9:00 A.M. to 5:00 P.M. Children $5.00; adults $3.00. Annual family memberships available.

The brainchild of Wesleyan alumna and Middletown mom Jennifer Alexander, Kidcity is devoted to integrated learning and play experiences for young children. Located just steps away from the city's main street, the museum offers 13,500 square feet of play space dedicated to the idea that parents and kids who play together will also learn together, grow together, and reach out to others together.

In early 2004 the museum enjoyed an exciting explosion of space and square-footage in its two linked buildings. A Deep Sea Playground, a treehouse village where elves may abide, and an outer-space lounge are among the wonderful new additions. "Please touch" is the rule in every area of the museum, with a dentist office, eyeglass shop, fire truck and fire station, market, jewelry shop, florist, and much more. Children can shop for groceries or ring up the sale, examine gemstones under a magnifying glass, or serve a meal at the Downtown Diner. Use the two-way radio or the phone system to chat with new friends or relay an important message to the library or bagel shop. Check out the nearby sailing ship or the farm yard and farmhouse. All of these areas on the first floor are specially designed for children through 5 years old.

On the second floor, exhibits especially for children 6 through 10 years old include a video theater where you can create your own show using lights, sound effects, props, and costumes. In the Build It play area, Velcro-covered foam blocks will challenge young architects who enjoy engineering and construction concepts; music enthusiasts may explore the unique instruments in the Global Music room, where a seesaw rainstick, an oversized steel drum, and a one-octave pipe organ are among the giant musicmakers that offer a chance to experiment. In the Invention Station are recycled odds and ends for making collages or inventions; while here, check out the changing displays of real-life applications of physics, science, and math. Perhaps you'll discover how to wire a bicycle chain or see how a toilet works. A Borrower's Library for those seeking quiet contemplation and a community room for parties or game playing are among the other amenities here. This museum is an outstanding example of how imaginative collaboration results in magical benefits for an entire community.

Deep River Navigation Company (all ages)

Harborpark, exit 14 or 15 from Route 9; (860) 526–4954. Advance reservations recommended for fall foliage cruises. Adults $25; children 3 to 11 half price; under 3 free. Free parking.

Foliage cruises on weekends from early to late October are currently the main focus of the two-hour and four-hour tours that leave from Middletown's Harborpark and go downriver. The longer cruise goes past Goodspeed Opera House in East Haddam and Gillette Castle in Hadlyme. Views of the glorious Seven Sisters hills are wonderful on these afternoon cruises suitable for the whole family. In fall 2003, cruises left Harborpark at noon and 2:30 P.M. Call ahead for tickets and the current schedule. Hot dogs, pizzas, snacks, and beverages are available on board. This cruise company also runs many other tours, beginning in Hartford and Old Saybrook. See those entries on page 123 and page 205. Call for a brochure, fares, and other information.

Oddfellows Playhouse Youth Theater (ages 4 and up)

128 Washington Street (Route 66); (860) 347–6143; www.oddfellows.org. Year-round. Tickets in advance or at door; adults usually $6.00–$8.00, children $4.00–$6.00.

The state's oldest and largest theater dedicated to works performed by and for children, this theater was started in 1975 by Wesleyan students. Now privately run, the recently renovated theater in a somewhat ordinary but refurbished early-twentieth-century red-brick building on one of Middletown's main drags is still spurred by the efforts and involvement of many Wesleyan folks. With a commendable mission to provide educational, multicultural entertainment that is accessible to all students, including disadvantaged and minority children, these productions are high-quality works enhanced by the expertise of professionals from all over the country who come to direct the young actors.

Among recent productions were a two-part adaptation of the Indian epic *The Mahabharata,* a production of *The Wizard of Oz,* and a showcase of immigration stories entitled *American Dream.* Great fun to watch or to perform in is the annual Children's Circus, held outdoors at 6:00 P.M. on the Friday of the first full week of August. Middletown schoolchildren ages 8 to 14 take a five-week summer camp to learn the necessary circus skills for this amazing production. All other plays are open to student actors from out of town, and all productions are open to the public. As many as two shows per month run throughout the school year; summer productions vary in number.

The Wesleyan Potters (ages 6 and up)

350 South Main Street (Route 17); (860) 344–0039. Open year-round Tuesday through Saturday from 11:00 A.M. to 5:00 P.M. Free.

One of Connecticut's finest craft centers, this prestigious studio was inspired by the work of a Wesleyan professor who began a pottery class for Middletown residents in 1948. Now housed in 9,000 square feet of studio and gallery space in an old Venetian blind factory, this cooperative includes 100 potters, weavers, basket makers, and jewelry artists who exhibit their work and hone their crafts here. They also teach a year-round schedule of classes and workshops, all of which are available to the public. The frequency of these classes nearly ensures that a visit here by a family could include observation of teachers and new crafters at work. Your interest is welcomed; just stop in the office between the gallery shop and the studios to ask someone to escort you to a spot from which you can observe without disrupting the class. Tuesday is probably the best day for seeing both potters and weavers; on Friday the place can be as quiet as a tomb. Call ahead to arrange a more detailed guided tour of the pottery and weaving studios (860–347–5925).

Amaizing

You've gotta check this out! In a four-acre corn field in Middletown, Connecticut's most **aMAIZEing Maze** has been planted and trimmed so that 2 miles of pathways lead visitors on a horse-high adventure every summer. Check out their Web site at www.CTmaze.com or call (860) 346–3360 for more information. From mid-July to early November, Saturday and Sunday, come to find your way—or get lost!

Where to Eat

Tuscany Grill. 120 College Street, also known as 600 Plaza Middlesex; (860) 346–7096. Open daily for lunch and dinner in an old theater building with high ceilings and brightly lit galleries. Light, fresh sauces over perfectly done pastas; well-seasoned soups; excellent thin-crust brick-oven pizza; good bread; simple but innovative salads. Children are warmly welcomed here. $–$$

It's Only Natural. 684 Main Street; (860) 346–9210. Restaurant, bookstore, and market, ION is perfect for families who crave the delicious taste and texture of wonderful entrees, soups, and sandwiches prepared freshly each day in this casual vegetarian eatery. Open Monday through Saturday from 9:00 A.M. to 8:00 P.M. and Sunday from 11:00 A.M. to 4:00 P.M. $

O'Rourke's Diner. 728 Main Street; (860) 346–6101. This place provides somewhere to go if the kids are up and at 'em early, that's for sure. Breakfast all day, real mashed pota-toes, perfect chicken salad club sandwiches, classic milkshakes. Tabletop jukeboxes and eager-to-please-the-kids servers make this a fun place for the family. Open Monday through Friday from 4:30 A.M. to 3:00 P.M. and Saturday and Sunday until 1:00 P.M. $

Eleanor Rigby's Gourmet Delicatessen and Café. 360 Main Street; (860) 343–1730. Cheerfully decorated and absolutely spotless, this breakfast and lunch spot provides an excellent salad bar, four homemade soups daily, sandwiches, salads, pastas, baked goods, and daily specials. Open Monday through Friday from 8:30 A.M. to 4:00 P.M. $

Vecchittos. 323 DeKoven Drive; (860) 346–2637. The place to go in all of Connecticut for Italian ice, this classic operation is run by three brothers who grew up in the house attached to the store. Choose a favorite ice (lemon, raspberry, chocolate, watermelon, banana, you name it) on a hot summer night. Noon till 9:30 P.M. from Memorial Day until the crowds go away sometime after Labor Day. $

Where to Stay

The Inn at Middletown. 70 Main Street; (860) 854–6300; www.innatmiddletown.com. Finally, a place to stay in the heart of Middletown! The city's former National Guard Armory has been restored and outfitted as a lovely 100-room inn. 12 two-room junior suites equipped with microwave and refrigerator; cribs available at no charge. Heated indoor pool, fully equipped fitness center, and a 100-seat restaurant **Tavern at the Armory** (dinner $$$–$$$$), which serves three meals daily. Specializing in traditional New England cuisine with seasonal favorites, it also offers a children's menu. Highchairs and boosters available. Walking distance to Kidcity Museum, downtown stores and theaters, Wesleyan campus, and harborfront activities. $$$–$$$$

Cromwell

Cromwell is a perfectly nice town of 12,000 friendly inhabitants, but not too much has happened near its busy urban-suburban State Route 372 thoroughfare to draw traveling families to the businesses and eateries that flank the roadside. On the town's historic Main Street, which is Route 99, there's more of a sense of community pride, and town leaders might want to jump onto the revitalization bandwagon with the small entrepreneurs here and use the town's riverfront position to a cultural and economic advantage. There's potential here, but for now there's just one great reason that all families should come to Cromwell.

Amy's Udder Joy Exotic Animal Farm Park and Nature Center

(all ages) 🐾

27 North Road; (860) 635–3924; www.freeyellow.com/members2/aujzoological. **Open May through Labor Day, Tuesday through Sunday 11:00 A.M. to 4:00 P.M.; weekends only at same hours after Labor Day until last weekend in October; please call in advance if you would like to visit after Labor Day. Admission for each person over the age of 1 is $3.00; pony rides (weekends only, from 1:00 to 4:00 P.M.) are an additional $2.00.**

One of those small attractions I thought I could write about without seeing, this is a sure hit for kids of all ages, but it sure isn't ordinary. I was expecting quack-quack, moo-moo, and other noisy fun—straightforward stuff, sort of like a day off for a travel writer. Kick off the Keds and write it straight from the armchair.

No such luck, at least not for me. When I first told my kids that owner Amy O'Toole had a llama, a yak, Barbados black belly sheep, and Tennessee fainting goats, they were in the car, ready to go, before I could say "and, now, for something completely different . . ."

Now ten years later, things *are* completely different. Amy's Udder Joy is a fully licensed, nonprofit zoological nature center and education facility with more than fifty rare, primitive, exotic, or endangered species from around the world, plus native wildlife. Along with the above-mentioned creatures are wallabies, fallow deer, African antelope, ostriches, emus, rheas, an Asian golden jungle cat, prairie dogs, a great horned owl, tarantulas, an American alligator, a porcupine, and many others. Now more than ever, it appears as if only Doctor Dolittle himself and the pushmi-pullyu are missing.

You can take a guided or self-guided tour. Excellent signage lets you know what you're looking at, and someone is always around to add to your education. One wonderful please-touch table invites children to stimulate their senses of touch and sight through examination of seashells, coral, cow horn, tree fungus, a honeycomb, a snakeskin, and other natural specimens. A saltwater touch tank nearby includes crabs and such, and a second touch table displays a skull collection.

The indoor and outdoor exhibits include more than 100 animals, plus approximately 200 chickens, geese, peacocks, and ducks, all of which are also rare or exotic. You can buy feed at coin-operated machines, and you can actually enter a special petting area to hold and feed baby chicks and geese and to pet the sheep and goats. The indoor barn exhibits include mammals, reptiles, arachnids, and small rock, mineral, fossil, and butterfly collections.

All drop-in visitors are welcome in this three-quarter-acre menagerie, but groups should call ahead if a lectured tour is desired. Bring a picnic lunch or snacks if you'd like to stay awhile. An enclosed picnic/party area can also be reserved for birthday parties or club meetings. Large and child-sized picnic tables are available for that use.

Every weekend during Amy's public season, children can ride the state's one and only living carousel. Four ponies are decked out with special hairduds, pretty blankets, and jeweled saddles and bridles. Amy plays calliope music over the loudspeakers, and the ponies give delighted young children four turns around the riding ring. I didn't plan to use the word "cute" in this book, but this is very, very cute.

And yes—the goats really do faint. Amazing.

Where to Eat

Baci Grill. 134 Berlin Road (Route 372); (860) 613–0601. Voted the best new restaurant in Middlesex County, this place welcomes families for Northern Italian pasta specialties, brick-oven pizzas, salads, chicken, veal, and seafood dishes, and more. Children's menu, $. Open for lunch and dinner daily year-round. $$–$$$

Where to Stay

Holiday Inn. 4 Sebethe Drive; (860) 635–1001. Nearly 150 units, restaurant, coffee shop, indoor pool, health club, sauna, and kids-stay-free deals. $$$

Radisson Hotel and Conference Center. 100 Berlin Road; (860) 635–2000. 215 units, restaurant, sauna, whirlpool, fitness center, indoor pool. $$$

Comfort Inn. 111 Berlin Road; (860) 635–4100. Nearly 80 units, with coffeemaker, microwave. Indoor pool, fitness room, sauna. Continental breakfast. $$

Super 8 Motel. 1 Industrial Park Road; (860) 632–8888. Nearly 120 units, including 5 suites. Continental breakfast. $$

Middlefield

I mean no disrespect at all when I say that Middlefield is very aptly named. Situated north of Durham close to the New Haven County line, it is an area of fields and farms, the pretty Coginchaug River, and parts of the Cockaponsett State Forest. Along with these features are three attractions particularly suited to families.

Lyman Orchards (all ages)
At the junction of Routes 147 and 157; store and events (860) 349–1793; pick-your-own information (860) 349–1566; lymanorchards.com. Open daily; seasonal hours; call for schedule.

A huge family-owned operation since 1741, this bucolic extravaganza includes apple, peach, and pear orchards, strawberry and pumpkin fields, raspberry and blueberry patches, an eighteen-hole golf course, an American-fare restaurant, and the Apple Barrel Farm Store. A grand destination in every season, the farm is very popular with families wanting to pick their own produce and see the countryside.

Many festival-style events are planned throughout the year, beginning in February with a Winterfest that celebrates maple syrup season. Come here for the Strawberry Jamboree in June, the Peach Festival in August, the Corn Maze in September and October, Apple Harvest Days in September, Pumpkin Harvest Days in October, the Apple Pie Contest in November, and visits from Santa at Christmastime. Food tastings, barbecues, hayrides, or horsedrawn wagon rides are planned on those festival days. The Apple Barrel store is filled daily to the brim with fresh produce, fresh baked goods, cheeses, maple products, fudge, freshly pressed apple cider, and gifts.

Come any time to enjoy the ducks on the pond and the fresh air and sunshine.

Wadsworth Falls State Park (all ages)
Route 157; (860) 566–2304. Open daily year-round from 8:00 A.M. to sunset. Day-use charge on weekends only from Memorial Day to Labor Day.

This state park has hiking trails and picnic areas, but its special attractions are a swimming area, which is available for ice-skating in the winter, and a beautiful waterfall with an overlook. One of the prettiest cascades in the state, Wadsworth Falls is a great place to spend a country afternoon. The swimming area and the falls are distinctly separate. Ask rangers or follow trails to the falls. You can also visit this 285-acre park to cross-country ski in winter and fish in the streams in summer.

Powder Ridge Ski Area (all ages)
99 Powder Hill Road off Route 147; (860) 349–3454; www.powderridgect.com. Open year-round. Package deals plus four-hour and eight-hour passes. Under-four ski free with adult. Call or check the Web site for rates and schedules.

Families toying with the idea of learning to ski should fret no more over the decision. Close to home and offering a wide variety of ski school packages, Powder Ridge bills itself as "the place where New England learns how to ski." Specializing in children's lessons, the ski school also caters to beginner and novice adults. Even if you know your stuff, it's a great spur-of-the-moment Friday night destination that saves you the trip all the way to Vermont.

Parents and kids will love the child-centered lessons. Skill stations allow kids to learn at their own pace and keep frustration at a minimum. Lessons are offered for children 4 and up. Children 4 and under ski **free** with a parent who has a full-price adult ticket.

Seventeen trails, five lifts, a slopeside restaurant, and a lodge with cafeteria are all part of the facility. State-of-the-art grooming and snowmaking equipment keep the slopes in optimum condition, often from late November through mid-March regardless of Mother Nature's cooperation. Night skiing, an equipment rental center, and a separate snowboarding park with halfpipe meet the needs and schedules of both beginners and skilled enthusiasts. Tubing enthusiasts can enjoy one of New England's largest snow tubing areas. Four runs, including a multiperson family tube ride and a kiddie chute, operate here. They supply the tubes, and the lifts take both you and the tube to the top—no huffing and puffing necessary. Tickets for tubing in 2004 ranged from $10 to $20.

In the fall, the lifts open to the public on the weekends for foliage rides, which usually cost $5.00 for adults and $2.00 for children 11 and under.

Durham

Durham has some of the prettiest farmland in the county. Centered on Route 17 just south of Middletown, it is famed for these farms, for its beautiful historical residences—and for its fair.

Durham Fair (all ages)

Durham Fairgrounds, Route 17, right in the village center; (860) 349–9495. Third weekend in September, beginning at 9:00 A.M. on Friday. Adults $10; children 10 and under free. Parking charge if you use someone's temporary lawn lot or free shuttle bus to free parking at the high school and other lots.

The fairgrounds are hardly noticeable most of the year as you drive past the green, but for three days annually, the joint is hoppin'. Like all country fairs, the Durham Fair celebrates the culture and traditions of Connecticut agriculture through literally hundreds of exhibits, demonstrations, and food and craft booths.

The largest agricultural fair currently held in Connecticut, it displays sheep, llamas, cattle, draft animals of *major* proportions, and every other barn and farm animal you can name. Look at the quilts, pies, fruits, and flowers. Ride the Ferris wheel and go through the Fun House. Eat candied apples, hot cashews, delicious chili, chicken, and chowder, and strawberry-topped Belgian waffles. Wander through the farm museum; buy something pretty at the crafts show. A terrific section for the youngest fairgoers includes kiddie rides and special programs for tots.

Over the aroma of fried everything rise the sounds of country music, announcements of contest winners, and screams from the midway. If your family has sleek, sophisticated city ways, put them aside for a day and come to the fair for a down-home good time. The ballet can wait, and your kids really ought to see the oxen and draft horses. They are a tribute to biodiversity, evolution, or Supreme Intelligence. Whatever your belief system, you have to be amazed at these creatures.

Where to Eat

Time Out Tavern. 100 New Haven Road; (860) 349–1721. Near the fork of Route 17 and Route 77 south of Durham center, this casual sports bar/tavern has a semi-casual family dining room perfectly suited to children. Reasonably priced American fare plus soups, salads, appetizers, and kids' menu. Open year-round daily for lunch and dinner. $$

Brennans Bake Shop. 325 Main Street; (860) 349–9751. This friendly establishment is a best bet for soup, sandwiches, wraps, grinders, and baked goods of all sorts. You can eat here or take out. Open daily year-round 6:00 A.M. to 3:00 P.M.; only ice cream and soft drinks after that, until 9:00 P.M. in season. $

Killingworth

Nearly completely residential and rural in nature, this hilly town south of Durham (take Route 79) supports a few small farms and nurseries and is usually missed altogether by tourists. Nevertheless, it has a popular site perfect for a day in the eastern woods, complete with plenty of pretty trails, a miniature covered bridge, and an ol' swimmin' hole.

Chatfield Hollow State Park (all ages)
Route 80, about 1.5 miles west of the rotary at the junction of Route 81; (860) 663–2030. Open year-round daily 8:00 A.M. to sunset. Day-use vehicle charge Memorial Day to Labor Day. Weekdays $6.00, weekends $7.00 for CT plates; $7.00 and $10.00 for out-of-state plates.

The hills in these parts are deeply etched reminders of the glaciers that passed this way thousands of years past; those icy masses carved out nooks and crannies well worth exploring in this pretty park. Crisscrossed by several miles of well-marked hiking trails that present a merely moderate challenge even to small children, the park also has a good-sized manmade pond for swimming and fishing fun in the summer months and ice skating, if the weather permits, in the winter. The pond's water is the color of iced tea, but don't let that stop you from plunging in. The clear, clean water is just tinged with the natural colors of the minerals loosed from the soil in the pond's basin.

Changing facilities, rustic flush toilets, and a picnic shelter provide a few comforts, but there are no showers and no concession. A privately owned mobile lunch truck is here all day most weekends in summertime and randomly other times.

Clinton/Westbrook/Old Saybrook

These three towns comprise Middlesex County's trio of Long Island Sound shoreline towns. Easy to group together because of their geography, they are also similar in other quintessentially Connecticut shoreline ways. Heavy with salt and briny mud smells of the sea and shore and marsh, the air here carries the sounds of screeching gulls, slapping rigging, lonesome train whistles, and bellowing foghorns.

These are the towns where you eat crabcakes and clam strips and play real mini-golf with windmills and lighthouses. Where you stroll along seawalls, have double-dip ice cream cones, and skip stones off the jetty. Where you walk barefoot, break out in freckles, and let the sun bleach your hair. These are the towns of summer.

Very, very low in true suck-'em-in tourist attractions, you can wander for hours along the shore roads that splinter south from the Boston Post Road. Also known as Route 1, footpath of the Pequot Indians and stomping grounds of the beach bums of Connecticut, this road is richer than a sea captain's treasure chest. Seafood shacks, antiques shops, ice cream parlors, and all those sort of half-rundown Cape Cod-y kinds of emporiums are designed to make you put on your browsing shoes.

Begin a tour in Old Saybrook, taking Route 154 south, bearing left on Main Street and continuing basically straight on College Street (both of which are actually still Route 154) toward the water.

Saybrook Point Park (all ages)
Follow College Street (Route 154) to its end at the park; (860) 395–3123. Open sunrise to sunset daily year-round. Free.

Proceeding down Route 154 you will find Saybrook Point Park and a few satellite sites. Stop for awhile in the big parking lot to your left as you approach the dead end in the roadway here, and walk to the seawall along the park's edge. It is here that nature provided the Connecticut River Valley her first big break. Down here near the mouth of the river, there's a sandbar that prevents huge ocean-going vessels from entering the river. Thanks to the sandbar that makes the Connecticut the largest river in America without a port, the river has stayed healthier than many others and her towns have retained many of their old-time characteristics.

At this popular destination for daytrippers, miniature golfers, and anglers, you will find great fishing spots on the seawall, long-range binoculars to help you get a better view of the boats and lighthouse, and benches and picnic tables that encourage you to linger here. From the paved walkway you can see the breakwater that protects the harbor, and you can watch the boats and gulls and swans. You can play eighteen holes at the **Say-brook Point Mini-Golf Course** (203–388–2407); it's affordable and well maintained, and picnic tables, lights, and bug zappers are there for your comfort.

You can also pick up a bite to eat at the Dock & Dine Restaurant or at their ancillary Quick Bites Gazebo, and you can see the artwork of the wonderful **Saybrook Colony Artists** (860–388–5010) at their gallery in the Connecticut River Room of the restaurant.

When you've soaked up the sights, get back in the car and follow Route 154 across the causeway and all the way around the peninsula (you'll turn sharply to the left immediately after you leave the Point parking lot). Enjoy the water views as you drive, then, when you arrive back at Route 1, turn left and drive toward Westbrook.

You'll have a real dilemma soon if you're hungry for lunch. You can stop in Old Saybrook at the restaurant voted best family dining in Connecticut by the readers of *Connecticut* magazine, you can head west a bit for the best pizza made anywhere between Providence and New Haven, or you can hold out until you reach the seafood king in Westbrook. See the end of this section for descriptions of all three restaurants. No matter which you choose, head for the beach when you're done.

Take a **Trolley**

Summer visitors may enjoy a tour of Old Saybrook on its seasonal trolley. It runs on the hour on weekends in June and September and daily throughout July and August. Among the points of interest are historic landmarks like Fort Saybrook Monument Park at Saybrook Point, the private area called Fenwick, the marinas, the railroad station, and downtown commercial areas. Stay on for the full tour and listen to the commentary from the driver, which makes the ride of interest to tourists. Rides are $1.00 or $3.00 for a full-day pass.

West Beach (all ages)

Seaview Avenue; (860) 399–3095. Open 8:00 A.M. to 10:00 P.M. Rest rooms, concession, showers in season.

After you eat, drive along the Boston Post Road and turn south onto Seaview Avenue in Westbrook. Highlighted by one of the prettiest views of the water and the offshore islands, this drive also takes you to what might very well be the best public beach in the tri-town area. Nonresidents are welcome to use the beach year-round, but they cannot park in the parking lot from late June through Labor Day weekend. In the summertime, nonresidents have to park elsewhere and walk to the beach. You can spend the day on the sand or stroll the long seawalk past the cottages that line the roadway across from the shoreline. This very clean beach is great for young children. Its swimming area has an extraordinarily sandy bottom that slopes very gradually toward deeper water.

When you leave the beach area, continue toward Clinton by driving west on Route 1. While no attractions set it apart as a place for families, it too has pretty views of the water from its various beach roads and marinas. A variety of restaurants, an ever-growing number of antiques shops, and an ice cream emporium or two make it a perfect town for whiling away a summer afternoon. Come on Thursday evenings in summer to the Gazebo at the historic Pierson School for the outdoor concert series. Programs generally begin about 6:30 P.M.

Ahoy! Saybrook Sails

Deep River Navigation Company; (860) 526–4954; www.marktwaincruises.com. The *Aunt Polly* departs Saybrook Point and sails upriver to Essex Harbor or downriver to Duck Island or to the lighthouses, at 11:00 A.M. and 1:30, 3:00, and 5:30 P.M. Daily from June 21 to September 1; weekends only through September. Cruises range from one to two hours; tickets are $4.00 to $6.00 for children; adults pay $8.00 to $12.00.

Captain John's Sport Fishing Center. (860–443–7259). Departs Saybrook Point for winter wildlife cruises to see bald eagles upriver. Naturalist on board. February–March.

Clinton Town Beach (all ages)
At the foot of Waterside Lane off Route 1; (860) 669–6901. Open year-round. Concession and rest rooms in season only. Day-use fee for nonresidents is $20 per vehicle, payable at the gatehouse from 9:00 A.M. to 3:00 P.M. only, from Memorial Day weekend through Labor Day weekend. No charge for nonresidents at other times.

Visiting families are welcome at this small crescent-shaped beach. Cross the wooden bridge at the foot of the narrow, pretty road that leads past some lovely old houses and enter the beach area. A children's playground, rest rooms, and a snack bar that provides simple summer beach fare are here. This is a nice, quiet beach perfect for families with young children.

Keeping Things Uniform

If the beach holds no interest for you, you might care to stop in Westbrook at the Company of Military Historians Museum at Westbrook Place on North Main Street. The nation's largest collection of American military uniforms is here, as are completely restored and operable military vehicles from World War II and other late-twentieth-century conflicts. Open year-round from 8:00 A.M. to 3:30 P.M. Tuesday through Friday and by appointment. Call (860) 399–9460. Free.

Cedar Island Marina and Esposito Beach (all ages) ⊘ ⊗ ⑭
Riverside Drive, Clinton.

Ending a tour of the beach towns at this lovely spot in Clinton could be the perfect close to your day. Take Grove Street south from Route 1 at the weathered blue sign that lists the harbor sites. This quiet, residential avenue reaches the water about a half-mile down, then turns onto Riverside Avenue, where you will find the marinas, restaurants, a great old lobster shack, a public boat ramp, and the tiny Esposito Beach. There is no lifeguard here and just a few benches on a pretty brick patio on this diminutive pier-side patch of sand, but it's a great place to let toddlers build a castle and get their feet wet while you watch the boats go by and decide which restaurant you might stop in for dinner. The view just before sunset across the boats and water to Cedar Island is the sort that artists come to paint. Savor it yourself in living color.

The **Pink Sleigh**

Last in Middlesex County is a little bit of magic before you head home. Best seen in the twilight when the air is crisp and your breath rises steamily from your throat is a haven of peace and beauty for anyone who delights in the wonder of Christmas. Housed in an old barn, this store is breathtakingly beautiful—a place where every small child will suck in his or her breath in awe of all its glitter and gold. Dazzling displays of every color and material fill the rustic two-story barn, which is in itself beautiful. Stepping into this place on a crisp autumn afternoon just as twilight falls is like stepping into an elfin workshop hidden in the hills.

Route 153 in Westbrook, ½-mile north of I–95 (860–399–6926). Open from early July until Christmas Eve on Tuesday through Saturday from 10:00 A.M. to 5:00 P.M., from noon to 5:00 P.M. on Sunday, and on Mondays also from Columbus Day to December 24. Extended hours in December on Thursday, Friday, and Saturday, when closing is at 8:00 P.M.

Where to Eat

Alforno Brick Oven Pizzeria and Ristorante. 1654 Boston Post Road in Old Saybrook; (860) 399–4166. Our family's favorite place for pizza on the shoreline. Thin, crisp crust, fresh toppings, excellent sauce, great salads, and good pasta. Unfortunately, the line goes out the door on weekend nights. If you can wait for a table, you won't be disappointed. $$

Bill's Seafood Restaurant. Route 1 in Westbrook; (860) 399–7224. If seafood wins the toss of the coin, cross the metal deck of the steel bridge and to your right is the conglomeration of structures known as Bill's. The food is good, the prices are reasonable, and the setting couldn't be more picturesque. Watch the swallows swoop and chatter; look for the ospreys nesting above the tidal marsh. The kids like to feed the ducks that hang out near the riverside deck, and there's a lighted Christmas tree all summer long out on the riverbank. So, if you're going to eat chowder, steamers, and clamstrips, you might as well do it here. The place hums most nights with live jazz, Dixieland, rock 'n' roll, and old-time banjo played by locally famed combos. $–$$

The Whole Enchilada. 1121 Boston Post Road, Westbrook; (860) 399–1221. Healthy Mexican is the fare in this bright, eat-in or take-out taco stand. Gazpacho, chili, burritos, soups, much more, all excellent. Just a few stools inside at a bar in cool weather; outside tables on a patio in warm weather. Open daily from 11:30 A.M. year-round. $

Edd's Place. 478 Boston Post Road, Westbrook; (860) 399–9498. For quick and delicious breakfast, lunch, and early, casual dinner or take-out, Edd's is terrific for soups, panini, spaghetti pie, lasagna, pies and muffins, and much more, at outdoor tables at the riverside or in a screened gazebo, open daily year-round. $

Aqua Restaurant. Riverside Avenue in Clinton; (860) 664–3788. This shoreside classic at Cedar Island Marina offers great views, a friendly ambience for families, and great adult-friendly food in addition to the traditional clams casino and fish and chips fare. There's no better place to watch the sailboats return to the marina. Open nearly year-round for lunch and dinner. $–$$$

Where to Stay

Days Inn. 1430 Boston Post Road, Old Saybrook; (860) 388–3453 or (800) 329–7466. 52 units with 6 suites, rooftop indoor pool, continental breakfast. $$–$$$

Sandpiper Inn. 1750 Boston Post Road, Old Saybrook; (860) 399–7973. 45 units, outdoor pool, beach passes. Nicely kept and popular with families. $$–$$$

Saybrook Motor Inn. 1575 Boston Post Road, Old Saybrook; (860) 399–5926. 24 units with refrigerators, beach passes. $$–$$$

Waters Edge Inn and Resort. 1525 Boston Post Road, Westbrook; (860) 399–5901 or (800) 222–5901. Fifteen acres on the Sound, 100 luxury units with beautiful beach, terraced lawns and gardens, tennis, indoor and outdoor pools, health club, spa, gorgeous-water-views public restaurant, entertainment, and planned activities for the kids. Year-round. $$$$

Westbrook Inn B&B. 976 Boston Post Road, Westbrook; (860) 399–4777. Often booked solid, this Victorian beauty has 9 rooms, 1 suite, and a two-bedroom cottage perfect for families. On the river with a dock and fishing; three minutes to beach, full breakfast on the wrap-around porch in fair weather. Gear available for boating, biking, and fishing. $$$

General Information

Connecticut River Valley and Shoreline Visitors Council. 393 Main Street, Middletown 06457; (800) 486–3346 or (860) 347–0028; www.ctrivershore.com.

Tourism Information Center. I–95 northbound in Westbrook. Staffed in summer months; maps, vacation guides, brochures.

Tolland County

Simple Dreams and Country Comforts

The hills of northeastern Connecticut have magic in them. As with Washington Irving's Catskills, something within these knolls has defied the physical laws governing the passage of time. The traveler is transported centuries backward just by being here. The magic of Tolland County lies not in what one *does* here. This is not a place well known for action. Rather, its magic lies partly in the sweet relief of having nothing to do here. It is, simply, a nice place just to *be*.

Families looking for the quieter pleasures of life in New England will find much to please them here. The museums are smaller and have fewer buttons to press, but they are no less excellent than their showy counterparts in the city. The activities have fewer moving parts and use little or no fossil fuel, but they'll invigorate the body, feed the soul, and leave time for the mind to restore itself.

Begin a circular tour of this county by starting in Coventry; its center is on Route 31, most easily reached from Route 44 to the north or Route 6 to the south.

TopPicks for fun in Tolland County

1. Nathan Hale Homestead

2. Museum of Natural History and Primitive Technology

3. Mansfield Drive-in

4. Connecticut State Museum of Natural History

5. Ballard Institute and Museum of Puppetry

TOLLAND COUNTY

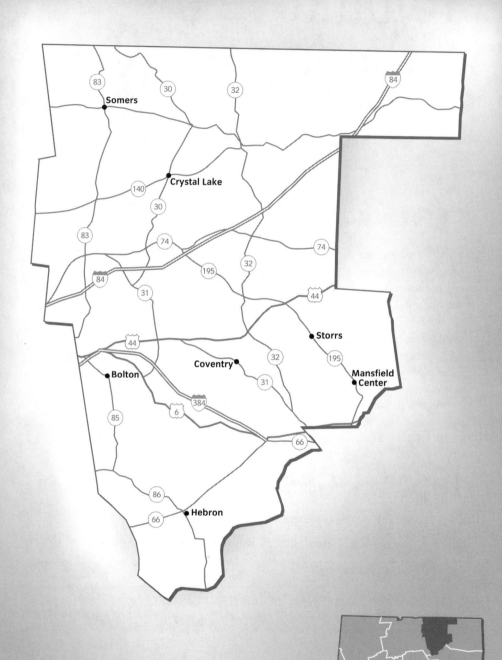

Coventry

Coventry is one of our family's favorite Connecticut towns. Centered on Route 31 neatly in the middle of the southern end of the county, its rolling, second-growth woodlands are laced by mile upon mile of twisting country road, beautiful in every season.

Like many of the towns in the area, Coventry's chief temptations are its scenic byways, farmstands, antiques shops, and inns. The slick stuff of the city is not to be found here. Still, Coventry provides a trio of attractions that will appeal to any family that enjoys history, nature, or . . . toys.

Coventry **Visitor Center**

Daytripping families may stop at the Coventry Visitor Center (860–742–1085) at 1195 Main Street, which is Route 31. Open year-round daily from 9:30 A.M. to 2:30 P.M., it is in the old brick post office in the heart of town. Maps, brochures from the tourism council, and the helpful assistance of the volunteers here can add to your exploration of this pretty place.

Nathan Hale Homestead (ages 6 and up)
2299 South Street; (860) 742–6917 or (860) 247–8996. Open Wednesday through Sunday from 1:00 to 4:00 P.M. from May 15 to October 15. Tours every half-hour. Adults $4.00; children $2.00.

The most famous spot in Coventry might be the home of Connecticut's state hero, Nathan Hale. On the fringe of the Nathan Hale State Forest off Route 31, the Nathan Hale Homestead is perhaps the most stately of Revolutionary-era historic homes in the country. Its situation on the property is a fitting memorial to the proud young man who lost his life in the service of his country in September of 1776.

Nathan spent his boyhood on this lovely property, raised here in apparent harmony with his nine surviving siblings. While Nathan was serving in the Continental Army, the house currently standing on the property was rebuilt to add space to the original smaller house in which the ten brothers and sisters had been raised. Sometime after the death of the first Mrs. Hale (I presume from exhaustion), Nathan's father, Deacon Richard Hale, married the second Mrs. Hale, a widow with seven children of her own. Clearly there was just cause for building a new homestead that represented not only breathing space but the prosperity that Nathan's father had achieved in their new, beloved land.

The homestead tour includes the grounds and the house. It begins with an excellent short film shown in the small eighteenth-century barn, which also serves as the gift shop, to the left of the drive at the left of the house. The house includes many Hale furnishings and belongings, including Nathan's musket, his shoe buckles, the trunk he left with his friend Asher Wright when he left on his mission, and the Bible he received as a gift on his seventeenth birthday. The tours are among the best we have heard for children in the state—filled with detail but quick and not above the heads of young listeners. You may even see a costumed character cooking at the open hearth, making soap, or toiling in the period herb and vegetable garden.

The Story **of a Hero**

At just twenty-one years of age, the young Nathan, a graduate of the class of 1773 at Yale and a teacher by profession, set out on the most dangerous mission known to his generation. Acting under the principles of freedom that drove the Patriot cause, Nathan, now a captain in the rebel army, walked on foot in the disguise of a poor schoolmaster to infiltrate the British encampment at New York City and bring the plans of the enemy back to General Washington. Apprehended within sight of the smoke from the American campfires, Nathan was relieved of the secrets he had written on a parchment hidden in his boot and was hung from the gallows without a trial for the crime of treason against the Crown.

Legend tells us that it was on this occasion, facing his death, that Nathan Hale uttered his most famous words: "I only regret that I have but one life to lose for my country." His body was left hanging for three days as a warning to other traitors and was buried in an unknown, unmarked grave in Artillery Field, now underneath the pavement near New York City's Sixty-sixth Street and Third Avenue. Back home in Coventry, years later, his father erected a headstone in his memory graven with these words: HE RESIGNED HIS LIFE A SACRIFICE TO HIS COUNTRY'S LIBERTY.

Several special days are planned annually. On Mother's Day the two Mrs. Hales appear to portray motherhood in the eighteenth century. Mothers are admitted at no charge. In early June Nathan's birthday is celebrated with birthday cake, special tours, and a performance by the Nathan Hale Ancient Fife and Drum Corps. On the first Sunday in June there is an Antiques Festival with one hundred or more exhibitors; in late July a Revolutionary War encampment takes over the grounds for a full weekend of camplife reenactments and a multicorps fife and drum muster. In late September a mourning day commemorates Nathan's death or some aspect of Hale family history. In October, a walking tour focuses on the homestead as well as the forest and other nearby historic sites.

The staff here also runs an exceptionally good Colonial Life Camp for children. A weeklong day camp, it involves kids in colonial games, crafts, weaving, cooking, clothes making, plant study, and the opportunity to role-play a Hale historical character. It is often a sellout program; call early in the spring for this season's fee.

History Lessons

Families with history buffs among them might also like to check out Coventry's Brick School House on Merrow Road. Built from 1823 to 1825, it served as a one-room district school until 1953. Now restored, it is furnished with nineteenth-century artifacts. It's open on Sunday afternoons from mid-May to mid-October. The Strong-Porter House at 2382 South Street, just down the road from the Hale Homestead, also appeals to history lovers. It includes local artifacts and memorabilia about Coventry and the Hales, their relatives the Strongs, and the Porters. The property includes carriage sheds, a barn, and a carpenter's shop. It is open Saturday and Sunday afternoons from mid-May to mid-October.

Caprilands (all ages)

534 Silver Street, off Route 44; (860) 742–7244; www.caprilands.com. Open daily from 10:00 A.M. to 5:00 P.M. Closed on major holidays. For the luncheons on Saturday at noon from May through December or for the high tea served on Sunday from April through December at 2:00 P.M., you must make reservations. Admission to the gardens is free. Luncheons are $20 per adult; teas are $12.

When you leave the Hale Homestead, bear to the left on South Street and drive down the road a piece until you reach Silver Street on your right. About a half-mile up on your left is Caprilands, a haven of fragrance and loveliness hidden in the woodlands but open to all the world. Especially appealing to children who have read Frances Hodgson Burnett's *The Secret Garden,* every corner of the fifty-acre herb farm has a themed garden of one sort or another, most with poetic names that conjure romantic images and make one half expect to meet some mythical creature along the pretty paths.

The reigning queen of this garden was Ms. Adelma Grenier Simmons—a lady who had worked at her venerable craft from 1929 to 1997. Surely heaven itself is prettier now that she is there, but her handiwork, creativity, and indisputably wholesome spirit of celebration are still everywhere apparent at Caprilands. In her place is a staff both knowledgeable and enthusiastic about every aspect of herb gardening. They'll send you home with hope and advice and excellent plants to get you and the kids going on a family garden.

In addition to the thirty-eight gardens, you will find a lovely tea shop, a basket shop, a large barn loaded with garden-related gifts, and greenhouses brimming with plants for sale.

Herbal luncheons are given in the beautiful eighteenth-century home on the property on Saturday at noon from May through December, but these are not children's affairs. Each five-course luncheon features foods prepared with fresh herbs, sauces, and vinegars made here and is preceded by a lecture and a tour of the gardens. High tea is served on Sunday at 2:00 P.M.

The grounds are most lush in late spring and throughout summer, with some raggedy edges showing by late autumn and dormancy in winter, but Caprilands nevertheless is open year-round. Christmas here is what Adelma called the fifth season of the year. No matter how bare the gardens look in December, the greenhouses and barn are alive with the magic cultivated here.

Special Joys Doll and Toy Museum (all ages)

41 North River Road directly off Route 31; (860) 742–6359. Open year-round, 11:00 A.M. to 4:30 P.M. Thursday through Sunday. Free.

This small museum housed in a pink Victorian home brims with artfully displayed collectible and antique dolls and toys, including such treasures as Steiff, Jumeau, Kathe Kruse, and Shuco dolls and animals. A few of these are animated; all are beautiful. Many of the dolls are placed among unusual pieces of antique or collectible doll furnishings, carefully arranged to illustrate room settings of the period most closely related to the era of the dolls themselves. Rare small accessories as well as antique room and shop settings are displayed along with the furniture. See a German butcher shop, several general stores, a French hat shop, an entire kitchen corner, and seven wonderful dollhouses. Tin and cast-iron toys, doll carriages, a German "shellhouse," a mechanical clown, and a beautiful display of cloth American folk dolls dating from 1860 are all part of this fascinating collection.

You can purchase items in the shop that shares the space devoted to the museum. Dolls, dollhouses, dollhouse miniatures, vintage doll clothes, and small toys await children and collectors.

Country Pleasures

Edmondson's Farm and Gift Shops at 2627 Boston Turnpike, which is Route 44, would love to see your family in their fields picking your own raspberries in August and September and riding their hay wagons in the fall to their pick-your-own pumpkin fields. Flowers, veggies, herbs, and Christmas trimmings are for sale all year-round. Fall is a favorite time here, when the air is crisp and so are the apples. They are open daily. Admission is **free;** fall hayrides have a fee. Call (860) 742–6124 to ask what you can pick this season.

Where to Eat

Bidwell Tavern. 1260 Main Street (Route 31); (860) 742–6978. Famous for its many styles of chicken wings, this classic 1820s tavern is a local favorite especially because it may be the only place in town. Notwithstanding the lack of competition, it deserves its reputation for good steaks, burgers, ribs, seafood, and even some vegetarian choices. Open for lunch and dinner daily year-round. $–$$

Where to Stay

Special Joys Bed and Breakfast. 41 North River Road; (860) 742–6359. If the day's activities have worn you plumb out, set a spell on the wooden swing at the Special Joys pink-towered bed-and-breakfast, which offers guests a private balcony, private entrance, and dining room. They have 3 immaculate, air-conditioned guest rooms (2 with private bath) with discreetly hidden televisions for those who really want to spoil the ambience. A glassed-in conservatory with a sparkling fountain overlooks the home's extensive rose and perennial gardens. Children over 6 are very welcome; pets are taboo. Full country-style breakfasts, often served in the conservatory, will jump-start the whole family. $$–$$$

Old Eagleville Inn. 670 Stonehouse Road; (860) 742–1872 or (800) 721–8058; www.oldeaglevilleinn.com. 4 guest rooms with private baths await families with children older than 5, in this antique saltbox home on seven acres. Canoeing on the river, cross-country skiing in season, fishing, and walking the pretty paths on the property make this a great country getaway. Full breakfast, and ice cream sundaes in the evening. No smoking indoors. $$–$$$

Mill Brook Farm. 110 Wall Street; (860) 742–5761. Seven acres open to wanderers; a wraparound porch for lollygaggers. 2 double rooms with a shared bath on this small, working sheep farm in the center of historic Coventry. Your hostess may invite you to the barn to help with the morning feeding, or she may show you how she cleans, cards, dyes, and spins her wool. She might even show you how she makes her wonderful stuffed Farm Bears. You might enjoy roasting marshmallows over the bonfire pit on summer or fall evenings or watching the muffins bake in the mornings. Children, pets, and smokers are welcome. $$–$$$

Hebron/Bolton

The trouble with Tolland County is that it's so rural that its towns are sort of rambling affairs without boundaries that are crystal-clear to the traveler. The boundaries exist, of course, but to find Point A in Town A, it might actually be easier to travel to Point A from Town B. And so on.

If you were to leave Coventry, for example, to find Gay City State Park (which is, from a north–south perspective, halfway between Hebron and Bolton), it would be absurd to travel to either Hebron or Bolton proper. You'd go to Andover first, and then on through the countryside to the park. You are much better off discovering and accepting this curious Yankee phenomenon right here in this slim volume because if you were to stop and ask an inhabitant of this strange land, they would likely smile wryly at your city-slicker type-A hang-ups and say something along the lines of, "W'aall, you found us so you cain't be too far off." And then you're on your own again.

The fact of the matter is that Gay City State Park is in Hebron, but even the state campground guide explains its position as 3 miles south of Bolton on Route 85. I say it's 4 miles west of Andover at the junction of Routes 31 and 85. The bottom line is that it's actually easy to find and very worthwhile no matter how you get there.

Gay City State Park (all ages)

Entrance on Route 85 in Hebron; (860) 295–9523. Open year-round 8:00 A.M. to sunset. Parking fee on weekends and holidays, $5.00 per car.

Adjoining the vast acreage of the Meshomasic State Forest, the park centers on the remains of an eighteenth-century mill village settled in 1796 by a religious sect led first by one Elijah Andrus and later by a man named John Gay. Quite successful and nearly self-sustaining, the community had, at its peak, a population of twenty-five families and a handful of thriving mills that produced lumber, woolens, and paper, among other goods.

For nearly eighty years, the industrious citizens of Gay City managed to overcome their various hardships, but by 1879 the struggle to sustain themselves became over-whelming. In that year, the last of their mills burned to the ground, and the citizens aban-doned the settlement. Soon the fields lay fallow, the silent ruins were home to wild dogs, and nature removed nearly every trace of human habitation. Now only some tumbling foundations, some cellar holes, a few gravestones, and the ruins of an old aqueduct remain.

When you enter the 1,569-acre park, leave your car at the parking areas near the pond and pick up a trail map from the rangers or in the wooden box near the trailhead. Ten trails in all lace through the park, but the easiest ones for children are the ones with the greatest concentration of historic spots. The park offers many recreational opportuni-ties, and you could easily spend a full day here. Swimming, fishing, hiking, and picnicking are perfect warm-weather possibilities. In winter, you can ice skate and cross-country ski. The state has provided picnic tables, drinking water, and flush toilets to make your visit comfortable. Leashed pets are permitted.

Fish Family Farm Creamery and Dairy (all ages)

20 Dimock Lane, Bolton; (860) 646–9745. Open Monday through Saturday, year-round, from 8:00 A.M. to 8:00 P.M. (6:00 P.M. in winter). Walking around is free, but they charge for the ice cream. You'll be willing to pay, believe me.

After a full day of hiking and swimming, you might need to replace some calories, and there's no better place to do that than at another of Connecticut's finest ice cream empo-riums. Now you can go to Bolton (you see, you didn't miss anything at all arriving at Gay City through Andover), straight north on Route 85. One of only four dairy operations in Connecticut that milks, pasteurizes, and bottles its own milk, the enterprising folks at this dairy also make their own ice cream.

Visitors are welcome to give themselves a self-guided tour around the place as long as the path taken is safe and doesn't endanger anyone. Groups can make an appointment for a one-hour guided barn tour. Forty-eight cows have to be milked here every day, and that's quite a sight by itself. Be here around 4:30 P.M. each afternoon if you'd like to see how that's done. On Monday the ice-cream making and bottling of milk is the big attrac-tion. A glass window in the farm store where you buy your ice cream is the best viewing place. The store also sells fresh local eggs and locally made pickles and honey. Best of all, though, is the ice cream—you won't get it any closer to the source anywhere in the state.

Where to Eat

Bolton Pizza and Family Restaurant.
270 West Street, which is Route 85; (860)
643–1014. Famed for its spinach pies and
calzones, this Italian eatery offers great food
at great prices to families. Stop across the
road at the Nutcracker Gift Shop (860–649–
7514) for Christmas decorations and an
amazing selection of nutcrackers. Next door
are the Bolton Cyr Riding Stables (860–649–
9075); ride first, then eat here. $–$$

Somers

Way up north in Tolland County just a stone's throw from the Massachusetts border is the
small town of Somers, pronounced like the season. Once the home of the Scantic Indians
and later settled by colonists who made use of the Scantic River to power grist and
woolen mills, it remains a quiet community with rural charm.

If you have been lingering in the south in the county, make your way up Route 85 to
the center of Vernon at Route 85's junction with Route 30. Take a right on Route 30, also
called Hartford Turnpike, and go to the second light to the shopping center called 30
Plaza. Stop at **Rein's New York Style Deli** (435 Hartford Turnpike; 860–875–1344) in the
shopping center and buy some wonderful take-out sandwiches, kosher pickles, German
potato salad, and whatever other picnic fixings you may need for a day in the country.
Then go northward on Route 83 to Somers.

Somers Mountain Museum of Natural History and Primitive Technology (ages 4 and up)

332 Turnpike Road; (860) 749–4129; www.somersmountain.org. Open on Sunday from 1:00
to 5:00 P.M. Adults $2.00; children and seniors $1.00.

Not far from the town center at the junction of Routes 83 and 190 is a small museum dedicated to the idea that all humans can learn to live in harmony with the earth and with
each other. A proud and touching reminder of the legacy of the Native American people,
its vast collection of artifacts has been gathered from all parts of North America. Museum
displays reveal the beauty and utility of the primitive artifacts used by civilizations and cultures whose lifeways are lost or threatened. Arrowheads, buckskin clothing and bags, war
clubs, moccasins, masks, baskets, jewelry, pottery, rugs, pipes, and tools are among the
items from the Pacific Northwest coast, the Southwest, the Eastern Woodlands, and the
Great Plains.

Mostly acquired through the efforts of the museum's founder, James F. King, this collection demonstrates respect for Native American ingenuity. The exhibits also include artifacts from the American Revolution, the French and Indian War, the Civil War, and the
eighteenth-century whaling industry.

Programs are offered regularly for a small fee (often $1.00 to $5.00); check the Web
site for the calendar of hands-on activities such as flint knapping, bow making, pottery
making, or taking a nature walk.

A small gift shop offers books, bird feeders, Native American music, Southwestern jewelry, and other works from local craftspeople. A picnic area on the grounds gives families the opportunity to rest awhile in this vernal setting; that's why you stopped at Rein's. You are also welcome to explore the lovely trails featuring edible and medicinal plants, a native vegetable garden, and a home built in the ancient Eastern Woodlands style.

Shallowbrook Equestrian Center (ages 4 and up)

Route 186; (860) 749–0749; www.shallowbrook.com. Open year-round; call for seasonal hours, events, and information on lessons.

Those of you who love horses probably already know about this place; it's the largest family-owned complex of its kind in the United States, it has the largest indoor polo arena in the nation, and it enjoys a national reputation as one of the country's best riding schools. Indoor and outdoor riding rings, a hunt course, indoor and outdoor polo courses, forty hours a week of scheduled riding lessons for all levels and ages of riders, facilities for carriage shows, rodeos, and gymkhana competitions, and much more keep participants and spectators alike arriving for the year-round special events on this beautiful fifty-acre site. Whether you come to watch the pageantry or the sportsmanship or to develop your own skills, you will find much to occupy the family at Shallowbrook.

Soapstone Mountain (all ages)

Soapstone Mountain Road. Open year-round dawn to dusk unless closed due to weather conditions.

If you want to save those sandwiches just a little bit longer, take Route 190 east from its junction with Route 83. Drive 1.2 miles to Gulf Road. Take a right on Gulf Road and drive 2 miles to the entrance of the Shenipsit State Forest. Pass the parking area and turn west onto Soapstone Mountain Road, which will twist upward to a beautiful vista just under a mile from Gulf Road. Stop at the overlook, then drive onward to a picnic area near the top of the mountain. Park here and enjoy your lunch. If the state forest trails are open at the time you visit, walk to the nearby weather-relay station and take the short trail to the wooden firetower beyond it.

Retrace your route to Gulf Road and take a right onto it so that you're going south toward **Crystal Lake,** which is just a few miles away at the junction of Routes 140 and 30. If you have the equipment, stop at Crystal Lake's public boat launch and public fishing area and see if you can land some trout. Crystal Lake Brook, which runs parallel to Route 30, is a major trout stream, stocked in early spring and open from the third Saturday in April to March 1. If the fish aren't biting, go east on Route 140 to Stafford Springs, and hook a right onto Route 32 toward Mansfield.

Mansfield

If you don't have a firm grip on the township concept, you'll have a great chance to process it fully in Mansfield. Composed of several village centers and a large university, it lies roughly between Routes 44 and 6 at the north and south and is criss-crossed by Routes 195, 275, 32, and 89.

I mention this because even if you have driven for miles you will know that you are still in Mansfield if you are between any two of these points, a fact that can become very important since the village names are Mansfield Depot, Mansfield Center, and Mansfield Four Corners. Plus Eagleville, Spring Hill, and Storrs (which is the home of the University of Connecticut and the name by which most out-of-towners refer to Mansfield). For the purposes of this book, we are going to group the university-related attractions under the town heading of Storrs, just a few pages onward.

Center **Marine**

If you'd like to rent a canoe, call Center Marine (860–423–1497) at 457 Storrs Road in Mansfield Center.

A day in Mansfield can include all four of the following attractions if you plan well: the Mansfield Drive-in Theater, the Gurleyville Grist Mill, the Mansfield Hollow Dam and State Park, and the Mansfield Marketplace, which is held at the drive-in.

Mansfield Hollow Dam and State Park (all ages)
Just about a mile east of Mansfield Center near the junction of Routes 195 and 89; (860) 455–9057. Open year-round from sunrise to sunset.

Created to protect the land around the 550-acre reservoir made by the damming of the Natchaug River by the Army Corps of Engineers, the park includes more than 2,300 acres of open space perfect for hiking, picnicking, cross-country skiing, and bird or wildlife watching.

Among the amenities are a field sports area, a picnic grove (with some pretty tall pines, tables, firepits, rest rooms, and seasonal water fountains), horseshoe pits, an interpretive nature trail, and miles of other hiking trails. Trash containers are not provided, so be prepared. The park is an alcohol-free facility, so leave the wine and beer out of your picnic fixings.

Unfortunately, because the lake is a public water supply, you can't swim here, but you can bring in your fossil fuel–burning powerboat at the public boat launch. As they say in New York, go figure. You can also fish here. I guess the fish don't mind the petrochemicals.

Follow the signs to the 1952 Mansfield Dam (you can walk to it along the top of the dike that runs through the first part of the park or you can drive to it on the roads). The dam is a fairly impressive structure, unless you've already seen Hoover, of course, and it overlooks the lake, the river, and Kirby mill, a stone structure dating from 1882. Tours of the dam are given weekdays from 8:00 A.M. to 3:00 P.M.; call (860–423–5603) to inquire about tour details.

Gurleyville Grist Mill (ages 5 and up)

Stone Mill Road; (860) 429–9023; www.mansfieldhistory.org/gurleyvi.htm. Open late May through mid-October on Sunday from 1:00 to 5:00 P.M. Free.

If historical structures intrigue you, head up Route 195, take a right onto Gurleyville Road and follow the signs to the mill. A mill site since the 1720s, this small stone building is the state's only remaining gristmill. Dating from 1830, it contains its original nineteenth-century machinery and is open for **free** tours, as is the nearby miller's house, once the home of Governor Wilbur Cross and now a museum of Mansfield history.

This is a short stop, unless you want to walk awhile on the nearby Nipmuck Trail, which follows the pretty twists of the Fenton River on which the mill is situated. To do that, park near the bridge that crosses the river and look for the blue blazes that lead northwest close to the west bank. The Nipmuck Trail is 39 miles long, but you can enjoy a short section right here near the mill. The riverside is a lovely place to stop for a picnic lunch. You can walk about a quarter-mile to a place where the trail crosses Gurleyville Road. From there you can retrace your steps to your car or continue up to Route 44 (about another mile) and then return to your car.

Mansfield Marketplace (ages 6 and up)

Mansfield Drive-in at 228 Stafford Road near the junction of Routes 31 and 32; (860) 456–2578; www.mansfieldmarketplace.com. Open from 8:00 A.M. to 3:00 P.M. on Sunday from March 15 through December. Rain or shine. Free. Small parking fee.

If you'd like to take a bit of history home with you, come to look over the antiques at the largest indoor/outdoor weekly flea market in eastern Connecticut. Don't be concerned that children won't have fun here. Of the 200 or so dealers who sell here regularly, a large percentage sell toys, crafts, candy, baseball cards, dolls, sporting goods, books, and other goods of appeal to families. Breakfast and lunch are offered for sale at the snack bar.

Mansfield Drive-In (all ages)

228 Stafford Road, which is at the junction of Routes 31 and 32; (860) 423–4441; www. mansfielddrivein.com. Open every Friday through Sunday evening in April, May, and September and every night in June, July, and August. Adults $7.00; children 4 through 11 $4.00. Wednesday night is Family Night: special per carload price, most recently $12.00. Opens at 7:10 P.M.

For fun in a time warp on this very site, come back in the evening for one of the first-run films playing on the big screen. If you were a child of the 1950s or '60s, you probably know how this works: the kids get into pajamas just before dark and pile into the Ford Country Squire, and the whole family cheerfully heads off to the drive-in to watch wholesome, family values–type movies under the stars.

If it's really warm, the kids spread a blanket on the roof of the car and pile on top, hoping to get a good view of anything interesting going on in the next car. There's lots of giggling involved and lots of popcorn, and when there's too much noise on the roof, Dad says something like "June, can you make those kids settle down?" and Mom says something like "Oh, Ward, they're just high-spirited," and everybody starts giggling again.

This drive-in is one of two remaining open in Connecticut and the only one east of the Connecticut River. The three screens offer "family" films, but call to be sure you share their opinion of appropriate films for your children. Often there are double features, with the earlier film being most oriented toward younger audiences. A full-service snack bar prepares dogs and burgers and such and hawks typical theater treats. Depending on your comfort level here, you can send the kids to play on the on-site playground. Rest rooms complete the package.

Storrs

Not surprisingly, the University of Connecticut provides several resources for family activities on its main campus at Storrs. If you enter the university near the information booth at the main entrance on Route 195, you can pick up campus maps and you can inquire about guided and self-guided tours of the campus. In addition to the attractions detailed below, you can visit the Kellogg Dairy Barn exhibits at the School of Agriculture daily from 10:00 A.M. to 4:00 P.M. and you can ask for the self-guided walking tour of the campus trees, which is actually pretty amazing. Planted with trees from all temperate parts of the world, the campus itself has achieved arboretum status, and its School of Horticulture maintains beautiful themed gardens, including one planted in the school colors. Be sure to visit the Little Stone House, which is constructed from stone taken from every town in the state of Connecticut and has an interior wall with a specimen stone from every state in the union. The Geology Park is made from stone taken from every working quarry in Connecticut and includes a set of Connecticut dinosaur footprints.

Connecticut Museum of Natural History at UCONN (all ages)

2019 Hillside Road, on the University of Connecticut campus, off Route 195; (860) 486–4460; www.mnh.uconn.edu. Currently under renovation, the museum is partially open now, on weekdays from 9:00 A.M. to 4:00 P.M. and Sunday 1:00 to 4:00 P.M. Call for current information before traveling to Storrs; be sure to ask for a calendar of special events, workshops, and activities. The Web site lists all events also. Visitors are welcome at the greenhouses Monday through Friday from 8:00 A.M. to 4:00 P.M. Suggested donation $1.00. The museum is a nonprofit department of the university and relies on public support for its programs.

The Connecticut State Museum of Natural History at UConn is a museum on the move! The museum, currently under renovation, is beginning its celebration of its permanent new digs with the opening of its new changing exhibition gallery. While the rest of the museum is readied for the reinstallation of one of Connecticut's finest natural history collections, a full program of activities continues. Family Days, nature walks and science workshops for families, Sunday lectures by scientists and scholars, summer camps for kids, and guided tours are all still on the calendar here.

At 75 North Eagleville Road behind the Torrey Life Sciences Building, the museum offers guided tours of the Department of Ecology and Evolutionary Biology's greenhouses, which house the most diverse collection of plants between New York and Boston. Nearly four thousand species thrive here, including cacti, succulents, bromeliads, and more than 500 species of orchids. Guided tours ($10 for nonmembers) of this wondrous green world are strongly recommended (for folks older than 10) and must be arranged in advance, or you can opt to guide yourselves. In either case, this may be the closest you come to a rain forest—it's lush, humid, and lovely.

William Benton Museum of Art (ages 8 and up)
University of Connecticut, 245 Glenbrook Road; (860) 486–4520; www.benton.uconn.edu. Open year-round Tuesday through Friday 10:00 A.M. to 4:30 P.M. Saturday and Sunday 1:00 to 4:30 P.M. Closed during exhibit changings or some academic breaks. Free.

Housed in one of UCONN's earliest buildings now on the National Register of Historic Places, this museum's two galleries are devoted to changing exhibitions and displays from the university's 4,000-piece permanent collection of American and European art.

The small size of the museum makes it a wonderful place in which to introduce young children to fine art, and the museum's changing exhibitions are of the highest caliber possible, often focusing on art from many cultures beyond the scope of its own collection. While directed mostly at adult visitors and students of fine art, some exhibitions are of great appeal to children; summer exhibitions often have a special family focus. The museum gift shop is excellent and features a special holiday festival sale from late November through late December.

Ballard Institute and Museum of Puppetry (all ages)
Willimantic Cottage, Weaver Road, UConn Depot Campus, off Route 44; (860) 486–4605; www.sp.uconn.edu. Open mid-April through mid-November Friday, Saturday, and Sunday from noon to 5:00 P.M. Adults $2.00; children $1.00.

One of the Benton Museum's special exhibitions was based on a collection so important and impressive, in fact, that a unique museum has been created to provide it a permanent home of its own. Named for professor emeritus Frank Ballard and dedicated to preserving and displaying the Ballard puppets as well as the puppets of other student, state, national, and international puppeteers, the museum also has as its purpose the aim to educate the public and promote the puppet arts.

Showcasing a collection of literally thousands of puppets from around the world, the institute and museum celebrate the wondrous art form of puppetry through changing exhibitions of marionettes, glove puppets, rod puppets, shadow puppets, and the props, paraphernalia, and publicity materials associated with puppet productions. Three of the museum's eventual five galleries are now open to visitors.

Honored by an award acknowledging its special contribution to the arts, the University of Connecticut is the only university in the nation with a degree program in puppetry arts. At the helm of that tradition for more than thirty years was Frank Ballard, directing the work of the latest generation of puppet creators. Ballard's own stories are inspirational tributes to the generous support he received from childhood onward as he carved out his life in the arts. He made his first puppet at the age of 5. Inspire your own kids—bring them to this must-see museum.

The astonishing array of puppets is of enormous appeal to adults as well as children, and the changing exhibitions and constant additions to this growing collection should encourage visitors to come often. Contact the Department of Dramatic Arts at the university for information about student puppet productions. In September or October, the museum usually has an Open House special performance or hosts the Connecticut International Festival of Puppet Arts, with renowned performers from across the globe presenting puppet performances for families as well as adults. Call for ticket information.

Jorgensen Auditorium (ages 4 and up) 🎵

2132 Hillside Road on UCONN campus; (860) 486–4226; www.jorgensen.ct-arts.com. October through May. Also Connecticut Repertory Theatre, (860) 486–3969.

This 2,630-seat contemporary theater offers top-drawer entertainment in the form of musicals, comedies, Broadway classics, dance, opera, and drama. The full season of productions features professional touring companies as well as nationally and internationally known soloists and symphonies. The 2003 to 2004 season included the Broadway musical *Annie, Get Your Gun,* the Kingston Trio, and other original shows suitable for the whole family. Single and subscription series are available; you can also design your own series. Children's tickets are $7.00.

The Jorgensen's Fleet Children's Series offers six productions each academic season, featuring favorite tales like *Miss Nelson Is Missing* and *Mike Mulligan and his Steam Shovel.* Recommended for children aged 5 through 11, these Sunday performances are at 1:00 and 3:00 P.M. Individual tickets ($12 adults; $10 children) are available.

Where to Eat

You can eat on campus at **Jonathan's,** which operates several eateries, including a couple of coffee shops, a fast-food-style restaurant and an upscale sort of sit-down dinner restaurant (both in the student union), and a traveling lunch truck. All operate daily in the academic year, but only on weekdays in the summertime. $

You can also try one of these local favorites:

Kathy-John's. 643 Middle Turnpike near the junction of Routes 195 and 44; (860) 429–0362. Sandwiches, burgers, soups, and salads plus breakfast dishes. Leave room for their famed ice cream and sundae creations. Browse here also among Kathy-John's inventory of books, gifts, cards, and rubber stamps. Open daily year-round from 10:00 A.M. to 11:00 P.M. $

Angellino's Restaurant. 135 Storrs Road, which is Route 195; (860) 450–7071. In a shopping plaza, but you just can't go wrong here. Pizza, great pasta, quick service, lots of families. $–$$

UConn Dairy Bar. 3636 Horsebarn Road Extension, UConn School of Agriculture; just north of Gurleyville Road on Route 195; (860)

486–2634. Sensational ice cream freshly made, year-round, by students. The price is lower than average, the portions are enormous, and the flavors change all the time—after all, these are creative college kids. Open Monday through Friday from 10:30 A.M. to 5:00 P.M. and on Saturday and Sunday from noon to 5:00 P.M. Open an hour or two longer in summertime. Closed on major holidays. $

Where to Stay

Best Western Regent Inn. 123 Storrs Road (Route 195) in Mansfield Center; (860) 423–8451. Near UCONN, 88 rooms with two double beds, indoor pool, fitness center. Continental breakfast. $$–$$$

Nathan Hale Inn. 855 Bolton Road; (860) 427–7888. Brand-new in 2001, this inn and conference center offers 100 guest rooms and 18 suites right on the UCONN campus. Restaurant, indoor pool, health club. $$$$

General Information

Northeast Connecticut Visitors District/Connecticut's Quiet Corner. 13 Canterbury Road, Suite 3, P. O. Box 145, Brooklyn 06234; (860) 779–6383; www.CTquietcorner.org. Free brochures, maps.

North Central Tourism District. 111 Hazard Avenue, Enfield 06082; (860) 763–2578 or (800) 248–8283; www.ctheritagevalley.com.

Windham County

River Valleys and Rural Byways

I don't know in what year some clever copy writer labeled Windham County the "Quiet Corner," but the name has stuck so thoroughly that you might think it is the official name of the region. Though parts of Tolland County share the name, at least in the state tourism materials, it is here in Windham that the full impact of the term hits the traveler. *It's quiet here.*

Although a portion of the county is sliced by I–395, which leads travelers toward Worcester, Boston, and points beyond, the area is little altered by the traffic. In fact, the whole twenty-five town region along the Quiet Corner's two major rivers has been designated the Quinebaug and Shetucket Rivers Valley National Heritage Corridor in recognition of its status as one of the last unspoiled and undeveloped areas in the Northeast. In keeping with that honor and spirit, the proprietors of the region's museums, shops, and inns have deliberately and successfully maintained the county's old-fashioned ambience, partly to please those very travelers who seek its peaceful thoroughfares.

TopPicks for fun in Windham County

1. Diamond A Ranch

2. Quaddick State Park

3. Roseland Cottage Children's Parties

4. Mashomoquet Brook State Park

5. Creamery Brook Bison

6. Prudence Crandall Museum

7. Wright's Mill Tree Farm

WINDHAM COUNTY

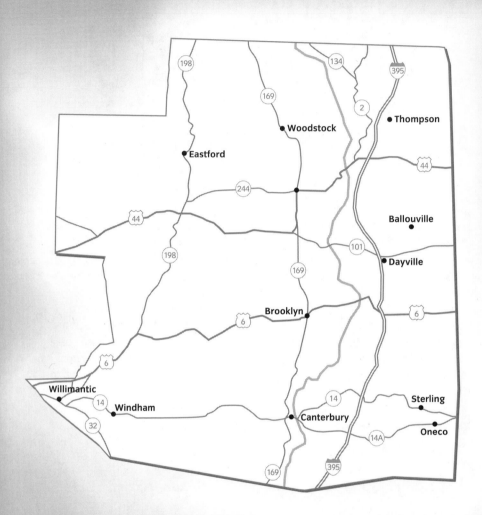

Families looking for fun in Windham County are going to find mostly simple pleasures. Kick back, take your shoes off, set a spell. Get ready to use your senses. This is the place to explore, to take a deep breath, to listen to the brooks, the breeze, and the birds. It's the place to contemplate how this land—all of this land, this whole now-United States—must have looked before 1636 when European settlers brought the native civilization out of the Stone Age and into the future.

Dayville

Beginning right in the heart of the county, take a ride up I-395 to Dayville, a barely-there village on the western side of the highway in the larger town of Killingly. This excursion will throw you right into the sort of down-home, laid-back, unhurried action typical of the county.

Diamond A Ranch (ages 3 and up)
975 Hartford Turnpike. From exit 93 off I-395, drive 1.1 miles east on Route 101 and look for the Diamond A; (860) 779-3000. Prices vary; call for current information. Rides range from one hour to three or more hours. Be prepared to give heights, weights, and level of ability for all riders.

Get on your dungarees and some sturdy shoes and head up the trail to Dayville for a day or weekend of fun in the great outdoors. On the belief that children are very nice people, the folks here offer guided trail rides and riding lessons for all ages on their gently rolling property.

Owner Alicia Summar has created some great opportunities for families with children aged 3 and up to enjoy the pretty terrain of her ranch. Trail rides ranging from one-hour outings to weekend excursions are offered nearly year-round, as long as there is no ice on the ground. Drop-ins are welcome, but reservations are recommended, especially during peak fall foliage season.

The trails at Diamond A traverse gentle hills and grassy meadows. They pass through an apple orchard and across numerous creeks. You can even ride through the canopy created by the trees at either side of the old Danielson-to-Providence trolley track that runs through the property. If you like horses and the New England woodlands and wildlife, come here.

For a family experience you won't easily top in terms of uniqueness, make reservations for the Wild West Trail Ride and Cookout, most often held in summer and fall. Specially designed for families with young children (but also adapted for teens), these trips are arranged by reservation only and usually consist of one- or two-family groups. Any day of the week, you leave the stables about an hour before dark and take a one-hour trail ride to a campsite in the middle of the woods. There, a blazing campfire awaits you, complete with a steaming iron kettle of beans and a big old coffeepot for brewing river coffee. You eat beef jerky, beans, and biscuits or cornbread, and you sit around the campfire for an hour or two and tell tales and sing campfire songs until it's time to head back to the stables.

Other trips are available as well, including a five-hour trail ride to a pizza restaurant overlooking a lake. Warm yourselves with pizza by the stone fireplace in the restaurant and then head back to the stables. Picnic lunches, birthday party rides, pony ride parties, beach rides, and moonlight rides are also offered. Overnight camping excursions leave from a trailhead in Natchaug State Forest and ride to the Lost Silvermine Horse Camp deep within the forest. All meals and supplies are included in the price of the trips; you just bring a sleeping bag and pillow.

Where to Eat

Tracks 101 Grille & Bar. Route 101; (860) 774–1313. Perfect for before or after a ride at the Diamond A. Reasonably priced, delicious prime rib, steaks, grilled chicken, pastas, lighter fare like salads, soups, finger foods, and other homestyle specials in a casually contemporary dining room of a quaint country house. Train memorabilia decorates the walls; in warm weather, you can dine *en plein air* near a water garden. Children's menu; breakfast on the weekends. Open Tuesday through Thursday 11:00 A.M. to 11:00 P.M., Friday and Saturday from 9:00 A.M. to 2:00 A.M., Sunday from 9:00 A.M. to 10:00 P.M. Closed Monday. $–$$

Zip's Diner. Junction of Routes 101 and 12; (860) 774–6335. Authentic stainless steel and spinning counter stools are here in this classic 1954 O'Mahoney diner. Open daily from 6:00 A.M. to 9:00 P.M. $–$$

A Shining Spirit

In the village of Ballouville, just a piece up from Dayville, off I–395 on the eastern side of the highway, there is—or at least, there *was*, until recently—a magical place called **Christmas Wonderland** at 101 Pineville Road, 2.25 miles from exit 94 off I–395.

Mr. Merwin Whipple's personal tribute to the glory and magic of Christmas housed a twelve-building miniature village, six display buildings, a granite chapel, and a showroom nearly as big as my house illuminated by 120,000 twinkling lights and animated by 350 moving displays and Christmas characters.

Sadly, Mr. Whipple put a for-sale sign on the property in 2003 and turned out the lights. Just in case someone exists with a generous spirit as bottomless as Mr. Whipple's was for thirty-five years, look for news in the next few years of the sale and reopening of this awesome display. Or just follow the glow.

Where to Stay

Holiday Inn Express Hotel and Suites.
16 Tracy Road, off exit 94, I–395; (860) 779–
3200. 78 rooms and suites, indoor pool, fitness room, restaurant, continental breakfast.
$$$$

Thompson

Some people think that Connecticut's most northeastern town of Thompson has the quintessential village of the Quiet Corner. Tiny and serene, it is lined with houses, churches,
inns, and merchants that still seem almost eerily reminiscent of the eighteenth century.
Were the town managers to outlaw automobile traffic, this village that grew alongside the
stagecoach route to Boston and Providence would be surreal indeed. A stroll along the
main avenue (Route 193) of town is pleasant for parents and patient children, but the real
family value in Thompson lies off the main thoroughfare.

Quaddick State Park (all ages)
**East Putnam Road off Route 44; (860) 928–9200. Open year-round from 8:00 A.M. to sunset.
Free, except parking fee on weekends and holidays from Memorial Day through Labor
Day, $7.00 charge per in-state plate; $10.00 out-of-state plates.**

Unless you've had your fill of simple pleasures, you'll find Quaddick a great place to spend
an afternoon. Located on East Putnam Road off Route 44, the land and the lake was once
the summer camp and fishing ground of the Nipmuck Indians. Later it was the Thompson
town farm, where elderly citizens spent their dotage in peaceful contemplation.

It's a fair bit noisier now, being actually one of the most popular state parks in the
county. Its 466-acre reservoir and sandy beach are the source of most of the activity. You
can swim, fish, water-ski, jet-ski, and sail or canoe here in the summertime. Those delights
are made easier with such facilities as changing houses, rest rooms, drinking fountains, a
boat launch ramp, a picnic pavilion, and a food concession. Canoes and paddleboats can
be rented by the hour or for a full day (the latter, $30). You can also hike through 116
acres on well-marked woodland trails or play ball or horseshoes on the sports fields.

In winter you can ice skate or ice fish on the reservoir as long as the weather permits.
Cross-country skiing is not possible on the trails, but you can hike or snowshoe if the spirit
moves you to take the kids out for a brisk walk in the crisp air.

Where to Eat

Jason's Restaurant. 274 Riverside Drive, at
the junction of Routes 12 and 193; (860) 923–
2908. Just about 8 feet from the gentle
French River, this restaurant serves casual
fare starting at 6:00 A.M. daily. Breakfast classics include eggs, pancakes, and Belgian waffles. For lunch and dinner, try seafood,
burgers, salads, sandwiches, grill specials,

and thirty-six flavors of ice cream. Eat inside in family-friendly dining rooms or outside on the deck overlooking the river in good weather. They close at 9:00 P.M. daily, leaving plenty of time for you to play a round of golf with the kids on their eighteen-hole miniature course. $–$$

Where to Stay

Lord Thompson Manor. Route 200, exit 99 off I-395, in Thompson; (860) 923–3886; www.lordthompsonmanor.com. Also set off from the main thoroughfare by a half-mile driveway, this beautiful estate was once a horse farm when it was used as a summer home. Now a magnificent inn, it welcomes children to its thirty-six-acre grounds (once landscaped by Frederick Law Olmsted), where a lovely walking path, a friendly inn dog, and lawn games await you. Among its 6 rooms and suites are 3 perfect for families: the Thoroughbred, the Morgan, and the Palomino, with queen-sized beds and cots brought in for the kids. Full country breakfasts, candlelit dinners, and picnic basket lunches set you up well for days of hiking, swimming, riding, or fishing nearby. Nightly rates only. $$$$

The Last **Green Valley**

The hills, valleys, rivers, and historic mill villages of the northeast corner of Connecticut constitute one of America's national heritage corridors, established by the National Park Service but managed by the twenty-one towns and many private organizations that lie within this portion of Windham County. Called the **Quinebaug and Shetucket Rivers Valley National Heritage Corridor,** the area extends from Norwich in New London County to south-central Massachusetts. Notable for its tranquillity, its pristine natural environments, and its historical importance as one of the birthplaces of the American Industrial Revolution, the region is much admired for its recreational opportunities and its preservation of natural and historic resources. Most of the important attractions within the corridor have been selected as destinations deserving treatment in this guide, but many others could also have been included had space permitted. For a complete understanding of this heritage corridor and its attractions, call the Northeast Connecticut Visitors Council at (860) 779–6383 or the Quinebaug and Shetucket Rivers Valley National Heritage Corridor, Inc. at (860) 963–7226. Ask for copies of these wonderful documents: the National Park Service brochure and map entitled *The Last Green Valley, The Green and Growing Guide to the Agricultural Treasures of the Q&SRVNHC,* the *Walking Guide to the Q&SRVNHC,* and *the Walking Weekend Guide.*

Corttis Inn. 235 Corttis Road, North Grosvenordale; (860) 935–5652. These folks call their house spacious; I call it enormous. You'll be back in the eighteenth century among period furnishings, having hot cocoa in front of the kitchen fire, skating on the pond, bicycling the country lanes, hiking or cross-country skiing the trails through 900—yes, 900—acres of their private property, waking up to the delicious smells of home-made blackberry jam on warm freshly baked muffins. Four rooms and a suite with private bath and private entrance are waiting for you and your children. No smoking. $$$–$$$$

Woodstock

Of all the Windham County towns, Woodstock may be the most gentrified, the most artsy, the most sophisticated. It is lovely, to be sure, and one can't blame the tourists for flocking here for the array of treats in store at every turn in the road.

Composed of several villages named North Woodstock, South Woodstock, and so on, the town center most noted for its picturesque qualities is Woodstock proper, a tasteful and sedate community located on beautiful Route 169. Atop the hill, its pretty town common beckons to the traveler with an eye for tranquil spaces. A leisurely stroll through Woodstock Center will reveal many lovely places in which to browse, buy country treasures, or pick up something tasty to eat. Our favorite shops are the **Christmas Barn** and **Resourceful Judith,** both on Route 169.

Roseland Cottage (ages 4 and up)

556 Route 169; (860) 928–4074. Open June 1 through October 15, including July 4 and Columbus Day, Wednesday through Sunday 11:00 A.M. to 5:00 P.M., with tours on the hour until 4:00 P.M. Adults $5.00; seniors $4.00; children under 12 $2.50. Reservations necessary for teas.

If you allow the children to wander awhile on the common, it shouldn't take them long to find Roseland Cottage just across the road. A candy-colored pink confection of a house, it is a most surprising attraction that may provide at least an afternoon's worth of entertainment. Built in 1846 in the newly fashionable Gothic Revival style, this magnificent home was the summer retreat of Henry C. Bowen, native to Woodstock but long and successfully a New York dry-goods dealer.

Though he made and lost several fortunes in his lifetime, Bowen never lost the sense of stewardship and philanthropy that characterized his actions. Founder of churches, abolitionist and supporter of the Union cause in the Civil War, advocate of the beautification of common property, and a lifetime teetotaler, Bowen was also a mover and shaker in all kinds of social and political circles and liked nothing better than celebrations. Roseland Cottage was the site of many lawn parties, bowling contests in the indoor bowling alley, and Fourth of July festivities that made all others look dull in comparison.

A visit to this house on one of its special festival days is everything but dull, an appropriate tribute to its former owner. In addition to tours of the luxurious "cottage," which retains most of its original furnishings, you can wander the labyrinthine pathways of the twenty-one formal gardens, have a picnic under one of the beautiful plantings on the lawn, and play games of the nineteenth century with other visitors.

Be sure to call for a current calendar of the popular family events planned throughout the summer. You may enjoy summer leisure activities, such as hoop rolling, ninepin, graces, and bilboquet. You might also play marbles, jacks, or croquet. The staff serves pink lemonade and cookies; families are encouraged to bring picnics and eat on the lawn. Storytelling or musical events may be a part of these special days. Admission is typically about $5.00 per person.

An annual Children's Victorian Tea ($15) features Victorian revelry for any child 7 or older. Discussions of the language of flowers and the history of teas, parasols, fans, and other Victoriana is part of the entertainment provided by the costumed hostess. You might not be able to resist coming to Tea with Mrs. Tiggy-Winkle, the delightfully incarnated hedgehog character from the tales of Beatrix Potter. Usually in mid-July, this very popular annual event is designed for children aged 4 to 7. You might also want to come for the Fall Festival of Fine Arts and Crafts, which features tours, a food court, clowns and jugglers to entertain the children, and a juried show of nearly 200 artisans. Attendance at this fabulous celebration often reaches 10,000; it is held annually on the weekend after Columbus Day.

The Woodstock **Fair**

Held from 9:00 A.M. to 9:00 P.M. on Labor Day weekend, this fair (www.wood stockfair.com) is one of the ten largest and one of the five oldest country fairs in the state. Each year at the fairgrounds on Route 169, you'll find a midway, tons of food, and practically continuous stage entertainment to enhance your enjoyment of the oxen pulls, horse shows, go-kart races, wood-chopping exhibitions, and hundreds of displays of premium livestock, prizewinning pies, gigantic vegetables, creative handiwork, and much, much more. As many as 200,000 other fairgoers will be here with you at this four-day festivity that begins on Friday and rocks steady through Monday. Adults $8.00, kids under 12 **free.**

Where to Eat

Stoggy Hollow General Store and Restaurant. 492 Route 198, Woodstock Valley; (860) 974–3814. This roadside wonder has omelets, salads with house-made dressings, homemade soups, fresh-baked breads, muffins, turnovers and pies, grilled specialty sandwiches, burgers, chicken pot pie, ham steaks, rib-eyes, pizza, and pasta and seafood specials, daily year-round from 7:00 A.M. to 8:00 P.M. most nights. Eat on the deck in warm weather and shop in the general store for locally made goodies. $

Fox Hunt Farms Gourmet and Cafe and Fox's Fancy Sweet Shoppe. 292 Route 169; (860) 928–0714. Four acres of picnic grounds make this a great place to stop and smell the roses. Hearty sandwiches are the specialty in the cafe, with all the extras you'd need to go with them. The sweet shop's old-fashioned frappes, floats, and ice cream treats will sweep you right off your best intentions. Open Tuesday through Sunday from 10:00 A.M. to 7:00 P.M. on weekdays and to 5:30 P.M. weekends. Sweet shop open to 10:00 P.M. May 1 to October 1. $

Java Jive. 283 Route 169; (860) 963–7477. This gourmet espresso cafe has an artsy, urban feel, but a down-to-earth motivation: Its profits are donated to Third World children in need of clean water and healthy food. Come here for coffees, fruit smoothies, fine pastries, confections, and healthy, moderately priced lunch and dinners. Open 7:00 A.M. Monday through Friday. Open 8:00 A.M. to 4:00 P.M. Saturday. Closed Sunday. $

Where to Stay

The Inn at Woodstock Hill. 94 Plaine Hill Road off Route 169, South Woodstock; (860) 928–0528; www.woodstockhill.net. This former Bowen Mansion has a wonderful cottage with 3 rooms, plus 19 rooms, all with private baths, in the main inn. Every inch of the house and fourteen-acre property is beautiful, and the elegant atmosphere is only enhanced by the casual and friendly attitude of the staff. Continental breakfast for all guests; lunch, dinner, and fabulous Sunday brunch available in the restaurant, which enjoys its own major reputation. All children welcome. $$$$

Beaver Pond B&B. 68 Cutler Hill Road, Woodstock; (860) 974–3312. Two guest rooms with a shared bath make this a nice place for families who want a private getaway. Eat a full country breakfast, then explore the options for hiking, fishing, and boating right on this property. $$

Pomfret/Pomfret Center

First settled in about 1700, Pomfret was known in the 1890s as the "other Newport" as visitors from New York City began summering in these pretty woods and building three-story cottages to help them rough it here. Just 5 miles south of Woodstock on Route 169, it is home now to private secondary schoolers, several pretty inns and B&Bs, a great herb garden, a handful of antiques stores, and a new vineyard. Among its best attractions for families are its famed Wolf Den Trail in its state park and its early mill historic site, but be sure to stop also at the Connecticut Audubon Center in Pomfret Center if you treasure the outdoors.

Mashomoquet Brook State Park (all ages)

Junction of Route 44 and Route 101 to Wolf Den Drive; park office: (860) 928– 6121. Open year-round daily from 8:00 A.M. to sunset for day visitors. Free, except for parking fee only on weekends and holidays between April 15 and October 15: $7 per in-state plate, $10 out-of-state plate. Camping reservations recommended especially for weekends and stays longer than two days; vacancies are filled on a first come, first served basis. $11 per campsite.

Nearly 1,000 acres are the combined area of the three sections that comprise this large park: Wolf Den, Saptree Run, and Mashomoquet Brook. Some great trails link the areas and make this one of Connecticut's most popular state parks. In addition to the typical activities of hiking, fishing, and picnicking, Wolf Den offers camping and Mashomoquet Brook offers swimming and camping. Wolf Den has thirty-five open sites with a flush toilet and drinking water from April 15 through October 15. Masomoquet Brook has twenty wooded sites with a composting toilet and pump water.

Several interesting features distinguish this park from other state recreation areas. The most famous of park attractions are the Table Rock and Indian Chair stone formations and the nearby **Putnam Wolf Den Trail,** accessible from Wolf Den Drive. Park in the park's second parking area. The 4-mile loop trail leads past the campground to the wolf den area. Guided walks are offered from time to time; call for a schedule if you'd like to get the full story of Israel and the Wolf. You can also get the scoop by asking the rangers for a self-guided tour map. After you've seen the site of this sinister encounter, check out the natural formations of **Indian Chair** and **Table Rock.** They are just a little farther along the Wolf Den Trail, which also crosses Mashomoquet Brook and then returns to the parking area.

Israel and the Wolf

General Israel Putnam became famous for more than just his role in the Revolution and his famed ride against the British down the 100 stone steps of his Greenwich hillside homestead. You see, he spent his young manhood in these parts, successfully pursuing the dual careers of innkeeper and farmer.

Legend has it that for several years young Israel and his neighbors were bothered by the killing instincts of a lone wolf that occasionally made a meal of the local livestock. One night in 1742 the wolf awakened the protective instincts of Israel by making off with more than just a few of Israel's sheep. Israel vowed to bring the killer down and assembled a ragtag army of neighbors to help him do it. For days Israel, his neighbors, and their hounds tracked the wolf, finally finding her lair in the face of a high cliff. In went the hounds braying and barking, and out they came again, yelping and mewling. None of them would re-enter the cave.

Israel himself decided to go in after the beast. After a few almost comic attempts to apprehend the criminal, Israel was finally successful. He shot her and dragged her out by the ears. Some say she was the last wolf to live in Connecticut. Today you can hike to her den via the Mashomoquet State Park's Wolf Den Trail.

Brayton Grist Mill and the Marcy Blacksmith Shop Museum
(ages 6 and up)

At the entrance to Mashomoquet Brook State Park on Route 44. Open weekends from late May through September from 2:00 to 5:00 P.M. Free.

Maintained by the Pomfret Historical Society, Billy Brayton's four-story gristmill is the state's finest example of a one-man, water-powered mill operation of the 1890s. The equipment for generating power to grind grain and shell corn survives in the exact locations where Brayton used them. The turbine, the millstone, and a corn sheller are among the items you'll learn about on a tour of the museum.

On the mill's fourth level, an exhibit of handcrafted tools represents the labor of the Marcy family blacksmiths, who plied their trade from 1817 to 1946 in an area known as Marcy Hollow at the side of Mashomoquet Brook. Orin Marcy opened the shop in 1830, using a water-powered bellows and triphammer. A collection of tools made by the blacksmiths includes some used in the manufacture of wheels and horseshoes. In fact, Orin's son, Darius, earned first prize for his horseshoes at the Chicago World's Fair in 1893.

Connecticut Audubon Center at Pomfret (all ages)

189 Pomfret Street (Route 169); (860) 928-4948. Open year-round; sanctuary open daily dawn to dusk; center open Monday through Friday, 8:30 A.M. to 12:30 P.M. and Saturday, 10:00 A.M. to 2:00 P.M. Free.

Folks who like birds are going to love this special refuge of nearly 700 acres of grassland and second-growth woodland that attracts many hard-to-find species year-round and seasonally. The Bafflin Sanctuary adjacent to the center is a beautiful area of meadows, forest, streams, and reclaimed farmland. Trails leading throughout the property offer many opportunities to observe wildlife and enjoy the Quiet Corner's uniquely preserved habitats. Owls, hawks, songbirds, and ducks are abundant, as are wildflowers and butterflies.

Daytime and evening field walks are common here, as are after-school and weekend workshops perfect for children and families. Preregistration is either required or strongly suggested for these. Changing natural history exhibits are inside the center, along with a classroom for special programs. Outside you may join a scheduled tour or walk on your own in this pristine environment. Bring the whole family; the trails are easy. Socks and water-resistant footgear are a great idea.

Where to Eat

Vanilla Bean Cafe. 450 Deerfield Road at the junction of Route 97 with Routes 169 and 44; (860) 928–1562. Ideal for families, this casual cafe serves from 7:00 A.M. daily to 3:00 P.M. on Monday and Tuesday, to 8:00 P.M. on Wednesday, Thursday, and Sunday, and to 9:00 P.M. on Friday and Saturday. It offers a huge breakfast/brunch on weekends and breakfast muffins and sandwiches the rest of the week. Lunch and dinner could be chili, quiches, hearty stews, sandwiches, homemade soups, or one of several daily specials. Entertainment on Saturday might be a folk artist or even an open mike—come and let the kids have fun. $

Where to Stay

Celebrations Inn. 330 Pomfret Street (Routes 169 and 44), Pomfret Center; (860) 928– 5492; www.celebrationsinn.com. Once a private school for girls and then the Old Pomfret Inn, this 20-room Victorian beauty truly welcomes children over the age of 9 to its 5 lovely guest rooms and suites with private baths and fireplaces. This elegant B&B is listed on the National Register of Historic Places. Its library and music and games rooms will beckon you to remain downstairs in the evening. Its gardens, patio, porch, and walking paths will call you outside after your full country breakfast. No smoking. $$$$

Eastford

West of Pomfret, taking Route 244 west from the center or going south on 169, then west on Route 44, take a side trip to Eastford, which is on Route 198. There's no doubt that Natchaug State Forest is the single biggest entity around here, and that's basically all that families might want to explore—at least after they stock up on all the wonderful agricultural goods produced in these parts by some of Connecticut's finest growers.

Buell's Orchard (all ages)

108 Crystal Pond Road, off Route 198, about 2 miles north of Phoenixville, via Westford Road; (860) 974–1150. Open Monday though Saturday from 8:00 A.M. to 5:00 P.M. and, in September and October only, on Sunday from 1:00 to 5:00 P.M.

If you'd like to pack some snacks for a day of hiking, start at Buell's, following the signs to the farm from the center of Eastford on Route 198. Beginning with blueberries in July and going forward to apples and cider in the fall, they also sell pears, peaches, pumpkins, Vermont cheese, maple syrup, and more. In season, you can pick your own apples, peaches, pears, and blueberries. After Labor Day, you can sink your teeth into one of Buell's Famous Caramel Apples. They are delectable sensations, but you may need orthodontic work after chomping your way through one of these. Come Columbus Day weekend for the annual Fall Festival and the opening of the pick-your-own pumpkin patch. Hayrides and **free** cider and doughnuts are part of the hoopla.

Natchaug State Forest (all ages)

Entrance 4 miles south of Phoenixville on Route 198; DEP office: (860) 295– 9523; park office: (860) 974–1562 or John Folsom, supervisor's office: (860) 928–6121. No charge at any time.

Certainly the largest of the treasures families will find in Eastford, this forest's name means "land between the rivers," a reference to its position at the junction of the Still and Bigelow Rivers. Bounded by Routes 44, 6, 198, and 97, it lies adjacent to the beautiful Natchaug River, formed by the confluence of the two smaller rivers. Its 13,000 pristine acres offer elbow room and more to the thousands of outdoor enthusiasts who use it for camping, fishing, picnicking, hiking, snowmobiling, cross-country skiing, and horseback riding.

Picnic sites overlook the river, and anglers of all ages enjoy the trout fishing allowed here from the third week in April to March 1. Besides its trails and picnic area, the State Forest Service provides outhouses and drinking water to day visitors as well as overnight visitors. Backpackers and horseback campers must pack in all supplies and register with the rangers. The Lost Silvermine Horse Camp is the site used by families with their own or rented horses. See Diamond A Ranch (earlier in this chapter) for a guided trip to this site.

Canoeing on the Natchaug is very popular. If you own a canoe, launch it just south of the junction of Routes 198 and 44 in Phoenixville, off General Lyons Road. A 7-mile run through a mix of flat water and quick water takes you past several dams and bridges to the take-out at England Road Bridge. This stretch is great for beginners; experienced canoeists might want to continue another 5.5 miles through several sets of rapids down to Mansfield Hollow State Park.

Family Camping on the Natchaug River

While the state forest campground offers the basic necessities for primitive camping, some families may enjoy the less limited amenities offered by two private campgrounds right on the Natchaug's riverbanks. **Charlie Brown Campground** (860–974–0142) at 100 Chaplin Road (Route 198) has 123 sites for tenters and RVers who need hookups, plus laundry, hot showers, a limited grocery store, and a recreation hall with Saturday night entertainment and planned activities in addition to the on-site opportunities for hiking, swimming, and fishing. Site rates are $23 to $29 nightly (higher on holiday weekends); weekly rates are available. **Peppertree Camping** (860–974– 1439) on Route 198 has 50 wooded sites along the river; it's a great place to launch canoes or tubes and a great spot for fishing the stocked river. It has all the amenities listed above, except for the rec hall and entertainment/activities. You make your own fun here. Nightly rates start at $23; weekly rates are available.

Where to Eat

Eastford Village Store. 192 Eastford Road (Route 198); (860) 974–2334. If Buell's Orchard doesn't have all you need for a picnic, head here. This country general store/cafe in the village center has everything you need to dine alfresco, or you can eat right here for breakfast or lunch. Home-cooked meals that taste like Grandma's are waiting for you. Open 7:00 A.M. Monday through Saturday and closed at 6:00 P.M. Monday through Friday and at 3:00 P.M. on Saturday. $

Brooklyn

Windham County contains one of the top ten scenic highways in the United States, selected for that distinction by Scenic America, an environmental organization that works, in part, to identify and protect scenic American roads. In 1996 the National Department of Transportation designated the road a National Scenic Byway. Historically known as the Norwich–Woodstock Turnpike, the 32-mile section of Route 169 that lies between Lisbon, in New London County, and Woodstock is just about as pretty as pretty can get. Part of that route goes through Brooklyn, a quaint village with beautiful New England churches and a monument to Revolutionary War hero General Israel Putnam in its center.

Farms and Family Fun

The Northeast Connecticut Visitors District has prepared an excellent brochure outlining the many dairies, produce farms, and orchards that offer tours, retail operations, or pick-your-own opportunities for families. Beekeepers, vineyards, sawmills, cider mills, llama farms, sugarhouses, farm fairs, and more are listed in this comprehensive publication. Call (860) 779–6383 and ask for the brochure with the same title as this sidebar.

Creamery Brook Bison (ages 2 to 12)

19 Purvis Road; (860) 779–0837; www.creamerybrookbison.com. Store open April through October from Monday through Friday from 2:00 to 6:00 P.M. and on Saturday from 9:00 A.M. to 2:00 P.M. and from November to March Wednesday through Friday from 2:00 to 6:00 P.M. and on weekends from 10:00 A.M. to 2:00 P.M. Call to schedule a farm tour or an ice-cream making activity. Wagon tours July to September, Saturday at 1:30 P.M. (no reservations necessary). Wagon tours, adults $6.00, children 3 to 11 $4.50, under 3 free; special rates (by reservation only) for groups of fifteen or more. Groups can also prearrange walking tours, ice-cream and butter-making activities, and wagon ride combinations.

Committed to educating the public about buffalo and dairy farming, this hundred-acre farm is also the home of seventy buffalo who roam its pastures and woodlands. You can visit here year-round simply to see the bison (early evening, around 6:00 P.M., is the best viewing time, when the herd leaves the cool woods and comes down toward the open field), you can come for a prescheduled tour of the farm, you can arrange an ice-cream–making outing, in which you help make hand-cranked ice cream and butter, or you can come on out from July through September for a wagon ride out into those cool woods to see the herd and this beautiful countryside. Along with Holstein and Jersey cows and the adult bison, you will more than likely see bison calves—too cute to resist. You can't pet these magnificent creatures—except for Thunderbolt, a friendly female penned and amenable to gentle petting. Learn about the history, habitat, habits, and myths of these once nearly extinct animals, and browse in the store for bison-related booty.

Birthday parties can also be arranged here. These typically include a wagon tour, ice-cream–making activity, and a birthday cake for eight children and two adults. If you don't have the time or occasion for a whole party, just stop for gourmet ice cream in the ice cream shop, open from 2:00 to 9:00 P.M. in the summer.

Brooklyn Fair (all ages)

Route 169, Brooklyn Fairgrounds; (860) 779–0012. Fourth weekend in August. Open Thursday 4:00 to 10:00 P.M., Friday and Saturday 8:00 A.M. to 10:00 P.M., and Sunday 8:00 A.M. to 6:00 P.M. Adults $7.00; children under 12 free. Parking, $4.00 per carload.

Every year in late August, Brooklyn's population soars as visitors from all over come to the oldest continuously active agricultural fair in the United States. Held for four days the weekend before Labor Day, it is perhaps the best country fair in the state. Just name the activities and sights you expect at a country fair. You'll find them all here.

I'll give you a partial list of what's in store for you: Oxen pull. Draft horse show. Skillet toss. Dog show. Circus. Midway. Pony pull. Cattle parade. Christmas tree show. Bingo. Barbecue. Tractor pull. Country dancing. Beekeeping exhibit. Children's games and contests. Art show. Stage entertainment for adults and children.

The list goes on and on. I'm not sure if these capture the diversity of sounds, smells, and sights that assault the senses at a fair of this sort, but I can assure you that your kids are going to love this event.

Don't be fooled by the low admission fees. Although the agricultural events are all free, you'll need a wad of currency for a day or evening here. That is unless you and the kids don't eat any food, buy any crafts or gadgets, or ride any rides.

Where to Eat

Hank's Restaurant. 416 Providence Road (Route 6); (860) 774–6071. Since 1972, this Brooklyn fixture has been serving up family-friendly food such as burgers, steaks, salads, soups, seafood, and pasta. A children's menu has typical favorites. Open Monday through Sunday at 11:00 A.M. and Sunday at noon. Close at 9:00 P.M. Sunday through Thursday, 10:00 P.M. Friday and Saturday. $

Where to Stay

Friendship Valley Inn B&B. 60 Pomfret Road (Route 169); (860) 779–9696; www. friendshipvalleyinn.com. Children over the age of 7 are welcome in this 1795 Historic Register home with five bedrooms, private baths, and hearty, homestyle breakfasts. If the weather's cold, hunker down by one of the fireplaces and keep warm. $$$$

Canterbury

Famed for its own architectural style and for Crandall Academy, founded in 1832 by Prudence Crandall, Canterbury is an almost completely rural town that appears nearly the same as it did a century ago. Six miles south of Brooklyn on Route 169, its pretty Congregational Church on the Green was built in the 1960s as a replica of the original one built in 1804, and its public library resides in the building that was the Canterbury district's one-room schoolhouse until the 1940s. Enjoy the beauty and learn from the history you'll discover in quiet Canterbury.

Prudence Crandall Museum (ages 8 and up)

On the green at the corner of Routes 169 and 14; (860) 546–9916. Open February 1 through December 15, Wednesday through Sunday from 10:00 A.M. to 4:30 P.M. Adults $2.50; children $1.50; children under 5 free. *(Note: This state-owned museum has recently been affected by state budget cuts. Check in spring 2004 for its reopening.)*

Site of the first New England academy for African-American girls, the Crandall Academy is now called the Prudence Crandall Museum. A National Historic Landmark, the 1805 structure is one of the several houses in Canterbury with the distinctive "Canterbury style."

Basically conforming to the Federal style, the house has twin chimneys and an elaborate two-story entrance ornamentation with a Palladian window on the second floor above the front doorway.

Far more famous than its architecture is the house's history and its mistress, Prudence Crandall. The story of Prudence's courage and the dignity of her students is told in tours of the museum. Exhibits explore topics such as local history, African-American history, the abolitionist movement, and women's rights. The museum also includes three period rooms, a gift shop, and a research library.

Families might especially enjoy Prudence Crandall Day, typically held on the Saturday of Labor Day weekend. This special festivity offers nineteenth-century children's games, craft demonstrations, musical entertainment, and refreshments and crafts for sale. On the first Saturday in November from 1:00 to 4:00 P.M., the museum usually hosts an annual Tea with Prudence Crandall. Local living history performer Donna Dufresne portrays Prudence in a forty-five-minute dramatic monologue and then interacts with the guests, who share tea and refreshments after the presentation. When the event is offered, advance registration is required.

The Story of the **State Heroine**

In the summer of 1831, twenty-eight-year-old Prudence Crandall was asked by a group of Canterbury citizens to establish a private academy in which she would teach local children. Crandall purchased a large house on the Canterbury green and opened her academy in January 1832. All went well for several months. Miss Crandall had the full support of the parents, who paid her $25 per quarter to teach their children reading, writing, arithmetic, grammar, geography, history, philosophy, chemistry, and astronomy.

Then, in the fall of 1832, Crandall accepted a new student. Sarah Harris, twenty years old, was Negro. Disapproval was immediate, and several families withdrew their children from the academy. Criticism was so harsh that Crandall dismissed the remaining students and reopened the school several months later as an academy for the instruction of "young ladies and little misses of color."

The first such school in all of New England, the academy added classes in French, drawing, painting, and piano. Outrage followed the earlier criticism as Miss Crandall made it clear that no distinctions were to be made in the education of white and black children. In May 1833, Prudence Crandall was arrested and jailed for breaking the Connecticut General Assembly's new "Black Law," which prohibited the instruction of any "colored persons who are not inhabitants of this State."

Though her case was dismissed in July, Crandall and her students suffered greatly at the hands of the citizens of the Canterbury area. The house was pelted with rocks and eggs. An attempt was made to set it afire, and its windows were broken in an angry attack in September, 1834. Only then, fearing the physical safety of her students, did Prudence close the school.

Prudence and her husband left Canterbury and settled in Illinois, where they remained until his death in 1874. Prudence bought property in Kansas with her brother and lived there until her death in 1890 at the age of eighty-seven. She taught throughout her life.

Wright's Mill Tree Farm (all ages)

63 Creasey Road, off Route 6, 169, or 14; (860) 774–1455; www.wrightsmillfarm.com. Open daily year-round from 9:00 A.M. to 5:00 P.M. No admission charge; hayrides $2.00 per person; trees and pumpkins sell at market rate.

Once the site of five seventeenth-century mills, this beautiful 250-acre property is an outstanding place to take the family in the fall and holiday seasons. Amid one of the prettiest New England settings we've seen, you can pick pumpkins, cut Christmas trees, walk the nature trails to the antique mill buildings, and soak up the aura of the olden days that seems to percolate from every pore of this refuge.

In spring and summer, families are welcome to explore the trails or picnic in the tranquil fields, but most daytripping families come here in autumn. The level of public activity rises sharply after Labor Day when the leaves begin to turn and thoughts turn to Halloween and Christmas festivities. The foliage is spectacular, and you'll find yourselves in high spirits on a horse-drawn Pumpkin Hunt Hayride through the splendidly crunchy leaves. No reservations are necessary, but there is a per-person charge for the ride to the pumpkin fields. If you'd rather walk, there's no charge to comb the fields for the perfect pumpkin.

Perhaps it will be winter that you find most enchanting here. I am certain that there is in all New England no setting more like a Currier and Ives painting than this one. The Grand Arrival of Santa in a horsedrawn sleigh at 11:00 A.M. on the Sunday after Thanksgiving heralds the opening of tree-cutting season. In the farm's thirty-one fields grow 150,000 trees of thirteen varieties; if you want to do the cutting yourself, the Amundsens provide maps, saws, and great little wooden carts for dragging in the most beautiful Christmas tree ever. You can also buy pre-cut trees, roping, holly-studded wreaths, garlands, and so on.

Santa or one of his elves gives every child a candy cane and listens to every Christmas wish list. During the week, the Amundsens often provide cookies and cider or cocoa for the little ones. The Silo Christmas Shop is brimming with ornaments; you can shop while the kids slide on the frozen pond—that is, if the weather cooperates. Come any day of the week during December from 9:00 A.M. to dark. There may be no better Christmas tree farm anywhere—come and see for yourself.

Sterling/Oneco

You're not likely to find the village of Oneco by yourself unless you're aficionados of driving the blue highways. We love to take the road less traveled, but the demands of our schedule rarely allow serendipity to manifest itself. One day, however, we got lucky in Windham County. Not far from exit 88 off I–395 in the township of Sterling rests the sleepy intersection of Route 14A and Newport Road. There you will find a Connecticut masterpiece—Whitford's General Store in Oneco village. Not far away are a few other sites worth a look if you'd like to stay in the area.

Whitford's General Store (all ages)
Route 14A at the junction of Newport Road; (860) 564–5215. Open year-round, Monday through Saturday from 6:00 A.M. to 10:00 P.M. and Sunday from 6:00 A.M. to 9:00 P.M.

Even if you have no other reason to come to Sterling township, bring the kids here and take a peek at the plethora of merchandise in stock at this throwback to the good old days. This place is brimful of everything under the sun, and the inventory is carefully maintained with the guiding philosophy that if they don't have it, you don't need it. Stroll the aisles of the big old house that has contained this store since 1879; they're lined with shelves of great old-time goods, some of which you might have thought no one manufactured anymore.

From almanacs to zippers, the merchandise will astound you. They have one-piece long johns with a trap door, night crawlers, fishing lures, blue jeans, barn boots, penny and nickel candy, cow manure—the list could take hours to recite. I know where you can buy pig and sow pellets, I just can't tell you whether you use them to feed 'em, cure 'em, or grow 'em. The proprietors know, though, and they'll be happy to tell you.

They'll also be happy to convince you to set a spell and have a plateful of their home-grown cooking. Try their gigantic grinders, fabulous fish and chips, huge hamburgers, outrageous onion rings, celebrated clam cakes, and a milk shake so thick you can stand your spoon up in it. Come in the morning for their Belly Buster, a grinder made with three eggs, sausage, bacon, ham, and cheese. You may have to carry the kids back to the car even if they share one of these. If the Buster doesn't satisfy, have a scoop or two of the Hershey's ice cream they serve on the wide veranda in the summertime.

River Bend Campground and Mining Company (all ages)

41 Pond Street (Route 14A), Oneco; (860) 564–3440; www.riverbendcamp.com. Open mid-April through mid-October daily from 9:00 A.M. to 5:00 P.M. Day visitors should call ahead in the off-season before Memorial Day and after Labor Day. Mining rates are $6.00 for children; accompanying adults are free. Gemstone panning is $4.50 per person. If you do both, the wildlife exhibit is free. Canoe rentals $8.00 per hour, $22.00 per day. Mini-golf and train rides, $1.00. Paddleboats and aquacycles, $8.00 per hour. Campsites, $28.00 and up nightly; cabin rentals, $55.00 and up nightly; weekly and seasonal rates available.

One of Whitford's nearest neighbors is this award-winning family campground, amusement center, and gem mine. In the campground business for more than thirty years and the entertainment/amusement business for more than a dozen, the host of this place has created a compromise between the Great Outdoors and Great Adventure, doing all he can to keep families safe and happy together in an outdoor environment. Located on the Moosup River and a thirty-five-acre pond, this center offers 160 campsites, some with rental cabins, trailers, and campers. You can rent a canoe or take a guided canoe trip, you can tour the indoor wildlife exhibit with diorama-style re-creations of life in the North American woodlands, and you can enter the walk-through gem mine re-creation to prospect for real gemstones from around the world or pan for gems and minerals in the outdoor sluice. A kiddie train, aquacycles, paddleboats, kayaks, archery, horseshoes, mini-golf, basketball, tennis, volleyball, a moon bounce, outdoor movies, bingo, and other interactive areas, activities, and special events keep this place hopping. Luckily, there's plenty of room for deciding whether you want to be in or out of the nearly continuous action.

Sterling Park Campground (all ages)

177 Gibson Hill Road, Sterling; (860) 564–8777. Open mid-April through mid-October. 130 sites; $32 nightly; weekly rates available.

The owners of Sterling Park Campground are proud of their commitment to providing wholesome family fun on the beautifully landscaped hills of their family campground. With a staff of friendly faces, they offer guests two heated pools (one just for kiddies), a rec hall, a children's playscape, mini-golf, a snack shack, a camp store, sports courts, and lots of pretty wooded or open campsites. You can arrive with your own camper or tent (electrical and water hookups are available) or rent their cabin or trailer. Free hot showers and a laundromat keep you comfortable throughout your stay.

Family movie nights, square dances, Saturday night dances, bingo games, hayrides, Kids Olympics, and Christmas in July with a visit from Santa are among the events on the busy calendar.

As if this all were not enough, the folks here decided a long time ago to set it all to music, at least once annually. Each year in June is the **Sterling Bluegrass Festival,** with foot-stomping, toe-tapping, knee-rocking music—the kind with banjos and guitars, mandolins and fiddles all singing sweetly in the great outdoors. A laid-back three-day affair that draws a moderate crowd, it features regional and local musicians. Call the campground for information, tickets, or camping reservations. For the festival, you're welcome whether or not you're campers.

Willimantic/Windham

Windham County has a sort of a little toe that pops westward from the lowest portion of its boundary with Tolland County. It is here in the toe that you'll find the small city of Willimantic and its sibling village of Windham. Situated on the banks of the Shetucket River, Willimantic's history is tied firmly to the textile mills that dominated three centuries of Connecticut industry.

Hill Towns and Mill Villages

The first textile mill in Windham County was built in 1806 by Smith Wilkinson on the Quinebaug near present-day Putnam. It was a small cotton mill that depended on the fluctuating level of the river to drive its wheels and turbines. Soon the technology developed to control the water through the use of reservoirs, dams, and canals. It was only a matter of time before every town and village on the rivers had a textile mill. Thousands of immigrants poured into the region to work in the mills and make their homes in the towns. The Quinebaug Mill, built in Killingly in 1852, was one of the largest mills. It had 61,340 spindles, 1,656 looms, and produced 28 miles of cloth each day.

An excellent driving-tour brochure, from which I have borrowed the title of this sidebar, of the principal mill sites remaining along Route 169 is available at the **Windham Textile and History Museum** or through the Northeast Connecticut Visitors District.

In fact, the history of many Windham County towns would have been totally altered were it not for the textile mills built along the Quinebaug and Shetucket Rivers in the eighteenth and nineteenth centuries. Today in Willimantic, families can visit one of these sites to learn more about life in Connecticut's mill villages.

Connecticut Eastern Railroad Museum

Train enthusiasts may enjoy knowing that the Connecticut Eastern Chapter of the National Railway Historical Society is currently building a railroad museum in Willimantic, with hopes of eventually creating an entire operating railroad village at the Bridge Street site. A roundhouse, a freighthouse, a section house, and other village buildings are being constructed or restored here, and track is being repaired or laid to allow passengers to ride on the restored trains in the chapter's growing collection. Children are welcome to try a replica pump car along a section of track, and special excursions on the Providence and Worcester Railroad are planned. Open from May through November on weekends from 10:00 A.M. to 4:00 P.M., the museum is a work-in-progress. Admission is $3.00 for adults; children 12 and under are free. Call ahead to see what has developed here recently. The address is 55 Bridge Street (Route 32); the phone number is (860) 456-9999; a Web site has been set up at www.cteasternmuseum.org.

Windham Textile and History Museum (ages 6 and up)

157 Union at Main Street, Route 66; (860) 456-2178; www.millmuseum.org. Open year-round on Friday through Sunday from Columbus Day to Memorial Day from 1:00 to 4:00 P.M. and Wednesday through Sunday 1:00 to 4:30 P.M. in the summertime. Closed major holidays. Adults $4.00; seniors and students $2.00; children under 6 free.

The Textile and History Museum examines the daily lives and culture of the people who labored in the mills. It also explores the stories of those who developed the technology and collected the money earned from the labor of immigrants at the height of the Industrial Revolution. Through its creative exhibits, the museum provides an excellent overview of the cultural and economic changes brought about by both the development and demise of the Connecticut textile industry.

Located in two buildings of the former Willimantic Linen Company, the museum has an authenticity unsurpassed by any other re-creations in the region. Dugan Mill houses exhibits that bring the visitor right into the last century, when tens of thousands of workers labored under difficult conditions and for very low pay. The exhibits include re-creations of an 1880s mill shop floor, equipped with a carding machine, a spinning frame, a loom, and a textile printer. At one end of the shop is the overseer's office, from which the workers were carefully monitored.

The museum's main building houses the Company Store, a re-creation of the very shop that on this site once served the needs of the employees. It now doubles as the museum gift shop. A laborers' tenement, a mill agent's mansion from the Victorian era, and the 1877 Dunham Hall Library are also housed in the main building.

Where to Eat

Willimantic Brewery and Main Street Cafe. 967 Main Street, Willimantic; (860) 423–6777. The dining room inside a historic post office is a dramatic setting for kid-friendly pub fare. Lunch and dinner, Tuesday through Saturday from 11:30 A.M. $–$$

General Information

Northeast Connecticut Visitors District/Connecticut's Quiet Corner. 13 Canterbury Road, Suite 3, P.O. Box 145, Brooklyn 06234; (860) 779–6383; www.ctquietcorner.org. **Free** tourism brochures such as annual Getaway Guide, seasonal Calendar of Events, a Waters Guide, a Bicycle Guide, a Walking Weekend Guide, and a Farms and Family Fun Guide.

Connecticut Department of Agriculture. 165 Capitol Avenue, Hartford 06106; (860) 566–4845. Produces pamphlets on pick-your-own farms, agricultural tours, farm activities, sugarhouses, and Christmas tree farms.

Connecticut Department of Environmental Protection. Office of State Parks and Recreation, 165 Capitol Avenue, Hartford 06106; Eastern District: (860) 295–9523. Publishes booklet describing state parks and state forests, with day-use and camping information for each site.

New London County

Coastal Voyages and Country Sojourns

The southeastern shoreline of Connecticut defies characterization. First, the county is comprised of a wide variety of habitats, so to speak. The hills and forests of its northern region are distinctly different from the meadows and marshes of its southern border along the Sound. Second, the population of the two areas is equally disparate. The peaceable hills to the north are much like Windham County in the state's so-called Quiet Corner, while the bustling towns of the shoreline reflect their long history of industry and commerce.

Both areas provide an abundance of attractions and activities for families. From fine art gallery to lighthouse museum, from woodland trail to fishing pier, with every level of sophistication and simplicity, New London's sights are as diverse as the county.

TopPicks for fun in New London County

1. Children's Museum of Southeastern Connecticut
2. *Sunbeam Express* Nature Cruises
3. Lyman Dolls and Toys Museum
4. Science EpiCenter and DNA Learning Center
5. Ocean Beach Park
6. USS *Nautilus* Memorial and Submarine Force Museum
7. Project Oceanology
8. Mystic Seaport Museum
9. Mystic Marinelife Aquarium
10. Maple Breeze Park

NEW LONDON COUNTY

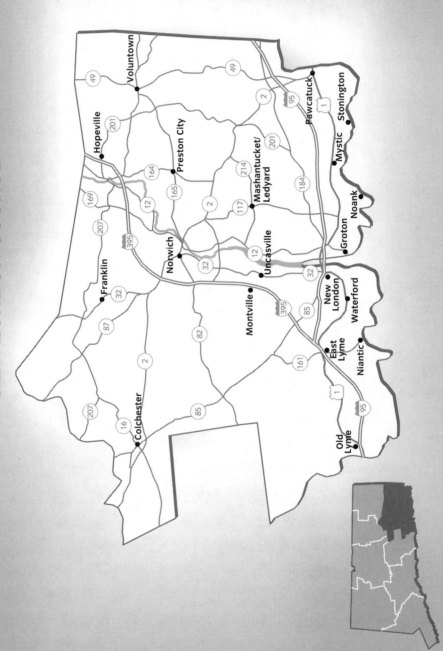

Country Daytripping

With a little planning, a good night's sleep, and a hearty breakfast packed in a picnic basket, you can tour the next four towns right smartly if you get an early start. Pick a weekend in late summer or early fall and have a brisk morning walk to the Salmon River from Day Pond in Colchester. Eat breakfast on the covered bridge, return to the pond, head to World Wide Games to stock up on gifts for friends and family, then grab an ice cream at Harry's. Ice cream for lunch is a great way to make your kids think that maybe you're still a lot of fun or maybe just half crazy so they'd better behave in case you do something really reckless. While you still have the kids raising their eyebrows in the backseat, take Route 16 to Route 207 through Lebanon to North Franklin. Chances are things are sleepy at Blue Slope Farm (unless you choose the weekends after Independence Day or Columbus Day), so just continue on Route 207 to Route 138 to Route 201 to reach Hopeville Pond State Park. Take out the fishing gear you packed along with the picnic goods, and throw a line and rest awhile until the trout start jumpin'. Pack up around 3:00 or so and continue on to Pachaug, where the cool woods in the late afternoon are just what you'll want to see. Skip the long hike—just drive up to near the top of Mount Misery and catch the breeze and the beauty of late afternoon. Now sweep southward on Route 165 and have a casual dinner at Village Pizza in Preston. When you can't eat another slice, mosey on up Route 164 and put up your feet at the Roseledge B&B where a feather bed for you, a full-size trundle for the kids, and a fireplace at your feet await you. ZZZzzz . . .

Colchester

At the crossroads of Routes 11, 2, 16, and 85, Colchester is typical of the northern communities of New London County. Elegant houses surround its green; small shops, a few restaurants, and pretty public buildings provide the hub of a structure that is primarily rural in nature. Don't let it fool you that Colchester calls its main drag "Broadway." This really is a country town.

Day Pond State Park (all ages)

Route 149; (860) 295–9523. Free admission, except for day-use vehicle charge of $7.00 (in-state plates) and $10.00 (out-of-state plates) on weekends and holidays. Open daily, year-round, from 8:00 A.M. to sunset.

That country flavor is clearly apparent out at Day Pond. In fact, though the dirt road to the park is clearly marked now, the last time we were here the sign was a paper plate nailed to a tree. Ain't no fancy city stuff here! Originally constructed by a pioneering family named Day, the pond is an antique mill pond, the water of which once turned an overshot waterwheel that powered the up-and-down saw of the family's sawmill. Now empty of all signs of industry, the pond is stocked regularly with trout and is popular with fishers, swimmers, and skaters. No boating is allowed on the seven-acre pond, which is also a spawning ground for migratory salmon.

As is typical at these parks, the state has provided telephones, rest rooms, picnic tables, a large picnic shelter with fireplaces, and drinking water for your comfort. A small nature trail across from the parking areas has a fourteen-point trail guide booklet that also contains maps of the whole park and its various trails. Call the number above to obtain that guide in advance of your visit, or if you're here on the weekend, ask the parking attendant for a copy.

A loop trail that begins at Day Pond is an easy walk for families; it connects with a trail through the Salmon River Forest to the Comstock Bridge on the Salmon River. If there is a ranger around on the day you visit, ask for a map to these trails or come equipped with the wonderful *Connecticut Walk Book,* published by the Connecticut Forest and Park Association (860–346–2372). You should also be able to find the trailhead yourselves by walking along Day Pond Road. The views of the Salmon River are beautiful; the trail actually hugs the river before reaching the 1873 covered bridge. The 4-mile combination of the two trails makes for a great day hike. Pack a lunch and eat at or on the bridge. Bring along a few night crawlers and a couple of poles and hooks, and you'll have the makings of a perfect country day.

World Wide Games (all ages)

75 Mill Street; (860) 537–2325. Open Wednesday through Friday from 10:00 A.M. to 5:00 P.M. and Saturday from 10:00 A.M. to 4:00 P.M.

Colchester is a great place for parents looking for game and craft bargains. Stop at the World Wide Games factory outlet store for the chance to pay up to 90 percent off retail for discontinued, slightly irregular, or damaged classic wooden board games, puzzles, brainteasers, and arts-and-crafts supplies. Grandparents can really buy up a storm here—they get a senior discount.

Where to Eat

Harry's Place. (860) 537–2410. On Route 16 back near the center of town is about as classic a roadside stand as ever stood on an American highway. Open only from April 15 to Columbus Day, Harry's Place has been called "the ultimate burger joint" by the *Hartford Courant*. No waistline-trimming foods are served here—just burgers dripping with "juice," excellent onion rings, french fries, dogs, and sauerkraut. Wash these down with soft drinks and shakes while you sit at the picnic tables near the road. Harry's Place has been "proud to serve" since 1918, so maybe there's a secret to longevity in this greasy gastronomy. Check it out, daily from 11:00 A.M. to 9:45 P.M. (10:00 P.M. at the ice cream window). $

Franklin

With great affection I have to say that this little town is out in the middle of nowhere, a comment I can make safely because I know that most of its inhabitants like it just fine exactly that way. There's not a lot here to make families jump in the car to get out this way, but one interesting site and a few events might make you tie in a visit with other plans elsewhere. Take Route 32 from Route 2 to reach the village. To reach Blue Slope Country Museum, take Route 2 to Route 87 and follow the signs.

Blue Slope Country Museum (all ages)

138 Blue Hill Road; (860) 642–6413. **Open year-round by special arrangement for school, scout, senior, and other special groups; open to the public twice yearly for weekend festivals in July (the weekend after Independence Day) and in October (the weekend after Columbus Day). Tours for special groups pay a group rate. Family groups can inquire about visits by appointment. On festival weekends, admission is $7.00 for adults and children over 12; children 12 and under** free.

Twice each year, Sandy and Ernie Staebner open their one-hundred–Holstein dairy farm to the public for a weekend of activities and wagon tours designed to let folks in on the bountiful history of farming and crafting that once flourished in these parts. Years ago there were more farms in New London County alone than there are in all of Connecticut today, and the Staebners have acquired an amazing collection of old-time tools, implements, and farm vehicles inside and outside of the 5,000-square-foot, two-story rustic museum building they constructed in 1990 to educate the public about that history.

Inside the museum are artifacts revealing interesting facts about the lives and labors of three centuries of farm families. Many objects are at least a century old, including looms, spinning wheels, drills, wooden water pipes, butter churners, weapons, milk cans, rakes, axes, sleighs, yokes, and toys. A library of eighteenth-, nineteenth-, and twentieth-century agricultural books and publications is also here.

If you come for the annual festivals, the place is truly steeped in history as forty to sixty volunteers, most of them dressed in period clothing, demonstrate the skills that farmers and crafters used throughout New England in centuries past. Spinning, weaving, candle dipping, stone splitting, mowing, quilting, basketry, broom making, soap making, quilling, tinsmithing, straw weaving, woodworking, and whittling are among the activities you might see reenacted. Special activities for children, such as butter making, tram rides around the farm, tours of the barns, and a Saturday-night barn dance are part of the fun. Food and refreshments are available for purchase, as are books and gifts related to the country theme.

Visiting groups arriving throughout the year miss out on most of that, but they get a guided tour that shows the evolution of farming technology and demonstrations of some of the museum's 4,000 tools and implements.

Hopeville

One of the small village centers that comprise the town of Griswold, Hopeville is just a bit more than a turn in the road. A rural and oddly reassuring enclave to those who live in hectic places, it's the home of one of northern New London County's most popular family parks.

Hopeville Pond State Park (all ages) ⓐ ⓐ ⓐ ⓐ ⓐ
Route 201; main office: (860) 376–2920; campground: (860) 376–0313. Open year-round. Day use is 8:00 A.M. to sunset. Day use is free, except for parking fee, $7.00 and $10.00 for CT plates and out-of-state plates, respectively, on summer weekends and holidays; camping April through October; campers currently pay $13.00 per night. You can reserve sites by mail or hope for a site on a first come, first served basis.

Located just east of Hopeville, a tiny village in the northern township of Griswold, this park is noted for its glacial geology and its excellent trails and forest roads created by the Civilian Conservation Corps in the 1930s.

Freshwater fishing, swimming, and boating are possible uses of Hopeville Pond, an antique woolen millpond used in the early nineteenth century. The trails, of course, are perfect for hiking, and a sports field encourages use by families who like nothing better than an old-fashioned reunion-cum-ballgame. As usual, the state has provided drinking water and toilets, plus changing houses, a food concession (in summer), and a boat-launch ramp.

Best of all, however, is the Hopeville Pond campground. Eighty-one wooded sites are perfect for family campers, and you could easily spend a week here without getting bored. Call the campground directly to check availability; this is a very popular site.

Voluntown

As you know by now if you've read any parts of this book consecutively, Connecticut has a vast amount of acreage set aside as protected public land. A huge chunk of that land is Pachaug State Forest, spanning six towns in this region and accessible from Route 49 just a short distance north of its junction with Route 138/165 in Voluntown. Pachaug is an Indian word meaning "turn in the river," and it is the pretty Pachaug River and its tributary, Misery Brook, that meander through the forest. Twenty-four thousand acres preserved here make this the largest protected site in the state and a great site for family camping and outdoor recreation.

Pachaug State Forest (all ages)

Route 49; (860) 295–9523. Open year-round. Campers don't need reservations, but they pay a nightly fee, currently $13.00. Day use is free, except on weekends and holidays between Memorial Day weekend and Labor Day, when residents of Connecticut pay $7.00 and nonresidents pay $10.00.

Entering the forest on Route 49, you will cross the Pachaug River and disappear for days into a veritable wilderness of greenery, 28,000 acres' worth. Most folks stay just at least long enough to soak up some of the beauty here and take it home with them in their souls.

Two separate campgrounds provide wooded sites for tenters who decide to soak overnight. You can haul in the motorhome, too, but no hook-ups are available. The park and forest service provides drinking water, toilets, canoe rentals, a boat ramp, and a horse camp. Once you're set up, you can hike, bike, canoe, bird-watch, swim, scuba dive, horseback ride, and picnic to your heart's content. You can also skate, snowmobile, snowshoe, or cross-country ski in winter.

Be sure to roam these rocky hills on the more than 30 miles of trails past interesting habitats such as a southern white cedar swamp, a rhododendron sanctuary, and the pond. A particularly great trail is the Nehantic Trail to the top of Mount Misery. From the east side of the parking area, it can be reached by beginning on a loop that will take you through the rhododendron grove (which blossoms abundantly in late spring, generally after the second week in June) and the cedar swamp, and then eventually hits the trail to the breezy, slightly balding top of the sorry-sounding mountain. If you don't feel like a moderate workout, you can also drive to within 200 yards of the summit. Most definitely, if you're looking for a little wilderness in this busy state, come here. You'll be amazed at how loud the quiet is.

Preston City

If you take Route 165 south from Voluntown, you'll end up in Preston, another rural enclave sought only by those travelers who reject the I–395 highway, which passes only a handful of miles to the west. At the junction of Routes 165 and 164, you should do yourselves a favor and take a right and drive north on 164 a few miles. Designated a scenic road for very good reasons, it leads past centuries-old farms and homesteads and the pretty Preston City Congregational Church—you won't be sorry you took a little detour before returning to head west again on Route 165 to the city of Norwich.

Roseledge Herb Farm B&B (all ages)

418 Route 164; (860) 892–4739 or (888) 996–7673; www.roseledge.com. Open year-round. Public tearoom open most afternoons; call for reservations if you'd like to arrange a luncheon tea. Room rates $95 to $135 nightly year-round. Stay two nights from Sunday to Thursday (excluding holidays) and get the third night free.

Whether you're stopping just for tea and fresh-baked goodies or stopping for the night, Roseledge Herb Farm B&B is the perfect endpoint of a country day. If you can, you'll spend the night right in one of those wonderful old houses on that beautiful stretch of Route 164, a 1720 farmhouse with fireplaces in every room, homemade soap in the baths, hearth-cooked foods (on occasional winter evenings), feather beds and trundle beds, goats and sheep, fresh-from-under-the-hen eggs, a charming tearoom for guests and visitors alike, and room galore for very welcome children. Join innkeepers Sandy and Gail Beecher for the morning chores—goats have to be fed, eggs have to be collected—or explore the herb gardens and barn. Pull out an old sled if it's snowing, play in the sandbox if it's not. Take a ride on Black Cherry, the tire-swing horse who awaits you at the cherry tree. Listen to stories read aloud from antique farm storybooks or just listen to the songs of the crickets and the bees. Take your shoes off, set a spell, and watch the grass grow.

Maple Lane Farms (all ages)

57 Northwest Corner Road, off Route 164, south of Route 165 junction; (860) 889-3766; 24-hour pick-your-own information: (860) 887–8855; www.maplelane.com. Open daily in season from 8:00 A.M. to noon, plus on Tuesday and Thursday from 4:00 to 7:00 P.M. Call ahead for field conditions. They supply containers.

Once 140 acres of overgrown pasture around an abandoned dairy farm, Maple Lane is now a thriving family farm with a marvelous spirit of confidence, abundance, and generosity fueled by hard work and determination. Share the positive energy by coming here for fresh strawberries, blueberries, raspberries, cut flowers, and pumpkins, plus tag and cut-your-own Christmas trees. Simply show up to buy, show up to pick your own, or call ahead and place an order for what you want them to pick for you.

Plucking sun-ripened strawberries on a clear June day may inspire young gardeners to set down a few plants of their own. Who knows? It may well be you yourself who's struck with farm fever in this stunning country setting that kinda makes you want to trade in the Volvo for a John Deere.

Free scenic hayrides are given on Saturday and Sunday in the fall from 9:00 A.M. to 4:00 P.M. During pumpkin season and strawberry season, a giant pumpkin and strawberry stand at the opening to the giant maze created from huge round hay bales for kids to play in.

Where to Eat

Village Pizza Family Restaurant. Route 165 in Fleming shopping center; (860) 887–1930. Spotless and perfect for families, this place is not just for pizza. Come also for Italian specialties including imported pastas, fresh sauces, chicken, veal, and seafood specials, salads, crusty bread, and a double helping of pride and friendly service. Open for lunch and dinner Tuesday through Saturday 11:00 A.M. to 10:00 P.M. and Sunday until 8:00. $–$$

Buttonwood Farm Ice Cream 471 Shetucket Turnpike (Route 165) in Griswold; (860) 376–4081. Open March 1 to October 31, this cheerful, crystal-clean roadside establishment offers more than forty flavors of top-quality farm-fresh ice cream every day from 1:00 to 8:00 P.M. (and sometimes later). Try the Forbidden Silk Chocolate or the Purple Cow. $

Where to Stay

Roseledge B&B. See page 253.

Hidden Acres Family Campground. 47 River Road; (860) 887–9633. This is a clean, busy, family-friendly place with swimming, fishing, and hiking opportunities and showers, toilets, laundry, camp store, recreation hall, and rental units to help ensure your comfort. $

Strawberry Park. Route 165; (860) 886–1944 or (888) 794–7944. This seventy-seven-acre family campground offers 440 campsites plus rental trailers that include kitchens, bedrooms, baths, and living areas. Some of the latter are positively luxurious; still, families provide their own linens, bedding, and cooking and eating equipment. Weekly and nightly rentals. Entertainment, swimming pools, game room. $$$

Norwich

A small city with the unfortunate distinction of being the birthplace of Benedict Arnold, Norwich has heretofore maintained a pretty low profile as far as tourism is concerned. But there's a new wind blowing on the Rose of New England these days. Pride in the city's active role in the Patriot cause, the production of woolens for Union uniforms in the Civil War, the importance of its shipping and manufacturing history, and its remarkable concentration of homes and public buildings of architectural importance have led to a deliberate attempt by city leaders to pull the city out of the doldrums.

Helped by a great number of forward-looking individuals plus a hefty bit of money garnered from the gaming done not far away on Indian lands, Norwich is making serious efforts to win the affection of travelers. The best of the family-fun stuff is listed below.

Slater Memorial Museum (ages 6 and up)

108 Crescent Street (Route 2), on the campus of the Norwich Free Academy; (860) 887–2505; www.norwichfreeacademy.com/slater_museum. Open year-round on Tuesday through Friday from 9:00 A.M. to 4:00 P.M. and on Saturday and Sunday from 1:00 to 4:00 P.M. Closed Monday and holidays. Adults $3.00; children under 12 free.

Founded in 1888, the museum inside this Romanesque edifice is the place to take the children if you think it may be awhile before you can take them to the Louvre, the Vatican, the Olympia Museum in Athens, or any other of the world's finest sculpture galleries.

Slater Memorial has a notable and beautiful collection of 150 plaster cast statues of famed sculptures from around the world. Among these exact replicas of Greek, Roman, and Renaissance masterpieces are *Aphrodite* (the so-called Venus de Milo), Donatello's *David,* and Michelangelo's *Pieta.* Although it's true that the plaster casting doesn't do justice to the luminous and satiny quality of the marble originals, I still can't overstate the beauty of these magnificent pieces; truly, if you are at all interested in having your children see the unbelievable genius of Michelangelo, Donatello, Verrocchio, Luca della Robbia, and others, save yourself the airfare and come here.

The museum also houses a wonderful collection of American art from the seventeenth to twentieth centuries, plus American Indian artifacts and Oriental, African, and European art and textiles. The American Rooms are period rooms that trace American history from colonial to Victorian days. The Gualtieri Gallery is especially appealing to children; it contains dolls, circus figures, and sculpture you can touch.

Mohegan Park (all ages)

On Mohegan Park Road, but with access from four different points; in my opinion, best entrance is at corner of Judd and Rockwell Streets near the rose garden; (860) 886–2381. Open year-round from 9:00 A.M. to sunset. Free.

With its walkways, plantings, statuary, and fountain, the 385-acre woodland park can be a nice spot to spend an afternoon. Walking trails, a bicycle/stroller path, picnic areas with grills , and pavilions and gazebos help to make the park a family destination.

Near the park's fairly large pond is a good-sized swimming area and a small beach perfect for young children; a play area with swings and such is also there. Popular with both families and area day camps, it can get crowded, but rest rooms and a concession make it workable for families, and it is certainly a clean, safe place for an afternoon swim. It is open from June 1 to Labor Day and for skating, weather permitting, in winter.

The lovely roses in the park's formal gardens at the corner of Rockwell Street and Judd Street are award-winning and are in bloom from late May through October, peaking in June and early July. You'll enjoy grassy paths among patterned beds and trellises showcasing more than 2,500 bushes in 120 varieties. The picnic shelter at the side of the two-acre rose garden is a nice place to stop with a bag lunch. Accessible from sunrise to sunset at no charge.

Powerhouse and Upper Falls Heritage Walkway (all ages)

On the banks of the Yantic River off Sachem Street and Sherman Street. Open daily year-round. Free.

Beginning near a restored powerhouse, this landscaped greenway is part of an ongoing attempt to preserve and restore the Yantic River and the various dams and mill buildings that contributed to Norwich's nineteenth- and twentieth-century history as a mill town.

The efforts to beautify and preserve the area include restoration of the dam, and thus the falls, the 1910 powerhouse, and the sacred site known as Indian Leap, where a group of Mohegans jumped to their deaths to escape the Narragansetts in 1643. Once a camping and fishing area of the Mohegans, the falls area includes the place where Uncas supposedly leapt the chasm with his enemies in pursuit. The 40-foot descent of the falls over large boulders and the natural chasm and the surrounding waterways are very pretty. On a recent summer day we saw great blue herons, egrets, a beaver and its dam, and many other species.

The 2-mile Heritage Walkway links the Upper Falls with Indian Leap, the Lower Falls, and the park and marina at Norwich Harbor. This signed walking path is part of the National Heritage Corridor, a protected green belt along the Quinebaug and Shetucket Rivers and their tributaries.

Dodd Stadium/Norwich Navigators (ages 4 and up)
14 Stott Avenue in Norwich Industrial Park; (860) 887–7962 or (800) 64–GATOR; www.
gators.com. April through September. Weekday and Saturday games at 7:05 P.M. Sunday
games at 1:05 P.M. Some variations. Call or check Web site for complete schedule and
directions to stadium. General admission tickets $7.00.

If you like baseball, come here for a taste of the great American pastime, with cheers led
by team mascot, Tator the Gator. New 6,000-seat stadium and lots of special events and
promotional giveaways at nearly every game make this a fun, easy way to watch the
sport, played by this AA affiliate of the New York Yankees.

Near-sellout crowds are attracted to these games played against affiliates of the Red
Sox, Twins, Marlins, and others. Come early and have a casual supper here—the snack bar
menu has the necessary hot dogs and popcorn, plus bratwurst, lobster rolls, soft pretzels,
and ice cream.

Special packages that offer some combination of meals and tickets make it easy to
have a baseball birthday party. A happy birthday message spoken by the public address
announcer or posted on the scoreboard can be arranged.

On the Waterfront

The waterfront/wharf area of Norwich continues to develop as a tourist area.
Located at the head of the Thames River on Hollyhock Island, the **Chelsea
Harbor Park** (860–886–6363) and the **Marina at American Wharf** have
been rebuilt with riverfront walkways, benches, picnic tables, barbecue grills,
and flower beds. **Putts-up Dock Mini Golf** (860–886–7888) has a volcano in
its midst; it fires every twenty minutes, to the delight of young visitors. Its
location across a good-sized waterway from the marina allows visitors to ride
the free shuttle on a pontoon boat to reach it and the **Howard T. Brown
Memorial Park** (860–887–2789) with gazebo, picnic areas, fishing pier, and
free concerts at lunchtimes and on Thursday and Sunday evenings in summer. **Americus on the Wharf Restaurant** (860–887–8555) is open only in
summer, daily for lunch and dinner. Special events, including an annual Harbor Day celebration in mid-August, have helped to encourage the continuing
revitalization of this historic area. Entrance is on West Main Street.

Where to Eat

Old Tymes Restaurant. 360 West Main
Street; (860) 887–6865. Casual ambience
with old-time artifacts on the walls and good
home-style American fare at reasonable
prices for families in need of breakfast, lunch,
and dinner. Try the southern-style favorites
like fried catfish and crab cakes, or just go
straight for the prime rib. Kids under 12 can
choose from child-friendly specials. Open
from 7:00 A.M. to 9:00 P.M. $–$$

Where to Stay

Courtyard by Marriott. 181 West Town Street; (860) 886–2600. 120 rooms, restaurant, indoor pool, health club. $$$$

Ramada Inn Norwich. 10 Laura Boulevard; (860) 889–5201 or (800) 272–6232. 127 deluxe units, restaurant and lounge with entertainment, indoor pool, exercise room. $$$

Comfort Suites. 275 Otrobando Avenue; (860) 892–9292 or (800) 847–7848. 119 suites with fridge, microwave; indoor pool, health club, game room; continental breakfast. $$$$

Royal Indian **Burial Grounds**

On Sachem Street off Route 32 is the tiny parcel of land that is the final resting place of Uncas, the Mohegan chief who befriended the European settlers and gave to them the land that became the city of Norwich. It lies on the left side of the street, very close to the corner as you enter from Route 32.

Montville/Uncasville

Just south of Norwich perched above the Thames River is the small town of Montville and its village of Uncasville, best known for their age-old connection to the Mohegan people. A visit here has a Native American focus.

Tantaquidgeon Indian Museum (ages 4 and up)
1819 Norwich–New London Turnpike (Route 32); (860) 848–9145. Open mid-May through late August, Monday through Friday from 10:00 A.M. to 3:00 P.M. The museum asks only for a donation from visitors.

Filled with stone, bone, and wooden objects used or made mostly by the Mohegan Indians, this museum in the heart of Mohegan territory also includes baskets, ladles, and bowls made by skilled Mohegan woodworker and basketmaker John Tantaquidgeon. Although the emphasis here is on the Mohegans and other Eastern Woodland tribes, the collection also includes artifacts from Native American peoples of the Southwest, the Southeast, and the Northern Plains. Pottery, rugs, dolls, tools, beaded bags, shoes, a beautiful canoe suspended from the ceiling, and other objects are among the items in this unique collection. The culture and history of each group are explained throughout the exhibits, which are housed in a building built in 1931 by Tantaquidgeon himself.

Look **Again**

This small museum may not look like much to city slickers, a fact I didn't address in the first edition of this book but felt compelled to in the second. Some readers headed to Montville and drove right past the modest structure nestled on a bluff essentially in the owners' backyard. A few of these drive-by tourists actually asked if I had been here—had I seen the place? Not nearly fancy enough for them, this fascinating place was mistaken for some one-man collection of artifacts of no importance. Wrong.

This museum, newly renovated in 2001, was founded by John Tantaquidgeon, the last of the Mohegan basketmakers and a direct descendant of Uncas, seventeenth-century chief of the Mohegans. The museum is now operated by the Mohegan Tribal Office on behalf of John's granddaughters, Ruth and Gladys Tantaquidgeon, ninety-four and one hundred-four years old, respectively.

Gladys is the oldest living Mohegan in the world. She is also Medicine Woman of the Mohegans, no mere honorary title but one rightfully bestowed on this amazing woman who studied the folkways and medicinal herbs and plants of the Delaware and other Algonkian Indians and authored a monograph on the Mohegan spiritual and medicinal healing practices. Gladys also dedicated decades of study to the lifeways and native arts and crafts of the Lakota Sioux, working on the plains to preserve and to teach to that nation's youngest generation the legacy of their forebears. Holding honorary anthropology degrees from Yale University and UConn, Gladys declined the invitation to accept a third degree from the University of Pennsylvania, where she had studied with that school's famed anthropologists. She is, frankly, one heck of an incredible woman, and visitors who are not too slick for this rustic museum might be lucky enough to learn a thing or two about her culture when they visit here. 'Nuf said.

Shantok, Village of Uncas, and Cochegan Rock (all ages) 🚹 👫 🏛
450 Massapeag Side Road, off Route 32, Uncasville. Open 8:00 A.M. to sunset year-round.

The Montville area is rich in the history of the Mohegans. If you drive north again from the Tantaquidgeon Museum on Route 32 to Raymond Hill Road, you will find Mohegan Hill and Cochegan Rock, which is said to be the site of secret meetings between Uncas and other Mohegan leaders. Cochegan Rock is reputed to be the largest boulder in New England.

Continue on Route 32 a very short distance to the area called Mohegan Hill (not actually clearly marked), where in Shantok, Village of Uncas (clearly marked), you will find the remains of the Mohegan fort of Chief Uncas and the sacred Mohegan burial ground. Here you may see the graves of the Tantaquidgeons and other descendants of Uncas. A stone monument marks the site of the ancient fort, and several small trails lead hikers along the banks of the Thames River, which flows past the edge of the park. Currently under ongoing restoration by the Mohegan tribe, the village should soon include a small visitor center with displays of artifacts, a re-creation of a Mohegan longhouse, and educational signage.

The large, open recreational areas of the park are available to picnickers, anglers (there is a stocked pond here), and ballplayers, but the fort and burial ground area is a sacred site. Visitors are welcome to explore it respectfully. Please do not picnic in this shaded, peaceful area. Feel free to enjoy the riverside pathways as the elder Mohegans still do, as a place of quiet meditation. Annual events such as a three-day Wigwam Powwow in the third or fourth week of August are also open to the public. The powwow features an elaborate Mohegan dance competition, Native American cultural exhibits, native foods such as succotash and clam and corn chowders, crafts and craft demonstrations, storytelling, and a theater production. Admission is **free.** Call (800) MOHEGAN or (860) 204–6144 for more information.

Nature's Art

The elaborate store off the beaten path in Montville is advertised as a "family fun attraction," but **Nature's Art** (1650 Route 85; 860–443–GEMS) is, in fact, a retail/commercial establishment designed as much to produce income as it is an activity center motivated to educate and entertain young minds. Families traveling nearby may enjoy a stop here; whether it becomes a true attraction or just a ruse to get you to plunk down cash remains to be seen. I know the owners mean to be pure in spirit. Apparently their love for natural history and the beauties of the Earth propelled their energies in creating this huge space devoted to nature's gifts. Outside are nature trails around a pond called Raptor Bay; life-size dinosaur replicas inhabit this space, and you pay admission to it near the complex's ice cream shop and picnic area. Inside, a whole gallery of life-size dinosaur skeleton casts awaits curious kids. Displays of real fossils, petrified wood, and such wonders as real dinosaur eggs line the walls of that room, which requires another admission ticket. In activity areas such as the Jackpot Mine visitors can dig for gems in a cave-like setting (starting at $9.99 for ten minutes); in Thunder Creek visitors pan for "gold" (starting at $6.49 for ten minutes); and in Bone Zone, $9.99 buys you thirty minutes in which to unearth a dinosaur skeleton. Birthday parties are popular in these sections. The rest of the enormous space is devoted to an amazing array of gifts. Jewelry, jewelry-making supplies, scientific toys, games, craft kits, fossils, rocks, and minerals are among the thousands of items for sale. You can even eat lunch or dessert in the store's Cobalt Café. It's quite a place—judge it for yourself from 9:30 A.M. to 6:00 P.M. daily year-round.

Old Lyme

A curious mix of authors, painters, and mariners inhabits Old Lyme, a lovely village that revels in its artsy reputation as well as its nautical one. It's no surprise that Old Lyme can employ the phrase "colony" to describe itself—it has long attracted residents who fall neatly into one or more of these three categories.

One of the earliest and most permanent of these groups was the artists who gathered at the home of Florence Griswold from 1899 until decades past the turn of the century. Known as the Lyme Art Colony, the folks who lived at Miss Florence's beautiful late-Georgian mansion played with light, color, and texture until they successfully settled upon characteristics later to become known as American Impressionism. J. Alden Weir, Childe Hassam, Henry Ward Ranger, William Chadwick, and many others perfected their brilliance here.

Florence Griswold Museum (ages 4 and up)

96 Lyme Street; (860) 434–5542; www.flogris.org. Open year-round. April through December, Tuesday through Saturday from 10:00 A.M. to 5:00 P.M. and Sunday from 1:00 to 5:00 P.M. January through March, Wednesday through Sunday, 1:00 to 5:00 P.M. Artist studio open April through October only. Adults $7.00; seniors and students $6.00; children 6 to 12, $4.00; children under 6 free.

Located on eleven beautiful acres next to the lovely Lieutenant River, this historic, soft-yellow mansion holds a magnificent collection of the works of the above-mentioned artists as well as related changing exhibitions that celebrate other artistry throughout the year. You may wander the upper gallery rooms of the museum unescorted, but a guided tour of the downstairs period rooms is given first. If children are in the group, their interests are taken into consideration as the gracious docents point out artwork and tell stories that capture young imaginations. Especially wonderful are the original paintings on the panels in the dining room and the restored studio of William Chadwick on the grounds.

Recently reacquired acreage and a handsome Colonial Revival house that was part of Miss Florence's original estate now includes restored gardens, marvelous exhibition spaces, a new museum shop in the Kreible Gallery at the riverside, and period rooms with furniture and personal effects of Miss Griswold. Visitors are encouraged to stroll and relax on the adjoining properties as the famed artists once did; you may even set up an easel and paint whichever of the lovely vistas catches your artist's eye.

The Hartman Education Center is the site of frequent programs for children as well as adults. On Sundays from 1:00 to 5:00 P.M., children can participate in hands-on *Encounters with Art,* learning about some aspect of Impressionism or painting *en plein air.* A Midsummer Festival includes activities for children, from typical fun like face painting and pony rides to unusual fun such as knot tying and scavenger hunts. Storytelling or Victorian games may accompany an art show, silent auction, lawn concerts, picnic suppers, ice cream, and more for the whole family.

Every December the mansion is decorated with Christmas trees in every room for a seasonal festivity called Home for the Holidays. Story readings and special tours of interest to children are offered to families who visit during this time. Lovely and very low-key, this celebration includes just beautiful trees and art.

Lyme Art

The **Lyme Academy of Fine Arts** (84 Lyme Street; 860–434–5232) and the **Lyme Art Association** (90 Lyme Street; 860–434–7802) have no articulated special focus for children and families, but both have ongoing exhibits in their galleries, plus classes, demonstrations, workshops, and lectures that may be of interest. Visitors are asked for a small donation. Both are open year-round, but hours vary. Call for a schedule. Other shops and small galleries on Lyme Street allow visitors the opportunity to see and purchase the work of talented local artists.

McCulloch Farm (all ages)

100 Whippoorwill Road; (860) 434-7355. Open daily, from 10:00 A.M. to 4:00 P.M. but advance calls are required. Twice yearly all-day events in spring and very early fall. Call for dates. Free.

One of Connecticut's hidden treasures is the oldest continually operating and largest Morgan horse breeding farm in the state. Visitors are more than welcome, but a call ahead ensures that someone here is able to give you a tour. Half a dozen or more foals are born here each spring, and you can see and pet them and their elegant parents nearly any day year-round. The farm itself is a Connecticut pearl—400 acres are yours to explore. While it's not maintained as a tourist attraction, its bridle paths lead through quiet corners where you may see wild turkeys, guinea hens, coyotes, and many birds and butterflies of the Eastern Woodlands. The owners kindly ask that you enjoy the property respectfully. They prefer no pets, no picnicking, and there is no hand-feeding of their magnificent Whippoorwill Morgans.

Come in the spring for Open Barn Day, when visitors are welcomed into the barns for a close-up look at the newborn animals. Come in early fall (sometimes the first weekend in September) for Versatility Day, a demonstration of the talents and tasks performed by the horses. Morgans from all over the country arrive for this eye-opening show. Both events are **free** to the public. No call ahead is required.

Ewe'll Love This

Beaverbrook Farm in Lyme, at 139 Beaverbrook Road off Route 156 about 5.5 miles north of Route 1, opens to visitors seven days a week year-round so that families can enjoy their handmade woolens, farmstead sheep cheese, yogurt, and cottage cheese—and their 600 sheep and lambs. In spring, the farm is fairly hopping with newborns; on the Saturday after Thanksgiving, come for Farm Day to see shearing demonstrations, take a horsedrawn hayride, buy country crafts from local artisans, and sample fresh meats and cheeses. For more information, call (800) 501–WOOL.

Sound View Beach (all ages)

Hartford Avenue off Shore Road (Route 156); (Parks and Recreation, in summer only: (860) 434–2760. Open 8:00 A.M. to 9:00 P.M. **Free** street parking or parking fee ($5.00–$10.00) at public and private off-street lots.

A wide, popular beach in the midst of a busy beach colony that looks like a throwback to earlier decades is great for playing or relaxing on a summer day or for strolling in autumn or winter. No coolers are allowed on the beach, there are no changing facilities or life-guards, and the only rest rooms are portapotties. Even so, tons of families come here, and on summer weekends the joint is hopping as the delightfully summery and slightly seedy arcades, amusements (there's even a carousel), snack bars, and restaurants along Hartford Avenue are crowded with visitors. The Carousel Shop, loaded with such beach needs as sunscreen, sunglasses, and ice cream, also rents and sells beach chairs, floats, and beach toys. They also operate the brightly painted (but small) 1925 carousel, which runs nightly from 7:00 to 9:00 P.M. all summer. One ride is $1.00, 12 rides are $10.00, and so on up to 100 rides for $65.00 for parties or fanatics.

For food, try the limited but beachy fare at whatever seasonal restaurants and snack bars may be open on Hartford Avenue. Be sure to have an Italian ice from Vecchitto's.

Where to Eat

Sherlock's 221. Route 1, Old Lyme Shopping Center; (860–434–9837). A cheerful new owner, a new name, and a new chef here make this family-friendly establishment welcoming and delicious. Tapas, gourmet pizzas, great salads, and an array of entrees make use of fresh local produce. Be sure to try the desserts, and stop at **The Happy Carrot Bookshop** (860–434–0380). Lunch Tuesday through Saturday; dinner Tuesday through Sunday. $–$$

HallMark Drive-in. Route 156; (860) 434–1998. An Old Lyme tradition, this is a classic shoreline shack specializing in fresh seafood, burgers, grinders, chicken, house-made ice cream and yogurt—even breakfast. Umbrella-shaded tables overlook the marsh so you can savor the salty air. Open year-round. Try the old-fashioned apple ice cream—extraordinary. $

Where to Stay

Bayberry Motor Inn. 436 Shore Road (860–434–3024). 11 spacious rooms with 2 double beds and kitchenettes with microwave, toaster, and cookware, continental breakfast, and picnic area create a beachy getaway for families. Passes to private beach association. Children under 12 stay **free.** $$

Old Lyme Inn. 85 Lyme Street; (860) 434–2600 or (800) 434–5352. This lovely country inn located in the historic village area welcomes children and pets to their no-smoking establishment. 2 of their 13 spacious rooms, all with private baths, have sofa beds, making them comfortable for families. Continental breakfast, inn restaurant and pub, entertainment, landscaped grounds. $$$$

East Lyme/Niantic

Though East Lyme actually extends northward several miles from I–95 (exit 72 northbound, exit 74 southbound), it is the activity in the southern part of town that attracts the most visitors. The village of Flanders centers on Route 1 where it bumps north of I–95. While a nice reminder of how the Boston Post Road looked before gas stations and fast-food joints overtook most sections, Flanders itself offers no attractions for tourists. Niantic, East Lyme's second village, south of both Route 1 and the interstate, is the center of activity. Take Route 161 south and explore it and the east–west Route 156 to gain a perspective on this shoreline gem of private homes and beaches, marinas and fishing piers, and small shops and restaurants.

Rocky Neck State Park (all ages)

Route 156 or exit 72 from I–95; (860) 739–5471. Open year-round 8:00 A.M. to 8:30 P.M. From Memorial Day to Labor Day, the weekday parking fee is $7.00 per CT vehicle, $10.00 per out-of-state vehicle; weekend rates are $9.00 and $14.00, respectively. Off-season visitors pay a weekends-only fee or no fee at all. The campground is open from April through September 30; its fees are $15.00 nightly for a party of four, $2.00 for each additional camper.

Few better places exist for beachcombing and shore camping than Rocky Neck State Park. Its full mile of beach frontage on Long Island Sound provides swimming, saltwater fishing, and scuba diving opportunities; its 150-plus campsites provide a home away from home for professional beach bums, amateur naturalists, and the children thereof.

Interpretive programs, junior naturalist activities, and a full summer calendar of nature walks and slide shows are offered for campers as well as day visitors. Hiking and picnicking are also common pleasures for both campers and day visitors. An interpretive trail points out examples of shore flora and fauna. The state provides picnic shelters, bathhouses, food concessions, lifeguards, first aid, and telephones. Campers have drinking water and bathrooms with showers and toilets.

Like other state parks, Rocky Neck is safe and clean, but its windswept bluffs and gorgeous views of the Sound and offshore islands clearly create a special attraction. The park is one of the prettiest of public shoreline areas managed by the state. Its beautiful stone pavilion, constructed in the 1930s, has pillars cut from Connecticut's other state parks and forests. From dawn to dusk in winter, the park's trails and open spaces can be used for cross-country skiing, and there is no better place to simply enjoy a fall afternoon.

Children's Museum of Southeastern Connecticut (ages 1 to 10)

409 Main Street; (860) 691–1111. Open year-round, Tuesday through Saturday, plus Monday in the summer or when school is closed, from 9:30 A.M. to 4:30 P.M., and on Sunday from noon to 4:00 P.M. Admission is $4.00 for each person 2 and up. *(Note: The museum is working on a plan to move to New London's Riverside Park in October 2004. Call ahead if you are planning a visit.)*

Among the shops on Niantic's Main Street is a small museum that is excellent for young children. Families from the far reaches of the state probably have a similar museum closer to home, but if you happen to be in the area or you live nearby, come at once.

More a play area and experience center than a traditional museum, the popular Children's Museum provides a fantastic opportunity to develop young imaginations. See how creative your children can be in hands-on centers where youngsters can role play in a kids-size hospital, fire station, and grocery store and explore the multicultural Global Village. Set your toddlers free among the slides and building toys in the Nursery Rhyme Land play area. Go outside to the newly renovated garden area and dig for fossils, play with the wondrous bubble table, or scale the climbing wall. Toddlers, teens, and parents alike will be mesmerized by the wonderful model train exhibit that depicts the real sights of the Connecticut shoreline and countryside. Push a button and make the trains go!

The museum's staff has created activities and exhibits that explore the sciences, the arts, safety and health, and culture and history in such centers as an arts-and-crafts area, a computer lab, and a Discovery Room with a live bee colony, a glow-in-the-dark-room, and an ant farm among its features. There's even a pipe organ here! Changing exhibitions keep folks coming to see what's new. This is a great rainy-day place if you are camping or vacationing in the area.

Niantic **Shoppers**

If your family is of a more strolling/browsing nature, cruise the shops and galleries of Niantic. Our favorites are the Silver Skate Christmas Shop (488 Main Street; 860–739–8913), the Made to Be Loved Doll Shop and Hospital (Route 156; 860–739–7756), and the Book Barn (41 West Main Street; 860–739–5715), which has 75,000-plus used books.

Millstone Discovery Center (ages 6 and up)

278 Main Street; (860) 691–4670 or (800) 428–4234. Open year-round Monday through Friday 10:00 A.M. to 4:00 P.M.; closed weekends and holidays. Free.

This family-friendly science center not far from the Millstone nuclear power plant shows visitors how nuclear energy can be safe and reliable. Hands-on and interactive exhibits and videos explain nuclear science and energy, show how reactors work and power plants operate, and demonstrate the production of electrical energy and tenets of electrical safety. Exhibits on conservation and the marine environment of Long Island Sound include aquariums and touch tanks and a nature trail. You can enjoy all of these by yourself or request a guided tour to the center.

Black Hawk II (ages 6 and up)

East Main Street (exit 72, left at Route 156, about 7 miles, under the bridge, into parking lot), Niantic Beach Marina; (860) 443–3662 or (800) 382–2824. June through October, daily sails at 6:00 A.M. and 1:00 P.M. Fare $33; children under 12 half-price. No reservations necessary.

Fishing trips out on the Sound are the specialty of this boat. Use your parental discretion as to whether your child is old enough to handle the excitement (and the equipment) necessary to hook a striped bass or a nice big bluefish. *Black Hawk II*'s crew and captain handle the driving, supply bait and set-up, rent rod and reel at $5.00 each if you don't bring your own gear, and turn burgers and dogs at the snack bar on board if you don't bring your own picnic. Free instruction is available for beginners. They stay out five to six hours in the sun, wind, and even in light rain, so bring sweatshirts, caps, and sunscreen. It's first come, first served and quite popular. Arrive 45 minutes before sail time on weekends and 35 minutes before on weekdays.

Where to Eat

Constantine's. 252 Main Street; (860) 739–2848. This clean, friendly, family-run establishment has great overstuffed sandwiches, house-made soups, salads, a children's menu, plus great seafood, chicken, veal, and steak dishes. Lunch and dinner, Tuesday through Sunday. $$–$$$

Flanders Fish Market and Restaurant. 22 Chesterfield Road (Route 161) in Flanders; (860) 739–8866. Cheerful, busy, and very casual, this place serves the best fish in town, plus lots of typical American fare appealing to kids. Open daily from 8:00 A.M. $–$$

Where to Stay

Ramada Inn & Suites. Route 161; (860) 739–5483 or (800) 942–8466. 62 units and suites, refrigerator, microwave, whirlpool, outdoor pool, beach passes, continental breakfast. $$$$

Niantic Inn. 345 Main Street; (860) 739–5451. Great for families; 24 roomy studios with dining and living areas and in-room fridge, continental breakfast. Beach practically out the door. $$$$

Best Western Hilltop Inn. 239 Flanders Road; (860) 739–3951. 90 units, some with refrigerator; outdoor pool, beach passes, continental breakfast. $$$

Elms Hotel. 27–37 Ocean Avenue; (860) 739–5545 or (888) 437–1117. Just a stone's throw from Crescent Beach, this century-old restored waterfront classic offers 30 rooms with microwaves, coffeemakers, and refrigerators; continental breakfast, picnic area with outdoor games; beach with shore fishing and swimming; children under 12 are **free.** Nonsmoking rooms available. $$–$$$$

Waterford

Waterford has a mall, lots of movie theaters, and an amazing complex called Sonalysts Studios, which may someday take Hollywood right off the map. Unfortunately, the mall and movies won't add much to a family vacation, and, right now anyway, neither will Sonalysts, since they don't offer tours. Waterford nonetheless offers a few attractions you might want to check out.

Sunbeam Express **Nature Cruise Center** (ages 4 and up)

Captain John's Sportfishing Center, 15 First Street; (860) 443–7259; www.sunbeamfleet. com. Seal and eagle watch, adults $30; children $15. Lighthouse cruise, adults $40; children $20. Children under 4 free. Family or other groups of ten or more get a discount. Reservations are recommended so the captain can call you if a cancellation due to bad weather is necessary; no deposit is required. The boats leave promptly; please check traffic conditions and plan to arrive thirty to forty-five minutes prior to departure.

Down at the docks on the Niantic River between Niantic and Waterford at Captain John's Sport Fishing Center, you can catch Captain John's nature cruises.

From mid-March to mid-May, Captain John leaves from the First Street dock on seal-watching trips; harbor seals and harp seals have returned to these waters in increasing numbers recently. The boat cruises Fishers Island Sound and other areas of eastern Long Island Sound in search of seals, waterfowl, and other wildlife. These cruises are narrated by a naturalist.

From February through mid-March, the boat leaves from the Dock & Dine Restaurant in Old Saybrook and heads up the Connecticut River for bald eagle cruises. These beautiful birds come from Canada to feed on the white perch they grab from the sections of the river that remain unfrozen south of Haddam. The seal and eagle cruises depart at 9:00 A.M. and return around noon. Also naturalist-guided, these excursions include many family groups. Each cruise highlights any wildlife you might see, from ospreys, herons, and other waterfowl to wild turkeys, fox, and deer on the riverbanks.

Throughout the summer season are eight to ten lighthouse cruises. Crossing the Sound through Plum Gut and across the Race, the five-hour cruise departs Waterford at 10:00 A.M. and 3:00 P.M. Guided by lighthouse historian Captain Ben Rathbun, the cruise highlights eleven lighthouses on both the Connecticut and New York shores.

The crew brings lunches, snacks, and soft drinks aboard for sale in the galley, or you can pack a lunch (no alcoholic beverages). Pack a Dramamine, a ginger capsule, or a wristband if you get seasick and dress appropriately for the weather. Bring a sweatshirt even in summer and winter gear at other times. The heated cabin of this 100-foot boat helps to keep you toasty, but despite the large windows the best viewing is still outside at the rail, so be prepared. Rest rooms are on board.

Colonial Village at Historic Jordan Green (ages 8 and up)

Rope Ferry Road and Avery Lane, off Route 156; (860) 442–2707. Open June 15 through September 15 from 1:00 to 4:00 P.M. and one festival day in May. Call ahead to confirm these limited hours. Free.

Close to the docks is the Jordan green and its replica colonial village with the 1740 Jordan schoolhouse, the 1840 Beebe-Phillips farmhouse, a blacksmith shop with a working forge, a corn crib, and a barn with farm implements, and historical artifacts. Two small apple orchards and an herb garden complete the historical exhibits. Tours include details of home, hearth, agriculture, and local history. A special festival is held for one day in May. Called "Sheep to Shawl," this event focuses on the shearing of sheep, the processing of their fleece, and activities related to creating the finished woolen thread and cloth. Traditional arts and crafts are demonstrated. Hearth cooking, food preservation, candle dipping, carpentry, and blacksmithing are among the activities you might see.

Harkness Memorial State Park (all ages)

275 Great Neck Road (Route 213); park information: (860) 443–5725; concert information: (800) 969–3400. Open year-round 8:00 A.M. to sunset. Daily parking fee in summer: $6.00– $7.00 CT plates, $7.00–$10.00 out-of-state plates for weekdays and weekends respectively; free from Labor Day to Memorial Day. Mansion open 10:00 A.M. to 3:00 P.M. on weekends only in May, June, and September and daily in July and August.

On the gorgeous seaside site of a former private estate, the park itself is a feast for the eyes. Pack a basket of goodies and spread a picnic on the lovely grounds surrounding Eolia, a recently restored forty-two-room mansion once owned by oil tycoon and philanthropist Edward S. Harkness and his wife Mary. Bequeathed to the state of Connecticut, the house is now open to the public from May 1 through Columbus Day. Visitors can explore the mansion at no extra charge beyond the park admission. Guided tours are given on weekends. The summer concert series held here in July and August features internationally and nationally known performing artists who entertain crowds of music lovers seated or sprawled on the lawn overlooking the sea. There couldn't be a better way to spend a summer night in Connecticut than to buy tickets for one of these performances and take a hamperful of bread, strawberries, and cheese to the seaside and soak up the notes. Sadly, these events are not free. Only that

would make them better for families. Even if you can't visit on concert nights, come for the day. A picnic area and fishing area are offered for day visitors, but no swimming is allowed, due to a strong undertow.

Where to Eat

Unk's on the Bay. 361 Rope Ferry Road (Route 156); (860) 443–2717. Close to the water and slightly more upscale than other family places, Unk's offers good food at fair prices. Open year-round daily for lunch and dinner. $–$$$

Sunset Rib Company. 378 Rope Ferry Road; (860) 443–7427. Sunset views of the sound and river complete with great ribs, chicken, pastas, salads, burgers, and more. Indoor and outdoor seating. Open daily for lunch and dinner from mid-March to late October. $$

Where to Stay

Oakdell Motel. 983 Hartford Turnpike, which is Route 85; (860) 442–9446. Immaculate roadside motel. 22 efficiencies; each room has a fridge, microwave, private bath, cable TV and phone, and either one or two double beds. Outdoor pool and grills. Complimentary continental breakfast. $$$

SpringHill Suites by Marriott. 401 North Frontage Road; (860) 439–0151. Two queen-size beds and a pull-out sofa in most rooms make this hotel great for families. In-room refrigerator, microwave, coffeemaker; continental breakfast, indoor pool, whirlpool, exercise room. $$$$

New London

Like its sister city, Groton, across the Thames River, New London has a long maritime history that has influenced its development into a center of commerce and industry. Settled in 1646 as Pequot Plantation by John Winthrop Jr., it was by 1846 the second largest whaling port in the world. Long a manufacturing and shipbuilding city, it offers an eclectic assortment of attractions of value to families. This guide touches just the highlights of New London. Be sure to contact the New London Visitors Information Service (860–444–7264) or New London Main Street (860–444–CITY) for maps, brochures, and walking guides to all of this 6-mile-square city's museums, historic sites, shopping areas, restaurants, and lodging choices. A look at the city's Web site (www.ci.new-london.ct.us) may be helpful, too.

United States Coast Guard Academy (ages 6 and up)

15 Mohegan Avenue off Route 31; Public Affairs Office: (860) 444–8270. Campus open year-round daily 9:00 A.M. to sunset. Visitors Pavilion open May through October 10:00 A.M. to 5:00 P.M. Museum open year-round 8:00 A.M. to 4:00 P.M. on weekdays and 9:00 A.M. to 5:00 P.M. on weekends and holidays. The *Eagle*, when in port, open Friday through Sunday 1:00 to 5:00 P.M. Free.

If you have someone in the family with an interest in the Coast Guard, you should know that New London is the home of its academy. The beautiful 100-acre campus overlooks the Thames River. The Academy has a museum and a visitor center that features a multimedia show on cadet life. Tours of the bark USCG *Eagle* are offered whenever it is in port. Dress parades and concerts by the Coast Guard Band are held on a seasonal schedule, usually on Friday at 4:00 P.M. in the spring and fall.

Lyman Allyn Art Museum (ages 4 and up)
Children's Art Park

625 Williams Street; (860) 443–2545; lymanallyn.conncoll.edu. Open year-round, except Monday and major holidays. Tuesday through Saturday 10:00 A.M. to 5:00 P.M., Sunday 1:00 to 5:00 P.M. Adults $5.00; students $4.00; children 8 and under free. The admission fee allows entrance to the Doll and Toy Museum as well. See next entry.

Like the New Britain Museum of American Art, the Lyman Allyn owns one of Connecticut's little-known but exceptional small art collections. The fine and decorative arts from America, Europe, Asia, and the South Pacific make this a perfect introduction to art history for young children. Located in a pristine setting near Connecticut College and the Coast Guard Academy, this beautiful neoclassic museum contains 30,000 pieces; some holdings of special appeal to children are an Egyptian falcon mummy and Native American artifacts. The museum's American collection is excellent. Take the kids on an art history tour of American style from the late 1600s through the Impressionism of the twentieth century.

The museum arranges special changing exhibitions with children in mind at least twice yearly, usually in the summer and between Thanksgiving and New Year's Day. Admission is free every Sunday afternoon, and the first Sunday of each month features special activities, such as live music performances, storytellings, poetry readings, or gallery tours. Outside on the museum's front lawn is the **Children's Art Park,** a sculpture garden designed to demonstrate the evolution of art. Children are welcome to climb on, play in, and ponder each object in the park. Back inside, a wonderful museum shop with gifts of great appeal to children and young artists is also here.

Lyman Allyn Dolls and Toys Museum (all ages)

Deshon Allyn House, 625 Williams Street; (860) 443–2545. Admission to the Lyman Allyn sites is $5.00 for adults; $4.00 for students; children under 8 free. That fee will admit visitors into both or either of the museums.

One of Connecticut's newest museums houses one of the state's most charming collections. An extension of the Lyman Allyn Art Museum, it is housed in the 1827 Deshon Allyn mansion, on the same grounds as the larger art museum. It invites children of all ages to enjoy an elaborate display of dolls and toys from yesteryear to the present.

The museum's notable collection includes nineteenth- and twentieth-century dolls, dollhouses, and toys. Freshly refurbished, the collection is inventively exhibited in settings that evoke the eras of the dolls and toys themselves. Hundreds of dolls, puppets, wind-up cars, tin boats, model trains, toy construction and emergency vehicles—even puzzles and cast-iron banks are part of the fun here.

Visitors will find exhibits designed to appeal to the child's imagination and creativity. Doll-sized farmhouses and farm equipment, along with livestock and miniature inhabitants, displays of tin boats and other maritime toys, road and highway vehicles, and fire, rescue, and other emergency vehicles are among the toys here. Doll lovers may wish to simply soak up the sights within the *Hall of Dolls,* home to more than a hundred antique puppets and dozens of more modern ones.

Sure to charm both young explorers and adult collectors, the Dolls and Toys Museum is a pleasing link to all the joys of childhood. Combined with visits to either or both the Lyman Allyn Art Museum and the Children's Art Park, this museum guarantees an enchanting family outing.

Science EpiCenter and DNA Learning Center (ages 4 and up)

33 Gallows Lane; (860) 442–0391; www.science-epicenter.org. Open year-round Tuesday through Saturday from 10:00 A.M. to 6:00 P.M. and Sunday from 1:00 to 5:00 P.M. Adults $7.00; children under 12 $4.50.

Emphasizing the life sciences and nature, this wonderfully creative museum gives children a chance to see, touch, and feel the principles of science demonstrated in its accessible and interactive exhibits, laboratories, and work stations. The invitation to learn and explore is irresistible in more than one hundred work stations related to discoveries about light, sound, microbiology, electricity, optics, animals, tools, and simple machines. A shop area includes an opportunity for children to build a wooden boat or a birdhouse, for example; in another, children learn about chromatography by experimenting with water and filter paper. An observation beehive and a marine touch tank are among the animal exhibits. Other special features are a science theater, a photographic darkroom, a DNA learning laboratory, a greenhouse, and access to the trails in the beautiful Connecticut College Arboretum (860–439–2140), where the science center is located. Spend a few hours inside, then have a picnic on the property, which includes trees and shrubs native to eastern North America.

What's the Story at **Connecticut College?**

The picturesque campus and liberal arts tradition at Connecticut College draw students from every corner of the nation. Families are also drawn here to the arboretum (www.arboretum.conncoll. edu) and to the Connecticut Storytelling Festival held annually in late April at the Connecticut Storytelling Center. For three days, professional and student storytellers gather for performances, workshops, and story swaps. Stories from traditions around the globe are told to audiences of adults and children. The opening story "concert" on Friday evening is often specially directed to families. Admission is charged. For information, call (860) 439–2764.

New London's **Historic Center**

You may also be interested in these important points of interest near or within New London's Historic District:

- **Fort Trumbull State Park.** Walbach Street; (860) 444–7160. Built on the site of Revolutionary War fortifications, Connecticut's newest state park has spectacular views of the river and sea. Guided tours, fishing pier, visitor center. Open year-round daily.

- **Nathan Hale Schoolhouse.** Foot of State Street. One of the two Connecticut schools where Hale taught before losing his life in the American Revolution. Open Saturday in summer.

- **Old U.S. Custom House.** 150 Bank Street; (860) 447–2501. Oldest customs house in U.S., now restored with museum on the customs service. Open Wednesday and Saturday, 1:00 to 4:00 P.M.

- **Whale Oil Row.** Huntington Street. Restored row of 1832 Greek Revival houses owned by whaling tycoons.

- **Starr Street Restoration Area.** Another row of Greek Revival homes laid out in 1835 on the site of a ropewalk.

- **Shaw-Perkins Mansion.** 305 Bank Street; (860) 443–1209. Built for wealthy Captain Nathaniel Shaw in 1756. Used as naval war office during Revolution.

- **Monte Cristo Cottage.** Pequot Avenue; (860) 443–0051. Boyhood home of Pulitzer and Nobel-Prize–winning playwright Eugene O'Neill. Great tour, but stories are sad and somewhat adult. Look for O'Neill's statue, sweetly portraying his boyhood, on rock overlooking the harbor just off the old Main Street, now renamed Eugene O'Neill Drive.

Hempsted Houses (ages 5 and up)

11 Hempstead Street; (860) 443–7949. Open mid-May to mid-October on Thursday through Sunday; tours are given from noon to 4:00 P.M. Adults $4.00; children $2.00.

This "compound" in the historic downtown area includes one of the oldest documented houses in America; both homes are among the few New London structures to have survived the burning of the city in 1781 by the British troops under the command of Benedict Arnold.

The 1678 Joshua Hempsted House is one of the oldest frame buildings in New England, and the diaries of ropemaker Joshua Hempsted, kept by him for more than forty years, have contributed greatly both to the excellent interpretation of the house itself and to our knowledge of eighteenth-century colonial American life. The newer, 1759 Nathaniel

Hempsted House is one of the most unusual historic homes in New England—it has two-foot-thick stone walls, a gambrel roof, and an exterior projecting beehive oven. Its mysterious French connections, the subject of recent research, are revealed in the intriguing tours.

Hands-on activities for children are offered on special weekends once each month. On Labor Day weekend a special focus is made on women's work of the eighteenth century. A Hempsted Thanksgiving is celebrated on the Saturday after Thanksgiving. Costumed docents, open-hearth cooking, and food samples are part of the celebration. In addition, an excellent colonial life summer camp is offered for children ages 8 to 12 or so.

Garde Arts Center (ages 4 and up)
325 State Street. For a calendar of events or other information, call (860) 444–6766; www.gardearts.org. For tickets, call the box office (860) 444–7373 or (888) ON–GARDE.

If you have never taken the kids to a real movie palace, the kind with gilded architecture and acoustics to spare, plush seats and a giant movie screen, go to the Garde, downtown in the historic district.

In addition to its noteworthy new and classic film series, the 1,500-seat theater presents nationally and internationally known live performing artists throughout the year. Select from a Broadway series and a Family Theatre series, plus country music, dance, and comedy series. Tickets to single performances are available as well.

Look closely at the upcoming season's announcements. At far more affordable prices than Broadway, the family can enjoy wonderful theater, dance, and more. The 1926 theater, by the way, has recently enjoyed a $19 million restoration/expansion that has transformed this already grand lady into a state-of-the-art performing arts center. See the beautiful results in its marvelous grand entrance and circular marquee that usher audiences into three floors of new and newly restored Moroccan-style lobbies.

New London **Waterfront Park**

A beautiful, wide, half-mile-long esplanade is the highlight of the new park along the Thames River in downtown New London. See historic sites, enjoy the activities of the ferry terminals, or soak up the views of the river and waterfront. A good place to enter the area is behind the railroad station near the Fishers Island Ferry or at City Pier at the foot of State. **Free** live entertainment and special events are frequent on the stage at City Pier Plaza; the new Children's Discovery Pier has permanent displays about local marine wildlife; Amistad Pier offers fishing space; and the Custom House Pier hosts vessels of all sizes, including tall ships and luxury cruise liners.

Ocean Beach Park (all ages)

1225 Ocean Avenue; (860) 447–3031 or (800) 510–SAND; www.ocean-beach-park.com. Access to the beach and park at no charge year-round, dawn to dusk. Entertainments and concessions open Memorial Day weekend through Labor Day weekend, 9:00 A.M. to 11:00 P.M. Admission collected through a parking fee of $9.00 on weekdays and $13.00 on weekends. Holiday parking is $20.00. Use of water slide, pool, lockers, and mini-golf involves extra per-person or per-family charges.

For the kind of family fun wherein everybody gets wet, come to a place that offers not one but *three* ways to get soaked. Right on the Sound, Ocean Beach Park is both old-fashioned public beach resort and newfangled party/conference/banquet facility.

A half-mile long, very clean white sand beach is the focal point of the park. Owned and maintained by the City of New London, Ocean Beach Park also has Connecticut's only wide wooden boardwalk down the length of the beach. It leads past food concessions, a pinball and electronic game arcade, a kiddie playground, volleyball nets, and an eighteen-hole miniature golf course complete with life-sized spouting sperm whale. Each player pays $4.00 to play this authentic seaside course.

A full staff of lifeguards and a first-aid station help make this a popular destination for families. Entertainment on the boardwalk on Friday, Saturday, and Sunday is provided for all park visitors. An immaculate Olympic-size swimming pool and a beautiful bathhouse with changing rooms, lockers, and showers are also available for individual fees ($4.00 pool).

New London **Sets Sail**

A variety of boats leave from New London docks. Check among these for the trips that best fit your family's interests and budget:

- **Block Island Ferry;** (860) 442–7891. Leaves from Ferry Street once daily from mid-June to mid-September for round-trips to Old Harbor, Block Island. *Anna C*, with enclosed passenger areas, and a galley for food and drinks, leaves New London at 9:00 A.M., arrives at Old Harbor at 11:00 A.M. Cars, walkers, and bicycles are welcome.

- **Cross Sound Ferry Services;** (860) 443–5281. Two Ferry Street. Vehicle and high-speed passenger service to Orient Point, Long Island.

- **Viking Fleet.** Montauk Ferry Dock near the New York City Ferry Terminal off Crystal Avenue; (631) 668–5700. New London to Montauk, Long Island, May to September. Links to Martha's Vineyard and Block Island.

- *SeaPony* **Express Sightseeing Cruises.** Crocker's Boatyard; (860) 443–0795. Look for this 36-foot lobster boat at Waterfront Park. Daytime, sunset, and moonlight cruises past submarines, lighthouses, and tall ships; custom charters. Web site: www.seapony.com.

Once home to several carnival-style kiddie rides, the park now has one remaining amusement park–style water slide. A triple-run, three-speed tower of serpentine slides, this is a humdinger of a ride and, with the exception of the beach itself, is the most popular attraction here. A height requirement of 46 inches helps to keep the ride safe for all visitors. Smaller children cannot ride double with a parent or sibling, and the folks in charge here are strict about the guidelines, so don't expect to be able to smuggle anyone through on tiptoes.

The three flumes begin about 50 feet up at the top of a challenging set of stairs, so depending on your speed and stamina in climbing those stairs, you'll get ten to fifteen runs down the flume of your choice in a half-hour time slot. Each person pays $7.00 for a half-hour or $17.00 for unlimited rides throughout a whole day. Our kids like the medium flume best; the fast one is fun, but small kids are tossed around a bit at the bottom of the run; we came home with a few elbows and knees rubbed raw. If you like quieter fun, take the nature walk to Alewife Cove and check out the birds from the observation deck.

Where to Eat

Fred's Shanty. Pequot Avenue, overlooking Thamesport Marina; (860) 447–1301. The quintessential seafood shack, immortalized in Mark Shasha's children's picturebook *Night of the Moonjellies.* Read the book and go have a great time getting into the act. Boats, gulls, "long dogs," fries, great seafood, burgers, outdoor-only seating. $

Recovery Room. 445 Ocean Avenue; (860) 443–2619. Great family place, a cousin to the equally wonderful Pizzaworks in Mystic and Old Saybrook. Terrific menu and atmosphere for children. Open year-round daily for dinner; Monday through Friday for lunch. $

Schooner's. 250 Pequot Avenue; (860) 437–3801. You'll spend a bit more money here, but you'll get great steaks, seafood, and chicken, and basics that please the whole family. Kids' menu. Indoor dining and an outdoor patio overlooking the Thames. Open for lunch daily from 11:30 A.M. to 3:00 P.M. and dinner daily from 5:00 to 9:00 P.M. $$

Bank Street Lobster House. 194 Bank Street; (860) 447–9398. House-made soups, great sandwiches, and terrific seafood for lunch and dinner daily. $–$$

Where to Stay

Holiday Inn. Frontage Road; (860) 442–0631 or (800) HOLIDAY. 136 units including 24 efficiencies, restaurant, outdoor pool, exercise room. $$$

Radisson Hotel New London. 35 Governor Winthrop Boulevard; (860) 443–7000. 120 recently renovated deluxe units with 4 suites, restaurant, indoor pool, exercise room. $$$$

Lighthouse Inn Resort and Conference Center. 6 Guthrie Place; (860) 443–8411. This 1902 mansion is set back just a short stretch from Long Island Sound and has access to the private Guthrie Beach Association just down the lane. The main mansion has 24 nonsmoking rooms, some spacious enough or families or with links to a second room. 24 more rooms are available in the inn's carriage house. Continental breakfast is complimentary; Timothy Grills is the noted chef at the inn restaurant. Inn is popular for weddings and other gatherings, so inquire about the hustle and bustle if you are hoping for a quiet place to stay. $$$$

Groton

Back on an even keel since the United States Naval Reserve Station decided to stay in town, Groton remains a busy center of naval and defense-related industry. Its long history as such defines its attractions as well. Surrounded on three sides by the waters of Long Island Sound, the Thames River, and the Mystic River, Groton has been a leading shipbuilding center since the eighteenth century. For much of the last century, it has been most famed as the home of the Electric Boat Division of General Dynamics, the leading designer and manufacturer of nuclear submarines.

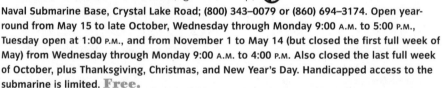

USS *Nautilus* Memorial and Submarine Force Museum (ages 3 and up)

Naval Submarine Base, Crystal Lake Road; (800) 343–0079 or (860) 694–3174. Open year-round from May 15 to late October, Wednesday through Monday 9:00 A.M. to 5:00 P.M., Tuesday open at 1:00 P.M., and from November 1 to May 14 (but closed the first full week of May) from Wednesday through Monday 9:00 A.M. to 4:00 P.M. Also closed the last full week of October, plus Thanksgiving, Christmas, and New Year's Day. Handicapped access to the submarine is limited. Free.

A visit to Groton has to include a visit to the USS *Nautilus*, the world's first nuclear submarine. The USS *Nautilus* Memorial at the U.S. Naval Submarine Base on Route 12 includes tours of the *Nautilus* and an award-winning museum that explores the history and technology of submarines.

Excellently presented in a state-of-the-art facility, the museum exhibits celebrate the achievements of the human mind in devising this technology. Children can stand in the re-created sub attack center and hear the sounds of battle. They can operate three working periscopes. They can watch films of submarine history, and they can explore mini-subs outside and models inside. Other outstanding exhibits explain the important uses of the submarine both in defense and underwater exploration.

Aboard the *Nautilus* you will explore the sonar and torpedo rooms and the navigation and control room. You will visit the crew's living quarters, the galley, and the captain's quarters. The impact of the huge size of the ship is somewhat lost due to the way it is moored to give visitors access, but, once inside, visitors will easily imagine life and work aboard this amazing vessel that explored beneath Arctic ice and the 20,000 leagues of the deep ocean.

Project Oceanology (ages 3 and up)

1084 Shennecossett Road, at foot of Benham Road, Avery Point Campus of UConn; (800) 364–8472 between 9:00 A.M. and 4:00 P.M.; www.oceanology.org. Public oceanography cruises from mid-June to Labor Day at 10:00 A.M. and 1:00 P.M. Seal-watching cruises, Febru-

ary through April, weekends only. Adults pay $19; children under 12 pay $16. Reservations strongly recommended; a Visa or Mastercard number is required to hold your reservation.

The lure of the sea may capture you once again in Groton. If so, head to the Institute of Marine Science at the Avery Point campus of the University of Connecticut, where you can board *Enviro-Lab II* or *III* for a two-and-a-half-hour cruise called Project Oceanology Study Cruises. These summer expeditions are among the best family activities offered in the state, especially for those families that have a child interested in marine biology.

Teaching more than 20,000 schoolchildren during the school year, *Enviro-Lab's* instructors are marine scientists who accompany each group of about twenty-five passengers for an afternoon or morning of study. Using the same methods the scientists use in their work, you will measure and record data about the geology and biology you observe. You will learn the uses of nautical charts and navigation instruments. You will collect and test water, mud, and sand samples. You will pull trawl nets and examine the plant and animals you catch. All the while you will be enjoying the beauty of the islands, lighthouses, and watercraft that surround your area of exploration. The crew and captain provide a wonderfully interesting narration about all that you observe.

Also available through Project Oceanology are cruises for observing grey and harbor seals in Fishers Island Sound. These weekends-only winter cruises are preceded by a twenty-minute slide presentation. They cost $19 for adults; children under 12 $16. Inquire also about the lighthouse tour to New London Ledge; that cruise is open to children older than 6; the fare is the same as other cruises.

In summer, be sure to wear sunscreen or a hat and sneakers. Bring a sweatshirt or a windbreaker. In winter, dress appropriately for cold weather, even though the boat has a heated cabin. Project Oceanology's headquarters are in a waterfront laboratory building near its boat docks. A seawater aquarium system, classrooms, a library, several labs, and a hostel are housed there, and a cafeteria where visitors can purchase snacks and lunches is available to daytrippers. You can also picnic on the campus before or after a cruise if you bring your own makings.

Bluff Point Coastal Reserve (all ages)

Depot Road off Route 1 (go to the very end of Depot Road under the railroad overpass to reach the parking lot). Open year-round from 8:00 A.M. to sunset free. For info, you can call the rangers at Fort Griswold.

Those who prefer to explore the shore on foot may do so at this beautiful park. From the parking area on Depot Road, it might take up to a half-hour to walk the 1.5-mile trail through its upland forest to the rocky bluff for which the park is named. Below the bluff lies the beach and tidal salt marsh. Saltwater fishing, beachcombing, and hiking are popular here, as is cross-country skiing in the wintertime.

You can also horseback ride, bring in a boat or jet-ski to launch from the sand ramp right into the water, and go shellfishing, scuba diving, snorkeling, and swimming. No lifeguards are here. This wonderfully wild place is a marvelous site from which to enjoy the sea and the sunset.

Fort Griswold Battlefield State Park and the Ebenezer Avery House

(all ages)

Monument Street and Park Avenue; (860) 445–1729. Battlefield and fort ruins open daily year-round 8:00 A.M. to sunset. The museum (860–449–6877) and monument are open from Memorial Day to Labor Day from 10:00 A.M. to 5:00 P.M. and from the weekend after Labor Day until Columbus Day on weekends only at the same hours. The Avery House (860–446–9257) is open only on weekends from Memorial Day to Labor Day from 1:00 to 5:00 P.M. Free admission to all sites at all times. Free guided tours available.

Revolutionary War buffs might want to visit this site of the 1781 massacre of American defenders by British troops under the command of Benedict Arnold. The fort includes ramparts, battlements, and buildings dating from the Revolution, and the view of the river is wonderful. For a view to beat all, climb the 134-foot monument. When you descend, visit the museum, which tells the story of the battle and also includes exhibits on early Groton and other elements of southeastern Connecticut history from Native American times through colonial settlement, the Revolution, the Civil War, and whaling days. Ask for the dates of the Revolutionary War reenactment in early September. This so-called Living History Weekend demonstrates camp lifeways, military drills, and more.

Also on the park grounds is the 1750 Ebenezer Avery House, which, in its original site on Thames Street, had been a repository for some of the wounded patriots. Moved to the park in 1971, its kitchen and weaving room are furnished as they might have been in the eighteenth century.

Thames River **Fireworks and Sailfest**

If you can get to Groton and New London in early July, coordinate your visit with the annual Sailfest, a three-day celebration of life on the water. Sailing regattas, musical entertainment, boat shows, craft shows, children's activities, and a parade through historic New London are on the schedule that touches both cities on the Thames. The crowning event has to be the absolutely fantastic Grucci Brothers Fireworks Show. Sponsored by the Mashantucket Pequot Tribal Nation, the fireworks are launched from three barges in the middle of the Thames River. This is a must-see show, but you have to like crowds. In this writer's opinion, Fort Griswold State Park is the best viewing site. Get there by 7:00 P.M. to stake a good spot.

Noank Village (all ages)

From Route 1 heading east out of the city of Groton, take Route 215 (Groton Long Point Road) south to the village of Noank. One of Connecticut's most picturesque shoreline enclaves, 300-year-old Noank has real beach-town flavor in its quiet, narrow streets, historic buildings, and shops and marinas. You could linger here all day if your idea of fun is wandering and wading at some low-key shoreline spots.

Esker Point Beach. Groton Long Point Road (Route 215) and Marsh Road; (860) 572–9702. Surely one of the prettiest points on the Connecticut coast, with a perfect beach for children and a picnic area so you can linger through a couple of meals to catch the sunset.

Noank Historical Society Museum. Sylvan Street; (860) 536–7026. Open July 4 through October 12 on Wednesday, Saturday, and Sunday from 2:00 to 5:00 P.M.

Spicer Park. Spicer Avenue, off Route 215, overlooking Beebe Cove. Grills, picnic area. Great spot for bird-watching.

Noank Play Area. In the village on Main Street. Playground and picnic area perfect for taking a break from a village stroll.

Where to Eat

Paul's Pasta. 223 Thames Street, Groton; (860) 445–5276. This friendly, casual place offers the best in pasta for lunch and dinner from 11:00 A.M. to 9:00 P.M. Tuesday through Sunday. $–$$

Abbott's Lobster in the Rough. 117 Pearl Street, Noank; (860) 536–7719. Fifty-plus years of extraordinary seaside ambience with beautiful views of bobbing boats and offshore islands. Eat out in the breeze and sun on picnic tables, under the striped tent, or inside the casual dining room. Lobsters, steamers, clams, oysters, shrimp, steamed corn, seafood sandwiches, barbecued chicken, hot dogs, and strawberry shortcake. Open May through Labor Day, noon to 9:00 P.M. daily, then Friday to Sunday through Columbus Day, from noon to 7:00 P.M. $$$

Sea Horse on Thames. 359 Thames Street; (860) 449–0074. For great water views and an eclectic menu for all the family, come for lunch from 11:30 A.M. and dinner, served to 9:00 P.M. Monday through Thursday and Sunday and to 10:00 P.M. on Friday and Saturday. Children's menu. $$

Mystic River Baking Company. 19 Pearl Street, Noank; (860) 536–0182. The best place for lunch, picnic and beach foods, delicious baked treats. Open daily March through December. $

Where to Stay

Best Western/Olympic Inn. 360 Route 12; (860) 445–8000 or (800) 622–7766. 140 rooms, restaurant, health club, sauna. $$$$

Mystic Marriott Hotel and Spa. 625 North Road; (860) 446–2600 or (866) 449–7390. Located on Route 117 close to the Noank area of Groton near the Poheganut Reservoir, this large, four diamond AAA-rated establishment has 285 generously sized rooms, including 6 suites perfect for larger families. Cribs available. Indoor pool, health club, coffee bar. Elizabeth Arden Red Door Spa on-site as well as the Octagon restaurant, which serves three meals daily. $$$$

Thames Inn and Marina. 193 Thames Street; (860) 445–8111. 21 efficiencies, 4 semi-efficiencies, overnight boat dockage and fishing, right on the Thames River. $$$

Mystic

If I were to name the ten towns in Connecticut that most typify the essence of New England, I surely would mention Mystic. Rich in history that harks back to the earliest days of the Connecticut Colony, it is a town that has witnessed the first of the difficult compromises between settler and native, the glory days of whaling and shipbuilding, the rise of industrialization and the decline of agriculture. Throughout this history Mystic has remained a vital community composed of diverse citizens engaged in the simple craft of building an American tradition.

For many years Mystic has been a tourist destination, most notably because of Mystic Seaport, among the nation's most outstanding maritime history museums. Now home to other notable attractions, Mystic is a destination for more tourists than ever before in its history. Even its wonderful downtown, until somewhat recently unknown to out-of-towners, is now a thriving center enjoyed by tourists as well as townies. Not an official political entity itself, Mystic lies on the shoreline, half in the town of Groton and half in Stonington along both banks of the Mystic River.

Mystic Seaport, the Museum of America and the Sea (all ages)

75 Greenmanville Avenue (Route 27), off I–95 exit 90; (860) 572–5315; www.mysticseaport. org. The seaport is open year-round, daily, except for Christmas Day. In summer, the schedule is 9:00 A.M. to 8:00 P.M.; from October to April, 10:00 A.M. to 4:00 P.M.; spring and early autumn hours 9:00 A.M. to 5:00 P.M. Adults $17.00; children 6 to 12 $9.00; children 5 and younger free. Second consecutive day is free. Family memberships are good bargains if you have more than two kids and you're coming twice in a year.

The first stop in Mystic for most visitors, the seaport's seventeen acres of historic buildings and re-creations represent a nineteenth-century New England whaling and shipbuilding village. An incredible array of educational and entertainment activities is offered here throughout the year. From rope making to printing to oystering, from sailor to chandler to merchant, the arts, crafts, and occupations of an early American seaport are demonstrated for visitors of all ages.

Horse and buggy rides, planetarium shows, sea chantey sing-alongs, chowder festivals, lantern-light holiday dramas, tall-ship tours, fine arts exhibitions, hands-on activities, and outstanding special events are key to the seaport's success. Summer camps, living-history workshops, boat excursions, and concerts are among the opportunities for families.

If you haven't already visited here, plan to do so soon. You may find yourself riding an early-twentieth-century bicycle, stitching a sailor's log book, or sampling a hearty New England stew. After your adventures, shop in the seaport's excellent five-part gift shop for a memento of your trip. In our family, I head to the shops to make holiday purchases while Tom pulls the girls out of the nineteenth-century world in which they've become entrapped. I can't recall a time when a visit here hasn't prompted one of the girls to say, "Oh, I wish we could live here!"

Lanternlight Tours at the Seaport

During the month of December (call for the exact schedule) the seaport offers lanternlight tours that reenact the scenarios that may have enlivened a similar town of the eighteenth century at holiday time long ago. Costumed reenactors set the scenes in a dozen or more sites throughout the village; your family eavesdrops on the goings-on as your guide leads you by lamplight through the darkened streets. You'll enter parlors, taverns, and shops, and even go down to the crew's quarters on the whaler *Charles W. Morgan*. The wind may wail, rain may lash at your cheeks, or perhaps snow will fall lightly on your path, but all seem merely enhancements to the special effect of these marvelous portrayals. Reservations are a must.

Sabino Mystic River Cruises (all ages)

From the Sabino Dock at Mystic Seaport; use south parking lot across from Seaport main entrance; (860) 572–5315. Call for rates and reservations after 10:00 A.M. Ninety-minute cruises every evening at 4:30 P.M., beginning mid-May; also every Friday and Saturday at 6:30 P.M. from late June. Also, daily half-hour cruises, leaving on the half-hour, from 10:30 A.M. to 3:30 P.M. from the third week in May to Columbus Day; extra cruises in mid-summer until 6:00 P.M. departure. Adults $5.25, plus seaport admission; children 6 to 12 $4.75 plus admission; children under 6 free. For the evening cruises, adults pay $10.25; children $8.75; no seaport admission necessary.

The *Sabino* is the last coal-fired passenger steamboat in operation. Built in 1908 in East Boothbay, Maine, for passenger service on the Damariscotta River, she is now a working exhibit of the seaport. Board as her steam whistle calls passengers to her double decks for a cruise back in time. Watch her crew shovel the anthracite coal into the glowing maw of her steam plant, then shift your gaze to the historic homes that grace the banks of the peaceful Mystic River. For the evening cruise, bring a picnic dinner aboard or ask about their boxed dinner and beverage service. Bring a sweatshirt or jacket and settle in for the one-and-a-half-hour journey down the river and into Fishers Island Sound.

Mystic Aquarium and Institute for Exploration (all ages)

55 Coogan Boulevard, off I-95 exit 90; (860) 572–5955; www.mysticaquarium.org. Open daily (except New Year's Day, Thanksgiving, and Christmas); admissions from 9:00 A.M. to 5:00 P.M. (visitors may remain until 6:00 P.M.) and in summer, admissions until 6:00 P.M. (visitors may remain until 7:00 P.M.). Adults $16; children 3 to 12 $11; children 2 and under free. Family memberships.

During recent years the Mystic Aquarium has been transformed into a state-of-the-art facility. Forty new or newly renovated exhibit areas have been configured to represent the trio of "islands" of marine life found across the globe: the estuaries, the coral reefs, and the upwelling zones. From a New England tidal marsh to a 30,000-gallon coral reef re-creation to a Roger Tory Peterson penguin paradise, the aquarium's indoor and outdoor exhibits focus on 4,500 mammals, fish, and invertebrates of the sunlit seas. With a focus on the vital importance of all the essential elements of a healthy ocean ecosystem, the aquarium also continues its primary mission of education, research, and conservation.

Families will be enthralled from one end of this complex to the other. The magic starts at the main entrance, with a 750,000-gallon beluga whale pool extending into the main lobby and providing the belugas with both deepwater areas and shallow cobble beaches. Vegetation and rockwork typical of the beluga's south-central Alaskan habitat are enhanced by mechanically produced fog. Indoor and outdoor exhibits include beluga whales, sharks, seals, sea lions, hundreds of species of fish, and invertebrates of every sort. The outdoor Seal Island and Penguin Pavilion exhibits are exceptional re-creations of the animals' natural habitats. The first represents the habitats of seals and sea lions of the North Pacific. The latter allows visitors to see both above and below water in the African black-footed penguin rookery. The skylit marine theater, Lions of the Sea, allows staff marine biologists to demonstrate the dramatic talents and capabilities of California sea lions. The Aquatic Animal Study Center concentrates on puzzling out the habits, behaviors, and needs of marine animals in order to help wildlife conservation efforts.

The aquarium has an exciting relationship with underwater explorer Robert Ballard in the Institute for Exploration, which introduces visitors to undersea technology, oceanographic exploration, and marine archaeology. Simulated deep-sea dives aboard a manned submersible include the sights and sounds that one might experience during a 12,000-foot descent; another exhibit shows the robotic and other technology being used to explore famed shipwrecks.

The aquarium also has an excellent gift shop/bookstore, which shoppers may browse without an admission ticket. Workshops, classes, and special events are held at the aquarium throughout the year.

Beluga Encounter

The Mystic Aquarium now offers a program that allows the public to swim with their whales. Adventurers 5 feet tall and over can make arrangements to spend time in the pool with the aquarium's beluga whales. An expensive adventure for most families, it may still be a once-in-a-lifetime experience worth the splurge to animal lovers. Call the aquarium for more details on this exciting program.

Olde Mistick Village (all ages)

At the junction of Route 27 and Coogan Boulevard, immediately adjacent to the aquarium; (860) 536–4941. Open year-round daily, from Monday through Saturday at 10:00 A.M. to 6:00 P.M. and on Sunday from noon to 5:00 P.M. Summer and holiday hours are often extended.

A shopping center built as a re-creation of a circa-1720 New England village, its pretty paths, reproduction freestanding shops, and ponds, fences, stone walls, and waterwheels make for a very pleasant shopping experience. Restaurants, tea shops, jewelry stores, clothing and toy shops, gourmet coffee and chocolate shops, and much more are here.

Olde Mistick Village is especially pretty in summer, when its ponds are busy with waterfowl, its gazebo is the site of **free** concerts, and its flowers and trees are in bloom. During December the village and its pretty, white New England church replica are aglow with holiday light displays, and various complimentary festivities and promotions in individual shops lure cheerful holiday shoppers along the luminaria-lined pathways.

Mystic Whaler Cruises (all ages)

P.O. Box 189, Mystic 06355; (860) 536–4218 or (800) 697–8420. Call for brochure or to obtain rates and reservations. Cruises range from $75 to $1,095 per person. Children of 10 years and older are welcome on overnight voyages at full fare. Children aged 5 to 10 are welcome on day sails and evening cruises at half-fare, with the understanding that parents are wholly responsible for the child throughout the cruise.

If you have the time and the money, these just may be the cream of the crop in terms of boat excursions along the entire Connecticut coastline. The cruise options are varied to suit nearly any desire; the schooner is an awe-inspiring 110-foot beauty carrying 3,000 square feet of sail, and, whether on a three-hour lobster cruise or a seven-day odyssey, the crew cheerfully invites both landlubbers and skilled show-offs to hoist the sails, plot the course, or take a turn at the wheel. If you can spring for an overnight sea trek, you can choose from five accommodations options, from the tiny Sloop to the Great Room that gives you a taste of life belowdecks for the common sailor to the Clipper cabins that provide skylights, private head and shower *en suite,* a sink with hot and cold running water, and a double bed. Three-hour lobster cruises include steamed lobster and fresh clam chowder served on deck under sail. Six-hour day sails include a hearty barbecue fresh off the on-board grill served while cruising Fishers Island Sound; if the wind is right, it includes a swim in a sheltered cove before returning to Mystic. Overnight sails of one, two, three, five, and seven days include such ports of call as Mystic herself, Block Island, Shelter Island, Sag Harbor, Newport, Cuttyhunk, and Martha's Vineyard. Full-moon cruises, pirate-treasure adventure cruises, lighthouse cruises, and art cruises that encourage you to bring along your art supplies and camera are among the maritime mini-vacations that Captain John Eginton plans to tempt you aboard. It might be worth it to skip the crowds at Disneyworld and have the adventure of a lifetime on your own pirate-getaway windjammer.

Denison Pequotsepos Nature Center (all ages)

109 Pequotsepos Road; follow Coogan Boulevard to its eastern end, take right on Jerry Browne Road, then right on Pequotsepos; (860) 536–1216; www.dpnc.org. Open year-round Monday through Saturday from 9:00 A.M. to 5:00 P.M. and Sunday from 10:00 A.M. to 4:00 P.M. Adults $6.00; children 6 to 12 $4.00; children 5 and under free. Trails are open dawn to dusk; leave a donation in the box. Pets, leashed, are welcome. Picnicking is allowed.

If you need a break from the busyness and the marine and historical themes, visit this 200-acre preserve with 7 miles of trails through woods and meadows and past ponds. Wildflower and fern gardens are among the areas created to encourage homeowners to create their own similar backyard habitats. Here in this habitat you may see otter, mink, and other mammals native to southeastern Connecticut, plus 150 species of birds, including bluebirds and scarlet tanagers.

The Pequotsepos natural history museum includes indoor native wildlife exhibits in woodland, wetland, and meadow habitats. Frogs, fish, birds, and reptiles are among the animals here. Be sure to stop in the *Night in the Meadow* Theater to experience a simulation of the sounds and sights in a meadow on a summer evening. Outdoor flight enclosures provide homes for nonreleasable owls. The Trading Post gift shop sells field guides, birding supplies, natural science materials for children, and locally made nature-related items. A full schedule of guided walks, summer camps for children ages 3 to 16, birding activities, and field trips can be obtained at the museum or found on the center's Web site.

A lovely added feature owned by the center is the beautiful Peace Sanctuary on River Road, about a mile away from the center, on the western bank. Atop rocky ledges, this wooded, thirty-acre preserve offers trails overlooking the Mystic River. Ask for directions when you visit the main center. Open at no charge from dawn to dusk, it is well named and especially lovely to explore during the early morning and close to dusk when the birds are most active.

Downtown Mystic (all ages)

West and East Main Street (Route 1); Water Street; Bank Street; Pearl Street; and other nearby streets.

A few years back only the locals knew the secrets of the "real" historic center of Mystic. Now the whole downtown area rocks and rolls with the tourist crowd that has discovered the no-longer-neglected inner core of the village. If your appetite for the sea has simply been whetted by the sights upriver, head downtown to Route 1 via Route 27 and the famed counterweighted bascule drawbridge that leads you to picturesque Mystic center. Linger awhile on the bridge itself (park the car somewhere else first) and watch the jellyfish and other flotsam. Stay to see the hourly raising of the bridge and the passage of the yachts and sailboats as they cruise up- or downriver. Then stroll the boutiques, art galleries, bookstores, candy shops, and restaurants. This wonderful village encapsulates a unique blend of old and new. Discover your own favorite places, but be sure to linger awhile at the incredible Mystic Army-Navy Store, the Mystic Art Association Gallery, Mystical Toys, near the Mystic River Park, the Mystic Drawbridge Ice Cream Company, and the incomparable Sea Swirl seafood shack. You'll find them all easily in the 1-mile historic district. If you can, come in mid-August for the Outdoor Art Festival, a two-day juried show of 300-plus artists who bring their wares from all parts of the nation to the sidewalks, parks, and riverbanks of downtown Mystic. Local vendors keep the shoppers and mere browsers on their feet with plenty of food and drink, and entertainment for all ages abounds throughout the festival scene.

Voyager Cruises (all ages)

15 Holmes Street; (860) 536–0416; www.voyagermystic.com. Daily from mid-May to mid-October at 10:30 A.M., 2:10 P.M., and 5:30 P.M. Adults $34 Monday through Friday afternoon, $36 Friday evening through Sunday; children under 18 $24 and $26, for weekday and Friday night/weekend cruises, respectively for all sails; children under 2 free. Reservations recommended.

The *Argia,* a replica nineteenth-century gaff-rigged schooner, takes passengers on two- to three-hour day sails in scenic Fishers Island Sound. This beautiful white bird glides gracefully across these sheltered waters, providing a gentle ride that cannot fail to relax and refresh a weary daytripping family. Beverages and light snacks are sold on board. You may also bring along a picnic lunch or dinner. If the majestic *Mystic Whaler* would break your bank, this more affordable option may be just right for a family cruise.

Into the Mystic **Cruises**

It seems there is no end to boat excursions out of Mystic, but the crowds are here to support them. Here are a few more options in case the others have failed to intrigue you:

Merry Charters/Mystic Coastal Cruises. (877) 248–6964.

Brilliant. Mystic Seaport (860) 572–5315.

Resolute. Mystic Seaport (860) 572–5315.

Breck Marshall. Mystic Seaport (860) 572–5315.

Where to Eat

Sea View Snack Bar. 145 Greenmanville Avenue; (860) 572–0096. Gulls circle the red-painted picnic tables, the sun glints on the river just beyond you, the view of the *Charles W. Morgan* can be wonderful, and the food is typical summer seaside shack cuisine, which means rings, wings, dogs, nuggets, fries, burgers, all sorts of seafood, and homemade chowder. $

Mystic Pizza. 56 West Main Street; (860) 536–6194. Who can resist? It's convenient, it's good, the menu has lots more than pizza, and it's famous, so be there, just for fun. Open for lunch and dinner. $

Seaman's Inne. Greenmanville Avenue, just outside the north entrance to the seaport; (860) 536–9649. This tavernlike restaurant is a great place for New England-y dishes like seafood pot pie and crab cakes and prime rib, plus soups, salads, stews, and sandwiches. Dixieland Sunday brunch offers southern-style fare and music. Open daily; lunch $; dinner $$–$$$$

Other **Mystical Attractions**

Mystic Carousel and Fun Center. 193 Greenmanville Avenue; (860) 572–9949. This family entertainment center (read "noisy, busy; pay-as-you-play" amusement arcade) has a full-sized operational carousel and antique band organ. Take a whirl! Open daily year-round.

Denison Homestead Museum. Pequotsepos Road; (860) 536–9248. If the seaport fails to satisfy a history craving, this unusual 1717 house might do the trick. Its rooms represent periods from the 1720s to the 1940s.

Williams Beach Park at Mystic Community Center off Mason's Island Road; (860) 536–3575. There's a saltwater beach, playground, picnic and snack pavilions, and grills. No charge. No lifeguards. Open June to Labor Day.

Where to Stay

Whaler's Inn. 20 East Main Street; (860) 536–1506 or (800) 243–2588; www.whalers innmystic.com. 49 truly lovely rooms right in the heart of downtown Mystic by the bridge. Homey ambience, children stay **free.** Complimentary continental breakfast. Three-diamond AAA rating. Great four-star restaurant called Bravo Bravo. $$–$$$$

Best Western/Sovereign Hotel. 9 Whitehall Avenue; (860) 536–4281 or (800) 363–1622. 150 units, 4 suites, restaurant, sauna, indoor pool. $$$

Howard Johnson Inn. 253 Greenmanville Avenue; (860) 536–2654. Crayola Kids Rooms with kid-friendly amenities like an easel and paints and crayons make a stay here fun for families. Those rooms also come with mini-fridge and microwave and plenty of room for mom and dad, too. Indoor pool. Vacation packages starting at $199 include room, 4 tickets to the seaport, aquarium, or the Mashantucket Pequot Museum; plus full breakfast and discounts to other regional attractions. $$$–$$$$

Seaport Campgrounds. Route 184, Old Mystic; (860) 536–4044. Spacious family campground for tenters and RVers. Swimming pool, fishing pond, playground, rec center, mini-golf, store, laundry, more. Open mid-March through late November. $

Mashantucket/Ledyard

I'm not sure whether to call this Connecticut's oldest town or its newest, but it certainly is one getting an awful lot of attention. Inhabited by Europeans since early in the seventeenth century and for centuries before that by Native American people such as the Pequots, the Mohegans, and the Narragansetts, the mostly rural town of Ledyard now contains a village called Mashantucket. A federal reservation of the sacred tribal land of the Mashantucket Pequot Tribal Nation, it is the center of activity in this otherwise quiet, forested landscape.

Visitors arrive by the busload to Mashantucket's most famous attraction: the Foxwoods Resort Casino. This author can't wholeheartedly recommend this complex as a family attraction, but many folks might disagree. Billed as the largest gaming (read "gambling") facility in the world, Foxwoods rises upward from Route 2 as if it were Oz itself—not a bad comparison since it sure is about as far away from Kansas as one might travel, speaking both materially and spiritually. Besides the thousands of ways you can part with your shirt here, there are a score or more of restaurants, a four-diamond high-rise hotel with pool and spa, a retail concourse of specialty shops, and Cinetropolis, a so-called city of theaters including wraparound screens, a Turbo Ride with hydraulic action seats, and Virtual Adventures, in which theatergoers participate in the action on screen. The choice is yours, but this author suggests a closer look at the simpler side of life in the Eastern Woodlands.

Mashantucket Pequot Museum and Research Center (all ages)

111 Pequot Trail, off Route 2; (860) 396–6800 or (800–) 411–9671; www.mashantucket.com. Open year-round daily from 9:00 A.M. to 5:00 P.M. (last admission 4:00 P.M.). Closed Thanksgiving, Christmas, and New Year's Day and the eves of each of those days. Adults $15; children 6 to 15 $10; children under 6 free.

Established with the goal of preserving Pequot history and culture, the Mashantucket Pequot Museum and Research Center is a must-see experience for all travelers to Connecticut. Nearly $150 million went into the research, planning, and construction of this fabulous showcase—an astonishing sum that is apparent in every pore of this amazing complex. Pack the family up as soon as you can and plan to spend a full day here.

You'll enter the museum and purchase your tickets in a rather modest lobby of warm woods and polished granite floors imbedded with seashells, but don't let that subdued ambience fool you. From there onward, you will be totally absorbed in a glorious yet graceful celebration of the Mashantucket Pequot tribal history and the natural history of their beloved land. Steps from the entrance lobby is an enormous glass and steel Gathering Space, open to the woodlands and the sky and home to beautiful, life-size dioramas representing the native people who have inhabited that exterior landscape for more than 10,000 years. Above your heads on the second level of the Gathering Space is a full-service restaurant offering Native American and traditional American cuisine, and not far away is a 185-foot stone and glass tower that provides sweeping views of the Mashantucket Pequot reservation.

Don't hesitate too long in these spaces, however. The real adventure lies ahead, and depending on the ages and interests of your group, you may need a good five or six hours to thoroughly explore the remarkable exhibits that await you. Your tour begins with an escalator ride through a simulated glacial crevasse complete with chilly temperatures and the sounds of howling winds. Traveling back in time to the Ice Age, you will learn how the movement of the glaciers shaped the land and how life began on the barren areas exposed when the ice caps melted. Time-traveling forward now, see a life-sized re-creation of an 11,000-year-old caribou kill; learn how the native people adjusted to the warming climate 8,000 to 3,000 years ago. Discover the ways the people used their woodland resources and adapted them to their needs for food and shelter. Traveling ever closer to our present time, walk through a wondrous 22,000-square foot re-creation of a sixteenth-century coastal Pequot village, featuring dozens of eerily realistic, life-sized figures engaging in everyday activities that demonstrate the fascinating lifeways and beliefs of the Pequot civilization. Immersed in the light, sounds, and even the aromas typical of the village culture, you will be transported to a nearly lost but not forgotten time.

Ledyard's Ups and Downs

The northeastern part of Connecticut was famed in the nineteenth century for the number of water-powered mills that sprang up along the banks of the Quinebaug and Shetucket Rivers, and even along lower tidal rivers such as the Yantic and Thames As a result, abandoned mill sites are not at all uncommon in these parts. Fully operational, restored sites are a rarity, however, and Ledyard has one to show off for you. Located near Lee's Brook in Sawmill Park on Iron Street, which is Route 214, this unusual water-powered up-down sawmill has been restored to the way it might have been when it was built by Israel Brown in 1869. Water levels on the mill's pond site are highest in spring and fall, so operation is seasonal, even though the park is open daily year-round and the public is welcome to enjoy its picnic tables and grills. If you visit during the operational seasons, you can see the vertical water wheel that turns the gears that move the up-down saw. This mill is still used to cut large logs into lumber. Demonstrations are given on Saturday from 1:00 to 4:00 P.M. during April and May and from mid-October through November. Also on this site are an operating shingle mill, an unrestored gristmill, and a blacksmith's forge. Call (860) 464–8888 or (860) 433–4050 for further information. Admission is **free.**

From there, you might explore an exhibit that re-creates through models and computer technology a seventeenth-century Pequot fort discovered in 1992 just yards from the present-day museum. You might stroll through an indoor and outdoor eighteenth-century Pequot farmstead, re-created on an acre of land right outside the museum walls. Step through the cabin door to an orchard and herb garden and learn about farming techniques and tools. Throughout the museum, watch any of a dozen or more films exploring such topics as food, wigwams, wampum, canoes, and Pequot history. (Note to Parents: The excellent short film *The Witness*, recounting the story of the Pequot massacre at Mystic, is unflinching in its graphic portrayal of this brutal event. You, however, may flinch more than a few times, and youngsters under the age of 10 may be disturbed by the violent nature of the film.)

You may be emotionally drained when you exit the theater if you have chosen to see the heartbreakingly honest *Witness*, but there is still much more to see. You can immerse yourself in exhibits describing the Reservation Period and the eighteenth-, nineteenth-, and twentieth-century struggles and lifestyles of the Mashantucket Pequots. You can visit the changing exhibition gallery, which usually features contemporary Native arts, artifacts from the museum's permanent collection, or traveling exhibitions from other collections and native cultures. In addition, there are two excellent research libraries, including an outstanding collection for children, and there are several classrooms, workshops, and a 400-seat auditorium with live performances, films, and lectures. A regular calendar of activities and demonstrations for children is planned throughout the year. Call to discover what may be on the agenda this weekend. No matter what parts of the museum you see or what activities you try, a visit here promises to be unforgettable.

Where to Eat

The Mashantucket Pequot Museum has both a full-service restaurant and a snack bar where you can get burgers, fries, and other light fare and beverages. Elsewhere along Route 2 from Stonington north to Ledyard are a variety of eateries. Here's one local favorite.

Ledyard Country Ice Cream. 680 Colonel Ledyard Highway; (860) 464–1055. Not far from the Ledyard firehouse on Route 117, this place is perfect for ice cream in the summertime, when the walk-up parlor opens its shutters from 1:30 to 9:00 P.M. Tuesday through Sunday. They also serve breakfast and lunch Tuesday through Saturday, breakfast only on Sunday. $

Where to Stay

Two Trees Inn. 240 Lantern Hill Road; (860) 312–3000 or (800) FOXWOODS. This is the self-billed "rustic" alternative to the glitzy hotels of the Foxwoods complex, also owned and operated by the Mashantucket Pequots. Two-room suites with a sitting room and sleeper sofa adjoined to a bedroom with one king-sized or two double beds make this lodge-style inn a good choice for families. Standard rooms are also available. Pool, gym, Branches restaurant. Complimentary continental breakfast. $$$–$$$$

Abbey's Lantern Hill Inn. 214 Lantern Hill Road; (860) 572–0483; www.abbeyslantern hill.com. Seven rooms and a cottage in contemporary country-style bed-and-breakfast in the countryside just far enough away from the glow of the casino. Private baths (some with Jacuzzis) and private decks or patios are among the amenities. Complimentary full breakfasts are served on weekends; conti-nental-style fixin's are available on weekdays. Young children are warmly welcomed, and well-behaved pets are welcome in the cot-tage. No smoking indoors. $$$–$$$$

Stonington

Nestled between the coves near the easternmost boundary of the state, Stonington is my favorite Connecticut town. Someday I would like to live here in a tiny house overlooking the sea, with lupines below my balcony and kitchen herbs in my dooryard. One of my daughters loves this place, too, so much so that she doesn't like me to write about it. "I don't want anyone else to go there," she says.

Just about 5 miles east of downtown Mystic by way of Route 1, it is very quaint, very New England, very evocative of the days of sea captains and West Indies trading ships. Close your eyes and see the little girls playing hoops and graces, the little boys in knee pants shinnying their way up the flagpoles. Hear the clip-clopping of the horses, the whoosh of the gas lamps, the clanging of the bell buoys. It's easy to imagine in Stonington.

Once you have crossed the bridge to the borough, park anywhere and just stroll—it's a great walking town. Weave your way down Water Street, stopping at the shops and gal-leries as you wander. Rest awhile at a cafe or coffeehouse. Enjoy the marvelous model rail-road in the Anguilla Gallery. Let the salty air lead you down to DuBois Beach right on the Point, and let the kiss of the sea breeze tease any stubborn knots from your work-worn shoulders. Hug one another and take a collective deep breath. Life doesn't get any better than this.

Old Lighthouse Museum (ages 4 and up)

7 Water Street; (860) 535–1440; www.stoningtonhistory.org. Open daily in July and August from 10:00 A.M. to 5:00 P.M. Open in May, June, September, and October from Tuesday through Sunday at the same hours. Adults $4.00; children 6 to 12 $2.00. Combination tick-ets to this and the Palmer House are $6.00 and $3.00, respectively.

Inside the 1832 stone lighthouse at the foot of the village are displays of whaling and fish-ing equipment, swords and cannonballs and other instruments of defense, nineteenth-century portraits, and much more. One exhibit focuses on the wonderful treasures brought back to Stonington by the captains of the China trade route. Another shows a col-lection of antique shoes found in the walls of old houses to protect them from evil spirits. The antique dollhouse, decoys, toys, and model ships are often especially interesting to children.

You can learn about the history of Stonington and its role in the War of 1812. You can learn about the railroad that once transferred passengers from sailing ships to river steamboats. You can even climb the tower of the lighthouse itself for a marvelous view of the harbor and the fishing fleet that still works in these waters.

Captain Nathaniel B. Palmer House (ages 6 and up)

North Water and Palmer Streets; (860) 535–8445; www.stoningtonhistory.org. **Open May through October on Tuesday through Sunday from 10:00 A.M. to 4:00 P.M. (last tour at 3:00 P.M.) and by appointment. Adults $4.00, children 6 to 12 $2.00. Combo tickets ($6.00 and $3.00) available for this and Lighthouse Museum.**

Home of the discoverer of Antarctica, this nineteenth-century mansion at the far north of the village has sixteen rooms filled with many examples of the clever architectural design work of the crafty captain himself. Better known for his success in the China trade and his discovery of the southernmost continent in 1820 in the relatively small sloop *Hero* while on a sealing expedition, the captain filled his elegant home with a variety of innovations and contraptions that intrigue young and old visitors. Lively stories told by the friendly docents tell of the many adventures of Nat Palmer and his also-daring brother Alexander; the tours take one hour. Be sure to climb to the top of the cupola to have a look at the glorious view.

The Blessing **of the Fleet**

Perhaps the quaintest and most touching annual event in Connecticut is the blessing ceremony that offers spiritual protection to the fishermen who still ply these waters for the seaborne bounty that provides to them a living and to us a feast. Held usually near the end of July, the two-day event begins under a tent at the town dock with a traditional lobster/clambake that builds everyone's stamina for an evening of dancing on the dock until midnight. The next morning the Fisherman's Mass is offered at 10:00 A.M. at St. Mary's Roman Catholic Church on Broad Street in the village, and then the street parade gets under way by 1:00 P.M., encircling the town before returning to the dock. A brief dockside ceremony precedes the bishop's boarding of the decorated fleet's lead vessel, which moves into the harbor for the bishop to bless each of the remaining boats as they pass in their own parade. Following the blessing, the vessels pass the breakwater and go out on the Sound, where the families of deceased fishermen toss into the sea floral tributes formed like broken anchors. When the boats return to the village, they are awarded prizes for the best decorations, and the dancing and eating resume until 6:00 P.M. Visitors of all faiths are welcome to join the celebration.

Where to Eat

The Yellow House. 149 Water Street; (860) 535–4986. Wonderful coffees and biscotti in a sunny space splashed with cheerful colors. Tasty sandwiches, tacos, quesadillas, soups, and other easy fare for children. Open daily from 6:30 A.M. to 3:00 P.M. $

Noah's. 113 Water Street; (860) 535–3925. Three solid meals a day at this warm and casual place with a downhome flair. Good cookin', served with a smile. The scrod melts in your mouth. $–$$

Where to Stay

Sea Breeze Motel. 812 Stonington Road (Route 1); (860) 535–2843. On a little arm of the sea, 30 units offer the basic necessities plus TV and air-conditioning. $$$

Randall's Ordinary. On Route 2 in North Stonington; (860) 599–4540. In addition to its famous open-hearth–cooked meals served in period costume, the seventeenth-century tavern on 27 acres has 18 guest rooms with fireplaces in the main inn, 9 in the adjacent barn restoration, and a unique silo suite with Jacuzzi and fireplace. Continental breakfast. Dinners, $39 prix fixe; breakfast and lunch also served daily to the public. Rooms $$$–$$$$

Inn at Stonington. 60 Water Street; (860) 535–2000. Top-drawer comforts are offered in this elegant 12-room inn in the center of Stonington Borough. Fireplaces, luxury baths. Exercise room, kayaks, and bicycles available. Complimentary continental breakfast. Mid-week specials offered on occasion will get you a third night **free.** $$$$

Pawcatuck

The easternmost village in the lower part of the county just before you cross the Rhode Island border on I–95, Pawcatuck is just a speck of a place officially in the town of Stonington. For families, it has some truly fun—just for fun—attractions.

Maple Breeze Action Park (all ages)

Off I–95 exit 92 at 350 Liberty Street, which is Route 2; (860) 599–1232. Open in May and June on weekends only from 10:00 A.M. to 10:00 P.M. and daily from July 1 through Labor Day at the same hours, weather permitting. Call to confirm hours early in the season or in questionable weather.

I promise you, on my honor, there is nothing—*nothing*—educational about Maple Breeze Park. There is no history, no legend, no folktale associated with this place. There is no scientific principle for you to understand, no mathematical concept for you to learn. There are absolutely no docents, costumed or otherwise. Just bring a bathing suit and prepare to have fun.

You can slide down either of two 350-foot water slides. Wide, smooth, and immaculate, these are tons of fun for anyone roughly taller than 40 inches. All riders must ride separately. You can also ride motorized bumper boats; you have to be 48 inches to ride alone, but smaller children can ride along with taller siblings or parents.

You can also play eighteen holes of miniature golf, also immaculate and meticulously landscaped. Nearby, for toddlers to about 8-year-olds, are motorized kiddie karts for racing around a track.

Use of the rides and games is administered through the purchase of tokens. Tokens for bumper boats and miniature golf cost less than $5.00 in 2003; the waterslide was $7.00 for a forty-minute turn. A snack bar and the Main Family ice-cream stand with twenty-four tummy-tempting flavors are on the premises.

Clyde's Cider Mill

On a crisp day in early fall when the apples are at their peak and the cider is at its sweetest, head to Clyde's (860–536–3354) on North Stonington Road in Old Mystic and watch this huge, steam-powered mill (the only such machine in the United States) press the amber juices from the apples that fill barrel after barrel to the brim. The whole place, in operation since 1881, is a National Historic Landmark. Sweet cider, hard cider, and the apples themselves are for sale, and on weekends especially there's always a crowd that adds to the aura of festivity here. Jams, jellies, honey, maple syrup, fudge, pies, breads, cornmeal, and local produce attract shoppers from near and far. Open daily 9:00 A.M. to 6:00 P.M. from early July until late December. Pressings are typically scheduled at 1:00 and 3:00 P.M. on weekends from September to Thanksgiving, plus randomly throughout the week.

Davis Farm Horsedrawn Hayrides (all ages)
576 Greenhaven Road; (860) 599–5859. Private rides for groups of approximately twenty passengers are $100.

Six beautiful pedigreed Belgian horses are enlisted during pumpkin season to take visitors along the 2 miles of trails through field and woodland on the lovely property of the Davis Farm. Held by the same family for more than 300 years, the farm produces and sells its own sweet corn, sweet cider, pumpkins, and other organically grown produce. Call to inquire about the late September through October pumpkin season. In some years, from the day after Thanksgiving through December, an enchanted Christmas hayride treks past 150 lighted and decorated Christmas trees and other seasonal scenes on the way to Santa's cabin in the woods. Call to inquire whether this seasonal event is on this year. Private carriage rides can also be arranged.

Barn Island State Wildlife Management Area (all ages) 🐾 🔺 🚶
Palmer Neck Road off Green Haven Road off Route 1. Call area supervisor John Lincoln at (860) 445–1729.

Take Green Haven Road south from the traffic light on Route 1 where the sign says BARN ISLAND STATE-OWNED BOAT LAUNCHING AREA. A nearly immediate left on Palmer Neck Road takes you past Wequetecock Cove and down to the shore, where the state manages an undeveloped wildlife area. Have a hike around this pretty site, where shorebirds nest and the marshes rustle. If you have a boat, launch it here and cruise the quiet inlets. Saltwater canoeing and kayaking are especially pleasant here. You can also fish here, usually without too many other anglers to disturb your serenity.

Where to Eat

Prime Time Cafe. 1 West Broad Street; (860) 599–3840. On the bridge overlooking the Pawcatuck River in downtown Pawcatuck, this brightly painted bistro-style restaurant serves breakfast, lunch, and dinner daily year-round. Everything is house-made and cooked to order. American cuisine; regional artwork; live entertainment on Thursday evenings $–$$

Where to Stay

Cove Ledge Inn and Marina. On Route 1 on Pawcatuck side of Stonington; (860) 599–4130; www.coveledgeinn.com. Right near the hub of a marina, this 16-unit waterfront motel on five acres is both picturesque and convenient, with fishing and boat launching easily available. 4 efficiency apartments, 2 guest houses, 2 luxury suites in lovingly restored vintage main house, plus motel rooms. Outdoor pool; playground; continental breakfast; kayak rentals. Special events planning such as reunions, weddings, and birthday parties. $$$

General Information

Connecticut's Mystic and More Convention and Visitors Bureau. 470 Bank Street, P.O. Box 89, New London 06320; (860) 444–2206; (800) TO–ENJOY; www.mysticmore.com. Maps, brochures, calendars.

Mystic and Shoreline Visitor Information Center. I–95 exit 90 at entrance to Olde Mistick Village; (860) 536–1641.

Mystic Chamber of Commerce. (860) 572–9578. For Mystic and Stonington Borough and area information.

State Welcome Center. I–95 southbound, entering state at North Stonington from Rhode Island; (860) 599–2056. Open daily year-round; rest rooms; staff in summer. Maps, state tourism guides, brochures.

Southeastern Connecticut Chamber of Commerce. One Whale Oil Row, New London 06320; (860) 443–8332.

Norwich Tourism and Main Street Office. 69 Main Street, Norwich 06360; (860) 886–4683 or (888) 4–NORWICH; norwichct.org.

Nutmeg Bed and Breakfast Agency. (800) 727–7592; bnb-link.com.

Visit **Mystic Web site** www.visitmystic.com.

Mystic Transportation and Visitors Center. Exit 90, I–95 (Route 27), Old Mystic; (860) 572–9949.

Mystic Welcome Center, Mystic Depot. Route 27/Route 1, Mystic; (860) 572–1102.

New London Visitor Center, at the Trolley Waiting Center. Eugene O'Neill Drive, New London; (860) 444–7264.

Index

Y